Conflict of Interest in the Professions

Practical Ethics
A Collection of Addresses and Essays
Henry Sedgwick
With an Introduction by Sissela Bok

Thinking Like an Engineer
Studies in the Ethics of a Profession
Michael Davis

Deliberative Politics
Essays on Democracy and Disagreement
Edited by Stephen Macedo

Conflict of Interest in the Professions
Edited by Michael Davis and Andrew Stark

Conflict of Interest in the Professions

Edited by
MICHAEL DAVIS
ANDREW STARK

UNIVERSITY PRESS

2001

OXFORD
UNIVERSITY PRESS

Oxford   New York
Athens   Auckland   Bangkok   Bogotá   Buenos Aires   Cape Town
Chennai   Dar es Salaam   Delhi   Florence   Hong Kong   Istanbul   Karachi
Kolkata   Kuala Lumpur   Madrid   Melbourne   Mexico City   Mumbai   Nairobi
Paris   São Paulo   Shanghai   Singapore   Taipei   Tokyo   Toronto   Warsaw

and associated companies in
Berlin   Ibadan

Copyright © 2001 by Oxford University Press

Published by Oxford University Press, Inc.
198 Madison Avenue, New York, New York 10016

Oxford is a registered trademark of Oxford University Press

Library of Congress Cataloging-in-Publication Data
Conflict of interest in the professions / edited by Michael Davis and Andrew Stark.
    p. cm.—(Practical and professional ethics series)
Includes bibliographical references and index.
ISBN 0-19-512863-X
1. Professional ethics.   2. Conflict of interests.   I. Davis, Michael, 1943–
II. Stark, Andrew, 1956–   III. Series.
BJ1725 .C66   2001
174—dc21   2001021983

9 8 7 6 5 4 3 2 1

Printed in the United States of America
on acid-free paper

CONTENTS

CONTRIBUTORS

THOMAS E. BORCHERDING
Economics
Claremont Graduate University

SANDRA L. BORDEN
Journalism
Western Michigan University

JOHN R. BOATRIGHT
Business
Loyola University of Chicago

LEONARD J. BROOKS
Management
University of Toronto

KATHLEEN CLARK
Law School
Washington University

ELLIOT D. COHEN
Philosophy
Indian River Community
    College

TYLER COWEN
Economics
George Mason University

MICHAEL DAVIS
Philosophy
Illinois Institute of Technology

DARREN FILSON
Economics
Claremont Graduate University

DONALD L. GABARD
Physical Therapy
Chapman University

JANE GALLOP
English
University of Wisconsin-
    Milwaukee

ERIC HAYOT
English
University of Wisconsin-
    Milwaukee

JEFF KING
English
University of Wisconsin-
    Milwaukee

KENNETH KIPNIS
Philosophy
University of Hawaii at Minoa

STEPHEN R. LATHAM
Law
Quinnipiac College

DAVID LUBAN
Law
Georgetown University

NEIL R. LUEBKE
Philosophy
Oklahoma State University

MIKE W. MARTIN
Philosophy
Chapman University

KEVIN C. McMUNIGAL
Law
Case-Western Reserve University

ERIC W. ORTS
Business
University of Pennsylvania

MICHAEL S. PRITCHARD
Philosophy
Western Michigan University

MERRILEE SALMON
Philosophy
University of Pittsburgh

ANDREW STARK
Management
University of Toronto

Conflict of Interest in the Professions

INTRODUCTION

Michael Davis

How important is conflict of interest to the professions? The answer is complex. Consider what recently happened to PriceWaterhouseCoopers (PWC), the world's largest accounting firm. PWC hired an outside investigator (at the urging of the Securities and Exchange Commission) to determine whether the firm was observing its own conflict-of-interest rules. The investigator reported that more than three-fourths of PWC's partners, including thirty-one of the top forty-three, had not properly sanitized their personal finances. The partners held financial interests in businesses that PWC audited; a few even owned stock in businesses for which they had direct auditing responsibility. Many of those partners were disciplined; some were told to leave the firm. PWC suffered a substantial loss of personnel and reputation. Failure to pay sufficient attention to conflict of interest was a disaster for PWC.

Soon after the PWC story reached its front page, the *Wall Street Journal* (January 19, 2000) ran an opinion piece challenging the utility of prohibitions of conflict of interest. Why not, instead, require auditors to take a long-term stake in any business they audit? An auditor with a long-term financial interest in the business audited would have a strong, personal incentive to ensure that the business is financially sound. The independence that conflict-of-interest rules are supposed to protect is a kind of indifference. That indifference does not guarantee effective auditing. Among important examples of audit failure over the past two decades, the *Journal* listed "Continental Illinois, LTV, Braniff, the entire savings and loan industry, Sunbeam, Waste Management, Oxford Health, and Cendant." Might not self-interested auditors have done better?

Professions and Conflict of Interest

That *Wall Street Journal* piece combines the two themes combined here as well. Conflict of interest is a problem only in a certain domain, one in which we do not want ordinary self-interest to guide the decisions of those on whom we depend; instead, we want those on whom we depend to be "independent," "impartial," "unbiased," or the like. This is the domain in which professions flourish. Why? If we think of a profession as a number of individuals in the same occupation voluntarily organized to earn a living by openly serving a certain moral ideal in a morally permissible way beyond what law, market, and morality would otherwise require, then the answer is obvious.[1] Insofar as a profession is successful at serving its chosen moral ideal, the profession provides an alternative to self-interest (the typical motive in an ordinary market). Whether the alternative is worth the trouble of organizing the profession is a distinct question, one requiring careful consideration of (among other things) the standards of conduct that define how the profession is to serve its moral ideal. Rules governing conflict of interest are part of those standards. They differ from profession to profession. The differences between them tell us much about the professions—and about conflict of interest in general. So, for example, to decide whether auditors should work under rules that eliminate conflicts of interest or should instead be required to maintain a long-term stake in any business they audit requires us to understand what auditors do, how they do it, and why they do it that way. We must also understand what conflict of interest is, what rules concerning conflict of interest do, and how they do it.

The sixteen chapters that form the body of this book can be divided into five parts, all but the second containing three chapters. The first three chapters deal with occupations in which the term "conflict of interest" first became popular—judging, government service, and lawyering. In "Law's Blindfold," David Luban uses a recent, highly publicized English case to argue that while we should try to eliminate all judicial bias, we should not try to eliminate all judicial conflicts of interest. We do not want justice to be too blind. Kathleen Clark's "Regulating the Conflict of Interest of Government Officials," though largely descriptive, includes an implicit warning. Much of the government's regulation of conflict of interest, especially the most demanding part, is concerned with avoiding the mere appearance of conflict of interest. Appearances are hard to manage. In "Conflict of Interest as Risk Management," Kevin

McMunigal treats conflicts of interest as a species of "perverse incentives." Using examples involving lawyers (some of whom were also government officials), he argues for assessing conflict-of-interest rules as devices for managing the risks that such incentives pose. Some conflicts of interest are worth the risk; they should be allowed. Some conflicts of interest are not; they should be prohibited.

The next part has three chapters that deal with occupations having more connection to business than judges, government officials, and lawyers typically have; the fourth chapter, concerned with corporate directors, is not about a (full-time) occupation at all. In "Conflict of Interest in Journalism," Sandra Borden and Michael Pritchard draw conclusions close to those of Luban, Clark, and McMunigal. This is not surprising. Journalism, though largely operating through businesses, is primarily about public affairs, much as law and government are. That is true of auditing too. In "Conflicts of Interest: The Accounting Profession," Leonard Brooks points out that while auditors are paid by those they audit, the audit is primarily for the public's benefit, not their employers'. Here is a perverse incentive, indeed. In "Conflicts of Interest in Engineering," Neil Luebke describes the conflict-of-interest rules under which engineers typically work, a combination of their own professional rules and those of their employers. What becomes clear from the rules he quotes is that many of those who employ engineers, especially business corporations, neither have a good understanding of conflict of interest generally nor offer their employees much guidance in dealing with particular conflicts of interest. A better understanding of conflict of interest should help those who employ engineers draft better rules.

Those who serve on the board of directors of a corporation, whether a for-profit corporation or a not-for-profit, generally do not do it as a full-time occupation. Many, especially those serving nonprofits, may do it without any pay beyond expenses. Directors are, nevertheless, enmeshed in a complex of regulation, mostly judge-made, governing conflict of interest. In "Conflict of Interest on Corporate Boards," Eric Orts surveys that complex. What he reports is a slow shift from substantive bright-line rules imposed by judges to disclosure procedures internal to the corporation that, except in extreme cases, insulate the corporation from judicial regulation. Judges seem to have moved (as McMunigal advises) from viewing all conflict of interest as irredeemably bad to a more nuanced view of them as business costs, allowable when the appropriate people have had the appropriate information in time to make a proper decision about them.

The three chapters in the third part are all concerned (more or less) with academics. In "Counselors who Teach and Teachers who Counsel," Elliot Cohen argues for a strict separation of the roles of counselor and teacher, pointing out how combining the roles can make it hard to perform either well. Jane Gallop's "Resisting Reasonableness" is almost a direct response to Cohen. Yes, combining roles has its risks, but, she argues, there are also benefits. What makes Gallop's argument both novel and especially piquant is that her focus is not on combining the roles of counselor and teacher, a question about which academics may disagree, but on combining the roles of teacher and lover, a question most academics might think long settled. Because much of Gallop's argument draws on personal experience, it is altogether fitting that her contribution end with a commentary by two of her own graduate students.

In "Conflict of Interest in Anthropology," Merrilee Salmon describes the changing relation between anthropologists and the people they study. There is, in that story, something analogous to Gallop's relation to her students, a complexity of motives and purposes that needs to be worked out case by case. While Gallop's subject is conflict of interest strictly so-called, Salmon's seems a bit wider, the construction of a professional role in which conflict of interest can be defined.

The fourth part is harder to describe. Neither stockbrokers, critics, nor show-business people are (as such) members of an organized profession; they seem more like the directors that Orts discusses. Yet, in "Financial Services," John Boatright describes a set of "perverse incentives" of a complexity beyond anything in the preceding chapters. He then describes the equally complex regulations that attempt to manage them, to create a structure in which they are (more or less) harmless. As with Orts' directors, professional codes play no part in these regulations. According to Tyler Cowen in "The Economics of the Critic," much the same is true of the critic, but the critic is also free from the regulation that Boatright's stockbroker works under. Indeed, by the time Cowen is done with his analysis, we seem to have something close to a free market in criticism. While there are conflicting interests, there seem to be no conflicts of interest (strictly so-called).

Something similar seems to be true of the Hollywood film "executives" described by Thomas Borcherding and Darren Filson. Even when one might most expect concern about conflict of interest (e.g., when an executive has sexual relations "on the casting couch" with actors seeking a part in a movie for which the executive is responsible), Borcherding and Filson argue that the movie industry's incentives give the executive sufficient interest in making the right choice (in principle at least) to make the risks of bad judgment arising from sexual relations with applicants too small to be worth concern. In one respect, the position of Borcherding and Filson resembles Gallop's; they see no reason to prohibit sexual relations between decision maker and subject of the decision. In another respect, however, their positions are almost opposed. Gallop wants to allow sexual relations between teacher and student because sex is too important to prohibit; Borcherding and Filson argue that the movie business tolerates it because sexual relations between executive and actor mean little to either.

The last three-chapter part is about health care: physical therapy, medicine, and prison health care. Having paid little attention to conflict of interest until quite recently, the health care professions are still struggling to sort out the place of conflict of interest in what they do. How much does the struggle reveal about the professions? In "Conflicts of Interest in Medical Practice," Stephen Latham (following much writing in medical ethics) tries to understand conflict of interest as a situation in which certain interests conflict. Surprisingly, many recent innovations in medical practice—for example, bonuses to physicians in a health maintenance organization (HMO) who do not refer "too many" patients to specialists—create conflicts of interest in this sense. These innovations have another aspect, one that may come as a shock: The innovations that Latham describes are making ordinary medical practice look rather like the practice of prison health care—at least as Kenneth Kipnis describes it in "Health Care in the Corrections Setting." All the incentives seem perverse in one way or another. It is, then, with some relief that we reach "Conflicts-of-Interest and Physical Therapy" by Mike Martin and Donald Gabard. The conflict of interest problems they identify look much more like those faced by lawyers, auditors, and engineers, as do the solutions developed by the relatively new profession of physical theory.

The book's final chapter, a reflection on what preceded it, is an invitation to think further about the relationship between professions and conflict of interest. In "Comparing Conflict of Interest Across the Professions," Andrew Stark, co-editor of this volume, offers a general theory of the relation between the character of an occupation and the type (and importance) of its conflicts of interest. Stark distinguishes two axes along which an occupation's conflicts of interest can be ranged. One axis has to do with role conflicts. Some occupations impose a conflict between the practitioner's role as judge and as advocate; others impose a conflict between the practicality role as diagnostician and as service provider. The other axis has to do with those for whom the occupation is supposed to work. For example, some professions have a fiduciary obligation to the public; some do not.

Insofar as this book has a thesis, one the seventeen chapters together support, it is that the question of how to deal with conflict of interest in an occupation quickly leads to questions central to deciding whether the occupation is, or should be, a profession. Each of the seventeen chapters tries, in addition, to say something helpful about what conflict of interest is. What should become plain as one reads these seventeen chapters is that a "standard view" has developed over the last two decades.[2] That view is the one a majority of the chapters rely on more or less—and the one a substantial minority reject in part. We may complete this introduction by summarizing that view's answers to the chief questions of conflict of interest: *What is conflict of interest? What is wrong with it? What can be done about it?*

Conflict of Interest on the
Standard View

A conflict of interest is a situation in which some person P (whether an individual or corporate body) stands in a certain relation to one or more decisions. On the standard view, P has a conflict of interest if, and only if, (1) P is in a relationship with another requiring P to exercise judgment in the other's behalf and (2) P has a (special) interest tending to interfere with the proper exercise of judgment in that relationship. The crucial terms in the standard view are "relationship," "judgment," "interest," and "proper exercise."

On the standard view, "relationship" is quite general, including any connection between P and another person (or persons) justifying that other's reliance on P for a certain purpose. A relationship may be quite formal (as that between PWC and a business it audits) or quite informal (as that between friends). A relationship can last a long time (as familial relationships generally do) or only a minute (as when one directs a stranger to a distant address). The relationship required must, however, be fiduciary; that is, it must involve one person trusting (or, at least, being entitled to trust) another to do something for her—exercise judgment in her service.

The legal distinction between agents and trustees is not important here. An agent is a fiduciary who is under the continual control of the principal (i.e., the principal may, at any time, issue new instructions). A trustee is not under similar control. For a time, at least, the trustee does not have to do what the principal says. So, for example, the trustee of an estate, while bound by the instructions of the will she administers, is a trustee precisely because she is not subject to further instruction, either from those who established the trust or from its beneficiaries.

On the standard view, judgment is the ability to make certain kinds of decision correctly more often than would a simple clerk with a book of rules and all, and only, the same information. Insofar as decisions do not require judgment, they are "routine," "mechanical," or "ministerial"; they have something like an algorithm. The decision maker contributes nothing special. Any difference between her decision and that of someone equally well trained would mean that at least one of them has erred (something easily shown by examining what they did). Ordinary math problems are routine in this way; so is ordinary entry bookkeeping.

When judgment is required, the decision is no longer routine. Judgment brings knowledge, skill, and insight to bear in unpredictable ways. When judgment is necessary, different decision makers, however skilled, may disagree without either one being obviously wrong. Over time, we should be able to tell that some decision makers are better than others (indeed, that some are incompetent). But we will not be able to do that *decision by decision*; we will not be able to explain differences in outcome in individual decisions merely by error—or even be able to establish decisively that one decision maker's judgment is better than another's in this or that case. Even if one decision maker is successful this time when another is not, the difference might as easily be the result of "dumb luck" as "insight." Good judgment is luck that lasts.

Anyone sufficiently adept in the exercise of judgment of a certain kind is competent in the corresponding field. Because part of being a professional is being competent in a certain field, judgment is an attribute of profession. Each profession is defined in part by a distinct kind of judgment. Accountants are especially adept at evaluating procedures for reporting finances; civil engineers, especially adept at predicting the likely serviceability of physical structures; teachers, especially adept at judging academic progress; and so on. Judgment is, however, not only an attribute of professions. Any agent, trustee, or other fiduciary may exercise judgment. One may even exercise judgment in a relationship as mundane as watching a neighbor's children while he answers the phone.

But not every relationship, not even every relationship of trust or responsibility, requires judgment. I may, for example, be asked to hold a great sum of money in my safe until the owner returns. I have a great trust. I am a fiduciary on whom the owner may be relying for her future happiness. But I need not exercise judgment to do what I should. My responsibilities are entirely routine, however much my ability to do as I should is, as Salmon puts it, "strained by a competing interest" in having the money for myself. I only have to put the money in the safe and leave it there until the owner returns and asks for it. I am a mere trustee, lacking the permissible options that make conflict of interest possible.

On the standard view, an interest is any influence, loyalty, concern, emotion, or other feature of a situation tending to make P's judgment (in that situation) less reliable than it would normally be, without rendering P incompetent. Financial interests and family connections are the most common sources of conflict of interest, but love, prior statements, gratitude, and other "subjective" tugs on judgment can also be interests (in this sense). So, for example, a judge has an interest in a case if one of the parties is a friend or enemy, just as the judge would if the party were his spouse or a business in which he owned a large share. Friendship or enmity can threaten judgment as easily as can financial or family entanglements. On the standard view, interests are not ends in view as much as factors tending to shape the ends one has in view.

Training or experience can sometimes protect members of an occupation from the effect of certain tugs on judgment. For example, would-be physicians quickly learn to view the body as a site of disease rather than sexuality. But there do seem to be limits to what training and experience can accomplish. So, for example, physicians have long preferred to send members of their own family to another physician rather than care for them themselves. They do that, in part at least, because they do not think their training has prepared them to keep adequate professional distance between themselves and someone emotionally close to them. Previous generations of physicians saw the bad consequences of supposing that family ties have no tendency to affect professional judgment. What in fact constitutes a conflict of interest is an empirical question, always open to revision as new evidence comes in. It is, therefore, a mistake (on the standard view) to make a final list of what constitutes the relevant interests. We should not, for example, say (as Luebke does) that by definition a conflict of interest must involve a financial or family interest. Definitions cannot settle empirical questions.

There are, of course, facts about a situation, such as loud noise or poor lighting, and even facts about a person, such as exhaustion or extreme anger, that, though rendering otherwise competent judgment unreliable, do not seem to be conflicts of interest. How are we to distinguish such facts from "interests"? For the standard view, this is neither a morally important question nor one difficult to answer. The question is not morally important because, on the standard view, threats to judgment arising from loud noise, exhaustion, or the like should be treated much as conflict of interest should (i.e., in one of the ways described in the next section). The question is not difficult because we can easily identify the conceptual boundary between, say, loud noise or exhaustion, on the one hand, and the influences, loyalties, and the like that, on the other hand, create conflicts of interest. Conditions such as loud noise or exhaustion do not threaten judgment in the way conflict of interest does. They make judgment unreliable by rendering it (temporarily) incompetent; we are, as we say, "unable to think." We might then actually fail a test of competence we would otherwise pass easily. Conflict of interest does not work like that. We remain able to pass any test of competence we could otherwise pass. What conflict of interest affects are the ends in view, the evaluation of this or that means, and other matters of judgment within the bounds of competence.

On the standard view, what constitutes proper exercise of judgment is a "social fact," that is, something decided by what people ordinarily expect; what P or the group P belongs to invites others to expect; what P has expressly contracted to do; and what various laws, professional codes, or other regulations require. Because what is proper exercise of judgment is so constituted, it changes over time and, at any time, may have a disputed boundary. For example, physicians in the United States today (probably) are expected to give substantial weight to considerations of cost when deciding what to prescribe, something not within the proper exercise of their judgment a half century ago.

What is proper exercise of judgment also varies from one profession to another. For example, a lawyer who resolves all reasonable doubts in favor of a client when presenting the client's case in court exercises her professional judgment properly. For a lawyer, truth is a side constraint. In contrast, a physicist who resolves all reasonable doubts in favor of his employer when presenting research at a conference does not exercise professional judgment properly. Physicists are supposed to serve their employers by serving science. For the physicist, truth is not a mere side constraint.

What is proper exercise of judgment may also vary from one client, or employer, to another. For example, one firm may leave its employees free to choose their flight even though the firm is paying for it; another may require employees to choose the least expensive flight consistent with arriving on time. Because employees are agents having a general duty not to waste their employer's resources, and because choosing among flights generally involves judgment, employees of the second firm will have less room for conflict of interest than do employees of the first. They will have less room for conflict of interest because their employer has restricted the domain of proper judgment more than the first did.

What Is Wrong with Conflict of Interest?

On the standard view, a conflict of interest is like dirt in a sensitive gauge. All gauges contain some dirt, the omnipresent particles that float in the air. Such dirt, being omnipresent, will be taken into account in the gauge's design. Such dirt does not affect the gauge's reliability. But dirt that is not omnipresent, the unusual bit of grease or sand, can affect reliability, the ability of this gauge to do what gauges of its kind should, and generally do, do. Such "special" dirt might, for example, cause the gauge to stick unpredictably. Insofar as dirt affects a gauge's reliability, it corresponds to the interests that create conflicts of interest. So, a conflict of interest can be objectionable for at least one of three reasons:

First, P may be negligent in not responding to the conflict of interest. We expect those who undertake to act in another's behalf to know the limits of their judgment when the limits are obvious. Conflicts of interest *are* obvious; one cannot have an interest without knowing it—though one can easily fail to take notice of it or misjudge how much it might affect one's judgment. Indeed, people with a conflict of interest often esteem too highly their own reliability (much as might a dirty gauge used to check itself). Insofar as P is unaware of her conflict of interest, she has failed to exercise reasonable care in acting in another's behalf. Insofar as she has failed to exercise reasonable care, she is negligent. Insofar as she is negligent, her conduct is morally objectionable.

Second, if those justifiably relying on P for a certain judgment do not know of P's conflict of interest but P knows (or should know) that they do not, P is allowing them to believe that her judgment is more reliable than it is. She is, in effect, deceiving them. Insofar as she is deceiving them, she is betraying their (properly-placed) trust. Insofar as she betrays their trust, her conduct is morally objectionable.

Third, even if P informs those justifiably relying on her that she has a conflict of interest, her judgment will be less reliable than it ordinarily is. She will still be less competent than usual—and perhaps appear less competent than members of her profession, occupation, or avocation should appear. Conflict of interest can remain a technical problem after it has ceased to be a moral problem. Even as a technical problem, conflict of interest can harm the reputation of the profession, occupation, avocation, or individual in question.

On the standard view, conflict of interest is not mere bias. *Bias* (in a person) is a determinable deflection of judgment. Bias, whether conscious or unconscious, is relatively easy to correct for. For example, if a gauge has a bias, we need only add or subtract a set amount to compensate. The gauge is otherwise still reliable. If a person is biased, we may be able to do something similar, discount for the bias ("take it with a grain of salt," as we say) or offer incentives to counteract it (as Borcherding and Filson suggest).

Conflict of interest is not bias but a *tendency* toward bias. Correcting for a tendency is harder than correcting for a bias. Consider our gauge again: Because of the special dirt in it, it has a tendency to stick. How do we correct for that tendency? Do we accept its first reading, strike the gauge once and then accept the new reading, strike it several times before accepting a reading, average all the readings, or what? How are we to know when we have what we would have had if the gauge were as reliable as it should be?

What Can Be Done about Conflict of Interest?

Virtually all professional codes, and many corporate codes of ethics as well, provide some guidance on how to deal with conflicts of interest. But many say no more than "avoid all conflicts of interest." On the standard view, such a flat prohibition probably rests on at least one of two mistakes.

One mistake is assuming that all conflicts of interest can, as a practical matter, be avoided. Some certainly can. For example, an accountant might, on becoming a PWC partner, put her assets in a blind trust. She would then not know what effect her audit decisions have on her own finances. Her "objective interests" could not affect her judgment. She would have avoided all conflicts of interest arising from her investments. She cannot, however, avoid all conflicts of interest in that way. The auditor may, for example, not have any practical way to avoid having her brother-in-law accept a management position at General Motors the day after she begins to audit (another part of) the company. Indeed, we might imagine her hearing of his good fortune only after his first day on the job, a week or two after she started the audit. She cannot put all her interests, including her family and friends, into a blind trust. And, even if she could, we would not think it proper; family and friends should not be abandoned in that way.

The other mistake on which a flat prohibition of conflict of interest may rest is the assumption that having a conflict of interest is always wrong. *Having* a conflict of interest is not like being a thief or holding a grudge. One can have a conflict of interest without being in the wrong. To have a conflict of interest is merely to have a moral problem. What will be morally right or wrong, or at least morally good or bad, is how one responds to the problem. There are three categories of possible response (apart from trying to avoid those conflicts that should be avoided).

One category of response is *escape*. One way to escape a conflict of interest is to redefine the underlying relationship. So, for example, a prosecutor foreseeing certain conflicts of interest might "recuse" himself, that is, establish procedures so that all litigation involving his assets, family, and the like that pass through his office bypass him. Another way to escape a conflict of interest is to divest oneself of the interest creating the conflict. If, for example, the conflict is created by ownership of stock in a certain corporation, one can sell the stock before making any official decision affecting it (and have nothing to do with the stock for a decent interval thereafter). This would (as Borcherding and Filson might say) realign the prosecutor's interests, eliminating altogether (what Mc-Munigal called) the perverse incentive.

Escape can be costly. Our prosecutor's recusal gives up the public advantage of having him contribute to certain official decisions. He will not even hear of matters he would ordinarily decide. Divesting avoids that cost, but perhaps only by imposing a substantial personal loss (because, say, the prosecutor would have to sell a stock when its price is low). If the prosecutor cannot afford divestment, and recusal is impractical, he may have to choose a third way of escape, withdrawal from the underlying relationship: He may have to resign his office.

The second category of response to a conflict of interest is to *disclose* the conflict to those relying on one's judgment. Disclosure, if sufficiently complete (and understood), prevents deception and gives those relying on P's judgment the opportunity to give informed consent to the conflict of interest, to replace P instead of continuing to rely on him, or to adjust reliance in some less radical way (e.g., by seeking a "second opinion") or by redefining the relationship (e.g., by requiring recusal for a certain range of decisions). But, unlike escape, disclosure as such does not end the conflict of interest; it merely avoids betrayal of trust, opening the way for other responses.

Procedures for disclosure can be quite elaborate (as Clark's description of the federal rules makes clear). Of course, we expect national governments to have elaborate regulations. So, it is worth pointing out that even an ordinary business corporation or municipal government can have relatively elaborate procedures. For example, the city of Chicago now requires every employee of the executive branch with significant responsibilities to fill out annually a two-page form disclosing close relatives, business partners, and sources of outside income. The forms are open to public inspection.

Disclosure may itself generate problems of privacy and confidentiality. If, for example, a condition of holding a certain public office is that the official list everyone with whom she has a significant business relation, she may have to provide information about people who, having nothing to do with government, thought they could avoid having their business relations put into a public record.

"Managing" is a third category of response to conflict of interest. Though managing is often the resolution reached after disclosure, it need not be. When disclosure is improper (because it would violate some rule of confidentiality) or impossible (because the person to whom disclosure should be made is absent, incompetent, or unable to respond in time), managing may still be a legitimate option. Suppose, for example, that the only surgeon in a hospital is called to the emergency room to operate on what turns out to be his former wife who, unconscious and near death, stands little chance of surviving unless he works quickly. Withdrawing would mean her death—and the end of large alimony payments. Disclosing the conflict of interest to her is impossible (because she is unconscious) and would, in any case, be unnecessary (because, if she were conscious, she would already know what he would disclose). Disclosing to his surgical team her relation to him (including the alimony) would invade *her* privacy while making absolutely no contribution to getting her informed consent. Perhaps the best the surgeon can do is to ask his team to watch him carefully, to keep an especially good record, and to call his attention immediately to anything that seems amiss, hoping his awareness of their watchfulness will curb any tendency in him to be careless with her. The best he can do is *manage* the conflict of interest. Managing is a partial realigning of interests. not enough to eliminate the conflict of interest but enough to make it seem likely that benefits will more than repay the costs.

What should be done about a conflict of interest depends on all the circumstances, including the relative importance of the decision in question; the alternatives available; the wishes of the principal, client, employer, or the like; common knowledge; the law; and any relevant code of ethics, professional or institutional. Some conflicts should be avoided; others escaped or disclosed; the rest, just managed.

Generally, conflicts of interest are easier to manage when they are "potential" than when they are "actual." A conflict of interest is *potential* if, and only if, P has a conflict of interest with respect to a certain judgment but is not yet in a situation where he must (or, at least, should) make that judgment. Potential conflicts of interest, like time bombs, may or may not go off. A conflict of interest is *actual* if, and only if, P has a conflict of interest with respect to a certain judgment and is in a situation where he must (or, at least, should) make that judgment.

In a friendly divorce, for example, the parties may prefer a less expensive proceeding in which they share a lawyer to a more expensive one in which each party has its own. The lawyer who undertakes to represent both parties in such a divorce can, of course, foresee that a dispute about the house, car, savings account, or dog may become unfriendly. From the beginning, the lawyer would be risking a moment when trying to put her professional judgment at the disposal of one party while trying to do the same for the other would affect her judgment in ways hard to predict. She would, that is, have a potential conflict of interest as soon as she agreed to represent both parties. But, while the divorce remains friendly, she has no actual conflict of interest.

Mistakes about
Conflict of Interest

Too frequently, discussions of conflict of interest begin with the biblical quotation, "Can a man have two masters? Can a man serve both God and Mammon?" On the standard view, this is the wrong way to begin. The reason one cannot have two masters is that a master is someone to whom one owes complete loyalty, and complete loyalty to one excludes any loyalty to another. Having only one master *is* a strategy for avoiding all conflict of interest, but it is a strategy making the concept of conflict of interest uninteresting. We must worry about conflict of interest only when having two or more masters—or, to say it without paradox, having none—is normal. Conflict of interest is an interesting concept only where loyalties are regularly and legitimately divided.

We often describe an inability to judge as someone less involved would as a loss of "impartiality," "independence," or "objectivity." Such descriptions often pick out a conflict of interest, but just as often do not. One can, for example, fail to be impartial, independent, or objective because one is biased or under another's control. Impartiality, independence, and objectivity have only a loose relation to conflict of interest.

Much the same is true of loyalty. One can be loyal even if one has a conflict of interest. A loyal agent who cannot reasonably avoid or escape a conflict of interest in some affair on which her judgment is to be deployed would disclose the conflict to her principal. That is what loyalty requires of her. Having fully disclosed the conflict and received the principal's informed consent to continue as before, she may continue, even though her judgment remains less reliable than it would otherwise be. There is no disloyalty in that; yet, the conflict of interest remains.

One can also be disloyal without having a conflict of interest. For example if you embezzle money from your employer because of greed, you are disloyal. You consciously fail to act as a faithful agent of your employer. Though your greed is certainly an interest conflicting with your employer's interests, conflict of interest does not explain why you took the money or what was wrong with taking it. You did not need to exercise judgment on your employer's behalf to know that you should not embezzle your employer's money; "don't embezzle" is part of common sense. There is a conflict of interests here, that is, a conflict between one of your interests and one of your employer's, but no conflict of interest. Conflicting interests do not necessarily constitute a conflict of interest.

On the standard view, a conflict of interest is no more a conflict between commitments or roles than between interests. So, for example, I do not have a conflict of interest (on the standard view) just because (in a fit of absent-mindedness) I promised to meet someone for dinner after promising to attend my son's soccer game scheduled for the same time. That conflict of commitments or roles does not threaten my judgment (though I must decide between them).

I would, however, have a conflict of interest if I had to referee at my son's soccer game. I would find it harder than a stranger to judge accurately when my son had committed a foul. (After all, part of being a good father is having a *tendency* to favor one's own child.) I do not know whether I would be harder on him than an impartial referee would be, easier, or just the same. What I do know is that, like the dirty gauge, I could not be as reliable as an (equally competent) "clean gauge" would be.

The same would be true even if I refereed a game in which my son did not play but I had a strong dislike for several players on one team. Would I call more fouls against that team, fewer (because I was "bending over backwards to be fair"), or the same as a similarly qualified referee who did not share my dislike? Again, I do not know. What I do know is that an interest, my dislike of those players, is sufficient to make me less reliable in the role of referee than I would otherwise be. Conflict of interest does not require a clash of roles; one role (referee) and one interest (a dislike of some players) is enough for a conflict of interest. Conflict of interest is (on the standard view) not a clash between roles or commitments but a clash between one's role or commitment and some interest. Nonetheless, a clash of roles or commitments can (like conflicting interests) be the occasion for a conflict of interest—as Cohen's chapter makes clear.

Beginning a discussion of conflict of interest with God and Mammon makes conflict of interest seem a concept as old as Jerusalem. In fact, the term—and, apparently, the concept—are barely half a century old. The first court case to use the term in something like the sense the standard view gives it was decided in 1949 (*In re Equitable Office Bldg. Corp.*, 83 F. Supp. 531 [D.C.N.Y.]). The *Index of Legal Periodicals* had no heading for "conflict of interest" until 1967; *Black's Law Dictionary* had none until 1979. No ordinary dictionary of English seems to have had an entry for "conflict of interest" before 1971. The first philosophical discussions of the term also date from the early 1970s.[3]

"Conflict of interest" seems to have begun as a mere variant of "conflicting interests." This older term designated a clash between a *public* interest (say, impartiality in a receiver or trustee) and some *private* "beneficial" or "pecuniary" interest (say, a receiver's wish to buy property at a bankruptcy sale he administers). The private interest was often said to be "adverse" (i.e., opposed) to the public interest. Early discussions tended to treat "conflict of interest" as if it were a transparent compound. Only in the late 1960s did lawyers begin explicitly to treat the term as an idiomatic expression connected with judgment. Other professions followed slowly. Meanwhile, the lawyers seem to have lost some of their early clarity.[4]

Because I regard "conflict of interest" as an idiom, I regard as a mistake the assumption Borden and Pritchard make that an analysis of "interest" developed for a theory of liberty applies automatically to conflict of interest. They need a substantial defense of that assumption, one coming to grips both with usage and history. If we were to follow Borden and Pritchard in limiting "interest" to ends in view, we should have to find a new word for "interest" in our analysis, leaving everything else the same and making the term "conflict of interest" look even more like an idiom than it does now. For now, I see no reason to abandon a useful term in order to satisfy a current trend in a distant part of political philosophy.

The term "conflict of interest" began to appear in codes of ethics in the 1970s.[5] Today the term is so common that we would find doing without it hard. Yet, if "conflict of interest," both the term and the concept, are as new as they seem to be, we are bound to ask why. So far we have no authoritative answer. The history of "conflict of interest" has yet to be written. The best explanation now available for the recent rise of the concept seems to be the replacement of the enduring personal relationships of master and servant by the briefer encounters characteristic of the free market, big city, and big business. We are now much more dependent on the judgment of others, much less able to evaluate their judgment decision by decision, and indeed generally know much less about those individuals than we would have even fifty years ago. Rules about conflict of interest are one systematic response to the risks of this new dependence.

Many potential or actual conflicts of interests are, out of politeness or timidity, misdescribed as "*apparent* conflicts of interest" or "merely apparent conflicts of interest." The term "apparent conflict of interest" need not be wasted in this way. On the standard view, a conflict of interest is (merely) *apparent* if, and only if, P does not have the conflict of interest (actual or potential) but someone other than P would be justified in concluding (however tentatively) that P does. Apparent conflicts of interest (strictly so-called) are no more conflicts of interest than stage money is money.

An apparent conflict of interest is nonetheless objectionable—for the same reason that any merely apparent wrongdoing is objectionable. It misleads people about their security, inviting unnecessary anxiety and precaution. An apparent conflict should be resolved as soon as possible. It is resolved by making available enough information to show that there is no actual or potential conflict. One might, for example, answer a charge of financial interest by showing that one does not own the property in question (or that one's investments are in a blind trust). When one cannot (even in principle) make such a showing, the conflict of interest is actual or potential, *not* (merely) apparent.[6]

Often, the basis of a charge of "apparent conflict of interest" is a gift or bribe. Of course, gifts are not in the same moral class as bribes. Gifts are a way of reenforcing, recognizing, or even starting friendship; they are an expression of such virtues as thoughtfulness and liberality. And, yet, just because gifts can start a friendship, they can add bonds of interest where none should exist (e.g., between a judge and a litigant or between a company's head of purchasing and the company's most ambitious supplier). For that reason, many governments, businesses, and other organizations have policies limiting business gifts to mere tokens. Some forbid such gifts altogether. Gifts are an important subject in any discussion of conflict of interest.

A "gift" *demanded* is a bribe (or "grease payment"), not a gift (strictly speaking). Bribes as such do not create conflicts of interest; generally, what they create is something more serious: disloyalty at least; at worst, crime. A *bribe* is a payment (or promise of payment) in return for doing (or promising to do) something one should not do (or, at least, should not do for that reason). When bribes affect judgment (as they often do), they affect it in a definite way, that is, in the direction promised. Affecting judgment in a definite direction creates a bias, not a conflict of interest.

Bribe *offers*, however, can create a conflict of interest. Offering your auditor a bribe may, for example, have so upset him that he is now inclined to doubt every entry in your books, even when documentation seems proper; he can no longer audit your accounts as efficiently as an ordinary auditor would. (Here "interest" is what Latham would describe as "passion.")

There is, of course, much more to be said about conflict of interest, but not here. This chapter is supposed to introduce the book, that is, to say enough about the seventeen chapters following to interest readers in them, to provide enough of a map to make the new territory seem inviting, and then to send them into it. The introduction should not be a substitute for the book it precedes.

Notes

1. For a defense of this definition, see Michael Davis, *Is Higher Education a Prerequisite of Profession?*, 13 Int'l J. Applied Phil. 139–48 (1999).

2. Michael Davis, *Conflict of Interest Revisited*, 12 Bus. and Prof. Ethics J. 21–41 (1993).

3. Neil R. Luebke, *Conflict of Interest as a Moral Category*, 6 Bus. and Prof. Ethics J. 66–81 (1987).

4. Kevin McMunigal, *Rethinking Attorney Conflict of Interest Doctrine*, 5 Geo. J. Legal Ethics 823–77 (1992).

5. See, especially, American Bar Association, *Model Code of Professional Responsibility* (1970).

6. Compare Andrew Stark, *The Appearance of Official Impropriety and the Concept of Political Crime*, 105 Ethics 326–51 (1995).

I

Law and Government

1

LAW'S BLINDFOLD

David Luban

The classical iconography of justice depicts her as a goddess and equips her with three symbols: the sword, the scales, and the blindfold.[1] Each of these captures one element of the rule of law. The sword indicates the coercive power of the court. The scales suggest that the job of the court is to weigh the competing claims in a controversy against each other. The many artistic representations of the scales usually show them in equipoise, with the pans empty: That is so we can see that the scales themselves are true and honest. The judge cannot start the proceeding with the pans out of balance: that would be pre-judgment—literally, and etymologically, "pre-judice."

What of the blindfold, a relatively recent addition to the traditional (and ancient) iconography, which entered common use only in the sixteenth century?[2] It signifies that Justitia bases her decisions only on the merits of the case, signified by the scales. She does not know who the litigants are; she is blind to their rank and station, their political connections, their virtues and vices apart from the case before her. She is oblivious to any signals sent by the sovereign about how he wishes the case decided; nor can she see gestures of threat or seduction that might affect her decision. More than any other symbol, the blindfold signifies that the judge must be wholly impartial, wholly disinterested, and wholly focused on the case before the court. Anything that compromises the judge's impartiality offends against justice.

This ideal undergirds judicial conflict-of-interest rules. Justitia is a divinity, but judges are all too human, and in real life they do not wear blindfolds. How can we guarantee their impartiality? We can forbid them from presiding over cases in which they are not impartial. I will call any rule directly forbidding judicial partiality a "direct ban rule." Most judicial codes of conduct contain a direct ban rule. For example, the American Bar Association's Model Code of Judicial Conduct (CJC) phrases its direct ban rule as follows: "A judge should disqualify himself in a proceeding in which . . . he has a personal bias or prejudice concerning a party or a party's lawyer. . . ."[3]

But in addition to relying on judges' ability to identify their own biases, other rules aim to screen them from temptation by forbidding them to remain on cases in which the incentive to partiality is great, typically because the judge or his or her family has a personal stake in the outcome. A judge with a conflict of interest in a case—an interest in the litigation that conflicts with the institutional interest in impartiality—must recuse (disqualify) him- or herself. Thus, in addition to the direct ban rule forbidding judicial partiality, ethics codes include indirect, or prophylactic, rules designed to reduce partiality by removing judges who face severe temptations toward partiality.

These indirect rules aim to curtail the same evil as the direct ban rule. They do so by prohibiting judges from remaining on cases in which they have a personal interest in the outcome, *whether or not the judge would actually give in to the temptation to partiality.* Actions that are not themselves evil are prohibited; henceforth, it is wrong not only for judges to be partial but also for them to sit in cases in which they have conflicts of interest. Now there are two evils, not just one. The first, judicial partiality, is (one might say) *malum in se;* the other, violating the prophylactic conflicts regulations, is *mala prohibita* (but no less *mala* for merely being *prohibita*). The distinction between the two may seem too obvious to labor, but it is often overlooked, and overlooking it can generate endless confusion. Journalists frequently unearth facts that point to a judicial conflict of interest and quickly infer judicial bias when there may be none; conversely, judges may be biased even though they are in technical compliance with the prophylactic rules defining conflicts of interest. Even though the rules prohibiting conflicts of interest and the direct ban rule prohibiting judicial bias are directed toward the same end—securing law's blindfold—they are distinct from each other and they define different offenses.

Financial and Familial Conflicts

The most fundamental of the prophylactic rules is that no one can be a judge in his own case: The temptation to bias is too strong. But the word "own" has an extended meaning. It refers not only to cases in which the judge herself is a litigant but also to cases in which her family or friends (or, for that matter, her enemies) are litigants, cases in which her family or former law partners are lawyers, and cases in which the judge has a financial stake in the outcome. In any of these cases, the judge should recuse herself or grant a litigant's motion that she recuse herself. According to the CJC, "a judge should disqualify himself or herself in a proceeding in which the judge's impartiality might reasonably be questioned."[4] Notice that the standard concerns not just the judge's own assessment of whether her impartiality might be compromised but whether a reasonable outsider might have doubts. A judge may know in her heart that her financial stake in the outcome will not compromise her impartiality a bit. But, as we have seen, the conflict-of-interest rules aim to protect judicial impartiality not merely by directly prohibiting judicial partiality but by forbidding judges from placing themselves in situations that might increase the risk of judicial partiality.

Canon 3E goes on to enumerate four specific situations that always require disqualification: (1) when the judge has personal bias or prejudice (this clause, recall, is the direct ban rule) or personal knowledge of disputed evidentiary facts; (2) when the judge or a former law partner or associate of the judge had at one time served as lawyer in the case, or the judge had been a material witness in it; (3) when the judge, the judge's spouse, or the judge's minor child has a financial interest in the case, or any other interest that could affect its outcome; and (4) when the judge or the judge's spouse "or a person within the third degree of relationship to either of them, or the spouse of such a person" is a party to the proceeding, or an officer or director of a party, or is a lawyer in the proceeding, or is known by the judge to have an interest that could be affected by the proceeding, or is likely to be a material witness in the proceeding.[5] This is not meant to be an exhaustive list, but it is certainly suggestive. One can argue about the details of these standards,[6] but the principle is straightforward and uncontroversial: No judge can remain in a case in which bonds of loyalty or self-interest would strongly tempt her to partiality.

The Appearance of Bias
or Impropriety

In addition to the direct ban on judicial partiality and prophylactic prohibitions on presiding over cases in which the risk of partiality is high, judicial ethics codes often forbid judges from presiding over cases in which there is an appearance of bias or an appearance of impropriety. Recall that Canon 3E of the CJC specifies that "a judge should disqualify himself in a proceeding in which his impartiality might reasonably be questioned." I observed earlier that this rule protects not just against judicial partiality but against temptations to partiality. It is also protection against the appearance of bias, because it makes the test of disqualification how things would look to a reasonable outsider.[7] The appearance of impropriety is a broader concept than appearance of bias: It includes the appearance of bias—the appearance that the judge has violated the direct ban rule—but also the appearance that the judge has committed any legal impropriety. (Thus when I discuss the appearance of impropriety, this should be understood to include the appearance of bias.)

Why prohibit mere appearances? The theory is that the appearance of impropriety is almost as bad as impropriety itself, because—as the old saw puts it—justice must not only be done but be seen to be done. Unless judges avoid the appearance of impropriety, public confidence in the fair administration of justice will be undermined.

That's the argument, at any rate. Unfortunately, the appearance-of-impropriety standard is a notorious old question beggar. It compels a judge to disqualify herself from case B even though her partiality is unsullied *and even though she has violated no conflict-of-interest regulation*, merely because the case *looks* (to whom? and after how much careful scrutiny?) superficially like case A, which involves a genuine violation of the conflicts rules. And then shouldn't case C, which looks superficially like B, compel recusal because of the appearance of impropriety? The problem is that "appearance" is a conceptual accordion that can expand as widely as suits the eye of the beholder—and the standard implicitly presupposes a beholder who has not analyzed the judge's conduct properly, because case B, by hypothesis, presents no genuine impropriety. For these reasons, the American Bar Association eliminated the appearance-of-impropriety standard from its code of ethics for lawyers in 1983; but it remains in the CJC (Canons 1 and 2).

In my view, the appearance-of-impropriety standard does have a legitimate place in judicial ethics—but not in the arena of conflicts of interest. A judge should not fraternize with known mobsters, drink alcohol during lunch in plain sight of jurors, or have sex in his chambers during office hours. Even if none of these things is unlawful, they all appear improper, and they may well undermine confidence in the judge's ability to administer justice. Some years ago, New York municipal judge Alan Friess made headlines because he tossed a coin to decide whether to sentence a convicted pickpocket to twenty days in jail (as the pickpocket suggested) or thirty days (as Friess proposed). Friess also took a show of hands of courtroom spectators to decide which of two elderly men accusing each other of harassment was more credible. In his most notorious case, the judge released a twenty-year-old female defendant into his own custody and brought her home. He did not last long on the bench, nor should he have. Whether or not these things were legally improper, they made his courtroom a laughing stock.[8]

Matters are different when it comes to conflicts of interest. As we have seen, prophylactic conflicts regulations do not prohibit per se evils—they prohibit actions that heighten the risk of partiality. Specifically, they prohibit judges from remaining on cases in which they or a member of their family has an interest. If it merely appears that the judge or the judge's family has an interest in the case, but on closer inspection the nexus is too slight to constitute a genuine interest, why should the judge disqualify him- or herself? Doing so merely wastes scarce judicial resources; it also makes the recusal motion a more potent weapon in the hands of litigants forum shopping for a judge they like. The appearance of conflict of interest is two levels removed from the actual evil of judicial partiality: An act that looks like, but is not really, a violation of a merely prophylactic rule should not undermine anybody's confidence in the justice system. To argue otherwise is to make judicial participation in cases hostage to the most cynical and suspicious elements of public opinion. Tabloids and talk radio should not set normative standards.

Even behavior such as Judge Friess's, which in my view legitimately warranted removal for appearance of impropriety, does not look as bad from close up as it did in the New York City tabloids. Friess explained that he called on the spectators to vote on the quarreling litigants' credibility only to dramatize to them that reasonable people might believe either of them; that his coin-flip sentence was a protest against the chaotic conditions of the New York courts; and that he took the female defendant home for a Thanksgiving dinner with him and his fiancée because she was ill, penniless, and frightened that her abusive boyfriend would kill her.

Ideological Conflicts

A philosophically interesting question concerns conflicts arising from a judge's moral, political, religious, or philosophical convictions—what I shall call, for short, ideological convictions. Occupying a prominent place in the pantheon of judicial infamy are the judges of the Weimar Republic, who were by and large right-wingers and anti-Republicans. For more than a decade they let their politics guide their judging; they meted out savage sentences to the German left and openly tolerated political murder by the far right, thereby paving the way for Hitler. Thomas Mann bitterly denounced "the jurisprudence of political revenge,"[9] and Bertolt Brecht quipped that Germany had metamorphosed from Goethe's land of *Dichter und Denker*—poets and thinkers—to the land of *Richter und Henker*—judges and hangmen. A judge whose ideological convictions prevent her from adjudicating a case fairly must recuse herself; after all, ideological commitment is as much an "interest" as money or personal loyalty and is just as capable of interfering with judicial impartiality.

The complication is that without a judicial philosophy no jurist can discharge his duties; as Chief Justice William Rehnquist once wrote, a judge whose mind is a *tabula rasa* is not so much impartial as incompetent.[10] The then Associate Justice was defending his own decision not to recuse himself from a case on which he had previously opined while working for the Department of Justice. His decision not to recuse may have been wrong, but his argument is surely correct. Particularly at the appellate level, we count on judges to have a consistent approach to statutory interpretation and to the Bill of Rights. Nor would we ask a former civil rights litigator such as Thurgood Marshall to disqualify himself from all civil rights cases, even though he was sympathetic to the pro-civil-rights side. Marshall's way of understanding civil rights was among his most prominent qualifications for the Supreme Court.

The dilemma, then, seems to be that judicial ideology simultaneously threatens judicial impartiality (and thus generates conflicts of interest) and creates the very possibility of judging. One response is to distinguish between a judicial philosophy, that consists of worked-out beliefs about purely jurisprudential issues and one that consists of beliefs about political ideology. Judges need the former and need to steer clear of the latter. However, I am skeptical that any such distinction is valid, because jurisprudential issues are seldom purified of politics. Consider as an example whether statutes should be interpreted according to their plain meaning even when it yields unappetizing or unreasonable results. This seems at first glance to be an issue of abstract jurisprudence or even hermeneutic philosophy. But judges who adhere to plain meaning usually offer a defense based on the theory of democracy: The plain meaning of a statute is the work of an elected legislature and should not be tampered with by unelected judges. That is a political argument and rests at bottom on a political ideology.[11]

One might argue that the solution to the dilemma lies not in judicial abstinence from ideology but, rather, in judicial openness to revising ideology in the face of recalcitrant cases. Ideological beliefs amount to disabling prejudices only when they literally prejudge a case—only, that is, when everyone (including the judge) knows ex ante how the judge is predisposed to decide, thereby signaling that he or she is not really providing what is aptly called a "fair hearing." The judges ideological convictions are a kind of noise that makes him or her hear one side more clearly than the other. That is a conflict of interest.

But, if the judge's judicial and political beliefs are themselves dynamic and evolving, if she is willing to hear, willing to rethink, willing to revisit her philosophy (or at least her mode of applying it in particular cases), then she has no real conflict of interest. The career of the late Supreme Court Justice Harry Blackmun, who began as a conservative mimic of Chief Justice Warren Burger and eventually metamorphosed into the Court's most liberal member, illustrates the possibility that judicial ideology can respond to experience. Moreover, some of the most famous episodes in U.S. judicial history involved judges who went against their own ideological grain—think, for example, of Justice Holmes, a sympathizer with Spencerian philosophy, who nonetheless cautioned in a dissenting opinion that "The Fourteenth Amendment does not enact Mr. Herbert Spencer's *Social Statics.* . . ."[12] Holmes always insisted that his so-called "liberal" dissents had nothing to do with liberal philosophy. When the Supreme Court denied citizenship to the Hungarian-born pacifist Rosika Schwimmer because of her beliefs, Holmes dissented, and Mrs. Schwimmer wrote him a touching thank-you letter. Holmes (hardly a pacifist!) wrote back, "You are too intelligent to need explanation of the saying you must never thank a judge. . . . If his decision was of a kind to deserve thanks, he would not be doing his duty."[13] In other words, a judge who deserves thanks has given in to a conflict of interest. If his decision is entirely the product of personal convictions, he has been inattentive to whatever the case itself has to teach.

The problem with this resolution of the dilemma is that it leaves matters entirely up to the judge. Notice that we are unwilling to leave it up to the judge in the case of familial or financial conflicts: We will not permit a conflict-ridden judge to remain on the case even if he assures us that his mind is open to the arguments of those who would injure him financially or defeat his family. In the terms of our prior discussion, when it comes to familial or financial conflicts of interest, we impose both the direct ban on partial judging and prophylactic rules designed to remove judges from temptation. In the case of ideological judging, however, we rest content only with the first. Why? I can see only four possible explanations, and none of them is satisfactory.

First, we may believe that blood and money are thicker than ideology—that political passions are less likely to compromise a judge's impartiality than love of lucre and family. As an empirical matter, this seems absurd: The greatest blood-lettings in human history have been motivated by politics and religion, not family or finance.

Second, it may be that we *want* political judging. Certainly it seems that way when U.S. senators and presidential candidates insist on ideological "litmus tests" for federal judges. But it is hard to square this view with the chronic criticism of judges imposing their own convictions instead of following the law. Other common law and civil law countries are even less tolerant of political judging than the United States.

Third, we may believe that a judge's prejudices are harmful only when they are, in the words of the CJC, "*personal* bias or prejudice concerning a party or a party's lawyer."[14] But why? If a judge is biased against all products-liability plaintiffs (believing them to be gold diggers), or against all affirmative-action opponents (believing them to be closet racists), the threat to impartiality is just as real as if the judge was biased against them personally.

Fourth, and perhaps most plausibly, we may simply be unable to devise disqualification rules that will let in honest judicial philosophy but exclude partisan or ideological prejudice. Canon 3E works because we can identify objective criteria of family or financial conflicts; there seem to be no comparable surrogates for ideological passions, except in the rare cases in which a judge belongs to some ideological organization that takes positions on litigation issues. (We shall see an example of this in the next section.) If it seems, then, that we are willing to tolerate intense judicial passions for politics, but are unwilling to tolerate even the possibility of judicial nepotism or greed (which may be less intense than political passion!), the disappointing reason may be that we live with unprincipled inconsistencies when we cannot figure out how to be consistent.

The Matter of Pinochet

A famous case from 1998 illustrates these difficulties at work. The case originated in efforts by a Spanish magistrate to bring General Augusto Pinochet, the former Chilean dictator, to trial in Spain for human rights violations that included the murder of Spaniards. In the fall of 1998 Pinochet underwent back surgery in London. While he was immobilized, the Spanish magistrate moved to extradite him, and the British government placed Pinochet under arrest while the motion was pending. The case was immensely controversial both in Chile—where the leftist government reluctantly joined with Pinochet's supporters to defend Chile's right to deal with its own political past—and in the United Kingdom, where former Prime Minister Margaret Thatcher joined with other conservatives to praise her old anticommunist ally. The case raised complicated issues of international law as well as British law.

Eventually, the case went to the Law Lords in Britain's House of Lords, where—in a momentous decision—a five-judge panel held 3–2 that Pinochet was extraditable. Then, sensationally, Pinochet moved to have the judgment set aside because one of the three-judge majority, Lord Hoffman, had a conflict of interest. Hoffman, it seems, had connections with the human rights group Amnesty International, which had supported the Spanish extradition request. A second panel of Law Lords heard the motion and agreed with Pinochet that the previous decision was tainted by Lord Hoffman's conflict and must be set aside. The case was reargued before a second five-judge panel, which also held against Pinochet but drastically narrowed the scope of the holding as well as the number of crimes for which Pinochet could be tried in Spain. The British Home Secretary subsequently determined that Pinochet was too psychiatrically deteriorated to be tried in Spain and returned him to Chile as a humanitarian gesture. Emboldened by the British court having ripped away Pinochet's aura of invincibility, the Chilean court system began the process of rescinding his immunity. As of this writing the determination of whether Pinochet can be tried in Chile is still pending in the courts.

Let us delve. Lord Browne-Wilkinson wrote the opinion in *In re Pinochet*, the House of Lords decision setting aside the first judgment that Pinochet was not immune from extradition.[15] His opinion sets out the following facts: For tax purposes, Amnesty International has bifurcated its British operation into two nonprofit corporations. Amnesty International Limited engages in advocacy, political work, and litigation; Amnesty International Charities Limited is a tax-exempt organization that does nonpolitical charitable work to advance human rights, work such as fund raising for human rights research—it explicitly avoids political work and advocacy. To keep them straight, I will call the three organizations "Amnesty" (the international umbrella organization), "Limited" (the British advocacy organization), and "Charities" (the nonpolitical charitable organization).

Lord Hoffman sits on the board of directors of Charities. As a director, he plays no role in setting policy for either Amnesty or Limited; indeed, Charities as a whole plays no policy-setting role. Apparently, Lord Hoffman's chief activity was fund raising; a letter soliciting funds from law firms for a new building for Amnesty went out over his signature. (Pinochet's lawyers responded with a contribution.) When Amnesty moved successfully to intervene in the Pinochet litigation, Lord Hoffman did not disclose his connection with Charities; apparently, British law does not require him to do so. In addition, the opinion notes that Lady Hoffman is a long-time administrative employee of Limited, but the Lords found it unnecessary to determine whether his wife's job created a conflict of interest for Lord Hoffman, because in their view his association with Charities required his automatic disqualification from the Pinochet case the moment Amnesty entered it as an intervener.

Why? British precedents require automatic disqualification when a judge has a pecuniary interest in a case because of the appearance of bias. The pecuniary interest is absent here, but Lord Browne-Wilkinson argues that Amnesty's nonpecuniary "interest . . . to establish that there is no immunity for ex-Heads of State in relation to crimes against humanity"[16] suffices to trigger automatic disqualification.

But how does Amnesty's interest transmogrify into Lord Hoffman's interest? Lord Browne-Wilkinson reaches this conclusion in three steps. First, he refuses to accept the legal fiction that Amnesty, Limited, and Charities are distinct entities. "The substance of the matter is that [the three organizations] are all various parts of an entity or movement working in different fields toward the same goals."[17] Second, if Lord Hoffman had been a member of Amnesty, he would be presumed to share its goals, including the goal of establishing Pinochet's extraditability. Third, it cannot make any difference that Lord Hoffman was a nonpolicymaking director of Charities rather than a member of Amnesty. "There is no room for fine distinctions if Lord Hewart's famous dictum is to be observed: it is 'of fundamental importance that justice should not only be done, but should manifestly and undoubtedly be seen to be done.' "[18]

At first glance, all this seems plausible and persuasive. At second glance, however, doubts begin to surface. Lord Browne-Wilkinson's argument turns on his analysis of two legal fictions: the fiction that Amnesty, Limited, and Charities are distinct entities because they have incorporated separately for tax purposes, and the fiction that all of Amnesty's policy interests are shared by all the people involved in the "entity or movement." Within the space of a single paragraph, Lord Browne-Wilkinson dismisses the first legal fiction, finding that the three organizations are substantially the same, and accepts the second fiction, finding that Amnesty members and Charities directors share Amnesty's interest in the litigation.

Why? It would be at least as plausible to argue exactly the reverse. Lord Hoffman might respond as follows:

> As a judge, I know full well that I cannot associate with an advocacy group, and that is why I did not join Amnesty. I accepted the seat on the board of directors of Charities only because Amnesty scrupulously ensures that Charities never participates in politicking or advocacy. When you, Lord Browne-Wilkinson, opine that both groups are "working in different fields towards the same goals," that is correct only in the broad sense that both groups want human rights abuses to stop. It isn't correct if you mean that Charities agrees with the positions Limited or Amnesty take on every discrete issue. In no way is Charities working, directly or indirectly, on the extraditability issue; nor do the people associated with Charities necessarily agree with Amnesty's position in the Pinochet case. We *have* no corporate position on the issue. When it comes to political issues, Amnesty, Limited, and Charities are distinct organizations in substance as well as legal form. The first legal fiction is really a fact.
>
> Furthermore, it's preposterous to presume that every member of Amnesty, let alone a non-operational director of Charities whose chief activity has been raising funds for a building, endorses Amnesty's litigation position in the Pinochet case. The human rights community is divided over whether extraditability will advance the cause; undoubtedly, Amnesty's membership is divided as well. Contrary to what you assert, 'the substance of the matter' is that no inference whatever can be drawn about *my* interest in the case by looking at Amnesty's interest. The second legal fiction is just that: a fiction.

I think that this reply is substantially correct, but Lord Browne-Wilkinson has the final word: *It looks bad.* The appearance of bias undermines the first decision's legitimacy, regardless of whether Lord Hoffman was actually biased, and regardless of what the best way to treat the legal fictions really is.

It would be hard to find a better illustration of the fundamental fuzziness of the appearance-of-impropriety standard. If Lord Hoffman clearly had a personal stake in Amnesty's litigation position—if, for example, he held a position of authority in Amnesty and had ordered its lawyers to intervene in the Pinochet case—it would have been, to say the least, entirely unethical to participate as a judge in the case. As it is, however, two layers of legal fiction and administrative fact separated the actual situation from this hypothetical impropriety. Is the resemblance close enough to constitute an appearance of impropriety? How close is close enough? There is simply no way to tell.

The Pinochet case also offers a striking illustration of the double standard we have observed between ideological conflicts of interest and interest-based conflicts. If Amnesty had not intervened in the case, or if Lord Hoffman had been a director of a different human rights group with no connection to Amnesty, then the Lords' argument for Hoffman's disqualification would vanish. Even if Lord Hoffman had been a full-time human rights activist and lawyer before becoming a judge, he would not be disqualified unless he had worked on Pinochet-related cases. Yet Lord Hoffman's potential bias against Pinochet arises from whatever convictions drove him to work for Charities, and those would presumably be the same or even stronger in regard to any of these alternatives. In the actual case, Amnesty's intervention merely provided the formalistic pretext for Pinochet's disqualification motion. The case was the rare one in which a party to the litigation is also the living embodiment of an ideology. If Hoffman's disqualification was correct, why should Pinochet have to rely on the happy accident of Amnesty's intervention to remove a potentially biased judge?

Curiously, I believe that in the end the Lords arrived at the right result, and indeed arrived at it for roughly the right reason. But the argument has nothing to do with the parsing of legal fictions, or the general validity of appearance-based disqualification. The right argument for the Lords to make, I believe, is this:

> This is a momentous case. Millions of people around the world are following its progress. Chilean reaction alone threatens to destabilize a fragile democratic compromise. Human rights law worldwide may be influenced by our treatment of this case. The case was decided by a single vote—Lord Hoffman's. Even though we are generally skeptical about disqualifying judges for apparent bias when there is little or no evidence of actual bias, the singular circumstances of this case make the slightest tinge of the appearance of bias unacceptable. If Pinochet is to be extradited, his supporters cannot be handed the makings of a martyr-mythology according to which he was railroaded by a biased British judge. We are fully aware that, should we permit this decision to stand, millions of people will know nothing about it other than that Lord Hoffman cast the decisive vote against Pinochet, and that Lord

Hoffman has some sort of official connection with Amnesty International. In ordinary cases, we would not and should not be influenced by the possibility that our decisions will be misunderstood and misrepresented by elements of the public. But this is no ordinary case. Our decision today, setting aside the earlier decision, is as singular as the case itself, and we explicitly confine it to today's facts. It is to set no precedent for future, less extraordinary, cases of judicial disqualification.

Perennial Institutional Conflicts

Let us pass on to less lofty matters than major human rights decisions. Thus far we have been surveying the most common and central cases of judicial conflict of interest. But conflicts of interest can include other less frequently discussed and more subtle ways in which Justitia's blindfold slips.

No conflict-of-interest rules can eliminate all possible temptations. One recurring temptation is built into the bureaucratic structure of legal institutions. Particularly in smaller jurisdictions, lawyers and prosecutors are repeat players—courthouse regulars—and judges will always be tempted to avoid friction with courthouse regulars because friction makes the job more difficult and life less pleasant. Thirty years ago, Abraham Blumberg published a famous study of an urban criminal court that detailed the many forms of complicity among courthouse regulars. Blumberg found that some judges would deny bail to defendants when defense lawyers signaled that they were having trouble collecting their fee from the client; for all I know, the practice might persist even now.[19] Less outrageously, trial judges are notoriously reluctant to impose sanctions on lawyers for abusive tactics, and they seldom use their contempt powers on lawyers who show up late to hearings and request continuances purely for the strategic purpose of inconveniencing the other side and its witnesses. I have spoken with judges who defend friction-reducing deference to lawyers on the ground that judges can be more effective at brokering settlements if they get along with the local bar. But, the ghost of Neville Chamberlain whispers in our ear, appeasement carries costs of its own, and good judges understand that their desire to maintain amicable relations with the bar should never interfere with their obligation to police the misbehavior of lawyers. To do otherwise is to give in to a conflict of interest: The judge has allowed his personal interest in tranquility to interfere with the interests of justice.

A second chronic dilemma facing elected judges arises from the ever-increasing cost of campaigning. Two decades ago, judicial elections were low-budget operations that seldom involved aggressive campaigning and rarely turned incumbents out of office. Judges now complain that campaigns have become contentious and expensive, requiring them to raise election-year warchests from the only people interested in contributing to them: lawyers and law firms that practice before their courts. The conflict-of-interest possibilities are obvious but the solutions are not. A selective ban on contributions by lawyers and law firms would be unconstitutional, and a ban on *all* contributions to judicial elections probably is as well; in addition, such a ban would unfairly prejudice judicial elections in favor of wealthy candidates. Making judgeships appointive rather than elective positions would eliminate the conflict, but it would be politically unpopular and paternalistic. Moreover, appointive judgeships have their own disadvantages, most notably tying the judicial office more tightly to party politics. The issue of campaign contributions remains vexed; it creates a knotty problem of institutional design, but, like other financial conflicts of interest, it raises no controversial issues of principle.

Two Concepts of Judging

The tension between a general judicial ideology and openness to the issues and merits of individual cases is just one example of a more basic tension in the judicial role. Even though a judge must be impartial between litigants, one common view of judging holds that the judge is not to be impartial between the litigants and the rest of society. The judge's duty runs entirely to doing justice to the litigants before the court, not pursuing the well-being of anyone else or of society as a whole. This is one of the basic lessons imparted at the National Judicial College, and one that gets repeated more than once. We may call it the *litigant-centered view of judging.*

According to the litigant-centered view, the judge's relationship to the litigants before the bench is analogous to a lawyer's relationship to his or her client. On the standard conception of the lawyer's role, the lawyer has at most an attenuated concern for the interests of third parties, of other clients or future clients, or of the justice system. A lawyer who allows his or her zeal to be deflected because of extraneous concerns has a conflict of interest. The litigant-centered view of judging implies that judges should treat the litigants collectively with the same regard that their lawyers treat them individually, and, as I shall suggest, this fact generates analogous conflicts.

According to the litigant-centered view, judges are required to resolve in a satisfactory way matters posed by the individual litigants before the bench that day. But it is also their responsibility to rationalize and improve the law and the institutions that administer it. These two judicial interests—to focus entirely on the particular litigants before the bench, and to improve legal institutions—can clash, or at least come into tension with each other. To put it another way, there is an alternative to litigant-centered judging, and that is what we might call the *utilitarian view of judging*. According to the utilitarian view, judges have (in Holmes's words) a fundamental "duty of weighing considerations of social advantage,"[20] because "the secret root from which the law draws all the juices of life" is "considerations of what is expedient for the community concerned."[21] If the utilitarian view is right, then excessive compassion for the particular litigants before the court amounts to a conflict of interest—a judicial loyalty that deflects attention from duty. Pari passu, if the litigant-centered view is correct, then judicial utilitarianism creates a conflict of interest—an ideological concern that interferes with the judicial injunction to do justice to the litigants in the court. Because the litigant-centered view and the utilitarian view both have undeniable merits, there seems to be a fundamental tension built into the very nature of the judicial role. No matter which path the judge pursues, there will be at the very least a plausible argument that the judge has been swayed by a conflict of interest.

If a courtroom were *fully private*—if its proceedings had no repercussions on other proceedings, other litigants, other disputes, or the law of the land—no conflict would exist, because the litigant-centered view would be obviously correct. Judges would decide cases very differently than they do now, and the interests of justice for the particular litigants would be the only interests guiding the judge. There would likewise be no conflicts if the courtroom were *fully public*—if the sole purpose of the proceeding was to settle a general question of law or of institutional design. For then the utilitarian view would prevail. Private arbitrations with rent-a-judges are our closest approximations to the fully private courtroom, though even there it is false that what goes on has no outside repercussions. Similarly, the U.S. Supreme Court is our closest approximation to the fully public courtroom, but of course even there it had better not be the case that the individual litigants count for nothing. Trial courts and courts of appeals are neither fully private nor fully public, and judges working in these settings must as a consequence confront the conflict between what we might call the private and public responsibilities of the judicial office.

This tension is well exemplified in a disagreement between Jerome Frank and Karl Llewellyn. Llewellyn had no use for judges who particularize justice to respect what he termed "the fireside equities"[22], Frank responded that judging should never depart very far "from mature notions of the ethical. Mercy, charity, compassionateness, respect for the unique attributes of the men and women who come before our trial courts—these would seem to be needed components of a civilized judicial process."[23] The source of their disagreement lies in the fact that for Llewellyn, the "settlement of disputes . . . is but a minor function of law" because "each case has a value chiefly for the light it sheds on the rights of ten or ten thousand people not in court."[24] Llewellyn, it appears, adhered to the utilitarian view of judging. Frank, on the other hand, argued the litigant-centered view that "individualization of cases . . . should be the aim of our own legal system. [This means] doing justice by giving consideration to their unique aspects."[25] More recently, Robin West has likewise argued that "we can rightly fault the pursuit of impartiality and universality when it is untempered by a judicial recognition of the particular claims of the particular litigants on the court's legal and moral imagination. . . ."[26] West argues that the pursuit of justice, untempered by an ethic of care and compassion for individuals, is not really the pursuit of justice at all.

Conflicts in Settlement

The conflict between litigant-centered and utilitarian judging appears in a variety of guises, and we may usefully think about seemingly disparate problems as instances of this tension. Two examples will suffice, both drawn from the role judges play in out-of-court settlements.

1. *Brokering settlements.* It has become a piece of conventional wisdom that a trial judge's most important responsibility is to try to settle the cases assigned to him or her. Trial, after all, is costly and time-consuming, and it makes litigants miserable. Federal Rule of Civil Procedure 16 requires federal judges to attempt to settle cases, and many judges believe that settlement provides higher-quality dispute resolution than trial. This "quality argument," I believe, is the most principled basis for favoring settlement over trial; the alternative arguments, based on the need to clear crowded dockets quickly, seem too eager to sacrifice justice for the sake of speed. The quality argument is overtly and straightforwardly litigant centered: It amounts to the claim that justice in the dispute between *these* litigants would be ill-served by trial and can best be achieved through judicial mediation leading to compromise.[27]

Owen Fiss, on the other hand, has argued that viewing the courts as organs of dispute resolution is sociologically unsound and morally unacceptable, and as a consequence he opposes the rush to settlement.[28] He worries that "when the parties settle, society gets less than what appears, and for a price it does not know it is paying. Parties might settle while leaving justice undone"[29]—where by "justice," Fiss makes clear, he means justice from the standpoint of society as a whole. The dispute-resolution picture of what judges are in the business of doing assumes (according to Fiss) that litigation originates in private disputes between private parties in an otherwise unstructured social field, whereas in reality every legal dispute implicates public values and carries public significance. Fiss's argument—that going to trial is necessary to resolve the issues of public morality each significant case represents—rests on a model favoring public over private judicial responsibilities, whereas the quality argument for judicial mediation originates in a concern for litigant-centered resolution of private problems. Settlements are compromises: Each party agrees to accept less than the law would award if the party prevailed at trial. In this respect, settlements make an end run around whatever principles the law embodies, and that is what bothers Fiss. Moreover, settlements retard the development of the law, because they create no precedents and leave issues unresolved.[30]

Of course, the decision to settle ultimately rests with the parties, not the judge, but judges still play two important roles in the settlement process. First, as I suggested, the judge often intervenes to help broker the settlement; second, regardless of who brokered the settlement, the judge must decide whether to accept its terms. The litigant-centered view of judging commends judges who mediate cases and recommends that judges exercise their power to police settlements in a deferential way, because the settlement terms are for the parties to determine.[31] From the standpoint of litigant-centered judging, a judge who believes that issues of public importance require the reasoned examination offered by a trial, rather than a quick settlement that both parties desire, has a conflict of interest. Just as a judge should be oblivious to what is popular, and unswayed by the demands of the sovereign, Justitia's blindfold should shield her from the interests of the popular sovereign.

Actually, aggressive judicial intervention to settle cases can create conflicts of interest from a litigant-centered viewpoint as well, if the judge, perhaps for utilitarian reasons, imposes settlement terms that one or the other party finds unwelcome. In that case, the judge's personal interest in sustaining settlement terms that for whatever reason she finds just may interfere with her objectivity. The characteristic method by which a judge pressures parties into settlement is to make the parties pessimistic about their chances at trial by dropping hints that the judge will resolve questions of law unfavorably to them, by debunking the quality of evidence they have to offer, and by suggesting that their cases are worth much less than they had hoped. By offering assessments such as these before oral presentation of the evidence (which allows the fact finder to assess the credibility of witnesses), or full-fledged rehearsal of the arguments, the deliberative process of trial gets replaced by what one trial judge has called a veritable "Ouija board."[32] The judge may then become personally invested in the terms of a settlement that she herself has brokered and less willing to entertain arguments from litigants that the settlement is unfair. This is plainly a conflict of interest, because the judge by this time has become, quite literally, a judge in her own case.

In one notable example, Judge Jack Weinstein pressured the parties in the massive Agent Orange litigation to settle for $180 million even though both plaintiffs and defendants had privately informed the judge that $200 million would be acceptable because "he did not want the settlement amount to signal that the case was stronger than it actually was, thereby encouraging groundless mass toxic tort litigation in the future."[33] This is a fundamentally utilitarian reason, although Weinstein's initial decision to pressure the parties into settlement was based on litigant-centered concerns.[34] Weinstein subsequently came down hard on plaintiffs who wanted to opt out of the settlement. Because too many opt-outs would unravel "his" settlement, it is hard to avoid the suspicion that by this time Weinstein was unable to be impartial in judging the legal merits of the opt-out cases—and Weinstein is widely believed to be the best trial judge in the United States. Such are the perils of settlement judging.

2. *Sealing the records of a case and approving secret settlements.* Defendants in products-liability cases sometimes offer plaintiffs generous settlements in return for a secrecy pledge. The plaintiff must promise not to discuss the case or the terms of the settlement and to return discovery material, because the defendant wishes to forestall future lawsuits by other consumers. Plaintiffs' attorneys complain that secret settlements often result in vital information about dangerous products being concealed from the public, sometimes for years. Attorneys nevertheless feel bound to negotiate secret settlements and recommend that their clients accept them, because they know that their clients have little chance of doing any better. If a lawyer chafes at the fact that her lips are sealed about a public health hazard, the standard conception of her role nevertheless instructs her that her public health concerns are nothing more than a conflicting interest.

And, on the litigant-centered view of judging—analogous, I have suggested, to the standard conception of the lawyer's role—the judge ought to go along with secret settlements that provide an injured plaintiff with generous compensation. Compassion for the plaintiff, and the defendant's desire for finality, seem to require no less. The judge ought to seal the records of the case if doing so is a term of the parties' settlement (as it is whenever the settlement is secret). Likewise, the judge should issue a protective order (a gag order) to prevent parties from discussing the case: After all, the case is nobody else's business.[35] Judges are more than willing to issue protective orders; one prominent federal judge wrote in a 1981 opinion that he was "unaware of any case in the past half-dozen years of even a modicum of complexity where an umbrella protective order . . . has not been agreed to by the parties and approved by the court."[36]

In short, judges usually do not think twice about secrecy in the settlement process because the litigants want secret settlements. This is litigant-centered judging with a vengeance: The litigants prosper but the public is harmed. If litigation is viewed—as litigant-centered judging suggests it must be—as a private matter between the parties, without wider repercussions or meanings, then the parties ought to be able to stipulate that the documents regarding their dispute be sealed. If, on the other hand, litigation brings a dispute into the public realm, or concerns a matter of general importance, then the documents too belong in the public domain.[37] Secret settlements clearly seem to be a context in which litigant-centered judging is inadequate, in which utilitarian judging seems to yield the better approach, and in which (consequently) the judge's compassion for the injured plaintiff seems to represent a conflict of interest—a case in which, if the judge yields to compassion for the plaintiff, the judge violates his or her duty to society.

Conflicts in Rulemaking: Hard Cases and Bad Law

It might be thought that the conflicts we have just been examining arise in large part because settlement is an anomalous judicial activity. Once we turn from settlement to adjudication, perhaps the anomaly evaporates.

It isn't so. The tension between litigant-centered and utilitarian judging arises even in the purest of adjudicatory contexts, judicial rulings on issues of law. The paradigm illustration is the so-called *hard case*, a case that is difficult to decide because if a judge tries to fashion the over-all best rule of law a terrible hardship, or inequity, is worked on the losing party.[38] An old adage has it that hard cases make bad law. The 1842 case in which this adage first appeared in print, *Winterbottom v. Wright*, is a perfect illustration. It was an action brought by an injured coachman against a firm that had contracted with the coach's operator to maintain it in safe condition. The court found for the defendant (based on privity of contract), arguing that allowing the plaintiff to recover for the defendant's negligence "might be the means of letting in upon us an infinity of actions," so that "the most absurd and dangerous consequences, to which I can see no limit, would ensue."[39] Judge Rolfe added in his opinion, "This is one of those unfortunate cases in which . . . it is, no doubt, a hardship upon the plaintiff to be without a remedy, but by that consideration we ought not to be influenced. Hard cases, it has frequently been observed, are apt to introduce bad law."[40]

This is a straightforward utilitarian argument of the kind that would appeal to Llewellyn. Holmes made the argument explicit in his dissent to *Northern Securities Co. v. United States*:

> Great cases like hard cases make bad law. For great cases are called great, not by reason of their real importance . . . but because of some accident of immediate overwhelming interest which appeals to the feelings and distorts the judgment. These immediate interests exercise a kind of hydraulic pressure which makes what previously was clear

seem doubtful, and before which even well settled principles of law will bend.[41]

It must be acknowledged that weighty arguments support this utilitarian view, according to which Justitia must blindfold herself to whatever accidental features of a case appeal to her feelings of compassion and therefore distort her judgment. One is a straightforward cost/benefit calculation: As we earlier quoted from Llewellyn, "each case has a value chiefly for the light it sheds on the rights of ten or ten thousand people not in court." If litigant-centered justice in hard cases leads to bad rules for those ten or ten thousand, it should be avoided. Judges should consider only the systemic effects of legal rules and honor only the public responsibilities of their office. There is also the argument that legal rules should be kept simple. They should be easy to follow and easy to apply even by undistinguished judges. That means rules cannot be overloaded with exceptions; they can cover only a few cases, and if so they should cover the commonplace cases, not the hard cases.

For the utilitarian, the analogy between litigant-centered judging and the standard conception of the lawyer's role offers no support to litigant-centered judging. For the standard view of legal ethics has some pretty unappealing consequences. We have just seen that it requires lawyers to negotiate secret settlements on behalf of their clients, at the expense of the public interest. Or take the example of a lawyer who, over the course of years, has established a reputation as a skilled but scrupulously fair negotiator. His reputation for fairness encourages other lawyers to trust him, and allows him to obtain better settlements for his clients, with less fuss and less expense, precisely because other lawyers know that his word is golden.

Now suppose that his current client wants him to settle her case on dubious terms, by bargaining ruthlessly and violating the trust his opposite number places in him. In other words, the client wants the lawyer to squander decades of reputational capital on her case, despite the fact that doing so is against the lawyer's principles and will make it impossible for him to bargain as effectively on behalf of future clients. On the standard conception of the lawyer's role, his desire to maintain his reputation for honorable bargaining is nothing more than a conflicting personal interest; for that matter, so is his concern about future clients. Nothing is supposed to matter except the interest of the current client.[42] Here, however, it seems clear that the interests of the one client should not outweigh the interests of the many clients to come. In just the same way, the interests of today's litigants in a secret settlement, with sealed documents, that prevent many other injured would-be plaintiffs from bringing suit, should not outweigh the interests of the many. And that conclusion is all judicial utilitarians seem to need to secure their argument.

Yet, as I argue next, the utilitarian view of judging is far from unassailable.

The Case against Utilitarian Judging:
The Role of Compassion

What, then, becomes of Jerome Frank's and Robin West's pleas for individualization and compassion in judging? One utilitarian response to Frank and West is that there really is no distinction between a judge doing justice to the litigants and a judge fashioning the best legal rules for society overall.[43] Doing justice to the litigants *means* applying general legal rules to the facts of their case, and the correct legal rules are those that are best overall. Judicial rulemaking occurs only when judges are addressing questions of law, and questions of law are general: They require no essential reference to facts specific to a single case.

At just this point, however, the case for judicial utilitarianism begins to weaken. As Frank and the other legal realists showed, the argument offers too simplistic an understanding of how questions of law get decided. Every judge knows that the facts of the specific case do enter into the formulation of legal rules. Legislation derives its legitimacy from the constitutional role of the legislature, and the democratic mandate of the legislators. By contrast, judicial rulemaking—"interstitial legislation," in Holmes's phrase—gains its legitimacy principally from the reasons judges offer in their written opinions. These, however, are not abstract arguments about social policy. Judges have no mandate to make social policy, only to decide cases. For this reason, judges must construct their arguments from the facts of the case they are deciding, and the persuasive force of their arguments derives in large measure from the felt sense that whatever rule the judge proposes yields the right outcome in *this* case, on *these* facts and *this* story.[44]

This is true even for the U.S. Supreme Court, the mission of which is explicitly to settle general questions of law. In one sense, everyone understands that the Court usually accepts cases because of the legal issues they raise, not because of their facts or the parties' grievances. But the Justices also understand the fact-bound character of judicial reasoning, and as a result they sometimes wait for years to address an issue until a case with "good" facts comes across the docket. Just as crusading lawyers bringing test cases shop around for attractive litigants with appealing facts,[45] the Supreme Court does as well.

For example, several Justices have been concerned for years about large punitive-damages awards and have made no secret of their desire to impose limits on punitive damages. When the Court finally imposed significant limitations on punitive damages, it did so in a case involving an immense punitive award to a wealthy physician who had sued because of a scratch on his luxury automobile.[46] Of course, the Court could have made any case the vehicle for its doctrine; the identical constitutional provisions and public policy arguments would apply in a case in which a jury had awarded major punitive damages against an unscrupulous corporate giant for screwing some poor-but-honest customer. But a pro-business decision in the latter case would have lacked plausibility and legitimacy. So the Court bided its time and waited for just such an unattractive plaintiff as a rich doctor whining about his scratched BMW. That way, it could be seen doing justice between *these* litigants, a much more reassuring posture than that of policy-minded judges sacrificing particularized justice on the altar of overall social utility.

It is hardly a secret that Justices often have a legal agenda that they intend to enact gradually, step by step and case by case, over a period of years. But the Court is officially bound by the constitutional requirement of issuing opinions only in genuine cases and controversies, and the rules of standing, which preclude anyone who has no tangible stake in the outcome from bringing suit, are meant to ensure that opinions cannot be issued merely because someone wants to settle an abstract question of law. These doctrines are intelligible only on the assumption that particular cases and real litigants matter, even to the U.S. Supreme Court. And, I am arguing, particular cases and real litigants matter even in abstract legal reasoning. Legal reasoning is never all that abstract: When judges devise tests of when a statutory condition is fulfilled, they do it by isolating the various "factors" that are relevant. These they assay out of the stories and fact patterns of real cases. If judicial reasoning deals with universals, it inevitably treats them as concrete universals.

In this sense, at any rate, all judging is litigant centered, because even abstract questions of law get decided by generalizing from the fireside equities of particular cases. Even utilitarian decisions are governed, perhaps more than the judges let on, by narrative detail rather than abstract argument. The only real question, and the one that separates the litigant-centered judge from the utilitarian judge, is the question of degree: How much should a rule be retrofitted to the particulars of the case?

What about Llewellyn's argument that what matters is not this case but the ten or ten thousand that its rule will effect? I have my doubts about this argument, because it presupposes that judges are in a position to know what effect their rules will have on the ten or ten thousand. The problem is that judicial predictions about the systemic effect of rules are at best good guesses and at worst prejudice or pretension. Here I agree with Jerome Frank:

> So in 1895, the Supreme Court, in holding unconstitutional the federal income tax law, was patently frightened by the prediction that such a tax would usher in communism, a prediction which proved absurd. . . .

When judges indulge in such glib soothsaying, they generally resort to "judicial notice," which . . . sometimes consists of wholly unverified impressions.[47]

Let us recall the stern judicial warnings in *Winterbottom v. Wright*. If an injured coachman can sue the coach maintenance service for his injuries, "the most absurd and dangerous consequences . . . would ensue." "We ought not to permit a doubt to rest upon this subject, for our doing so might be the means of letting in upon us an infinity of actions." "If we were to hold that the plaintiff could sue in such a case, there is no point at which such actions would stop."

Seventy-four years later, Judge Cardozo overturned *Winterbottom* in his most famous opinion, *MacPherson v. Buick*, which inaugurated the modern law of negligence.[48] Civilization did not become notably more discontent, and the dire prognostications in *Winterbottom* were revealed for what they were: sheer judicial incapacity to imagine a social world governed by less ruthless rules for allocating risk than those of Dickens's England.[49] Judges are not social scientists, and even social scientists have a miserable track record when it comes to predicting the future. Judicial utilitarianism, much more than litigant-centered judging, requires judges to exceed their very limited competence. It flatters them into behaving like oracles.

The worry about judicial utilitarianism is, in a nutshell, that it requires judges to worry too much about bad law and not enough about hard cases. Perhaps this is a consequence of Justitia's blindfold, which blocks out everything in the hard case that makes it hard. Yet it is important to realize that people have seldom regarded the blindfold as an unqualified good. Justice blindfolded can be justice hoodwinked—a figure of pathos as well as a figure of nobility. A 1554 painting by Pieter Brueghel depicts blind justice surrounded by a panorama of ghastly executions—a perfect emblem of the fact that Justitia is as blind to the damage she wreaks as she is to the temptations of prejudice.[50] Likewise, a 1497 engraving by Albrecht Dürer shows Justice, seated with her sword and her scales, being blindfolded by a Fool.[51] Dürer, like Brueghel, was thoroughly aware of the human costs of blind justice. Sometimes hard law makes bad cases.

Conclusion

I began with the most straightforward judicial conflicts of interest, those involving the personal and financial interests of the judge. Because they are straightforward, they are relatively easy to forestall through prophylactic disqualification rules. But other conflicts of interest raise knottier problems. Some involve the mere appearance of conflict of interest, and these I do not believe are genuine conflicts at all. Some involve a conflict between a judge's moral and political beliefs and the requirement of impartiality. Such conflicts cannot be remedied by codified ethics rules, because to screen off the source of the conflict is to screen off the judge's mind and conscience. Some conflicts are seemingly ineradicable features of the institutional setting in which judges work. Finally, I have argued that there is a basic tension between a judge's public and private responsibilities—between her duty to advance "social advantage" and her duty to do justice to particular litigants. Most obvious in the context of settlements, it appears in judicial rulemaking as well, in the inconsistent demands to show compassion in hard cases and to make good law. From the standpoint of either judicial utilitarianism or litigant-centered judging, responding to the other theory's demands represents a conflict of interest akin to an ideologically based conflict. Yet, I have suggested, there is no easy way out, because neither litigant-centered judging nor utilitarian judging is entirely satisfactory. This last form of conflict of interest, then, represents a structural tension—a deep unanswered, perhaps unanswerable, question—at the core of the judicial role. It is the question of whether, in the end, we actually want law blindfolded.

Notes

1. For a fascinating analysis of artistic and poetic representations of justice, from which I take these observations, see Dennis E. Curtis & Judith Resnik, *Images of Justice*, 97 Yale L. J. 1727–72 (1984).

2. Id. at p. 1757.

3. American Bar Association, *Model Code of Judicial Conduct*, Canon 3E (1)(a).

4. Canon 3E(1).

5. Much of this rule has been codified in the federal disqualification statute, governing federal judges. 28 U.S.C. § 455.

6. For example, the "third degree of relationship" test forbids judges to sit in a case involving their niece's spouse, but does not forbid them from sitting in a case involving their first cousin. This seems irrational.

7. The U.S. Supreme Court has construed the "might reasonably be questioned" language to include appearances of impropriety, even when there is no actual impropriety, in Liljeberg v. Health Services Acquisitions Corp., 486 U.S. 847 (1987).

8. E. R. Shipp, *"Burnt-Out" Judge Leaves the Bench*, N.Y. Times, Jan. 16, 1983, at 42.

9. Quoted in E. J. Cohn, *Manual of German Law*, vol. I (rev. ed. 1968), 29, 43.

10. Laird v. Tatum, 409 U.S. 835 (1972)(memorandum of Rehnquist, J.); see also William Rehnquist, *Sense and Nonsense About Judicial Ethics*, 28 Record of Ass'n of Bar of City of N.Y. 708–13 (1973).

11. See the debate between Antonin Scalia and his critics, in Scalia, *A Matter of Interpretation: Federal Courts and the Law* (Princeton: Princeton University Press, 1997).

12. Lochner v. New York, 198 U.S. 45, 75 (1905) (Holmes, J., diss.).

13. Holmes to Schwimmer, Jan. 30, 1930, quoted in Liva Baker, *The Justice from Beacon Hill: The Life and Times of Oliver Wendell Holmes* (New York: HarperCollins, 1991), 625.

14. Canon 3E(1)(A) (emphasis added).

15. Judgment in In Re Pinochet, *http://www.parliament.the-stationery-office.co.uk/pa/ldjudgmt/jd990115/pino01.htm*.

16. Id. at p. 10.

17. Id. at 11.

18. Id.

19. Abraham S. Blumberg, *The Practice of Law as a Confidence Game*, 1 Law & Soc'y Rev. 15–39 (1967).

20. Holmes, "The Path of the Law," in *Collected Legal Papers* 184 (New York: Peter Smith, 1952).

21. Holmes, *The Common Law* 31–32 (Boston: Little Brown, 1963).

22. Karl Llewellyn, *The Common Law Tradition* 268, 272 (Boston: Little Brown, 1960).

23. Jerome Frank, *Courts on Trial: Myth and Reality in American Justice* 389 (Princeton: Princeton University Press, 1949).

24. Karl Llewellyn, *The Effect of Legal Institutions Upon Economics*, 15 Am. Econ. Rev. 671 (1925). Frank comments that this statement is "far too unqualified." *Courts on Trial*, note 23 *supra*, at 343 n. 4.

25. *Courts on Trial*, note 23 *supra*, 378.

26. Robin West, *Caring for Justice* 51–52 (New York: New York University Press, 1997).

27. But there are grounds for skepticism about both the quality and the efficiency arguments. See Marc Galanter, . . . *A Settlement Judge, not a Trial Judge: Judicial Mediation in the United States*, 12 Law & Soc'y 1–18 (1985); Marc Galanter & Mia Cahill, *Most Cases Settle: Judicial Promotion and Regulation of Settlements*, 46 Stan. L. Rev. 1339–91 (1994). For a defense of judicial mediation in many cases, see Carrie Menkel-Meadow, *Whose Dispute Is It Anyway? A Philosophical and Democratic Defense of Settlement (In Some Cases)*, 83 Geo. L. J. 2663–96 (1995). Menkel-Meadow correctly observes that legal justice, meaning whatever the law would rightly decide if a case were adjudicated, need not be the same as justice in a more basic ethical sense, whereas settlements that depart from the law can achieve justice in the latter sense. This is a sophisticated version of the quality argument.

28. Owen Fiss, *Against Settlement*, 93 Yale L. J. 1073–90 (1984).

29. Id. at 1085.

30. I have discussed Fiss's argument at greater length in David Luban, *Settlements and the Erosion of the Public Realm*, 83 Geo. L. J. 2619–62 (1995).

31. Or, rather, the litigant-centered view commends judges who mediate cases in a fair way, ensuring that the weaker party is not bullied into abandoning legal rights. Some commentators have observed that when power imbalances between the litigants is too great, litigant-centeredness requires the formality of trial. Richard Delgado et al., *Fairness and Formality: Minimizing the Risk of Prejudice in Alternative Dispute Resolution*, Wis. L. Rev. 1359–1404 (1985).

32. H. Lee Sarokin, *Justice Rushed Is Justice Ruined*, 38 Rutgers L. Rev. 341 (1986). One thinks of Lon Fuller's claim that "the distinguishing characteristic of adjudication lies in the fact that it confers on the affected party a peculiar form of participation in the decision, that of presenting proofs and

reasoned arguments for a decision in his favor. Whatever heightens the significance of this participation lifts adjudication toward its optimum expression. Whatever destroys the meaning of that participation destroys the integrity of adjudication itself." Lon L. Fuller, "The Forms and Limits of Adjudication," in *The Principles of Social Order* 92 (Kenneth I. Winston, ed., Durham, NC: Duke University Press, 1981).

33. Peter H. Schuck, *Agent Orange at Trial* 159 (1986). I have discussed this issue at greater length in David Luban, *Heroic Judging in an Antiheroic Age*, 97 Colum. L. Rev. 2064–90 (1997).

34. Weinstein worried that if the Agent Orange case came to trial, the veterans would get nothing, because the scientific evidence that Agent Orange caused their injuries was too weak.

35. Federal Rule of Civil Procedure 26(c) authorizes judges to "make any order which justice requires to protect a party or person from annoyance, embarrassment, oppression, or undue burden or expense."

36. Zenith Radio Corp. v. Matsushita Elec. Indus. Co., 529 F. Supp. 866, 889 (E.D. Pa. 1981).

37. Luban, *Settlements and the Public Realm*, note 30 supra, at 2648–59.

38. "Hard case" means "hardship case." This is, according to *Black's Law Dictionary*, the oldest meaning of the phrase. Ronald Dworkin, in his celebrated essay "Hard Cases," introduced a different meaning: A hard case is one that "cannot be brought under a clear rule of law." Ronald Dworkin, "Hard Cases," in *Taking Rights Seriously* 181 (2nd ed., Cambridge, MA: Harvard University Press, 1978). This is not the sense I will use.

39. 152 Eng. Rep. 403, 404 (1842) (Lord Abinger, C.B.). This case was very influential in retarding reform in products liability law.

40. Id. at 405–406.

41. 193 U.S. 197, 400–401 (1903).

42. On this point, see Robert J. Condlin, *Bargaining in the Dark*: The Normative Incoherence of Lawyer Dispute Bargaining Role, 51 M. L. Rev. 1–104 (1992); Ronald J. Gilson and Robert H. Mnookin, *Disputing Through Agents: Conflict and Cooperation Between Lawyers in Litigation*, 94 Colum. L. Rev. 509–65 (1994).

43. I don't mean to be taking a controversial position here on the question of whether judges make laws rather than applying them—the hot-button issue of "judicial activism" and "judicial legislation." No one—or at least no one who knows anything whatever about the legal system—doubts that judges must make law. Judgemade law comes in the form of "tests"—rules that state operational criteria for applying legislative law. To take an example chosen nearly at random, the RICO statute (18 U.S.C. § 1962) criminalizes "patterns of racketeering activity"; judges must devise tests of when several racketeering acts form a pattern. Because all statutes employ general words (e.g., "pattern"), every statute requires judicial test making—rulemaking—if courts are to implement it.

44. As I have written elsewhere, the life of the law is neither logic nor experience, but narrative. David Luban, *Legal Modernism* 211 (Ann Arbor: University of Michigan Press, 1994).

45. For example, a prominent conservative public interest firm, which has been conducting a campaign against affirmative action, carefully screens dozens of potential plaintiffs, looking for Ms. Right: a telegenic, apolitical, blue-collar white woman denied university admission despite good grades and test

scores. David Segal, *Putting Affirmative Action on Trial; D.C. Public Interest Law Firm Scores Victories in War on Preferences,* Wash. Post, Feb. 20, 1998, at A1.

46. BMW v. Gore, 517 U.S. 559 (1996).

47. *Courts on Trial,* note 23 *supra,* 343.

48. 111 N.E. 1050 (1916).

49. Of course, contemporary tort reformers believe that exactly these concerns have come to pass in our "litigation explosion." But they are mistaken. For an eye-opening contemporary survey of the actual data on tort lawsuits, which contradict the "litigation explosion" picture in almost every particular, see Marc Galanter, *Real World Torts: An Antidote to Anecdote,* 55 Md. L. Rev. 1093–1160 (1996).

50. Curtis & Resnik, note 1 supra, at 1757.

51. Reproduced in Curtis & Resnik, note 23 *supra,* at 1740, figure 6. The engraving is also reproduced on the dust jacket and paperback cover of my own book *Lawyers and Justice* (Princeton: Princeton University Press, 1988), where I was struck by the thought that the Fool may have represented a lawyer hoodwinking Justice.

2

REGULATING THE CONFLICT
OF INTEREST OF
GOVERNMENT OFFICIALS

Kathleen Clark

Conflicts of interest have been a matter of concern in the United States since its founding. The U.S. Constitution itself contains three provisions restricting conflicts of interest: one forbidding federal officials from accepting gifts, employment, or titles from foreign governments; another prohibiting members of Congress from being appointed to a federal office that was created or whose salary was increased during that member's term in Congress; and a third preventing members of Congress from receiving an increase in salary until after they stand for reelection.[1]

During and after the Civil War, in response to wide-scale influence peddling and procurement fraud, Congress passed a wave of conflict-of-interest legislation. Among other reforms, Congress made it a crime for government employees to act as agents or attorneys on behalf of parties who had monetary claims against the United States. These statutes remained on the books, with few prosecutions, for nearly a century. During the 1950s, however, they significantly complicated the government's ability to hire consultants on a temporary or intermittent basis. In 1962, Congress enacted legislation that recodified and reorganized the nineteenth-century statutes.[2] This legislation also created a new category of government employment for persons employed by the federal government on a temporary or intermittent basis and provided that the conflict-of-interest laws would operate more leniently on this type of employee.[3]

The next major change in the federal conflict-of-interest laws came after Watergate with passage of the Ethics in Government Act of 1978.[4] This act required certain employees of the government to disclose their finances, placed restrictions on postgovernment employment for executive branch employees, and established the Office of Government Ethics, which promulgates conflict-of-interest regulation for the executive branch. In response to continued perceptions of abuse in both the executive and legislative branches, Congress passed the Ethics Reform Act of 1989, which imposed tougher postgovernment employment restrictions on certain high-level executive branch officials, created postemployment restrictions for members of Congress and highly paid congressional staff, established a rule restricting the ability of employees in all three branches of government to accept gifts, and banned honoraria for almost all government employees.[5] More recently, both Houses of Congress adopted new rules restricting the ability of members and staff to accept gifts.[6]

The current federal rules on conflicts of interest are highly detailed and complicated and include statutes, regulations, and executive orders. In some cases, the distinctions that these rules draw seem excessively legalistic. For example, the government has issued detailed regulations distinguishing donuts from sandwiches and lobbying on behalf of a private university from lobbying on behalf of a private high school.[7] This chapter describes the conflict-of-interest rules regarding gifts, financial interests, outside compensation, and postgovernment-employment activities.

Acceptance of Gifts

Federal law contains both a broad restriction on employees' receipt of gifts and several narrower restrictions. The general federal gift statute applies to government employees at all levels: from the file clerk and truck driver right up to the cabinet secretary.[8] The gift statute identifies three categories of persons who may not give gifts to federal employees. One category of prohibited givers consists of those persons "whose interests may be substantially affected by the performance or nonperformance of the [employee's] official duties."[9] This part of the statute focuses on the individual employee's responsibilities.

A second category of prohibited givers consists of anyone "seeking official action from [or] doing business with . . . the [employee's] employing entity."[10] Here, the statute focuses not on the particular employee but on the agency in which the employee works. The gift statute may take such a broad approach out of concern that any employee in an agency could have some indirect effect on agency decision making or could obtain confidential government information for the gift giver. The government also may simply prefer the bright-line test provided by the current statute rather than the individualized analysis required under the fiduciary model. Especially when dealing with restrictions that do not impinge upon employees' fundamental rights, the broader, bright-line approach may be more appropriate than one requiring individualized analysis.

A third category of prohibited gift givers consists of anyone who "conduct[s] activities regulated by [the employee's] employing entity."[11] Once again, the focus is on the employee's agency rather than the particular duties of the individual employee. What is peculiar about this provision is that it applies only to employees of the executive branch and not to members or employees of Congress. Why the gift ban should be more restrictive with executive branch officials than legislative branch officials is not readily apparent. But Congress has recently made significant strides in tightening its gift rules. It now more severely restricts the receipt of gifts from the one class of persons who routinely attempt to affect the exercise of discretion by members of Congress and their staff: lobbyists.[12] Members and staff are now prohibited from accepting gifts of personal hospitality, transportation for work-related events, or contributions to their legal defense funds from lobbyists.

Government employees also are prohibited from accepting gifts from foreign governments, even if there is no relationship between the foreign government and the employee's responsibilities or his or her agency's powers.[13] The foreign gift ban is illustrative of the tendency to treat foreign entities more restrictively than their domestic counterparts in ethics regulations.

Other federal gift restrictions take aim at specific classes of employees. One prohibits meat inspectors from receiving anything of value from anyone engaged in commerce.[14] On its face, this statute purports to prohibit the inspectors from accepting even trivial gratuities, such as cups of coffee, from meat processors and also purports to prohibit inspectors from receiving birthday gifts from their families. The courts, however, have construed the statute to apply only when the gift has more than nominal value and when there is some nexus between the gift and the employee's official duties.[15]

In summary, most of the executive branch restrictions on gifts are substantially broader than what would be necessary to prevent conflicts of interest. Rather than using the individualized analysis regarding a particular employee's loyalty obligations, they provide a general standard applicable to all agency employees. They also place a broad ban on gifts from foreign governments. Although these restrictions do not appear to be strictly necessary, neither do they seem to cause particular hardship to government employees. In the legislative branch, on the other hand, up until recently gift restrictions have not been strict enough to prevent officials from abusing public office. But the new congressional gift rules are much closer to that suggested by conflict-of-interest analysis.

Employees' Financial Interests

The federal ethics rules dealing with employees' financial interests are contained in a general financial conflict-of-interest statute applicable to the executive branch and independent agencies, its implementing regulations, and the House and Senate rules and in certain agency-specific statutes. The general financial conflict-of-interest statute prohibits executive branch and independent agency employees from participating "personally and substantially" in a "particular matter" in which the employee (or a member of her family) has a financial interest.[16] Although the statute itself does not define "personally and substantially," the implementing regulations do, and they require direct and significant participation by the employee.[17] The statute also fails to define "particular matter," but it does provide several examples, such as a contract, claim, and accusation. These examples suggest that "particular matter" is limited in scope to discrete controversies involving a small number of parties. The implementing regulations define the term "particular matter" as

> encompass[ing] only matters that . . . [are] focused upon the interests of specific persons, or a discrete and identifiable class of persons. [It includes matters that] do [] not involve formal parties and may include . . . legislation or policy-making that is narrowly focused on the interests of such a discrete and identifiable class of persons.[18]

This definition reflects a more general trend in government ethics rules to exclude from coverage those governmental actions that are broad in scope: legislation, general policymaking, regulation writing, and sometimes rulemaking. The reasons for this trend are both theoretical and practical. The theoretical justification is that conflicts of interest are likely to be most serious in situations in which the governmental action is directed at particular parties or affects a small number of persons. As a decision decreases in scope, two things become more likely: (1) a decision could be influenced by an employee's intention to benefit his or her own financial interests rather than to promote the government's interests; and (2) the nongovernmental entity could influence such a decision. On a practical level, as decisions increase in scope, the more likely it is that an employee could have some sort of direct or indirect financial interest. Laws or regulations of general application will affect nearly everyone in the country, and if all government employees with an interest in that decision were disqualified from participating in the decision, no one would be left to make the decision. The executive branch regulation's definition of "particular matter" represents a compromise between the desire to insulate government decisions from employees' personal financial interests and the need to ensure that someone in government can make the decision.

The executive branch regulations also provide a reasonable resolution to the issue of how attenuated the effect on the employee's financial interest must be to trigger disqualification. Disqualification is required only if the matter under consideration will have a "direct and predictable effect" on her financial interest.[19] Under the regulations, the magnitude of the employee's gain or loss is immaterial.

The general financial conflict of interest statute does not apply to the legislative branch,[20] and the House and Senate rules provide only an incomplete protection against conflicts of interest. The Senate rules prohibit a senator or a Senate employee from using his or her official office to introduce or aid the progress of private bills that further only the employees own pecuniary interest or those of his or her family or a limited class of persons including his or her family.[21] As long as legislation affects the financial interests of others, a senator may help pass legislation which also affects his or her own personal financial interest. The House rules contain even fewer restrictions. Members of Congress are not required to divest their financial holdings or put them in a blind trust. As a result, members of Congress sometimes play key roles in passing or blocking legislation that has a direct impact on their investments.

Although no governmentwide statute or regulation requires employees to divest financial holdings that would otherwise require them to disqualify themselves under the disqualification provisions, certain regulations and agency-specific statutes do require divestment. The Senate rules require the staff (but not the members) of committees to divest "any substantial holdings which may be directly affected by the actions of the committee."[22] Executive agencies are authorized to issue regulations prohibiting all or some agency employees from specified classes of financial interests where such an interest "would cause a reasonable person to question the impartiality and objectivity with which agency programs are administered."[23] Agencies also can prohibit a specific employee from acquiring or holding a particular financial interest or class of interests where the employee's possession of such interest would require her disqualification from matters "central or critical" to the performance of her official duties.[24]

Some agency-specific statutes prohibit all or certain agency employees from having financial holdings in companies regulated by the agency. For example, Federal Communications Commission (FCC) employees may not have a financial interest in any company engaged in the business of radio or wire communication.[25] Although these restrictions on stock ownership may not impinge upon any constitutionally protected right, they are extremely broad, in terms of both the number of employees affected and the breadth of the restrictions that each of these employees must face. They impose restrictions where a conflict of interest-based rule would not, such as prohibiting an FCC-employed mail clerk from owning stock in AT&T. These agency-specific statutory restrictions are not tailored to apply only to agency employees who exercise discretion that could affect specific investments. They impose unwarranted hardships on government employees by restricting their freedom unnecessarily and make it harder for the government to recruit personnel.

To summarize, the general financial conflict-of-interest statute and its implementing regulations address the conflict-of-interest concerns raised by executive branch employees' financial interests. Some of the agency-specific rules go further than conflict-of-interest concerns would require and impose unnecessary restrictions. The rules for Congress, on the other hand, are entirely inadequate to address the conflicts of interest that members of Congress routinely face in dealing with legislation that could affect their financial interests.

Receipt of Outside Compensation

Some government employees earn income from activities they engage in outside their federal government jobs, such as sitting on corporate boards, helping to run a family business, driving a taxi, writing books or articles, and giving speeches. For the purpose of conflict-of-interest analysis, I divide these activities into two categories: those involving nonexpressive conduct and those involving expressive conduct. The analysis for these two categories is quite similar, but because of the unique history of government regulation of employees' expressive conduct, I examine them separately.

Compensation for Nonexpressive Conduct

The federal government imposes five different types of restrictions relevant to this analysis. The first type of restriction, the salary supplementation statute, prohibits an employee from receiving compensation from a nongovernmental source for his or her governmental work.[26] When for example, an employee, acting in her governmental capacity, receives compensation for her government work from a nongovernment source, there is the possibility that the prospect of receiving such outside compensation might influence her decisions about what activities to engage in as part of her government job. It would be improper for her to make a decision on the basis of the nongovernment party's ability or willingness to pay her. The salary supplementation statute prevents such conflicts.

The second type of restriction prohibits certain agencies' employees from being employed by any company regulated by that agency.[27] This prohibition resembles the general gift ban in two respects: (1) its prohibition applies to all employees at an agency rather than focusing the prohibition on only those employees who actually have discretionary power; and (2) it covers all entities regulated by the agency rather than only those entities that specifically could benefit from the employee's exercise of discretion. This regulation is broader than that suggested by conflict-of-interest analysis. A rule aimed only at conflicts of interest would not prohibit an FCC mail clerk from also working as a clerk for MCI, but a statute prohibits it.[28] This restriction on outside compensation burdens a more significant liberty interest for government employees than does the restriction on their receipt of gifts. Nonetheless, the ease of applying the rule to all agency employees rather than just those with discretion may justify the broader rule.

A third type of restriction on outside employment prohibits high-level employees from receiving compensation for professional work that involves a fiduciary relationship.[29] This prohibition cannot be derived directly from conflict-of-interest principles, but it may stem from a generalized sense that conflicts between an employee's government and private employment are more likely to arise if he or she owes fiduciary obligations to someone other than the government.

Two additional types of restriction on outside income bear no relation to conflicts of interest. One prohibits certain officials from engaging in any paid or unpaid work outside their government job. Members of the FCC, for example, may not engage in "any other business, vocation, profession, or employment while serving as . . . members."[30] A similar prohibition applies to all full-time presidential appointees.[31] This type of restriction might be justified on the grounds that it ensures that these positions receive the employees' full attention.

Another restriction limits outside earned income to 15 percent of their government salary for members of Congress, all staff of the House of Representatives, highly paid Senate staff, and highly paid political appointees in the executive branch.[32] This restriction does not protect against conflicts of interest because it does not prevent members of Congress from working for parties who could be affected by legislation. In fact, it is not at all clear what purpose this restriction serves.

Compensation for
Expressive Conduct

In the past, some government employees routinely have received compensation from nongovernmental sources for such expressive activities as giving speeches, writing articles and books, and teaching. Outside compensation may cause a conflict of interest for the employee if the employee is acting in a governmental capacity when she engages in expressive conduct and receives compensation from a nongovernment source. Such compensation obviously could influence the employee's decisions on what to say and where to say it. Employees may be more likely to give such a speech to an organization that can pay them rather than one that cannot. When the employee is engaging in expressive conduct in her governmental capacity, outside compensation for that speech is prohibited by the salary supplementation statute.[33]

The Ethics Reform Act of 1989 banned outside compensation for speeches and articles by government employees.[34] Congress enacted this honoraria ban in response to concerns that the receipt of honoraria by members of Congress posed a conflict of interest. Industry groups and trade associations with an interest in legislation were paying members of Congress to speak at the groups' conventions and meetings. The concern was that the honorarium was a payment to ensure influence with or access to that member. The legislation, however, banned honoraria not only for members of Congress and other high-level officials with extensive discretionary power to influence policy but also for all other government employees, including file clerks, receptionists, and truck drivers. It applied to all speeches and articles, even when the speech was not given in the employee's governmental capacity, when it was unrelated to the employee's responsibilities, and when the source of compensation could not be affected by the employee's exercise of discretion. As the examples in the implementing regulations made clear, the act prohibited honoraria even when no reason existed to believe that the honoraria would constitute a conflict of interest.[35]

In 1995, the Supreme Court found the honoraria ban to be an unconstitutional burden on the First Amendment rights of executive branch employees at or below the GS-15 salary level and struck it down as applied to those employees.[36] The Court left the ban in place as applied to executive branch employees above GS-15, as well as all legislative and judicial branch employees. In 1996, the Justice Department issued a memorandum noting that most of the people affected by the original honoraria ban were now excluded from its application and concluding that the honoraria ban could not be applied to any government employees.[37] Two and a half years later, the Office of Government Ethics (OGE) rescinded its regulations implementing the honoraria ban.[38]

Nonetheless, the Office of Government Ethics has kept in place other regulations restricting the receipt of compensation for expressive conduct. Back in 1991, perhaps anticipating that the honoraria ban would be struck down, OGE issued somewhat narrower regulations restricting compensation for "teaching, speaking and writing."[39] Some of these restrictions closely track conflict-of-interest analysis. For example, an employee may not receive compensation for teaching done in that employee's governmental capacity; where the invitation was extended because of the employee's "official position rather than [her] expertise"; where the person inviting or compensating the employee "has interests that may be affected substantially by performance or nonperformance of the employee's official duties;" or where "the information conveyed . . . draws substantially on . . . data that are nonpublic."[40] On the other hand, some of the restrictions appear to be overbroad, such as the prohibition on compensation where the subject deals with "any ongoing or announced policy, program or operation of the agency."[41] Thus an employee of the Securities and Exchange Commission cannot receive compensation for writing a book about the regulation of the securities industry even if the employee deals only with employment issues at the Commission.[42]

Postemployment Activities

It is quite common for government officials to stay in government for only a few years, and then return to the private sector. While this "revolving door" between the public and private sectors causes some reformers to see possible corrupting influences, other commentators have noted that this flexibility does benefit the government. It is able to attract highly talented professionals, often at salaries lower than what they could obtain in the private sector. After several years of valuable government experience, the professionals return to the private sector, their places being taken by other less experienced and less expensive employees. Such a pattern of employment is possible only if the government refrains from imposing tight restrictions on those who leave government service.

The restrictions on postgovernment employment represent a compromise between the goal of facilitating flexibility and the goal of limiting conflicts of interest. Most of these restrictions are found in a criminal statute that contains permanent, two-year, and one-year bans on certain types of postgovernment employment activities for former executive and legislative branch employees.[43] A few additional restrictions on certain high-level executive branch officials are found in an executive order issued by President Clinton.[44]

A former executive branch employee who "participated personally and substantially" in a particular matter involving a specific party or parties while in government is permanently barred from lobbying anyone in government about that matter after leaving government.[45] In this context, lobbying means making an appearance before or a communication to a government employee on behalf of someone else with the purpose of influencing the government. This lobbying restriction does not prohibit a former government official from advising a client on how to lobby the government. Thus, this restriction is aimed at preventing influence peddling rather than the revelation of confidential information. In all cases, it is irrelevant whether the former government employee is compensated for these services.

There is also a two-year ban on former executive branch employees lobbying anyone in government about a particular matter involving a specific party or parties if that matter was under the employee's "official responsibility" while he or she was in government.[46] Thus, someone with supervisory responsibility who was not directly involved in a matter is nonetheless barred for two years from contacting anyone in government in an effort to influence the government's handling of the matter.

Certain "senior" executive branch officials are barred from lobbying anyone in their former agency on *any* matter for one year after leaving office.[47] An even smaller group of "very senior" executive branch officials is barred from lobbying not just their former agency but also senior employees of all executive branch agencies.[48] This restriction seems to recognize that at the very highest levels, former officials may have influence not just within their agency but with political appointees and other high-level officials in other agencies as well. There is a one-year ban on former members of Congress and certain highly paid legislative branch employees lobbying particular officials within the legislative branch.[49] In addition, President Clinton imposed significant new restrictions on high-level political appointees, including a five-year ban on their ability to lobby their former departments and a lifetime ban on their ability to lobby on behalf of foreign companies.[50] More recently, there has been discussion of loosening these restrictions, but no action has been taken as of the time of this writing.

In the limited arena of foreign trade, there are restrictions not just on lobbying but on providing any kind of advice or assistance to those outside the federal government. Former executive and legislative branch employees who participated in trade negotiations are prohibited for one year from providing any kind of aid or advice regarding trade to anyone other than the U.S. government.[51] The former U.S. Trade Representative and his or her deputy are permanently prohibited from lobbying on behalf of foreign governments and political parties or providing them with any advice on how to influence the U.S. government.[52]

Conclusion

Since the 1960s, several waves of federal ethics reform have produced innumerable detailed ethics rules that are often difficult to follow. Some of these rules are aimed squarely at significant conflicts of interest, whereas others bear little relationship to protecting the public trust.

This chapter has examined current ethics regulation in four areas: employees' receipt of gifts, their financial interests, their receipt of outside compensation, and postgovernment-employment activities. In general, Congress has overregulated executive branch ethics and underregulated its own. But in recent years, both the Senate and the House of Representatives proved their ability to address their own ethics problems by tightening restrictions on gifts, one of the areas in which congressional ethics regulation had been so lax that it did not protect the public trust.

Notes

Based in part on Kathleen Clark, *"Do We Have Enough Ethics in Government Yet?: An Answer from Fiduciary Theory,"* 1996 U. Ill. L. Rev. 57, and Kathleen Clark, "Be Careful What You Accept from Whom: Restrictions on Gifts and Compensation for Executive Branch Employees," *In The Lobbying Manual: A Compliance Guide for Lawyers and Lobbyists,* (William V. Luneburg, ed, 1998).

1. U.S. Const. art. I, § 9, cl. 8; *id.* art. I, § 6, cl. 2; *id.* amend. XXVII.
2. Act of Oct. 23, 1962, Pub. L. No. 87–849, 76 Stat. 1119 (current version at 18 U.S.C. §§ 201–218).
3. 18 U.S.C. § 202(a).
4. Pub. L. No. 95–521, 92 Stat. 1824 (1978).
5. Ethics Reform Act of 1989, Pub. L. No. 101–194, 103 Stat. 1716.
6. House Rule XXVI cl. 5(a)(1)(B) (H.R. Res. 9, 106th Cong., 1st Sess. (1999)); Senate Rule XXXV (S. Res. 158, 104th Cong., 1st Sess. (1995)).
7. 5 C.F.R. § 2635.203(b); 18 U.S.C. § 207(e)(1); *id.* at 207(j)(2).
8. 5 U.S.C. § 7353.
9. 5 U.S.C. § 7353(a)(2).
10. 5 U.S.C. § 7353(a)(1).
11. *Id.*
12. Senate Rule XXXV; House Rule XXVI.
13. U.S. Const. art. I, § 9, cl. 8; 5 U.S.C. § 7342.
14. 21 U.S.C. § 622.
15. United States v. Mullens, 583 F.2d 134 (5th Cir. 1978); United States v. Seuss, 474 F.2d 385 F.2d 385 (1st Cir. 1973).
16. 18 U.S.C. § 208(a).
17. 5 C.F.R. § 2635.402(b)(4).
18. 5 C.F.R. § 2635.402(b)(3).
19. 5 C.F.R. § 2635.402(c).
20. 18 U.S.C. § 208(a).
21. Senate Rule XXXVII, § 4.
22. Senate Rule XXXVII, § 7.
23. 5 C.F.R. § 2635.403(a).
24. *Id.,* § 2635.403(b)(1).
25. 47 U.S.C. § 154(b)(2)(A)(ii).
26. 18 U.S.C. § 209.
27. 47 U.S.C. § 154(b)(2)(A)(iv).
28. *Id.*
29. 5 U.S.C. app. III § 502(a)(3).
30. 47 U.S.C. § 154(b)(4).
31. Exec. Order No. 12,731 (1990).
32. 5 U.S.C. app. III § 501(a).
33. 18 U.S.C. § 209.

34. Pub. L. No. 101–194, 103 Stat. 1716.

35. For example, an air traffic controller employed by the Federal Aviation Administration could not receive payment for writing an article about sheep ranching in New Zealand. 5 C.F.R. § 2636.203(a) example 5.

36. United States v. National Treasury Employees Union, 513 U.S. 454 (1995).

37. Memorandum from Walter Dellinger to the Attorney General re: Legality of Government Honoraria Ban Following *U.S. v. National Treasury Employees' Union* (Feb. 26, 1996).

38. 63 Fed. Reg. 43067 (Aug. 12, 1998).

39. 5 C.F.R. § 2635.807.

40. 5 C.F.R. § 2635.807(a)(2)(i).

41. 5 C.F.R. § 2635.807(a)(2)(i)(E)(2).

42. *Id.,* at example 4.

43. 18 U.S.C. § 207.

44. Exec. Order No. 12,834, reprinted in 5 U.S.C. § 7301.

45. 18 U.S.C. § 207(a)(1).

46. 18 U.S.C. § 207(a)(2).

47. 18 U.S.C. § 207(c).

48. 18 U.S.C. § 207(d).

49. 18 U.S.C. § 207(e).

50. Exec. Order No. 12,834.

51. 18 U.S.C. § 207(b).

52. 18 U.S.C. § 207(f)(2).

3

CONFLICT OF INTEREST AS RISK ANALYSIS

Kevin C. McMunigal

Lawyers, like all professionals, do their work subject to the pushes and pulls of a constellation of incentives. The thrust of some is benign, reinforcing the lawyer's motivation to serve her client well. Competition from other lawyers, for example, creates an incentive for the lawyer to serve her client faithfully lest the dissatisfied client hire a different lawyer. The possibility of a malpractice suit also gives the lawyer reason to fulfill her professional duties to her client.

Other incentives, though, exert pressure that threatens the fulfillment of a lawyer's professional duties. A persistent problem in all professions, these perverse incentives are commonly called "conflicts of interest." In the practice of law, they can arise from something as routine as an insurance company hiring a lawyer to defend a policyholder or as extraordinary as the $4.2 million book deal prosecutor Marcia Clark negotiated for writing a book about the O. J. Simpson case. Sources of such perverse incentives seem limitless. Relationships with family, friends, or other clients, simple greed, even the laudable ideal of reforming the law to better serve society, all may tempt the lawyer to disserve a client.

The legal profession takes conflict of interest seriously. There are detailed ethical rules on conflict of interest as well as published cases and bar opinions by the hundreds. Legal ethics treatises and law journals devote hundreds of pages to an expanding academic literature on the topic, and law students typically spend several weeks studying it in a required course on professional responsibility. And lawyers who violate conflict-of-interest rules may incur serious sanctions—money damages, loss or reduction of a fee, discipline by the bar, and disqualification by a judge from representing a client.

Despite this effort and attention, the legal profession has struggled and continues to struggle to articulate a clear, coherent response to the threat that perverse incentives pose to the fulfillment of a lawyer's duties. In the words of one commentator, interpreting the nuances of legal conflict-of-interest rules can "seem as abstruse as explicating the Dead Sea Scrolls."[1] The frequency with which commentators choose words such as "arcane," "intractable," and "morass" to describe those rules is an index of their ambiguity, complexity, and incoherence.

The primary problem with legal conflict-of-interest doctrine is that it fails to recognize conflict of interest as a type of risk analysis aimed at setting acceptable risk levels regarding perverse incentives. As a consequence of this failure, the legal profession does not squarely confront the difficult questions risk analysis entails or formulate a coherent and consistent theoretical approach to setting acceptable risk levels. Legal conflicts doctrine, for example, gives a confusing set of mixed signals about what magnitude of risk arising from a perverse incentive is acceptable and fails to acknowledge explicitly the role justifiability of risk taking plays in setting acceptable risk levels.

Harm versus Risk

Failure to distinguish clearly between harm to the fulfillment of professional duties and risk of such harm is the most fundamental problem in legal treatment of conflict of interest. A tendency to collapse harm and risk obscures the fact that conflict of interest is essentially an exercise in risk analysis and masks the need to address the questions that lie at the heart of risk analysis. To understand this failure and possible remedies, one must first grasp the difference between harm rules and risk rules.

To see how a harm rule differs from a risk rule, consider the following problem far from lawyering. Player brawls—fights in which multiple players from each team assault one another—have marred the playoffs of the National Basketball Association (NBA) in recent years and received extensive media coverage. How might the NBA stop player brawling?

One strategy would be to adopt a rule that any player who strikes another player during a game is suspended or fined. This is a harm rule—it requires a player to actually strike another player for sanctions to be imposed. Like the crimes of homicide, rape, or robbery, such a rule directly proscribes and punishes the evil it seeks to prevent and requires the occurrence of that evil to trigger its operation.

The NBA might also seek to prevent brawling through a more indirect strategy by forbidding conduct that precedes and increases the risk of brawling. The NBA might decide, for example, that players leaving their team's bench when a fight begins on the basketball court increases the risk that the fight will escalate into a brawl. The NBA would then adopt a rule that any player who leaves the bench during a fight is suspended or fined, regardless of whether he actually brawls. Like the crimes of conspiracy, attempt, and solicitation, the "leaving the bench" rule anticipates a harm which may or may not in fact occur.

To explain the essential nature of conflict-of-interest rules and distinguish them from other ethical rules, some commentators describe them as "preventive." But the preventive label only clouds the distinction between harm and risk. Both a harm rule and a risk rule help prevent harm, but they do it in different ways. A harm rule works to prevent harm through a threat of sanction aimed at potential offenders, those in a position to choose to engage in or refrain from the evil the rule seeks to prevent. In the language of the criminal law, a harm rule does its preventive work through deterrence.

A risk rule, by contrast, works to prevent harm by keeping potential offenders from being in a position to be tempted or to be able to engage in the target evil it seeks to prevent. Rather than influence a potential offender's choice, a risk rule takes the choice away from the potential offender. In the language of the criminal law, a risk rule does its preventive work through incapacitation. In short, a harm rule punishes sin whereas a risk rule insulates a potential sinner from temptation.

The legal profession often simultaneously deploys harm and risk rules to keep lawyers out of trouble. The bar, for example, disciplines lawyers who steal or misuse client funds. But it supplements the deterrence that such discipline generates with another line of defense to protect client money. It forbids lawyers from commingling client funds with their own funds, regardless of whether that commingling results in actual harm to the client, because of the risks commingling poses.[2] One finds another example of the legal profession's simultaneous use of harm and risk rules in the area of solicitation of new clients. Rule 7.3(b)(2) of the *Model Rules of Professional Conduct* prohibits a lawyer from engaging in coercion, duress, or harassment when soliciting potential clients, a harm rule. Another part of Rule 7.3, though, sets forth a risk rule. Rule 7.3(a) generally bans all personal solicitation for pecuniary gain—regardless of whether the lawyer actually uses coercion, duress, or harassment—based on what Rule 7.3's Comment calls the "potential for abuse inherent" in such personal solicitation. Model Rule 7.3(b)(2), in other words, is triggered by the *occurrence* of coercion, duress, or harassment while Model Rule 7.3(a) is triggered by *risk* of coercion, duress, or harassment.

Conflict-of-interest rules operate as part of a similar dual system deployed to protect lawyer's obligations to their clients. There are, for example, ethics rules apart from conflict-of-interest rules which require a lawyer to "provide competent representation,"[3] to "act with reasonable diligence,"[4] and to maintain a client's confidences.[5] If she represents a client incompetently, fails to exercise diligence, or breaches confidentiality, the lawyer is subject to sanction under these rules. One might view the deterrence such sanctions provide as adequate to prevent breaches of these rules. But the legal profession also deploys conflict-of-interest rules to help prevent breaches of duties such as competence, diligence, and confidentiality by keeping lawyers out of situations that pose an unacceptably high level of risk of compromise of these obligations. But the legal profession often blurs the distinction between these two lines of defense, one based on harm and the other on risk, as the following paragraphs demonstrate.

An Identity Crisis

The ultimate objective of conflict-of-interest rules is clear: preventing failures to carry out professional duties. But how do rules about conflict of interest pursue this objective? Is the prohibition against conflict of interest essentially a harm rule or a risk rule? Unfortunately, it tries to be both.

In law and other fields, the term "conflict of interest" is commonly used loosely to encompass both harm rules and risk rules dealing with perverse incentives, often without distinguishing clearly between them. This unresolved "identity crisis" about the strategic thrust of rules against conflict of interest can result in considerable confusion.

Take, for example, the exchanges in the news between former Secretary of Agriculture Michael Espy's defenders and Special Prosecutor Donald Smaltz prior to and during a criminal trial at which Espy was acquitted of conflict-of-interest charges. The indictment in the Espy case charged that Espy had solicited and accepted $35,458 worth of gifts such as tickets to sporting events, meals, luggage, crystal bowls, and artwork from companies whose businesses were regulated by the Department of Agriculture. Espy's defenders emphasized that the favors he received did not influence his behavior as Secretary of Agriculture, that the perverse incentives those favors created actually did no harm to Espy's fulfillment of his obligations as Secretary of Agriculture. Implicit in that defense was the view that the federal illegal gratuities statute under which Espy was charged is a harm rule. Smaltz, in contrast, emphasized that Espy violated the statute even if he did nothing in return for the favors he received. Smaltz saw the federal illegal gratuities statute as a risk rule. Though both Espy's defenders and Smaltz were talking about conflict of interest, one side focused on harm, the other on risk. Consequently, they simply talked past one another.

To get a better sense in a legal context of the contrast between the harm interpretation of conflict of interest and the risk interpretation, consider two hypothetical high-profile criminal cases. In the first, the defense lawyer early in the case enters into a lucrative deal with a publishing firm to write a book about the case. Assume also that the lawyer in this case then leaks confidential information about the case to generate publicity and increase future book revenues.

There are two problems here. The lawyer (1) engaged in risky conduct—the book deal, and (2) leaked confidential information. Lawyers find it relatively easy to distinguish these two problems because the legal profession consistently places each in separate conceptual compartments governed by different rules. Lawyers refer to the book deal as a conflict of interest and to the information leak as a breach of confidentiality. Though obviously closely related in that the conflict of interest created by the book deal was the motive for the confidentiality breach, lawyers talk and think about the two problems in this first hypothetical case as distinct conflict-of-interest and confidentiality problems.

In the second hypothetical high-profile criminal case, assume that the defense lawyer again enters a lucrative book deal and that subsequently the prosecution offers the defendant a guilty plea, acceptance of which is clearly in the defendant's best interest. But because a trial will generate publicity increasing the value of her book deal, the lawyer in the second case advises the client to decline the prosecution's offer.

Again, there are two problems. The lawyer (1) engaged in risky conduct—the book deal, and (2) gave advice serving her own interests rather than her client's. Unlike the first hypothetical case, lawyers have a problem distinguishing these two problems because the legal profession's ethical concepts and vocabulary do not facilitate making such a distinction. As defined in a recent treatise on legal ethics, "a conflict of interest exists not only when an interest has an *actual impact* on the lawyer's representation, but also when a *substantial risk* for an adverse impact occurs."[6] Under this definition, both the high-risk situation created by the book deal's perverse incentives and the resulting tainted advice qualify as conflicts of interest. The legal profession collapses both problems in this second hypothetical case—one involving risk, the other harm—into the conceptual compartment of "conflict of interest."

There are times when legal ethics rules do clearly distinguish risk from harm, as in the rule governing when a lawyer may and may not sue a former client. Known as the substantial relationship test, it forbids a lawyer from representing a client if that client's *interests are adverse* to a former client of the lawyer and the representation of the new client would be *substantially related* to the representation of the former client.[7]

This rule is explicitly based on risk of misuse of confidential information gained in the former representation. Here the legal profession again deploys dual harm and risk rules. The duty of confidentiality continues after representation ends, barring the lawyer from revealing confidential information of a former client to a new client or using it against the former client. But the legal profession also forbids the lawyer from being in the situation of representing a client with adverse interests in a substantially related case because of an unacceptably high risk of violation of the former client's confidentiality. In other words, the substantial relationship test is explicitly based on avoiding risk of misuse of confidential information, using the two factors of adverse interest and substantial relationship to define the area of unacceptably high risk.

More typical of the legal profession, though, is the blending of risk and harm. The legal ethics treatise quoted previously, for example, states that "a conflict of interest exists not only when an interest has an *actual impact* on the lawyer's representation, but also when a substantial *risk* for an adverse impact occurs." Similarly Rule 1.8 of the *Model Rules of Professional Conduct*, titled "Conflict of Interest: Prohibited Transactions," contains a mixture of harm and risk rules. Rule 1.8 (a), for example, allows a lawyer to enter into a business deal with a client, clearly a high-risk situation, as long as the terms of the deal are "fair and reasonable to the client." This is a harm rule. The lawyer is allowed to engage in risky behavior as long as the client is not harmed by being treated unfairly or unreasonably. Rule 1.8 (b) is another harm rule. It forbids a lawyer from using confidential client information "to the disadvantage of the client." But the following rule, Rule 1.8 (c), is a risk rule, forbidding the lawyer from preparing an instrument giving the lawyer "any substantial gift from a client." And Rule 1.8 (d) provides another risk rule, forbidding the lawyer from entering into a media deal, such as the book contract mentioned in the hypotheticals above, "prior to the conclusion of the representation."

Even if one succeeds in distinguishing risk from harm, questions remain. How much risk is acceptable? What reasons for taking that risk are legitimate? The remainder of this chapter examines these questions.

How Much Risk?

Once one adopts a risk approach, the next task one faces is to distinguish between acceptable and unacceptable risks. Initially it may seem attractive to direct lawyers to avoid all perverse incentives, and some cases and bar opinions espouse such a view. But upon examination, the exhortation to lawyers to avoid all temptation to disserve a client is just verbal posturing. Legal ethics rules routinely allow lawyers to put themselves in certain risk situations which could be forbidden, such as lawyers entering business deals with clients and joint representation of criminal defendants.

Moreover, it would be impossible to eliminate all risks from perverse incentives in the practice of law as it is impossible to completely insulate lawyers from such incentives. Perhaps the simplest way to illustrate this point is to examine the incentives that arise from the various ways lawyers can be paid for their services. An hourly fee creates a perverse incentive for the lawyer to overwork a case, to put in more time than the case requires, in order to increase the lawyer's income from the case. It also creates a perverse incentive for the lawyer to resist or delay settlement when settlement is in the client's best interest in order to increase the lawyer's hours and thus her income. A flat fee creates the opposite risk, a perverse incentive for the lawyer to underwork a case, to invest fewer hours than the case requires, in order to maximize the lawyer's effective hourly compensation. A flat fee also creates a perverse incentive for the lawyer to settle the case quickly, even when settlement is not in the client's best interest, in order to minimize the number of hours worked.

A contingent fee also creates financial temptation to disserve a client, especially if the lawyer and client have different levels of risk aversion. The client may wish to take a case to trial either because a principle is at stake or because the client is more willing than the lawyer to risk losing at trial. The fact that the lawyer will receive no compensation under a contingent fee if she loses the case at trial might lead the lawyer to ignore the client's wishes and settle the case in order to eliminate the risk of losing all compensation. Even lawyers whose fees are not paid by the client are subject to temptations to disserve their clients. A lawyer who represents a client for free, for example, may be motivated by ideals and a desire to change the law which encourage the lawyer to resist settlement even when settlement is in the client's best interest.

Because it is impossible to insulate lawyers completely from incentives that tempt them to disserve a client and the legal profession is unwilling to eliminate certain risks even when that is possible, such as those arising from lawyer-client business deals, a conflict-of-interest rule must tell a lawyer which risks are unacceptable and therefore proscribed. Drawing the line between acceptable and unacceptable risks is in fact the central mission of conflicts doctrine, but it receives little explicit attention.

The primary criterion for distinguishing unacceptable from acceptable in conflict-of-interest doctrine, as in other areas of risk analysis, is the magnitude of the risk, how *much* risk is acceptable. The perverse incentives lawyers are exposed to in their work are continuous, not dichotomous in nature, existing in degrees that vary greatly. But much of what is said and written about conflict of interest ignores this fact, treating conflict of interest as if it were dichotomous—one either has a conflict of interest or one does not. Such commentary, because it fails to recognize problems of conflict of interest as ones of degree, often fails entirely to address the issue of what degrees of risk are acceptable and unacceptable.

Legal rules often suffer from verbal imprecision in dealing with questions of degree. Statutes describe the sort of unacceptably risky driving which can result in criminal conviction with words such as "carelessness." The tort law's concept of negligence has traditionally been defined simply as "conduct which involves an unreasonably great risk of causing damage."[8] Words such as "careless," "negligent," or "unreasonable" do little to convey what magnitude of risk is unacceptable.

The legal profession has been similarly ambiguous about the magnitude of risk which the conflict-of-interest rules prohibit, giving a confusing set of mixed signals scattered across the probability spectrum. Some authorities, for example, speak in terms of *possible* impairment, such as the Model Rules' prohibition of situations in which the representation "may be materially limited." Others speak in terms of *probable* impairment, such as the *Model Code of Professional Responsibility* provisions banning situations in which the lawyer's judgment is "likely to be affected."

Recently the legal profession has taken positive steps toward remedying these inconsistent signals about magnitude. An American Bar Association (ABA) Commission charged with amending the *Model Rules of Professional Responsibility*, the primary model for lawyer ethics rules in the United States, has proposed a draft which clearly states that the risk must be "significant" in order to qualify as a conflict of interest. The American Law Institute (ALI) in its recently completed Restatement of the Law Governing Lawyers uses the word "substantial" to describe the amount of risk which results in a conflict.[9] Both "significant" and "substantial" are improvements over the inconsistent signals about the magnitude of acceptable risk currently found in conflict-of-interest rules, cases, and commentary.

Reasons for Taking the Risk

Though the recent work of the ABA and ALI on conflict of interest has made progress in focusing on risk in defining conflict of interest and clearly articulating the magnitude of risk needed to qualify as a conflict as "significant" or "substantial," it still fails to capture an essential ingredient in how conflict of interest should be and at times actually is analyzed—the justifiability of taking the risk. In failing to address this factor, the ABA's and ALI's recent work replicates the failings of the Model Rules and the Model Code, neither of which include justifiability in their general rules about conflict of interest.

Conflict-of-interest analysis is an exercise in defining acceptable risk levels. In thinking about risk, our attention naturally tends to focus on the magnitude of the risk and the recent work of the ABA and the ALI conforms to that tendency. But in making judgments about the acceptability of risk, we actually rely in many instances on both the size of the risk and any reasons for taking the risk. Our judgment about the acceptability of driving over the speed limit, for example, may vary depending on whether the driver is simply seeking a thrill or rushing a critically injured person to a hospital emergency room. Whether a dangerous surgical procedure is acceptable may depend on what the procedure is likely to accomplish as well as the risk associated with not performing the procedure.

Though it is ignored in the recent ABA and ALI rules and in the lawyer ethics codes which predated them, justifiability of risk taking features prominently in much current conflict-of-interest analysis. Contingent fees, for example, as pointed out earlier, often pose significant risks of impairing a representation but are found acceptable, at least in part, because they are useful in giving clients without resources access to counsel. And joint representation of criminal defendants, though fraught with risk, is often found acceptable because it is thought useful to the clients in presenting a unified front, saving money, and increasing access to a defendant's counsel of choice.

One way to incorporate the idea of justifiability would be to add it to the definition of conflict of interest. A conflict would exist if there is "a substantial *and unjustifiable* risk" that the representation will be impaired. Another way to incorporate it might be to continue to define conflict of interest solely in terms of magnitude, for example, as a substantial or significant risk, but to add the notion of justifiability to a consent provision which required the lawyer to determine that the risk, though significant, be justifiable in order to obtain client consent to proceed.

These suggestions are based in part on the view that justifiability should play a role in conflict-of-interest analysis. But they are also based on the fact that by failing to mention justifiability, current legal ethics rules and the rules recently drafted by both the ABA and ALI fail to capture a significant aspect of how lawyers, judges, and ethics committees actually talk and think about conflict of interest. In failing to capture this aspect of current practice, these rules are potentially misleading.

Possible Remedies

How could the legal profession better distinguish risk from harm in conflict of interest? One constructive step might be to jettison the semantically ambiguous phrase "conflict of interest" and the array of modifiers which have been attached to it in an attempt to cure its ambiguities. Examples include "potential," "actual," "latent," "acute," "deep," "relevant," "subjective," "objective," and "per se." The most pervasive of these are "actual" and "potential." As pointed out previously, questions of conflict of interest, like all risk analysis questions, are matters of degree. Such issues are notoriously difficult to resolve with verbal precision, a difficulty masked but not avoided by use of words such as "actual" and "potential." These terms shed little if any light on what magnitude of risk qualifies as a conflict of interest. Therefore, they should be discarded entirely.

Alternatively, and perhaps more practically, we could restrict the term "conflict of interest" to risk rules governing perverse incentives, referring to harm rules by the underlying duty on which each is based, such as independent judgment, confidentiality, and competence. We could also separate risk rules more clearly from harm rules. For example, the *Model Penal Code* reserves a section for treatment of the anticipatory offenses of conspiracy, attempt, and solicitation, clearly distinguishing them from harm offenses, such as homicide. Similarly, risk rules could be given a distinct place in an ethics code, rather than mixing risk and harm rules together as current codes do.

Conclusion

The legal profession has given detailed attention to issues of conflict of interest, perhaps more than any other profession. But ambiguity and incoherence nonetheless continue to plague the legal profession's treatment of conflict of interest, just as they plague the subject of conflict of interest outside the legal profession. Disentangling the notions of risk and harm, focusing on conflict of interest as risk analysis, and squarely confronting the questions risk analysis entails would go a long way toward remedying both the ambiguity and the incoherence and allow the legal profession to focus its energy and attention on the admittedly difficult issues entailed in setting acceptable risk levels for perverse incentives which threaten to undermine lawyers faithfully serving their clients.

Notes

1. Stephen Gillers, *Conflicts: Risky New Rules*, Am. Law., Sept. 1989, at 39.
2. See Model Rule 1.15(a).
3. Model Rule 1.1.
4. Model Rule 1.3.
5. Model Rule 1.6.
6. Nathan M. Crystal, *An Introduction to Professional Responsibility* 85 (1998) (emphasis added).
7. See Model Rule 1.9
8. *Prosser and Keeton on the Law of Torts* 169 (5th ed. 1984).
9. *Restatement (Third) of the Law Governing Lawyers Section 201* (Prop. Final Draft No. 1, 1996).

II

Professions within Businesses

4

CONFLICT OF INTEREST
IN JOURNALISM

Sandra L. Borden & Michael S. Pritchard

Journalists should be free of obligation to any interest other than the public's right to know.
       —*Code of Ethics*, Society of Professional Journalists

Codes of ethics for professional journalism associations and individual news organizations typically include conflicts of interest among their ethical prohibitions. For all their attention to this ethical problem, however, these codes do not offer an analysis of the concept. It seems to be assumed that we all know what conflicts of interest are, the circumstances in which they are likely to arise, and the values that are at stake. This is a concern because signs of potential conflicts of interests may go unnoticed by journalists who, as a consequence, may find themselves involved in undesirable, but possibly avoidable, conflicts of interest. As we shall see, the consequences to the public interest and to the profession's credibility in such cases can be substantial.

What Is a Conflict
of Interest?

So, what is a conflict of interest in journalistic practice? Each of the following seems to raise a concern about possible conflicts of interest:

- Amy Andrews covers environmental issues. The Environmental Protection Agency has accused her grandfather's industrial firm of contaminating the local groundwater. Should Amy cover this story?
- Caroline Carson is the consumer reporter for the local television station. A group of major developers would like to convince the county commission to rezone an area so that a multi-purpose mall can be constructed. The proposed mall will have an amusement park, fine restaurants, and a wide range of quality shops. The developers invite Caroline, her husband, and her two children to an all expense-paid weekend at a similar mall they have developed in another part of the state. Should Caroline accept the offer?
- Upset by unfavorable coverage in one local paper, a car dealer terminates its advertising with that paper and offers to advertise with another local paper, provided that the second paper "treats it decently." Should the offer be accepted?

Conflicts of interest in journalism arise in circumstances in which there is reason to be concerned that the judgment and performance of journalists might be unduly influenced by interests they have that lie outside their responsibilities as journalists. Each of these imagined cases raises this concern.

Following the general contours of Michael Davis's (1991) analysis of conflicts of interest, we offer the following conceptual framework for understanding a conflict of interest as it applies to an imagined journalist, Chris:

- Chris is a journalist with responsibilities to convey the news informatively and in ways that are truthful, fair, and least likely to mislead the public.
- Fulfilling these responsibilities requires exercising *good judgment* with regard to gathering, editing, reporting, and displaying the news.
- Chris's role as a journalist justifies others relying on her exercising good judgment with regard to gathering, editing, reporting, and displaying the news.
- Chris is in a situation in which, because of interests *other* than those related to her journalistic responsibilities, there is reason to believe that her judgment could be compromised, involving either self-deception or a deliberate attempt to ignore or suppress unfavorable information.

In discussing the responsibilities of journalists, we confine our attention to the United States, where the press is given special constitutional support that helps define those responsibilities. We draw attention to factors that make conflicts of interest problematic, and we suggest possible ways of either avoiding or managing conflicts of interest in journalism.

The Primary Interest of Journalists

Journalists, however else they might be characterized, have responsibilities grounded in their protected social function of gathering, interpreting, presenting, and disseminating information needed for individuals and communities to make sound judgments about matters of personal, political, and social importance.[1] It is this essential function and its performance on behalf of society that marks the *primary interest* that a journalist, *as* a journalist, is expected to serve and that distinguishes journalism as a profession. In fact, it is with this public good in view that the Constitution sets the press apart as the only private enterprise with special protection in the Bill of Rights; the Congress is specifically enjoined from abridging the press's freedom in the First Amendment.

This constitutional privilege is one basis for responsibility on the part of journalists. Louis Hodges (1986) refers to this as a *contractual* basis, because the broad freedom granted in the United States to the press implies a "covenant with the society" (p. 19). Indeed, Hodges notes, U.S. journalists have few responsibilities *assigned* to them by society. These tend to be stated negatively (e.g., "Do not libel") and only specify the bare minimum we can expect from journalists. But, for the most part, contracted responsibilities are left broadly open to interpretation. Because of such latitude, society is vulnerable to the judgment of journalists. After all, in today's world, we are highly dependent on journalists for furnishing information that enables us to make meaningful decisions about our lives, and we have little choice but to trust that journalists will strive to meet our needs and interests in this regard.

Conflicts of interest jeopardize this trust. Take the case of Amy Andrews. If Amy covers the accusation that her grandfather's firm is contaminating the ground water, she is in serious danger of focusing on her allegiance to her grandfather rather than on communicating clearly and accurately to the public about the possible hazards of the alleged water pollution. Few of us have the time or ability to engage in the kinds of investigative work needed to inform ourselves about such environmental concerns. We rely on journalists to do this. If Amy fails to exercise good judgment as a *journalist*—if, for example, she buries the story or understates the seriousness of the allegations—she deprives individuals of the information they need to make sound decisions. Depending on what they take the circumstances to be, individuals may wish to consider responses ranging from complaining to their senator to simply drinking bottled water.

If people cannot trust a journalist to "give it to them straight," they are stripped of their ability to make well-informed choices. They will not know whether the information provided is a reliable basis for decision making; their options are curtailed. In short, conflicts of interest can diminish our autonomy and even have concrete, harmful consequences for us. These problems arise directly from the unequal nature of the relationship between journalists and the individuals who depend on them, and this inequality places greater responsibility on journalists. As Hodges (1986) notes, "The greater our power or ability to affect others becomes, the heavier becomes our moral duty" (p. 16).

As much as journalists have to rely on their own discretion when fulfilling their contracted and assigned responsibilities, they face an even greater burden in this regard when it comes to fulfilling what Hodges (1986) calls their *self-imposed* responsibilities, those that journalists adopt on their own as expressions of their vocation. Here, there are no prohibitions handed down, no promissory expectations to guide one's actions. Rather, journalists are basically on their own when it comes to defining and carrying out such responsibilities. In light of the ambiguity inherent in human communication—the difficulties involved in expressing oneself clearly, listening attentively, comprehending well, being emotionally responsive, and so on—even conscientious journalists who single-mindedly pursue their journalistic responsibilities can easily fail to exercise their discretion wisely. For a journalist whose judgment has been swayed by an outside interest, the possibilities for intended or unintended harm are almost endless.

Consider our second case, the business editor who has been offered an all-expenses-paid trip to the prototype mall. Let us assume that Caroline takes it upon herself always to disclose to her readers whenever she has accepted free tickets or other complimentary items in order to cover a story. Just how candid is Caroline likely to be when she returns? Following her usual policy, we can expect her to state somewhere in her story that the developers flew her to the mall at their expense. But will she take the extra step and disclose that her family went along for the ride? Will she write in detail about any other perks she and her family received that made their experience of the mall especially enjoyable? It would be easy to leave out or downplay such aspects of the trip. She might also ignore or downplay less than enjoyable moments of the trip. She might not knowingly or intentionally do this; such is the danger posed by outside interests that interfere with the responsible use of journalistic discretion.

Sound Professional Judgment

Journalistic codes of ethics try to get at the concerns we have sketched here when they urge journalists to maintain their *independence*. But they also are getting at these concerns when they direct journalists, in the words of the code of the Society of Professional Journalists, to "seek the truth and report it." If people depend so heavily on journalists, journalists must at least be truthful, and regardless of how much discretion they enjoy generally, discretion about pursuing the truth is not negotiable.

Critics may rejoin that "the whole truth and nothing but the truth" is unattainable. This may be conceded, but it is beside the point. Seeking the truth and making a sincere effort to report the truth insofar as one has been able to ascertain it can be expected. This is what truthfulness requires. Furthermore, although "the whole truth and nothing but the truth" may not be attainable, departures from truth are often readily determinable; and deliberately reporting what one knows to be false is not acceptable. Thus, as Sissela Bok (1989) maintains, truthfulness (which addresses questions of intent and commitment) can serve as a reasonable norm. She concludes: "We must single out, therefore, from the countless ways in which we blunder misinformed through life, that which is done with the intention to mislead; and from the countless partial stabs at truth, those which are intended to be truthful. Only if this distinction is clear will it be possible to ask the moral question with rigor" (p. 8). Given the journalist's role as conveyor of reliable information, commitment to truthfulness is essential even though this commitment cannot guarantee reliability.

More than just the intent to write truthfully is required, however. Other criteria enter into what may be considered professional judgment in journalism—criteria that increase the odds that something approximating truth will result and that people will reach reasoned conclusions about issues that concern their lives. Besides being truthful, information supplied by journalists should meet these criteria: All relevant viewpoints should be considered, any complexities involved should be acknowledged, the assumptions underlying key arguments should be made plain and should be widely recognized as valid, the key terms should be precisely and consistently used, and so on. These are the criteria for sound arguments. When journalists, intentionally or not, engage in fallacious reasoning themselves, they fail to demonstrate sound professional judgment.

Fallacious reasoning often is highly persuasive. In fact, the "informal fallacies" discussed in basic logic texts (e.g., hasty generalization, appeal to authority, *ad hominem*, appeal to popularity, and begging the question) are so named precisely because we commonly fall prey to them. But there are many other, nameless, ways in which the truth we seek may be obscured. This places a heavy burden on the conscientious, truth-seeking journalist. Jay Black, Bob Steele, and Ralph Barney (1999) cite Carl Friedrich's observation that "since everyone is fallible in making decisions, society needs the collective judgments of many fallible people to produce valid social decisions and solve social problems. The journalist is the central figure in improving the odds that good decisions will be made. He or she provides key information that will assist the populace in giving informed consent to public proposals" (p. 18).

It is precisely because "the whole truth and nothing but the truth" is unattainable that conflicts of interest pose such a basic threat to the primary interest of journalism. As Davis (1991) points out, conflicts of interest arise when professional *judgment* or *discretion* is required. Journalists are to do for us what we cannot do for ourselves (viz., gain access to and widely communicate information on matters of personal, political, and social importance). We *trust* journalists to be thorough in investigating and presenting the news. Even though news reports may be based on fallacious reasoning, the reasoning underlying those reports may not appear in the reports themselves. Readers and listeners may simply assume that journalists have used good judgment in assembling their stories. So, journalists need to be wary of their own susceptibility to bad reasoning in selecting information and preparing news reports for us. One way of characterizing a conflict of interest, in fact, is that one has a *vested interest* in *seeing* things in ways favorable to one's interests. Unguarded confidence that one's interests do not, or will not, exercise this distortion is unwarranted. Self-deception is a prominent worry. But even if one were right in believing that one's own judgment is not unduly influenced by outside interests, it does not follow that the public can know this: The problem of public trust remains unresolved. Thus, given the great challenge of approximating "truth" as best one can we have all the more reason to be concerned about conflicts of interest.

Loyalty to Clients and Employers

In characterizing journalistic conflicts of interests, we have been concerned to focus on the social responsibilities of journalists rather than on loyalty to employers or even clients. In regard to clients, we might think of the public as constituting the journalists' "clients." This is the approach of Michael Bayles (1989), who has pointed out that journalism is substantially different from other professional contexts in which the client is a known individual with whom the professional has an interpersonal relationship. However, focusing on the client in this impersonal way may invite depictions of the public that are more convenient than accurate (as when a journalist assumes that members of the public are lazy citizens or only interested in reading fluff). Focusing directly on journalists's responsibilities to promote well-informed decisions, on the other hand, can serve as a reminder that journalists can be expected to provide members of the public with reliable information, not simply what they want to hear or what they are willing to spend time reading or watching. Instead, what must be envisaged is an "ideal" audience—an audience that accepts, and demands, the standards of truthfulness, fairness, and thoroughness that we have been advocating. Whether actual audiences appreciate this is beside the point. So, even if it were the case that the public has only superficial interests in the news, this would not really change journalists's responsibilities *as journalists*. Understanding journalism within the context of service to society is what gives it its professional character.

Another set of interests that we might include among journalists' primary interests are those of their employers. Most journalists are employees, and the employer/employee relationship carries with it certain obligations. However, problems arise if we include obligations to one's employing organization among the primary interests that journalists *as journalists* should serve, as organizations typically have at least some goals that may threaten journalism's democratic responsibilities. Having journalism's set of primary interests be internally inconsistent is undesirable. But, even if the goals of news organizations always were compatible with journalism's primary interest in serving the information needs of democratic societies, we still would not want to identify the journalist's primary interest with his or her employer's interest in having a profitable enterprise. After all, it is not by virtue of being employed by a news organization that one is properly called a journalist. This criterion does not distinguish journalists from other employees in the same organization, such as ad salespersons, newspaper carriers, secretaries, and janitors. Even those who are involved in "making the news" per se are not always to be considered journalists, as in the case of composing room personnel who might set small agate type for local sports roundups in the daily newspaper. Such a role does not entail the independent journalistic judgment we are requiring here. What distinguishes journalists, *as journalists*, from other employees are their special democratic responsibilities. That is not to say, of course, that journalists might not experience conflicts of interests as *employees* (as may be true in cases of moonlighting). But as a *journalist*, interests of the employer are *secondary*.[2]

Secondary Interests
in Journalism

A conflict of interest involves being involved in circumstances that give others reason to worry about whether one's judgment is actually vulnerable to secondary interests that tend to make that judgment less reliable than others are entitled to expect. Further clarification of what is meant by "interests" is in order. Suppose a journalist is scheduled to conduct an interview that is crucial to preparing a news story, but she realizes that conducting a thorough interview will jeopardize her going to a concert with her friends. Does the fact that she has a strong desire to join her friends mean she has a conflict of interest? If her realization that she must conduct the interview causes her to be bitterly disappointed and somewhat depressed, does this mean she has a conflict of interest? We do not think so, not even if her disappointment and depression do, in fact, interfere with her judgment. Not every factor that might interfere with one's judgment creates a conflict of interest. Incompetence, brain tumors, fatigue, emotions, moods, or even eager anticipation of a weekend getaway can all interfere with a journalist's ability or willingness to discharge her responsibilities, but they do not pose conflicts of interest. This is because they are not *interests*. An interest is something we pursue, act in behalf of, or act for the sake of.[3]

What is necessary for a conflict of interest is *another* interest, the presence of which inherently threatens to interfere with the *independent exercise of judgment* that journalists need to maintain in trying to satisfy their *primary* responsibilities as journalists. Let us say the same journalist is assigned to cover a local election and then discovers that her brother is a late entry. In the context of her journalistic responsibilities, her interest in her brother's success is a *secondary interest*. To call interests secondary is, in the context of a conflict of interest, to say that such interests could, but should not be allowed to, affect the journalist's commitment to satisfying the primary interest that defines the journalist's responsibilities. If secondary interests are allowed to become a significant factor in the journalist's functioning as a journalist, they can be expected to make it more difficult, if not impossible, for the journalist to maintain independent journalistic judgment.

Were it not for this primary interest in independent journalistic judgment, there need be nothing wrong with pursuing the secondary interests. Supporting one's brother's political campaign usually is not inappropriate. The basic point is that interests that create a conflict of interest must all be interests that are at least allowable to pursue were it not for the conflict itself. Deliberately spreading false information about a political candidate, for example, usually is inappropriate. It is not the sort of interest that is an element in a conflict of interest (which is not to say that it cannot interfere with one's independent judgment).

One reason conflicts of interest, seen in this way, constitute a special category of concern is that the conflicting interests, taken separately, are legitimate. Indeed, it is not even accurate to say that secondary interests should be necessarily of lesser importance to an individual journalist than her primary interests as a journalist. After all, the role of journalist is only one of many roles that a journalist has. Nevertheless, from a journalistic standpoint, however important a journalist's secondary interests might be "overall," they must not be allowed to compromise the primary interest that defines the responsibilities one has *as a journalist.* It may even be appropriate for secondary interests to take on primacy for the journalist (e.g., one's relationship to a loved one), but this is when it is important for the journalist to step out of the journalistic picture, or at least to alert others to the threat this poses to meeting one's journalistic responsibilities. For journalistic practice to work as it should, these other interests must remain secondary—that is, they must not be allowed to interfere with the primary interest of truthful, fair, and thorough presentation of the news.

Other Threats to Journalists' Primary Interest

It is important to bear in mind that bias does not necessarily indicate a conflict of interest. For example, a journalist writing for *American Spectator* could cover public affairs from a distinctively Republican right perspective and not be guilty of a conflict of interest. Likewise, an environmental reporter could advocate tougher pollution laws in his or her stories without being guilty of a conflict of interest. What all these journalists are demonstrating, of course, is bias, and this is what readers expect. Deliberately taking a stand or advocating a cause does not preclude commitment to truthfulness, fairness, and thoroughness in reporting. Not only is it not necessary to be wholly "objective," in the sense of purging oneself of all bias, it could not be confirmed even if it were somehow achieved. There is no impartial, third person (god-like) perspective against which we can measure the "objectivity" of stories—we must check each other's work, but again from something less than a godlike perspective. This is another reason that seeds of suspicion sown from conflicts of interest can damage trust.

Of course, strong allegiances to an opinion or world view also can damage trust, as they do tend to warp journalists's professional judgment when used deliberately as a yardstick to make journalistic decisions. For example, the *American Spectator* reporter might distort the Democratic Party's position on an issue, or the environmental writer might leave out facts that would cast doubt on passage of those antipollution laws. But the problem in each of these examples is not that the journalist in question has failed to be studiously neutral. The writing of each, in fact, is opinionated by definition. More to the point, the problem is not that the journalist has favored some legitimate nonjournalistic interest over his or her primary interest as a journalist. Purposely distorting information and short-circuiting public deliberation cannot be considered *legitimate* interests. The moral culpability in these instances would lie, rather, in breaking commitments these journalists and/or their organizations made to readers regarding their reliability as sources of information, thereby deceiving the readers. These are ethical problems, to be sure, but they are not conflicts of interest.

It is also important to note that although journalists may have difficulties fulfilling all their responsibilities, and they may satisfy some at the expense of satisfying others, this does not ordinarily constitute a conflict of interest. At issue is not how many different responsibilities one might have, or even whether it is possible to fulfill them all. For example, being assigned more stories than one can write in time for a deadline places a journalist in conflict, but this is not a conflict of interest. Patricia Werhane and Jeffrey Doering (1995) refer to this as a conflict of *commitment* rather than a conflict of interest. For a conflict of interest, it is *what* the secondary interest is (e.g., protecting one's relatives) that explains why the primary interest is threatened rather than simply the lack of time to fulfill all of one's responsibilities.

How Should Journalists
Handle Conflicts of Interest?

Many news organizations have policies that prohibit accepting gifts, getting involved in politics, and other situations that pose conflicts of interest in journalism. Indeed, *recusal*, that is, removing oneself from the circumstances that threaten to interfere with journalistic judgment, is a good way of handling conflicts of interest. As we have seen, conflicts of interest arise in circumstances in which we cannot assume that the journalist's judgment can be trusted. Therefore, it is most prudent to avoid such circumstances altogether.

However, these matters can be complicated and controversial. An example is the reassignment of education reporter Sandy Nelson to the copy desk of the *Tacoma (Washington) Morning News Tribune* in 1990 after she founded a political action group and promoted a ballot initiative to protect gays from housing and employment discrimination (Sherman, 1997). Clearly, Nelson was pursuing legitimate political interests. What is at issue in determining whether her actions created a conflict of interest is whether her secondary interests inherently conflicted with her primary interest as a journalist. Nelson and her supporters argued that her primary and secondary activities did not conflict with each other because the ordinance Nelson supported was not directly related to her responsibility for covering education. Even if this were true, however, there remains the concern that Nelson's highly visible political role created the impression that she somehow represented the newspaper as a whole. If this impression were believed, the public's trust in the institution's *collective* judgment could be seriously compromised. This concern cannot be dismissed easily if Nelson and her fellow journalists were to function well in terms of their primary responsibility as journalists.

Nelson refused to give up her leadership position in the gay-rights initiative as a condition of remaining in her assignment as a reporter (Sherman, 1997). This indicates, at least, that Nelson did not prioritize her journalistic role over her citizen role. That is understandable enough. A journalist's responsibilities as a journalist should not necessarily supersede those of all other roles. Indeed, Nelson was quoted in the *Tribune* in 1997 as saying, "I would give up journalism before I would give up political activism" (Epler, 1997, p. A1). Still, we do expect that journalists, at least while acting as journalists, will hold their journalistic responsibilities foremost. If this is true, it might have been reasonable for Nelson to have voluntarily accepted a change in her journalistic tasks in order to ensure that her journalistic judgment would not be jeopardized by her political activities, or at least that public trust in her newspaper would not be undermined. Not only did Nelson refuse to cease her highly public political activity, she sued the newspaper under a state antidiscrimination law. Nelson's case went all the way to the Washington Supreme Court, which upheld the newspaper's right under the First Amendment to reassign her in the interest of maintaining its credibility. The U.S. Supreme Court refused to hear Nelson's appeal.

Another case much discussed in journalistic circles was the decision by *New York Times* Supreme Court reporter Linda Greenhouse to march in a pro-choice demonstration in Washington in 1989. As was the case with Nelson, Greenhouse's actions reflected not just on her but also on her newspaper. Some argued that Greenhouse's public advocacy of the pro-choice position undermined the trust her readers could have in her judgment, as well as the collective judgment of the *Times*. Greenhouse's case differs from Nelson's in two critical ways, however. First, Greenhouse's job was to cover the very body that is most directly involved in the abortion issue. Therefore, the probability that her coverage of the Supreme Court, at least in relation to this issue, could be unduly swayed by her legitimate interest in supporting a political cause was high. Second, Greenhouse did not take a leadership position in the pro-choice cause; she merely was one of hundreds of marchers.

Given the complexities of this case, it might be unreasonable to outright prohibit Greenhouse from any participation in a political cause that is obviously so important to her. As in Nelson's case, a more appropriate approach might be to *manage* the conflict by restricting (rather than prohibiting) the journalist's secondary activities. For example, Greenhouse could have pursued her legitimate political interests in a way that did not distract from her primary interest as a journalist if she had shown support for the pro-choice cause by making a monetary donation rather than participating in a highly visible march. Furthermore, the donation could be made to an organization such as Planned Parenthood, which provides general health services for women in addition to abortions, rather than, say, a political action committee directly involved in lobbying for pro-abortion laws. We also might want to distinguish between support given as a member of an organization (e.g., Professional Women Communicators) and support given as an individual. The collective stand taken by an organization may not accurately reflect the stand of any one member; therefore, it would be less likely that a journalist could compromise the trustworthiness of her journalistic judgment on the basis of an action taken in her behalf by a group. If Greenhouse were unwilling to curtail her pro-choice activities along these lines, then reassignment to a less visible journalistic job might be warranted, as was the case with Nelson.

Should such relatively discreet outside activities be *disclosed?* If they do indeed make the journalist's judgment suspect, the answer is yes. Those who depend on the journalist's judgment are entitled to know of any possible reasons why they might not be able to rely on that journalist. However, this is an imperfect solution: Drawing attention to the conflict has the effect of nullifying the benefits offered by the mitigating strategies we have suggested. The key would be an accurate assessment of the probability of impaired judgment/credibility posed by the actual conflict versus disclosure of that conflict, a difficult task at best.

Nevertheless, disclosure is a worthwhile alternative in lieu of a blanket prohibition against all outside activities, despite the concerns raised by the Nelson and Greenhouse cases. For example, we would think it unacceptable if a journalist were to wash her hands of any responsibility to be involved in her children's education because some day the school or the PTA might be the subject of a news story.

An exemplary instance of the disclosure approach occurred at the institutional level in 1978, when the *Lewiston (Idaho) Morning Tribune* ran a full-page story disclosing and analyzing the various outside interests of its publisher, editors, and reporters (Tate, 1978). The article, reprinted in *Columbia Journalism Review* (Tate, 1978), enumerated then-publisher A. L. "Butch" Alford, Jr.'s sources of income and discussed his questionable involvement with the state Board of Education, the United Way, and other projects, as well as how his involvement had affected coverage of these entities. Alford was quoted in the article as saying, "It's the first time in my association with the paper that we've thought to look at ourselves. This is a healthy thing. I hope as a result of this editorial coverage of ourselves we can see the weaknesses in our own process" (Tate, 1978, p. 44). The article did not result in the wholesale abandonment of the staff's outside activities. Indeed, prohibiting staff from exercising their rights as citizens might have been unjust and might have skewed their judgment in another direction. As *Lewiston Morning Tribune*'s night managing editor, Perry Swisher, commented in the 1978 story, "I do not like cloistered, celibate people writing about people who are neither cloistered nor celibate (Tate, 1978, p. 46)." All conflicts of interest cannot—and perhaps should not—be avoided. But when they cannot be, disclosure is the least the public can expect.

Institutional Conflicts of Interest

So far we have concentrated mainly on conflicts of interest that arise for individual journalists and how these conflicts might reflect on the news organizations that employ them. However, it is also possible for a news organization itself to find itself facing a possible conflict of interest. This greatly complicates matters.

Consider our earlier example of the car dealership that offers to advertise in a newspaper provided it is "treated decently." This proviso may seem innocuous, as the request that one be treated decently seems reasonable enough. However, the dealership is making this offer because of dissatisfaction at how it was treated by another paper. This may suggest that the dealership's request for "decent treatment" is actually a request for preferential treatment (e.g., avoiding stories that might cast the dealership in an unfavorable light). That is, the newspaper might be expected not to treat the dealership by the same principles of truthful and fair reporting as any other company.

If a newspaper explicitly or implicitly accepts such terms, it creates at least a potential conflict of interest for itself. However, it does not follow that individual reporters employed at the newspaper have a conflict of interest when it comes to reporting on matters that affect the interests of the car dealership. They might not even know of the agreement with the dealership. Nevertheless, their reporting may be affected by this agreement. They might not be assigned stories that concern the dealership. Or the stories they write might not be published, or they might be judiciously "edited" by someone else. In any case, individual recusal or even disclosure will not remedy the conflict of interest. In fact, if *all* reporters were either to recuse themselves or disclose the conflict of interest, this would simply ensure that the newspaper would keep its agreement with the dealership and make the public wary of its new coverage policy.

Known agreements, explicit or implicit, to treat sponsors "decently" are not necessary for creating public distrust. The simple fact of ownership by a larger organization can accomplish this. A case in point is the Disney acquisition of ABC News. In 1998, ABC decided not to air a story alleging that Disney's theme parks and resorts have convicted pedophiles in their employ. According to Elizabeth Lesly Stevens (1998/1999), it is not entirely clear why the story was withdrawn.[4] Possibly it was for perfectly appropriate journalistic reasons. However, there was little ABC could do to convince doubters that its decision was not unduly influenced by interests that threaten to compromise its primary journalistic responsibilities. Here is why.

In late September 1998, only days before the decision not to run the story was made, Disney Chairman Michael Eisner said on National Public Radio's *Fresh Air*, "I would prefer ABC not to cover Disney. . . . I think it's inappropriate for Disney to be covered by Disney. . . . [B]y and large, the way you avoid conflict of interest, is to, as best you can, not cover yourself. . . . We don't have a written policy. . . . ABC News knows that I would prefer them not to cover [Disney]." (Stevens, 1998/1999, p. 95) Although not a blanket disapproval of ABC coverage of Disney, Eisner's statement clearly expresses the preference that ABC not seek out stories about Disney—favorable or unfavorable.

Because there was no written policy, it is entirely possible that when David Westin became president of ABC in June 1998, he was unaware of Eisner's preferences. It was shortly after assuming that post that he approved of ABC reporters investigating allegations that theme parks had problems with convicted pedophiles in their employ. However, Stevens points out, it is unlikely that Westin was unaware of Eisner's stance at the time he withdrew the story, especially in light of Eisner's September 29 statement on National Public Radio.

Meanwhile, others at ABC have steadfastly insisted that ABC News is committed to independent news coverage. In a panel discussion in October 1997 at the Columbia University Graduate School of Journalism, ABC News's senior vice president for editorial quality, Richard Wald, insisted, "We do not play around with the integrity of the central question of our lives, which is to report fully and fairly what we know" (Stevens, 1998/1999, p. 96). This is consistent with assurances made by all three major networks—ABC, NBC, and CBS—when they were acquired by large corporations. All three, says Stevens, assured the public that they "would always act independently of any wider corporate interest or agenda" (Stevens, 1998/1999, p. 96).

Even after Westin's decision to quash the Disney story, ABC spokeswoman Eileen Murphy told *Brill's Content*, "Our statement that we cover Disney like any other company has been consistent all along. We are all saying the same thing." But, Stevens contends, not everything Murphy says is consistent with this. "We certainly cover them [Disney] when the news breaks," Stevens quotes Murphy. But, Murphy continues, "Generally, we would not embark on an investigation focused on Disney." Stevens (1998/1999) comments, "Many companies would certainly welcome such an exclusion" (p. 103).

Acknowledging that there is no evidence that anyone at Disney directly was involved in killing the story, Stevens (1998/1999) concludes: "But what is clear is that Westin, in judging the Disney pedophile story fatally flawed by some unspecified measure of editorial quality, committed at the very least the sin of being more 'fair' to Disney than other companies and public officials ABC has subjected to harsh inspection" (p. 103).

What can ABC News say in response to concerns that its handling of the news is tainted by a conflict of interest resulting from its relationship to Disney, its owner? According to Stevens, none of the ABC News executives or staff were willing to speak publicly about the Disney story. However, Stevens (1998/1999) cites a portion of a written statement by Westin:

> In reviewing the script, I applied basic principles of journalism—neutral principles—without regard to either the reporter or the companies being reported on. I concluded that the script did not meet ABC News editorial standards. I consulted with some of the most senior and respected journalists here at ABC News, who concurred in the judgment. That the Walt Disney Company, among others, was involved in the story did not influence the decision in any way. I remain entirely confident in the decision. (p. 98)

Stevens is not reassured by this statement. Conceding that there may have been no direct interference from Disney, she concludes, "More likely than overt pressure from Disney is another more troubling scenario, one in which Westin moved proactively to avoid grief from his bosses" (Stevens, 1998/1999, p. 98). Her own take is that despite the fact that she has not had access to the full script, a convincing case can be made that the story was well reported, interesting, and satisfied standards typically used in deciding whether to broadcast stories—about other companies.

So, what should the public conclude about this incident? Should Westin simply be taken at his word that his decision was not unduly influenced by Disney? It would be difficult to argue this. Ownership by Disney seems clearly to create the potential for conflicts of interest to arise, not only in this case but in many others as well (given Disney's widespread interests). In the present instance, a reasonable case can be made for the appearance of a conflict of interest, and this appearance cannot be resolved simply by an expression of confidence on the part of the decision maker. No matter how sincerely made, self-deception remains a possibility.

There are further implications. Although the investigative journalists in the Disney pedophile case evidently felt no constraints from the Disney connection in preparing their script, the fact that the story was quashed could well have an effect on future reporting—both theirs and others at ABC News. Whether intended or not, what happened seems to send the message: "Don't bite the hand that feeds you." Even if reporters do not take this to heart, public doubt remains. The problem is not simply that of maintaining one's journalistic integrity; there is also the problem of maintaining public trust.

Not that this credibility gap is anything new. At its core, the Disney problem is essentially the same one that has existed since journalism emerged as a bona fide industry after the Civil War (Dicken-Garcia, 1989; Schudson, 1978). Large increases in newspaper circulation and profitability were accompanied by increasingly complex organizational structures that gradually differentiated the role of the editor from the printer at the beginning of the nineteenth century and then also from the accountant by midcentury (Dicken-Garcia, 1989). Just as "fact" gradually became strictly separated from "opinion" in U.S. journalism (Stone, 1968), so the editorial function of journalism became strictly separated from its business function. This solution was never airtight, of course, but it placed into effect normative constraints that substantially minimized institutional conflicts of interest, both real and perceived (Soloski, 1989). It is this mind-set that most likely explains why ABC reporters felt free to pursue the pedophile investigation involving its parent company.

However, the solution of strictly demarcating editorial and business functions has become less effective as corporate linkages have become harder to disentangle and as management trends in journalism have begun to emphasize the integration of organizational functions (Underwood, 1993). It may not be possible to turn back the clock, but two solutions proposed by Werhane and Doering (1995) might help. First, changes can be made in institutional policies that reflect both the current realities and the limited success of past strategies. For example, there is no reason why managers (who often have no journalistic background) cannot be trained to be sensitive to journalistic concerns so that the bottom line does not drive every decision without consideration of other factors. Those who function in editorial roles cannot be oblivious to a company's strategic concerns, but their independence is best maintained if business managers limit their influence to allocating resources and setting targets—then let the journalists decide how best to function within those constraints. For those entanglements that cannot be avoided, Werhane and Doering suggest another possible solution—public guidelines. If there is going to be an understanding, for example, that ABC will not proactively investigate Disney, it should be explicitly stated so that managers, journalists, and the public know what to expect. This solution does not do away with the conflict but significantly blunts the moral problem.

Conclusion

As we have used the term, "conflicts of interest" are situations in which there is reason to worry that the independent judgment and performance of journalists *as journalists* may be compromised by interests that lie outside their journalistic role. This is not to say that their judgment and performance necessarily will be compromised in such circumstances. Perhaps in many cases they will not. However, neither the journalist nor the public is in a good position to provide such assurances. So, concerns about reliability and trust remain.

We have distinguished conflicts of interest from other kinds of situations that pose ethical problems for journalists. We specifically excluded bias from our analysis of the concept of conflicts of interest, even though conflicts of interest in journalism commonly are associated with departures from "objectivity." The broad spectrum of journalistic practice ranges from traditional community newspapers to commentary on CNN. Although truthfulness, fairness, and thoroughness are reasonable standards across this spectrum, absence of bias is not.

We have tried to demonstrate, through example, the sorts of circumstances that make analyzing conflicts of interest complex. These included consideration of the legitimacy of secondary interests, consideration of the cost that a conflict of interest has in terms of public trust, and consideration of differences between conflicts at the individual and institutional levels. Our examples of individual conflicts of interest centered on political activism as a potentially distracting secondary interest, at least insofar as highly visible activity by individual journalists tends to undermine public trust in their judgment, as well as in the collective judgment of their news organizations. However, these are by no means the only kinds of conflicts of interest that arise for journalists. More common may be those posed by the so-called revolving door, in which people who previously worked in other occupations change careers and become journalists. Almost inevitably, there will be secondary interests associated with these journalists' previous commitments that may pose a conflict of interest. Institutional conflicts such as those highlighted in the Disney case, however, promise to multiply, given current market trends toward corporate mergers. These kinds of conflicts of interest seem most difficult to address because journalists do not have much choice regarding the organization of their work and because there is little hope of convincing the public that institutional conflicts of interest do not actually influence coverage even when they, in fact, do not. This is an area of special concern in the future.

Conflicts of interest deserve careful scrutiny from both journalists and the public. As we noted earlier, conflicts of interest may escape detection precisely because the secondary interests that oppose themselves to journalists' primary responsibilities are worthy in their own right. It is crucial that conflicts of interest be recognized so that they may be avoided or—when this option is not reasonable—so that they may be managed with a minimum of damage to the crucial mission journalists perform.

Notes

1. The quintessential American journalist is one who reports and presents the news in an impartial manner to a mass audience. However, other types of journalists might report for trade publications that reflect the distinct perspective of an industry; others might write for political or environmental publications that advocate in favor of a specific cause; others might publish newsletters that supply technical information. In fact, there is a wide range of communication specialists who might be considered journalists. We concentrate here only on the first type.

2. For further discussion of the distinction between primary and secondary interests, see Thompson (1993).

3. For further discussion of what distinguishes interests from other factors that might interfere with judgment, see Feinberg, (1984) and Pritchard (1996, at 1309).

4. The account that follows is based on Stevens (1998/1999).

References

Bayles, M. D. (1989). *Professional ethics* (2nd ed.). Belmont, CA: Wadsworth.

Black, J., Steele, B., & Barney, R. (1999). *Doing ethics in journalism: A handbook with case studies* (3rd ed.). Boston: Allyn & Bacon.

Bok, S. (1989). *Lying: Moral choice in public and private life.* New York: Vintage.

Davis, M. (1991). Conflict of interest. In D. Johnson (Ed.), *Ethical issues in engineering* (pp. 317–326). Englewood Cliffs, NJ: Prentice-Hall.

Dicken-Garcia, H. (1989). *Journalistic standards in nineteenth-century America.* Madison:University of Wisconsin Press.

Epler, P. (1997, February 21). Newspaper can restrict activism of workers; the *News Tribune* has right to limit reporters' political work, state high court rules. *The (Tacoma, WA) News Tribune,* p. A1.

Feinberg, J. (1984). *Harm to others.* New York: Oxford University Press.

Hodges, L. W. (1986). Defining press responsibility: A functional approach. In D. Elliott (Ed.), *Responsible journalism* (pp. 13–31). Beverly Hills, CA: Sage.

Pritchard, M. S. (1996). Conflicts of interest: Conceptual and normative Issues, *Academic Medicine, 71*(2), 1305–1313.

Sherman, K. (1997, October 7). Supreme Court declines to consider reporter's appeal; state verdict will stand upholding newspaper's right to reassign writer on basis of political activity. *The (Tacoma, WA) News Tribune,* p. B10.

Schudson, M. (1978). *Discovering the news: A social history of American newspapers.* New York: Basic Books.

Soloski, J. (1989). News reporting and professionalism: Some constraints on the reporting of the news. *Media, Culture and Society, 11,* 207–228.

Stevens, E. L. (1998/1999, December/January). "mouse.ke.fear," *Brill's Content,* pp. 95–103.

Stone, M. E. (1968). *Fifty years a journalist* (reprint). New York: Greenwood.

Tate, C. (1978, July/August). Conflict of interest: A newspaper's report on itself. The *Lewiston Morning Tribune's* examination of its own staff gained national attention. Here is the text of its report. *Columbia Journalism Review,* 44–48.

Thompson, D. (1995). Understanding financial conflicts of interest, *New England Journal of Medicine, 329*, 573–576.

Underwood, D. (1993). *When MBAs rule the newsroom: How the marketers and managers are reshaping today's media.* New York: Columbia University Press.

Werhane, P., & Doering, J. (1995). Conflicts of interest and conflicts of commitment. *Professional Ethics: A Multidisciplinary Journal, 4* (3 & 4), 47–81.

5

CONFLICT OF INTEREST IN THE ACCOUNTING PROFESSION

Leonard J. Brooks

The accounting profession is one in which accounting designations or certifications are received from professional associations, societies, or institutes to signify appropriate education, training, examination, ethical screening, and a commitment to follow the professional body's ethical code. Not only do professional accountants[1] have to be competent; they have to subscribe to the ethical values and standards put forward by their professional body. If they do not, professional accountants will not live up to the ethical standards expected by the public, and their reputations as well as those of their professional colleagues will suffer. As a profession, they will not be able to offer credible services and will lose the ability to command a competitive premium relative to other professionals who do.

Moreover, professional accountants offer complex expert services that are virtually impossible for a layperson to evaluate. Therefore, to preserve the credibility of the profession, it is particularly essential that clients be able to rely on professional accountants to act in their interest. Unfortunately, many interests conflict with those of current clients and the professional accountant must not favor one of these interests over the others or else the profession's credibility could be eroded.

In fact, a professional accountant is called on in his or her professional code to "hold himself or herself free from any influence, interest or relationship in respect of his or her client's affairs, which impairs his or her professional judgement or objectivity or which, in the view of a reasonable observer would impair the member's professional judgement or objectivity."[2] Consequently, a conflict of interest is any influence, interest, or relationship that could cause a professional accountant's judgment to deviate from applying the profession's standards to client matters.

To assist the professional accountant in sorting out how to balance and/or manage competing interests, professional accounting bodies have developed principles and rules that are embodied in codes of conduct, as well as generally accepted accounting and auditing standards (GAAP and GAAS)[3], and standards of professional practice. Securities commissions also keep watch on and have promulgated standards of independence to ensure the objectivity and integrity of professional accountants. Accounting firms have developed internal practices to ensure that employees are aware of and protected from independence-compromising situations, both in appearance as well as in substance.

Professional accountants, however, must be careful not go to any possible length to act in the best interest of their current client. In this regard, the professional accountant faces quite a different ethical regime and limits than does a lawyer. These topics are examined here under the headings of the professional accountant's mandate, fiduciary responsibilities, and credibility; ethical regime; limits to serving clients; frequent conflicts of interest; and resolving and managing conflicts of interest. New regulations and professional prouncements are reviewed, which confirm the earlier discussions in this chapter.

Mandate, Fiduciary Responsibilities, and Credibility

Professional accounting societies were created to provide a means of signaling the public that the persons receiving the professional designation have been certified as technically competent on accounting and related matters such as taxation and business practices. This certification became attractive when accounting techniques and related matters became sufficiently complex that more than a layperson's expertise was desirable in achieving successful treatments. Moreover, the matters being dealt with were considered sufficiently important to the persons and companies directly involved that specific standards of expertise were necessary to facilitate transactions. Members of the public were also indirectly involved through their jobs and investment of savings in the activities of the organizations using accountant's services and raising capital based on those services, so there was a public interest in the provision of competent, accurate, reliable, and trustable accounting services. Members of the professional accounting society were attracted to join the society because it signaled their competence and reliability—really their credibility—and provided a competitive advantage compared to noncertified accountants.

In most jurisdictions, the right of a society to grant a designation that signals certification of the possession of skills, competencies, and values important to the public is overseen by the state. Although the society may be self-governing and self-disciplining, the right to offer designations is conferred by the state and the activities of the society are scrutinized to make sure they are in the public interest. If they are not, the autonomy of the professional society may be curtailed, or another society, association, or institute may be given competing rights. Some professional accounting societies have been granted the right by the state to set accounting and auditing standards as well, which is a source of professional reputation that may also be transferred to another organization. Consequently, the rights enjoyed by professional accounting societies and their members are conferred by government in return for the provision of services considered to be in the public's interest.

The mandate of a professional accountant is then to provide services that can be trusted by the members of the public to serve their interests. This means that the public's interest must be put first when a professional accountant is confronted by a choice that conveys value to one interested group or person to another. For example, it would be against the public interest to overstate current profits to raise current share prices to the benefit of current shareholders who would sell at inflated amounts to the detriment of those future shareholders who would pay too much. To be involved in such a misstatement would lead to a lack of trust in the activities of the professional and his or her colleagues in the profession.

The professional accountant's mandate involves maintaining the confidence and trust of the members of the public. This describes a fiduciary relationship and thus qualifies the professional accountant as a fiduciary. It is interesting to note that in addition to ensuring that he or she maintains the confidence and trust of the public, the professional accountant must do the same for each client served. Sometimes the interests of clients conflict with those of the public and others, and the professional must choose his or her actions carefully indeed so as not to be branded as a "faithless fiduciary" and/or to bring disrepute to the profession.[4]

Historically a professional designation has signaled that the holder can be expected to perform services in a credible and trustworthy manner that befits a fiduciary. Dealing effectively with ethical challenges including conflicts of interest is essential to the maintenance of the reputation and rights enjoyed by the profession and its members. Guidance in meeting such challenges can come from the professional's own values and also the ethical regime in which the professional operates.

Ethical Regime

The ethical framework for the decisions of a professional accountant is derived from a number of sources, including the following:

the code of conduct of the professional society

the disciplinary proceedings of the professional society

generally accepted accounting principles (GAAP)

generally accepted auditing principles (GAAS)

security commission pronouncements

disciplinary hearings of the commission

codes of conduct of employer organizations

normal standards of practice

expectations of the public

The code of conduct of a professional accounting society usually covers the following:

fundamental principles

general rules

specific rules and interpretations

discipline

The Code of Professional Conduct[5] of the American Institute of Certified Public Accountants and the Rules of Conduct[6] of the Institute of Chartered Accountants of Ontario apply directly and indirectly to the largest number of professional accountants in the United States and Canada. They provide representative guidance sources in which fundamental ethical principles are developed. Both the Code and the Rules also extend these principles to provide general and specific rules. The Codes of Conduct for professional accountants indicate that members should (1) at all times maintain the good reputation of the profession and its ability to serve the public interest, (2) perform with integrity, due care, professional competence, independence, objectivity, and confidentiality, and (3) not be associated with any misleading information or misrepresentation.

The intent of these elements of the AICPA Code and ICAO Rules is to provide guidance to professional accountants that will safeguard the fiduciary rights of those who use the accountant's services directly or indirectly. All users are entitled to fair and unbiased services that maintain their confidences and that they can trust.

It is important to note, however, that a professional accountant is not free to use only his or her own judgment in choosing accounting treatments or auditing practices. In fact, that judgment must be exercised within the boundaries of GAAP and GAAS and of the pronouncements of securities commissions. These determine the content and form of financial disclosures and the procedures for their audit. It should be pointed out to the nonaccountant reader that GAAP and GAAS are not trivial; they are voluminous and continue to grow as business complexities increase. Moreover, there are several sets of GAAP and GAAS—usually one per country—and another set developed by the International Federation of Accountants (IFAC). Fortunately, the underlying principles are generally the same, although specific treatments and techniques differ. The objective is to cause the choice of accounting treatments that are predictable and also neutral or unbiased with respect to the interests of various users—and in so doing cause the choice of treatments that protect the public's interest. Consequently, a professional accountant confronted with a choice that might favor one user's interest over another should choose from acceptable alternatives sanctioned by GAAP or GAAS and thus avoid or minimize favoring one interest over another.

In other words, the professional accountant must adhere to a set of rules aimed at neutrality and at protecting the public interest—he or she should not go to absolutely any lengths to serve a specific client's interests unless the public interest is also served. This is quite different than the behavior expected of a lawyer involved in litigation. Barristers or litigators are expected to put only their client's best case forward in court (subject to the rules of the court) because it is expected that the opposing lawyer and the judge/jury will find the flaws, if any, and make justice prevail. Although it is true that barristers cannot use unlawful means or information they know to be untrue, they often do not ask their clients if the clients are guilty and thus are prevented from arguing untruths. Professional accountants, however, are not allowed to hold back or ignore unflattering information called for by GAAP or GAAS. Because there is no expert challenge system similar to an opposing lawyer and judge to filter what an accountant does, there is a much greater requirement for accountants to self-adhere to rules protecting the public interest.

Professional accountants must also be wary of assessing the risks of uncertainties affecting accounting and auditing estimates too much in favor of the positions of current clients or their management. Even though such judgments may be within legal bounds, securities commissions and the public expect professional accountants to protect the public interest. If accountants fail to act properly, they may be subject to class actions or independent civil actions and criminal proceedings, as well as fines, prevention from or restrictions on practice, and/or sanctions by securities commissions and by discipline committees of professional accounting bodies. The professional accounting designation or certification may also be withdrawn.

Limits to Serving Clients

The professional accountants' ethics regime restricts the range for appropriate judgments on client matters in the ways noted earlier. In addition, there are several other aspects of the accounting environment that affect appropriate behavior in regard to clients that require comment, such as the following:

letters of engagement

presentation of best case in taxation discussions and other negotiations

legalities

postengagement time-frame restrictions

Professional accountants are encouraged to draft letters of engagement for clients to reissue on client letterhead to the professional accountant setting out the terms of each assignment. Usually, these letters of engagement specify the duties involved so that the client and the professional know what to expect. Assignments are therefore not of open or unlimited scope. Additional work beyond the terms of existing engagements would need to be covered by additional letters of engagement. This practice is intended to protect the client from false understandings and unlimited bills and the professional accountant from charges that he or she did not do what was expected or should be prepared to do additional work.

Codes of conduct make it clear that professional accountants cannot be party to any misrepresentations or illegalities, so they cannot mislead taxation authorities or be party to tax evasion. They can, when a matter is in doubt[7], advise their clients as to their best course of action to avoid paying tax unnecessarily provided the suggested action is legal and does not involve misrepresentations. If a professional accountant finds that a client has misrepresented or illegally evaded tax, he or she must counsel corrective action, and if no such action is forthcoming, the accountant must resign. At present, professional accountants are not required to report the evasion or illegality to taxation authorities, but if another accountant is found to have breached his or her professional code, the breach is to be reported to the professional society. It is noteworthy that only in late 1998 were some professional accountants freed by amendment in some jurisdictions to argue their client's best case with taxation authorities, but this change does not permit misrepresentations and illegal treatments.

It is also evident from the foregoing comments that professional accountants must not be involved in illegalities or fraudulent behavior. In the taxation context, this means that it is unacceptable to falsify expenses or income to reduce tax payable.

These limits to how far a professional accountant should go in satisfying his or her immediate client represent implementation of the ethical principles of fair treatment, adequate notice, integrity, and fiduciary responsibility. Moreover, these limits respect the fact that the professional accountant must be aware of the rights of other stakeholders and keep the public interest uppermost in mind when advising clients.

One additional point of difference from the legal regime facing lawyers is the ability of a professional accountant to take on competing clients, whereas a lawyer cannot except under certain conditions. For example, a lawyer cannot take on competing clients unless there is prior knowledge and consent by both. Because the lawyer has a duty of disclosure to both clients, there can be no information held back from either as confidential, and if a dispute arises, the lawyer may be prevented from serving either client even if there is prior agreement about which client the lawyer will serve. In other words, a lawyer can serve competitors but not on issues on which there is a conflict between them. Nor can a lawyer take on a new client on issues involving a prior client after resigning from an engagement involving those issues with the prior client, whereas an accountant can. The reason is that the accountant is responsible to the stakeholder-neutral rules of GAAP and GAAS rather than to the lawyer's requirement of using all facts to put the best case forward for the client.

Frequent Conflicts of Interest

With the foregoing background, it is useful to consider the most common conflicts of interest for accountants. Using a stakeholder framework, these conflicts of interest can be categorized as per table 5.1.

Profit versus the Public Interest

Many of the conflicts professional accountants face involve favoring their own interest at the expense of others. For instance, a professional accountant is in a position to provide substandard services to save money and increase his or her own profit. Alternatively, he or she can accept offers of cheap goods or services from clients, thus benefiting him- or

Table 5.1 Conflicts of Interest for Professional Accountants: Categories, Spheres of Activity Affected, and Examples

Stakeholder Categories	Sphere of Activity Affected	Examples
Self vs. others	Services offered	Conflicting services, shaving quality
	Improper use of influence	Improper purchases of client goods
	Misuse of information	Improper investments by relatives
Self and others vs. others	Services offered	Overinvolvement with management or Directors erodes objectivity
Client vs. client Employer vs. employer	Services offered	Serving competing clients at the same time
Stakeholder vs. stakeholder	Misuse of information (confidentiality)	Whistleblowing, reporting to government or regulators

Source: L. J. Brooks, *Business and Professional Ethics for Accountants* table 5.1 (South-Western College Publishing, 2000).[8]

herself. This could put the accountant in the position to be asked for a favor in return that would erode his or her independence and perhaps cause harm to other investors or government that represents the public interest. Similarly, information received by professional accountants in the practice of their duties is supposed to be kept confidential and not used for investment by the professional accountant or his or her relatives or friends. Constant vigilance is required to avoid the lure of personal gain, as well as the appearance of it.

Two aspects of this battle against the lure of personal gain deserve further comment at this point. First, professional accountants must be on guard against their desire to be businesspeople rather than professionals. For businesspeople profit or market share is the central goal, whereas for professionals the welfare of the public interest or the client should be more important than the professional's personal wealth. Professional accountants who forget this are often lured into "lowballing" fee quotations or providing fixed fee estimates that do not allow for adequate investigations of regular matters or unusual problems or create unreasonable pressures on staff to meet work deadlines or budget deadlines. Second, professional accountants must not use information from clients to invest because they could be guilty of "insider trading" or of improperly signaling the marketplace about their client's affairs. To avoid any such suppositions, most auditing firms require their personnel to agree not to invest in clients even when those clients are served by other personnel in other cities.

Overinvolvement, Assurance Services, and Multidisciplinary Firms

Sometimes the professional accountant becomes overinvolved with senior management at a client, to the extent that the professional's skepticism and critical perspective are suspended. Friendship, partnerships, the prospect of social interaction, or admiration may all have an impact on the professional's independence of judgment to the detriment of the public interest. In addition, care must be undertaken to ensure that a professional accountant or his or her firm does not become so dependent on the revenue from one client that decisions contrary to the client's interest become difficult to make.

One recently emerging development that exacerbates the overinvolvement problem is the trend for professional accounting firms to expand their consulting services and to become multidisciplinary firms that embrace legal and engineering consultancies as well as other professional groups. This increase in nonattest activity that does not have the need for independence as its central focus has the danger of replacing service responsive to the public interest with practices devoted to the increase of the multidisciplinary firms' profit. An example of this could be a new perversion of risk management in tax matters, where the client is advised to take a questionable action based on the probability that government tax auditors are unlikely to appear because of other time demands, not because the tax treatment is in doubt.[7] An additional aspect of a multidisciplinary firm that could cause difficulties is the potential conflict between the professional codes and practices of accountants, lawyers, and engineers. For example, accountants are not expected to blow the whistle on clients, but engineers are required to report any endangerment to life from a dangerous process or poorly maintained building[9]—which profession's rules should prevail? Similarly, lawyers have a different standard of confidentiality that prevents them from advising competing clients, whereas professional accountants do it frequently. In addition, the new vision for the future of U.S. and Canadian professional accountants envisages more "assurance services"[10] beyond auditing that will rely on the skepticism and credibility of the accounting profession but will also bring extremely high pressure on the maintenance of independence because of mounting pressures for profit and the requirements of multiple professions. We are also already seeing some assurance services downgraded to review or consulting services to lessen the legal liability involved in a effort to bolster profits. Increased attention to ethical principles for managing such conflicts of interest will be essential to the maintenance of the accounting profession's reputation in the future, as well as the reputations of the other professions involved.

It is noteworthy that the American Bar Association (ABA) has studied the issue of whether lawyers could practice within a multidisciplinary firm (MDF). In the summer of 1999, the ABA resolved that lawyers could do so provided essentially that their ability to follow their legal code of ethics was not impinged upon. It will be interesting to see how this is operationalized when one of the MDF's audit clients (A) which uses the MDF's in-house lawyers takes over another one of the MDF's clients (B) which also uses the MDF's lawyers, or when A sues B. Will MDF's lawyers have to withdraw from one or both clients? Will the courts view MDF's audit confidences as an extension of the MDF's lawyers' position?

Confidentiality

One important aspect of providing services in which the public can place trust involves the appropriate treatment of information about a client's affairs that could be harmful to the client's interest if it became known to competing interests or misused. To protect the interests of each client, as a general rule information about client matters must be kept confidential. A number of techniques that are discussed next are available to assist with this objective. They have been successfully employed for some time in the accounting profession, thus allowing professional accountants to serve more than one client with competing interests.

When a professional accountant or his or her firm serves a client, that client is entitled to rely, within certain parameters, on that person or relevant group of persons to use their expertise and act in the client's best interests. The client has the right to expect the professional to act in good faith with regard to the objectives of the assignment but always subject to the profession's code of conduct and associated relevant rules.

For example, a client has the right to expect that confidential information shared with his or her professional accountant will be kept confidential and will not be disclosed except when subject to court or disciplinary proceedings. So far, professional accountants are not generally held to be agents of the crown or state and are therefore not required to report client misdeeds to the government on a proactive basis. This confidentiality regime is usually justified on the practical basis that if it were absent, clients would not be sufficiently forthcoming to enable professional accountants to accumulate the knowledge about the client's affairs to do a thorough job,[11] and clients would turn to other less qualified and possibly less ethical experts for advice to discuss gray-area issues. Similarly, a professional accountant would have to refrain from advising other clients with competing interests.

If a professional accountant seeks to significantly change the relationship agreed to or reasonably expected by a client, fairness demands that the professional accountant should inform the client so that the client can make alternative arrangements for his or her affairs and will not be harboring false expectations. A significant change would be one in which the client's interests would suffer tangible harm as a result, and the client should be informed before tangible harm can occur.

If the professional accountant wishes to continue serving the client, then consent to the new relationship/arrangement should be obtained. If the professional accountant wishes to terminate serving client A but does wish to begin to serve or continue to serve another client (B) who has competing or conflicting interests with A, it is imperative that the interests of A as they stood at the end of the engagement not be eroded. This means, for example, that any confidences shared up to the end of the engagement should not be revealed. On the other hand, in fairness to the professional accountant, client A should not be able to block the termination of the engagement and the assumption of work for client B, provided the fiduciary interests of A will not be violated in the future. Adequate measures would have to be undertaken, and remain in place, for example, to ensure that A's confidential information will not be revealed to or used on behalf of B. The professional accountant would have to be able to provide assurance that such fiduciary interests had not been eroded in the future.

Serving Multiple Clients

It is difficult to serve two or more competing clients at the same time because it is hard to avoid the appearance, at least, of favoring one stakeholder at the expense of the others. When both clients know about the assignments, they should be advised to have an informed, independent assessment of the result. When the professional is convinced that measures can be taken to protect the interests of both clients, and they are aware of the assignments, the professional should still take actions that would mitigate the possibility of an outcome that is biased in favor of one or the other. Such management techniques are the subject of the next section of this chapter. This stance of placing responsibility to the public foremost differs from the stance of the legal profession on the matter of taking assignments for competing clients.

In fact, professional accountants have been dealing with clients with potentially conflicting interests for a long time. Often this is with the knowledge and consent of all clients, but it is also common for either knowledge or consent, or both, to be absent. Table 5.2 sets out illustrative examples.

The first and second cases are readily justified on the basis of practicality. There are simply not enough professional accountants in North America to provide exclusive or conflict-free service to each client. In addition, however, provided no misuse is made of confidential information, no harm will be caused the clients involved. Finally, it should be noted that adherence to a strict no-conflict-of-interest regime (which bar-

Table 5.2 Instances When Auditors Serve Multiple Clients without Their Knowledge or Consent

Nature of Assignment	Knowledge/Consent Missing
Audit of banks and of bank customers.	Both. Although bank auditors are known to the public, no permission is ever sought from other clients even when audit firm changes are made.
Audit of nonbanks and of their customers and/or suppliers.	Both. No effort is made to inform clients or to obtain consent regardless of whether the clients are public or private entities.
Audit of two competing clients (GM and Chrysler).	Measures to protect confidences are usually explained; consent may be sought.
Investigation by company auditors of allegations against executives who are also tax return clients.	No knowledge or consent sought so as not to tip off the executives so that they can cover up their alleged misdeeds.
Investigation of executives by nonauditor, professional accountants that have other professional assignments with the executives.	Same as last case.

risters have) would open the door to preemptive strike behavior. Trivial assignments could be used to prevent some accounting firms from taking on important work, thus exposing the public interest to professional accounting units that might not have the critical mass or research resources to take on large-scale or highly complex assignments.

The second-last case warrant further explanation. Insofar as an auditor relies on the audited entity's internal controls when forming an audit opinion, it is the auditor's responsibility to ensure that internal controls are adequate.[12] Moreover, it is an auditor's responsibility to follow up on allegations of fraud to make sure their implications are understood.[13] In addition, it is the professional accountant's responsibility not to be involved with any misrepresentations. For all these reasons, the duty of auditor to an executive client is overtaken by his or her duty to the public, and knowledge of or consent for the investigation is not considered essential or even desirable.

If a company's auditor is not used to investigate allegations about an executive, and another professional accountant is employed (the last case), the investigating accountant could not advise the executive prior to at least beginning the assignment and securing relevant records without tipping off the executive and possibly obviating the assignment.

If, in this latter case, the investigating accounting firm found that the executive whose activities were to be investigated was also a client, the accounting firm would have to weigh its duties to the executive, to the company requiring the investigation, and to the public interest. To the executive client would be owed the duty not to use confidences gained in a client–professional accountant relationship. To the company client would be owed an unbiased investigation. To the public interest, and to the accounting profession, would be owed the duty not to be involved in any misrepresentation. There are possibilities—either the executive client is guilty or not guilty, or there is doubt about the guilt. If he or she is not guilty, then he or she cannot be harmed by the investigation. If there is doubt about guilt, then provided the investigation will not breach confidences, the professional accounting firm's duty to the company client, to the public and to the profession is to discover the facts and report them. If the facts implicate the executive, the firm is not obligated to act in the executive client's best interest and misrepresent the situation. Thus, provided prior executive client confidences are protected (e.g., by employing a firewall, as discussed later, and using different professionals from a different part of the accounting firm), the accounting firm can ethically undertake the investigation.

In summary, current practice by professional accountants includes many assignments where the same professional or firm acts for clients that might or do have competing interests and where notification and/or informed consent are not considered necessary or advisable. Moreover, acting in the best interest of a client does not mean that a professional accountant or firm should advocate in the manner of a lawyer for a current or past client, nor does it involve misrepresentations. A professional accountant or firm is responsible to a current or past client only for advice or service that reflects integrity, objectivity, and competence within the rule of law and the rules of GAAP and GAAS and the professional's code of conduct. Advice or service based on those fundamentals is in the public's best interest, which represents the highest level of duty owed by the professional accountant.

Employees versus Profit and the Public Interest

Professional accountants do not all serve as auditors with client responsibilities. Some serve as employees and face the conflict between loyalty to one employer or to another. This would be the case when they are moonlighting, or when they are shifting employers and are making use of intellectual property from one to help the other. This, of course, is unethical unless the involvement is approved by both employers.

Professional accountants definitely face problems that other employees do not. Because of their adherence to their professional code, and their expertise in financial matters, they are required not to be involved in misrepresentations and must ensure that their analyses have integrity so that users are not misled. Employees without responsibilities under professional codes of conduct are not required to protect the public and the reputation of a profession in their activities on behalf of the company.

Whistleblowing and Resignation

With specific exceptions, professional accountants are not expected to blow the whistle on individuals or companies to governmental authorities. The exceptions involve reporting on financial institutions in financial difficulty (in Canada), and on the laundering of money for drugs or terrorism (in the United Kingdom). Generally this failure to inform on many other activities contrary to the public interest is rationalized by the need for auditors to be able to discuss issues with clients on a confidential basis because they would not otherwise have access to information important to audit judgments and financial disclosures. On the other hand, as noted earlier, professional accountants are expected to report to the professional society any fellow professional who breaks their code.

When a professional accountant finds that a client or employer has done or is about to do something that is not appropriate according the professional's code of conduct, it is his or her duty to try to get the problem rectified. If the client or employer is unwilling to do so, the professional must resign in order not to be connected with a misrepresentation or other significant ethical misdeed. Unfortunately, this puts the professional in the position of not being able to reveal confidences about why he or she resigned even to prospective employers. Because these confidences cannot be revealed to the public either, only the ethical miscreants benefit and the public interest suffers. Ideally, this flaw in professional codes will be addressed soon to assist professional accountants in dealing with this unfortunate conflict of interests.[14]

Real, Potential, and Imaginary Conflicts of Interest or Harmful, Potentially Harmful, and Imaginary Conflicts of Interest

Usually, conflicts of interest facing professional accountants are referred to as *real* (where harm has been caused), *potential* (where real harm might be caused in the future), *or imaginary*. Moreover, it is said that a professional accountant must be wary not only of *real* conflicts of interest but also of *potential* conflcits, as well as those that are *imaginary*.

It is worth noting, however, that this terminology is not helpful in promoting a good understanding of conflicts of interest. For example, a conflict of interests refers to a condition where a fiduciary *might not* act in the best interests of a client because of bias in favor of other interests. However, even if the potential for bias to influence behavior is present, actions might not be influenced because of a principled character, awareness, training, and other countervailing factors. Conflicts of interest provide some motivation or tendency for biased actions but do not ensure that harm will be caused. Thus there may be a "real" conflict of interests, but no harm may ensue. Consequently, it would be useful to adopt the following terminology in the future:

harmful conflict of interest (where bias has caused harm to the client)

potentially harmful conflict of interest (where bias might cause harm)

imaginary conflict of interest

This revised terminology can clarify several issues. For example, it is possible for competitors to have competing general interests but no specific direct conflicts of interests. A professional accountant with clients that are competitors without specific conflicts of interest is focussed on applying rules designed to protect society (GAAP) and not to put the best case forward for one or the other. Consequently, the conflict of interest involved would be imaginary. If a transaction or action arose which pitted one client against the other, the condition could be considered a potentially harmful conflict of interests but harm would not necessarily follow if appropriate steps to manage the situation were to be taken.

It is worth noting that allegations in the media of a conflict of interest are often unnecessarily harmful to a professional accountant or his or her firm, even when no harm may come to the clients involved. Rarely do the media differentiate between an imaginary, a potentially harmful, or a harmful conflict of interests. Any form of conflict of interests is almost always considered to be prima facie evidence of harm to clients in media stories. Moreover, once a professional accountant's reputation is stained, it is hard to recover. Consequently, it is often as hard to remedy the negative reputational impact of a potentially harmful or imaginary conflict of interest as it is to recover from a harmful conflict of interest.

Resolving and Managing Conflicts of Interest

Proper handling of conflicts of interest is fundamental to the maintenance of fiduciary relationships. Consequently, it is covered in auditing and professional ethics texts and curricula, as well as in rules/codes of conduct for professional accountants. In addition, at least the largest professional accounting firms have additional codes of conduct or practice that offer the firm's guidance thereon. Members of a multioffice firm often sign a document in which they promise not to discuss the affairs of, or trade in securities of, clients of any office in their firm, and they maintain a restricted list of client's names for reference. Members of the firm are told that even if they do not personally possess information on a client's activities, they may be presumed to do so by the interested public. There is little doubt that professional accountants are aware of the importance of conflicts of interest and their potential impact.

Professional accountants employ several techniques in the management of conflicts of interest to minimize potential harm, including:

codes of professional bodies and firms

training sessions and reinforcing memos

client lists and sign-off procedures

scrutiny of securities trading, particularly related to new issues

firewalls or Chinese walls to prevent information flows within firms

reporting and consultation with senior officers

avoidance

rules for serving clients with potentially conflicting interests

rules for taking on new clients or providing new services, and for termination of client relations

The "firewall" or "Chinese wall" concept deserves further comment. This practice uses the analogy to an impervious wall to describe those measures and methods that would prevent the transmission of client information from one part of an organization or consortium to another. Such firewalls[15] or Chinese walls are not tangible in a three-dimensional sense but refer to a multidimensional set of measures such as the following:

instructions to keep information confidential

instructions not to read, listen to or act on specific types of information

educational programs and reinforcements by top management

monitoring and compliance sign-off procedures

scrutiny of insider or key-person trading of securities

physical barriers to information transmission, such as:

    separate computer- or physical-storage systems

    segregation of duties to different personnel

    segregation of information in a different location or building, etc.

    different lock systems

appointment of a compliance officer who would monitor the effectiveness of the wall

disciplinary sanctions for breach of the wall

Chinese walls or firewalls have been a normal part of business and professional operations for many years. For example, when a client is involved in the preparation of a public offering of securities, those members of the offering team (lawyers, professional accountants, and underwriters) are expected not to divulge advance details of the underwriting to the other members of their respective firms or to anyone else. The public issuance of securities, as presently known, would be impossible without the Chinese wall construct. Fortunately, even though in the final analysis a Chinese wall relies on the integrity of the professionals involved for its effectiveness, such arrangements are considered effective to protect the public interest and to safeguard the interest of current clients as well as former clients.

International Aspects

Accountants increasingly find themselves operating internationally with foreign clients or employers, or in foreign jurisdictions with domestic clients. In these situations, the professional accountant faces the problem of whether to adhere to his or her original domestic code of conduct; the code of conduct of the foreign jurisdiction involved; or the Code of conduct[16] of IFAC, which is a group recently constituted to develop international standards for ethics, GAAP, and GAAS; or the most stringent of these or securities commission guidelines.

It is clearly in the interest of the professional accounting firm involved to specify its desired approach to guide its employees and clients. However, the individual professional accountant involved may be bound by the code of conduct of his or her domestic professional society, particularly if the professional accountant has held him- or herself out as a member of that domestic society. Consequently it is most appropriate, if deviation is necessary, to adopt the rules of a more stringent guideline than the domestic guideline rather than one that is less stringent. If there is doubt about the applicability of the professional's domestic standard or the local standard, professionals should consult their domestic society. Such consultation, in fact, is excellent advice for domestic as well as foreign matters.

New Regulations and Professional Pronouncements

Under mounting pressure from high profile lawsuits, from increasingly complex business pressures and a growing array of assurance services, and from controversy over the need for large accounting firms to split from their consulting practices, the Canadian Institute of Chartered Accountants (CICA) and the U.S. Securities and Exchange Commission (SEC) each released new guidance on conflicts of interest for accountants. Specifically, the CICA issued *Conflict of Interest: A Task Force Report*[17] in September 2000. It explored the issue of fiduciary duty and recommended that the Canadian rules of professional conduct be changed to reflect their findings and to incorporate them into the guidance related to restricted control of confidential information, engagements involving two or more clients, and the institution of a framework and process for dealing with client conflicts of interest. The use of Chinese walls and explicitly agreed to "cones of silence" are considered to be effective means of managing conflicts of interest even though the courts might be skeptical about their efficacy. The report suggests that there are three types of conflict of interest: professional—those that offend professional rules of conduct; legal—those that arise out of fiduciary duty, contractual agreements or legal process; and business conflicts—those that relate to enhancing profit or furthering a career. Conflicts should be identified as early as possible and managed properly or avoided. Recommendations are generally in agreement with the discussion presented earlier in this chapter except for an expectation that serving two clients will generally require obtaining informed consent from all parties.

In its *Final Rule: Revision of the Commission's Auditor Independence Requirements*,[18] the SEC required accounting firms with SEC registrants as clients to observe new standards to ensure that bias does not influence the objectivity of their audit judgments. Such firms are expected to (1) be concerned with whether "a relationship or the provision of a service: (a) creates a mutual or conflicting interest between the accountant and the audit client; (b) places the accountant in the position of auditing his or her own work; (c) results in the accountant acting as management or an employee of the audit client; or (d) places the accountant in a position of being an advocate for the audit client"; (2) employ quality control systems to prevent misuse of confidential information; and (3) take immediate corrective action if inadvertent impairment of independence occurs. The SEC also required the restriction of a client's confidential information based on a "need to know criteria," which, in addition to the presence of quality control measures such as Chinese walls, was considered sufficient to permit the accounting firms to continue to provide many non-audit assurance services rather than to have to sell off or discontinue them. In this regard the SEC went to considerable length to specify which services were acceptable for retention by audit firms and which were not. Although the new SEC rule is intended to apply to large accounting firms, it will doubtless form the touchstone for further thinking of conflict of interest matters.

Both the CICA and SEC documents are well worth studying. Both confirm the relevance of discussions earlier in this chapter. In addition, the International Federation of Accountants (IFAC) and other professional accounting bodies are also in the process of issuing new pronouncements.

Conclusions

Professional accountants have a responsibility as fiduciaries for providing credible, trustworthy services that serve the public interest as well as the interests of their clients or employer and their profession. Necessity demands that such services are based on the integrity, objectivity, independence, due care, professional competence, and confidentiality of each accountant. Professional accountants realize that conflicts of interest cannot be entirely avoided and therefore must be effectively managed. In making decisions concerning conflicts of interests, professional accountants would be well advised to put the public interest first, ensure that no real harm can come to current clients, and avoid situations that are potentially harmful when possible. In the end, such safeguards will depend more on the ethical awareness and integrity of the specific professionals involved than on their technical competence. As a start, the professional accounting community should persist in revisiting the subject of conflicts of interest to raise awareness, point out the variety of possible conflicts and adopt more meaningful terminology for these conflicts, such as "harmful," "potentially harmful," and "imaginary" conflict of interests. New regulations and professional pronouncements are a step in the right direction.

Notes

1. A professional accountant differs from a person with accounting or bookkeeping skills in that a professional has a legally recognized designation or certification from a professional association and must subscribe to ethical values as laid down in the association's code. The most common professional accounting designations are Certified Public Accountant (CPA), Chartered Accountant (CA), and Certified Management Accountant (CMA). CPAs and CAs are licensed by some jurisdictions to serve as auditors and to render opinions as to whether financial statements present fairly the activities of the organization.

2. *Rules of Professional Conduct and Council Interpretations*, Institute of Chartered Accountants of Ontario (ICAO), Toronto, 1997, Foreword, p. 505, updated continuously

3. See, e.g., the pronouncements in *CICA Handbook*, Canadian Institute of Chartered Accountants (CICA), Toronto, Canada, undated continuously; *FASB Statements on Accounting and Auditing Standards*, Financial Accounting Standards Board (FASB), Norwalk, Conn., updated continuously.

4. For example, the management or current directors may want to choose a method of revenue or expense recognition that while recognized as being within GAAP, may nonetheless fail to present fairly the financial affairs of

the organization and therefore mislead the public and future shareholders in it. The professional accountant must stand up for the public in such circumstances.

5. *Code of Professional Conduct*, American Institute of Certified Public Accountants (AICPA), New York, 1999, see Principles and Rules sections.

6. ICAO, note 2 supra.

7. This doubt must be real in the professional judgment of the professional accountant, for he or she must be prepared to defend against charges of involvement with an illegality (fraudulent or otherwise) or misrepresentation.

8. Brooks, *Business and Professional Ethics for Accountants* table 5.1 (2000).

9. Presumably, this difference in treatment is due to the higher priority attached by society (and therefore the engineers) to physical well-being as opposed to financial well-being. Society is willing to endorse the reporting of one, but not yet the other.

10. See the report of the Special Committee on Assurance Services on the AICPA Website that defines several assurance services including assessing information systems reliability and providing assurance concerning e-commerce through the WebTrust seal of approval.

11. J. C. Robertson and W. J. Smieliauskas, *Auditing & Other Assurance Engagements*, 707 (1998).

12. *Id.* at 192.

13. *Id.* at 861.

14. See, e.g., L. J. Brooks, *Ethical Codes of Conduct: Deficient in Guidance for the Canadian Accounting Profession*, 8. J. Bus. Ethics 325–36 (May 1989).

15. A firewall may also represent a barrier within a computer system designed to keep information separate and prevent unauthorized access to it.

16. *Code of Conduct for Professional Accountants*, International Federation of Accountants (IFAC), New York, 1999, website: www.ifac.org

17. *Conflict of Interest: A Task Force Report*, The Canadian Institute of Chartered Accountants, Toronto, 2000.

18. *Final Rule: Revision of the Commission's Auditor Independence Rule*, U.S. Securities and Exchange Commission, NY, February 5, 2001, website: *www.sec.gov/rules/final/33-7919.htm.*

6

CONFLICT OF INTEREST IN ENGINEERING

Neil R. Luebke

On the basis of several sorts of evidence, conflict of interest is an important topic of professional ethics for engineers. The codes of ethics of major U.S. engineering professional societies include provisions dealing with conflicts of interest, although the wording and the amount of specificity vary. Conflict of interest is the largest category of ethical problems to be addressed between 1958 and 1998 by the National Society of Professional Engineers' Board of Ethical Review. Then, too, virtually every major corporation that employs engineers has policies governing conflicts of interest, and engineers in military or government service usually work under statutes or administrative rules that apply to conflicts of interest.

This chapter examines the treatments of conflict of interest by both professional engineering societies and a sample of major corporations that employ hundreds of engineers. As might be expected, the two groups of organizations have differing orientations in approaching the topic, which might in turn cause difficulties for professional engineers who are corporate employees. On the other hand, although there is considerable agreement on paradigm instances of conflict of interest, there is also some variation in definition, rationale, categorization of instances, and recommended courses of action. *ASME v. Hydrolevel* is discussed primarily to review the American Society of Mechanical Engineer's (ASME's) conflict-of-interest policies developed in the aftermath of the U. S. Supreme Court's 1982 decision.

Definition and Related Considerations

The rationale for ethical provisions regarding conflicts of interest in professional settings rests in the nature of the professions themselves and the values they implicitly represent. Although other characteristics can be noted, it is fundamental that a professional puts his or her educated abilities of skill and judgment at the service of another party or parties who, in turn, customarily entrust the professional with a measure of authority to carry out the service. Especially with regard to engineering, many would add that "the public" is also a party to be served. Thus, technical competence in the exercise of abilities and moral integrity in the service rendered to clients, employers, and the public are two principal values which together might be termed "professional reliability." Technical competence by itself is not sufficient for reliability, for we can imagine a thoroughly skillful engineer who cannot be trusted to use the skills in legitimate ways on behalf of clients. Similarly, one can imagine a person of extraordinary integrity who, at the same time, is unable to work at an appropriate level of engineering competence. Because clients employ and trust engineering professionals to act in the client's interest, usually entrusting them with information and limited authority, and the public trusts them to act in socially beneficial or at least nonharmful ways, trustworthiness is clearly a major element in professional integrity. Conflicts of interest occur when a professional's dutiful and proper service to the client, employer, or public is threatened to be compromised by certain other "interests," possibly resulting in biased judgments or willfully contrary actions. Failure to avoid or to act properly in a conflict-of-interest situation violates the professional relationship with a client/employer, erodes the trustworthiness of the professional or professional firm in the eyes of both the client and the public, and may cast a shadow on the profession generally.

Several elements in the preceding paragraph may be elaborated. First, conflicts of interest can arise only for persons who have or are given authority to act in service to, and usually on behalf of, other parties.[1] In a broad sense, then, they can arise only for a person (or firm) insofar as that person (or firm) plays a fiduciary role. Engineers and other professionals play fiduciary roles in varying degrees. A chief consulting engineer overseeing the design and specifications for a major project may be positioned to confront more conflicts of interest than a fledgling, employed engineer merely carrying out prescribed tests on manufacturing materials.

Second, the "interests" in question should be understood, in accordance with the historically older sense of the word, as "material" or "objective" interests such as financial holdings, business associations, or family relationships rather than as "psychological" or "subjective" interests such as penchants for rock music, sunny beaches, the Boston Red Sox, or champagne. On the other hand, as the biblical "where your treasure is, there your heart will be also" is probably true, the material interests are assumed to have psychological accompaniments. Hence, the material interests may operate—using a term from another writer in this volume—as "perverse incentives," setting up a conflict-of-interest situation.[2] Yet, when we look for evidence of conflicts of interest we examine bank accounts, stock holdings, and family ties, not the results of psychological preference tests.[3] It is disclosure of facts of the former type, not the latter, that professionals are expected to make to their clients or employers. To interpret "conflict of interest" as meaning the opposition between psychological interests of two parties makes the extension of the term so broad as to be virtually useless.[4]

Third, conflict-of-interest policies that identify the relevant moral wrong as either an act of "disloyalty" or a diminution of "quality of judgment or service" play on ambiguities in these two terms. Insofar as an engineering professional should be a "faithful agent" of a client/employer, the professional should be committed (i.e., "loyal" in one sense) in professional service to the best interests of the party, and failure to avoid or act properly in a conflict-of-interest situation could be interpreted as a violation of loyalty in this sense. On the other hand, "disloyalty" normally connotes an intentional transfer of allegiance away from a previously pledged party. To categorize all actual conflicts of interest as acts of disloyalty is to assume the acts derive from anti-client/employer motives, whereas they might result from ignorance or insensitivity. Furthermore, categorizing them as instances of disloyalty may mislead policy writers into applying the term "conflict of interest" to such acts as buying a competitor's product or voicing dissatisfaction with one's employer.

In a similar way, the claim that a failure to act appropriately in a conflict-of-interest situation is wrong because it would impair the quality of the professional's judgment or service may play on the ambiguity of "quality." Quality can be judged on the basis of technical competence or on the basis of whether the judgment provides the best service *to the client*. What is often worrisome in conflict cases is not that the professional lacks competence but that the competence might be used on behalf of a party other than the client/employer/public. Of course, favoritism may result in decisions that are indefensible on objective grounds, but the issue is not a professional's lack of technical competence but, rather, a lack of integrity.

Finally, a few words should be said about appropriate responses to a conflict-of-interest situation. Of course, if the conflict situation can be foreseen and is serious, it should be avoided in most cases. Sometimes avoidance is not possible or at least not possible given reasonable limitations of knowledge. There may also be some cases, such as dearth of professionals in a given area, in which conflict situations should be tolerated for the sake of maximal use of limited professional services. Except for situations in which avoidance should have been practiced, there is usually nothing wrong with merely finding one's self in a conflict of interest; the ethical questions usually concern the choice (and often timing) of one's response. The minimal response, which may be sufficient in many cases, is disclosure of the facts of one's situation to some or all of the possibly affected parties. A second step, assuming some amount of disclosure, is recusal or some degree of nonparticipation by which one effectively removes one's self from the conflict situation. An extreme form of this step may be resignation. An alternative response when possible, again often assuming some amount of disclosure, is divestment of the threatening interests. Stock holdings can be sold and business associations can be terminated; however, family relationships are not so easily treated.

Corporate Policies

It has become standard for large corporations to issue policy manuals setting forth standards for employee conduct, especially by administrative and professional employees. Although issues differ among industrial groups, typical manuals of companies employing a large number of engineers usually address confidentiality, conflicts of interest, equal employment, health and safety, and political contributions. Following is a brief examination of what some representative corporate manuals say about conflict of interest.

As the examples show, corporate definitions of conflict of interest tend to stress one or both of two concerns: loyalty and objectivity.[5]

1. A conflict of interest arises when an employee's loyalty to the company is prejudiced by actual or potential personal benefit from another source. (from a major chemical corporation)
2. A conflict of interest occurs whenever an associate [i.e., employee] allows the possibility of direct or indirect personal gain to influence his or her judgment in the conduct of [company] business. (from a major automotive corporation)
3. The principle of conflicting interests is simple . . . don't compete with the company and don't work for competitors. . . . A conflict of interest is any situation that could cast doubt on your ability to act in an objective manner. Every employee has an obligation to avoid

financial or other outside relationships that could be adverse to the interests of the company. (from a major petroleum corporation)

4. It is [the corporation's] worldwide policy that, without prior management approval, [corporate] employees should not engage in activities that conflict with or are inconsistent with [the corporation's] activities or business interests or that could cause a reasonable person to believe that their judgment, loyalty to [the corporation] or objectivity in the conduct of their [corporate] business activities and assignments might be adversely affected. (from a major manufacturing corporation)

5. A conflict of interest or adverse interest arises when an officer or employee has such a substantial personal interest in a business transaction or in an organization which is party to a business transation with the Company that their judgment or the performance of their duties may reasonably be affected or may reasonably appear to be affected thereby. (from a major engineering corporation)

6. The firm's professional integrity requires that these decisions ["which involve large expenditures of money by the Firm or its clients"] be made objectively, unbiased by personal friendships or favors. (from a major engineering corporation, which does not use the tem "conflict of interest" in its policy)

Example 1 mentions only loyalty, examples 2 and 6 mention only objectivity, but examples 3 and 4 mention both. Example 5 alludes to objectivity in judgment but also refers to duties generally. Interestingly, the expanded discussions of examples 3 and 4 do not seriously consider a situation in which objectivity and loyalty might clash. Presumably, such a situation might be taken to fall under the usual blanket "confer with your supervisor" directive. However, instances abound, from the well-known Challenger shuttle and DC-10 cargo door cases to more everyday "Dilbert" experiences, of clashes between engineers' objective concerns for safety or quality in design and (read "loyalty to") management decisions. I am not contending that a conflict of objectivity with loyalty should be called a conflict of interest; I am only suggesting that policy statements that use both terms in their definitions raise an important ethical issue they often fail to address.

Types of behavior usually cited as violating the policies commonly include the following:

1. Accepting gifts (in a broad sense covering favors) given to the employee or a member of the employee's immediate family by a party doing business with the company. Sometimes a gift is deemed permissible when it is under $50 to $100 in value or meets other guidelines. Some policies require checking with a supervisor before accepting a gift of any size; several prohibit any gift of cash. One major electronic manufacturer places gifts in a section entitled "Dealing with Customers and Suppliers," separate from the section on conflict of interest.

2. Exercising direct authority over a relative or over business relations with a company employing a relative, especially if the relative's compensation can be affected by the employee's decisions. Usually disclosure to a supervisor is required in such a situation, with the possibility of reassignment of responsibility.

3. Owning shares in a competing firm or a supplier or working for a competing firm or supplier. Some companies make explicit exceptions for ownership through mutual funds or ownership of publicly traded stocks under a given percentage of the total class outstanding. Aside from the exceptions, disclosure to and permission by the company is usually required.

4. Serving on the board of directors of a for-profit organization unless it is clear that no conflict of interest can occur and that the experience will be beneficial to the company. Often company approval is required for any for-profit board. Serving on boards of, or participating in a major way in, nonprofit charitable or educational organizations is usually permitted although some companies require prior notification and approval by a company official.

Several corporate policies include as examples certain types of behavior that, although usually wrong, seem to me not to be cases of conflict of interest. They are usually violations of trust motivated by desire for private gain; hence, they are seen as acts of disloyalty by the policies that define conflict of interest in terms of loyalty. By contrast, I prefer to categorize them as abuses or misuses of company resources rather than as conflicts of interest. The three most common examples are (1) unauthorized use or distribution of confidential or proprietary information, (2) unauthorized use of company equipment including software, and (3) unauthorized use of company title or affiliation to promote a personal business. As I see it, these examples seem morally more analogous to stealing than to being biased in judgment, and corporate policy statements would likely make a stronger ethical case against them by categorizing them separately rather than lumping them along with instances of stock ownership in competitors. The latter has no aroma of theft.

The Asme v. Hydrolevel Case

The most notable case of conflict of interest to affect an engineering society is *American Society of Mechanical Engineers* v. *Hydrolevel Corporation*, settled in 1983 after an antitrust judgment by the U.S. Supreme Court in 1982.[6] Even though all parties agreed that ASME did not financially benefit by the actions that led to the case, the courts found in favor of Hydrolevel, which ultimately settled with ASME for $4.75 million. As a result, ASME made major changes in its practices and policies. These policies may serve as a worthwhile example to other professional societies that could confront conflicts of interest on the part of their volunteer officers.

The Case

Since 1915, as a result of concern with a growing number of boiler accidents and the inability of the boiler manufacturing industry to regulate itself, the ASME has developed, published, and periodically reviewed a set of rules governing the construction of boilers. Almost all states and the majority of Canadian provinces have now incorporated the ASME Boiler and Pressure Vessel (B-PV) Code into law. Although ASME neither "enforces" the code nor renders judgments regarding the conformity of specific products, the importance of the code has given ASME—and derivatively the members of its code committees and subcommittees—considerable power over the boiler industry. As a large share of the committee members are themselves volunteers who are employed by boiler manufacturers or related firms, the possibility of conflicts of interest seem obvious. What follows is a summary of the case. More detailed versions are readily available.

Since the 1920s, McDonnell & Miller (M&M), a Chicago firm had dominated the market for low-water boiler fuel cutoffs, producing mechanical devices incorporating a bulb floating on the surface of water within a chamber attached to the boiler. As dry-firing is a cause of many boiler explosions, the B-PV Code requires the cutoff device to shut down the fuel supply when the boiler water reaches the lowest visible level of the gauge glass. In 1965 Hydrolevel began marketing an electrical probe device ("Safgard"), mounted vertically inside the boiler, that used the boiler water as a ground for an isolated circuit. To compensate for the turbulence of the boiling water causing nuisance shutoffs as the water neared its lowest permissible level, the company installed a time-delay in some of its products. Hydrolevel's devices received the approval of Underwriters' Laboratories and Factory Mutual Engineering Laboratory as well as passing independent tests by the New York Telephone Company. Presumably the Hydrolevel control was not in violation of the B-PV Code. By 1970 Hydrolevel had begun to make inroads in the market dominated by M&M.

In March 1972, two meetings were held in Chicago that set in motion the events leading to the court decision more than a decade later. Present at both meetings were Eugene Mitchell, vice president of sales for M&M, John James, vice president of research for M&M, and T. R. Hardin, vice president of Hartford Steam Boiler Inspection and Insurance Company. M&M President James Solon was present at the second meeting. Hardin and James were, respectively, chair and vice chair of the ASME subcommittee on Code Section IV Heating Boilers. The upshot of the meeting was a brief, carefully drafted letter—to be sent by Mitchell on April 12—asking the ASME whether the code requires "that the cut-off operate immediately when the boiler water level falls to the lowest visible part of the water-gauge glass, or is it permissible to incorporate a time-delay feature in the cut-off so that it will operate after the boiler water level reaches some point below the visible range of the gauge glass?"[7] This letter was referred by B-PV Committee Secretary W. B. Hoyt to subcommittee chair Hardin, who included in his response, to be sent by Hoyt on April 29, the statement: "If a time-delay feature were incorporated in a low water fuel cut-off, there would be no positive assurance that the boiler water level would not fall to a dangerous point during a time delay period."[8] Subsequently, M&M used this statement in a memo that named Hydrolevel and told M&M representatives that "A time delay of any kind in the firing device circuitry would very definitely be against the ASME Code . . ." and "A time delay would defeat the intent of the ASME Code and this should definitely be brought to the attention of anyone considering the device which included a time delay in the low water cut-off circuitry." Hydrolevel began to experience rejections which, after several months, were traced to the M&M memo.

Hydrolevel President Russell Rymer insisted that ASME clarify or retract the April 29, 1971, letter, and the matter was referred to the Section IV subcommittee meeting in May 1972. Hardin had resigned as chair and had been replaced by James, who recused himself from the subcommittee deliberations and vote on Rymer's request. The subcommittee voted to reissue the letter minus its trouble-causing statement. However, when the matter came before the main committee, a new letter was drafted in which James was able to effect a slight revision. This letter was sent to more than 300 people in the boiler market. Although Hydrolevel seemed to have been satisfied with the new ASME response, a few years later, in July 1974, *The Wall Street Journal* published a story critical of the ASME and especially James's role in the Hydrolevel matter.

Shortly thereafter, the ASME Professional Practice Committee investigated and concluded at the end of 1974 that James had acted properly in absenting himself from the subcommittee meeting when the Hydrolevel complaint was dealt with. However, ASME investigators had not learned of the earlier meetings in Chicago or of James's revision in the final ASME letter. These facts came out in a hearing held by the Senate Judiciary Subcommittee on Antitust and Monolopy in March 1975. Some ASME members favored revisiting the case, but ASME was soon put on the defensive by a second *Wall Street Journal* story in April 1975 alleging both that ASME had been duped by M&M and that its own internal investigation was a sham. The ASME Professional Practice Committee began a second investigation but was halted when, on August 23,

1975, Hydrolevel brought suit against M&M (now owned by ITT Corporation), Hartford Boiler Insurance, and ASME on the grounds, among others, of conspiracy to restrain trade in violation of the Sherman Antitrust Act.

In 1978, M&M and Hartford reached an out-of-court settlement with Hydrolevel for a total of $800,000, but ASME, convinced that as a non-profiting not-for-profit organization it should not be held liable for the actions of its volunteer members, chose to proceed with the legal case that came to a jury trial in U.S. District Court for the Eastern District of New York in January 1979. Less than two weeks later, the six-person jury found the ASME in violation of the Sherman Act and awarded Hydrolevel $3.3 million. In accordance with the provisions of antitrust law, the judge trebled the judgment after deducting the $800,000 already received in settlement, making the judgment against ASME $7.5 million. By the time of the verdict, Hydrolevel had gone out of business and had only a month earlier sold its material assets as scrap for $55,000. Rymer, hospitalized for a heart condition, suffered a fatal seizure upon hearing the jury decision.[9]

After losing appeals in both the 2nd Circuit Court of Appeals in November 1980 and the U.S. Supreme Court in May 1982 (6–3 decision, with Justice Blackmun writing the majority opinion), the case returned to the original District Court for a retrial to settle damages. Justice Blackmun's opinion stated that when ASME "cloaks its subcommittee officials with the authority of its reputation, ASME permits those agents to affect the destinies of businesses and thus gives them power to frustrate competition in the marketplace." Prior to a final court decision on damages, ASME settled out of court in October 1983 for $4.75 million. By this date Hardin had died and James had resigned from ASME. ASME policies also underwent change. As Charles Beardsley, editor of *Mechanical Engineering* magazine, puts it, "In the wake of the Hydrolevel ruling, the Society has changed the way it handles codes and standards interpretations, beefed up its enforcement of conflict-of-interest rules, and adopted new "sunset" review procedures for its working bodies."[10]

Current ASME Policies

ASME, which initially had adopted a special Conflict of Interest Policy in March 1976, revised the policy later in 1976, in 1979, in November 1982, and again in 1984. Since then, it has undergone revision about every three to four years. The policy version discussed here (ASME Policy P-15.8) was last revised in November 1996.[11]

The policy's Preamble begins with the sentence "Each individual acting for or in the name of ASME is in a position of trust." It goes on to assert that the "Policy is intended to further assure the objectivity and public confidence in the integrity of all Society deliberations and statements," at the same time acknowledging "that competent and knowledgeable individuals of recognized abilities, qualifications and interest who participate in professional activities may have potential conflicts of interest." It covers not only volunteer members of committees and decision-making bodies but also staff members, in short, any individuals acting for or on behalf of ASME.

It is important to note that the policy expands on ASME's Code of Ethics originally adopted in 1976, replacing an earlier code adopted in 1947. Both the 1947 Code (which did not use the term "conflict of interest") and the 1976 Code discussed conflict of interest only in terms of unfaithful service to clients or employers, or to governmental bodies. Neither code mentioned avoiding the appearance of conflict of interest nor had wording that would have covered the type of act that led to the Hydrolevel lawsuit. Not only does the current Conflict of Interest Policy explicitly treat both topics, but the ASME's current Code of Ethics (last revised June 1998) includes some provisions, obviously written in harmony with the policy wording, that also handle the topics. Thus, the Code's Fundamental Canon 4 now states, "Engineers shall act in professional matters for each employer or client as faithful agents or trustee, and shall avoid conflicts of interest or the appearance of conflicts of interest." Specific to the *Hydrolevel* case, the Code's Interpretation Criterion 4.h. states, "Engineers working on codes, standards or governmental sanctioned rules and specifications shall exercise careful judgment in their determinations to ensure a balanced viewpoint, and avoid a conflict of interest."

The policy sets up some key procedures. It establishes the ASME Board on Professional Practices and Ethics as the oversight body having authority to review and judge questions or alleged instances of conflict of interest and either to direct letters of admonishment to offenders or to refer matters to ASME's executive director. Second, it requires every person elected or appointed to represent ASME in any capacity to be sent a copy of the appropriate ASME policies and to sign a statement of acceptance of the policies. A person who does not sign such a statement is not permitted to hold office. Third, individual members of ASME bodies should disqualify themselves from participating in deliberations and decisions when it is clear that their judgment may be affected by a conflict of interest, although the policy does allow them to attend and participate "on the same basis as any nonmember of the committee or other body." Fourth, if the individual member believes there may be an appearance of conflict of interest, he or she should either (1) explain the situation to the group and obtain a three-fourths majority on a secret ballot in order to continue without recusal or (2) in some special circumstances, bring the matter directly to the oversight body mentioned above. Any appeal or unresolved case that emerges from procedure (1) is also to be brought to the oversight body.

Although these procedures may require extra paperwork for ASME members and staff and may strike some as overly bureaucratic, their rationale seems clear and the provisions themselves appear ethically acceptable. The procedures are similar to honor pledges sometimes required of college students. In both cases, we can assume general agreement on the unacceptability of the targeted practice—cheating or self-serving judgment. The point in both cases is to focus attention and to raise consciousness regarding the target practice, thus reducing although not eliminating the possibility of violations. Of course, a related purpose in the ASME case is to reduce ASME's liability should any violations occur.

To my mind, the most objectionable part of the ASME Conflict of Interest Policy is its definition of "conflict of interest" and the seeming derivation of a technique of "balancing interests" as a practical remedy in potential conflict situations. Although waffling a bit in some of the wording, the policy takes the position that "whenever a person owes a loyalty to multiple interests or organizations," a conflict of interest may occur "only when loyalty to one interest would impel a course of action different from that impelled by another interest" (Section II, A & B). First, the definition is too broad, and even more so by leaving the term "interest" undefined. Second, it makes conflict of interest a matter of competing loyalties rather than one of a violation of professional or civic duties. Third, the balance-of-interest strategy may be a wise organizational ploy, but it is not derived from the definition nor is it likely to be a remedy for actual conflicts of interest.

Although the writers of the policy may have intended that its statements apply only to persons "acting for or in the name of ASME . . . in a position of trust," the phrase is not repeated in the definition, nor are the notions of fiduciary duty or violation of trust so repeated. As put, the definition applies equally well to persons or groups who have not necessarily violated a fiduciary duty but nevertheless have been impelled on courses of action that uphold one interest in opposition to another, for example, union workers who go on strike or a company that relocates for economic reasons leaving its former hometown in civic shambles. Taking "interest" in its broader subjective or psychological meaning, the engineer who has to choose between attending an NCAA basketball play-off series or attending a voluntary, company-sponsored technical refresher short course (or vice versa) could also be described by the policy as having a conflict of interest.

The policy writers might reply that they are concerned with conflicting loyalties (to different group or organizational interests) not with conflicting interests themselves. But this seems to me a difference in words without a difference in action. The test for "acting loyally to X" would seem to be the same as those for "acting to support X" or "acting in X's best interests" or "being impelled by an interest in X's welfare." Insofar as loyalty can be interpreted as some sort of duty to a group (not necessarily a fiduciary duty though), the definition would seem to turn all conflicts of interest into conflicts of duties. This move seems to be made explicitly in the last part of Section II.D. But, clearly, not all conflict-of-interest situations are conflicts of duty. For example, suppose I am a corporate vice president in charge of materials purchasing and suppose a recently deceased uncle whom I barely knew bequeaths me a small fortune in the shares of a materials supply company. I think there would be general agreement that I am in a conflict-of-interest situation (and would probably be advised to sell my shares), even though I have absolutely no loyalty or duty to the supply company and may actually think the supply company is a low-class producer of second-rate goods.

The third qualm I have about the policy is its attempt to link its definition of conflict of interest with the practical strategy of striving for balanced or diversified representation on committees and other selected organizational groups. Diversified representation is often an effective strategy to elicit a variety of viewpoints and to reduce the likelihood of a faction domination. However, it does not seem to me a safeguard against an individual member having a conflict of interest. Indeed, the policy seems to admit such yet, at the same time, optimistically claims that the conflict would be rendered ineffective because of the "balance of interests" represented on the group. The policy states that the balance of interests "minimizes the instances of appearance of conflict of interest by preventing situations in which a single interest group could control the action on an issue." This sentence would seem to shift the concern over conflicts of interest from the individual to the group. Amazingly, the policy then seems to make a reverse move in justifying a tolerance of appearance of conflict in order to achieve a balance of interests. In appointing a balanced committee, it urges, "an individual's identification with the particular interest shall not be grounds for raising the issue of the appearance of conflict of interest. This is particularly so because the removal of one or more individuals representing a particular category of interest on conflict of interest grounds could upset the planned balance of economical and technical interests" (Section II. C). Apparently the policy writers also had qualms about the balance strategy overcoming the conflict of interest problem, for they add (Section II.D) the following thought (my editing): "It is nevertheless the duty of volunteers acting for or on behalf of the Society to be aware of the possibility of a conflict of interest . . . and to refrain from participating in Society decisions . . . when continued participation would unreasonably jeopardize the integrity of the decision making process."

Codes of Engineering
Professional Societies

Although corporate codes frequently differ in their emphases on company loyalty in contrast to objectivity in judgment, professional society codes tend to differ in their recommendations to avoid, disclose, or both. The ASCE Code and the ASME Code, both following the Code of Ethics and Guidelines originally published by the Engineer's Council for Professional Development (now distributed by the Accreditation Board for Engineering and Technology), have identical wording that includes both recommendations: "Engineers shall avoid all known or potential conflicts of interest with their employers or clients and shall promptly inform their employers or clients of any business association, interests, or circumstances which could influence their judgment or the quality of their services" (Section 4.a of the ASCE "Guidelines to Practice" or the ASME "Criteria for Interpretation"). Both avoidance and disclosure are also stated in the Code of Ethics of the Institute of Electrical and Electronic Engineers (IEEE) and in the Code of the American Institute of Architects. On the other hand, the codes of National Society of Professional Engineers (NSPE) and the 1984 "Model Guide," published by the American Association of Engineering Societies, specify disclosure but are silent on avoidance.[12]

In 1974, the NSPE included avoidance in its code statement but subsequently changed it.[13] As with several other code modifications over the years, this change grew out of the experience of the NSPE's Board of Ethical Review (BER) in applying the code to specific cases. In case 85–6, the BER rendered a judgment on a situation in which an engineer was retained by the state to perform feasibility studies on a possible highway spur that would run near the residential area in which the engineer's home was located. The engineer disclosed the facts to the state agency and the state permitted the engineer to continue the study. The engineer ultimately recommended in favor of the spur and it was constructed. The BER concluded that the engineer did not act unethically because in accordance with the current code (1) he properly disclosed his interest to his client and (2) the NSPE code no longer stated an absolute requirement to avoid conflict of interest.

The BER discussion contrasts case 85–6 with a similar case 69–13 which was given an opposite ruling under a previous version of the code that included the wording "The Engineer will endeavor to avoid a conflict of interest with his employer or client, but when unavoidable, the Engineer shall fully disclose the circumstances to his employer or client." The later BER speculates that had the later version of the code been in effect in 1969, the earlier BER might have ruled differently. The 1969 case dealt with a civil engineer who had been retained to recommend a water and sewer system in the general area of property he had earlier inherited.

Here the BER interpreted the code strictly to avoid as well as to disclose, holding that disclosure was not sufficient and that the engineer should either dispose of the landholding or decline to provide services. Reflecting on this case, the 1985 BER goes on to state

> In no sense should this change be interpreted in any way to suggest a retreat by this Board or the Code of Ethics from its deep concern for dilemmas relating to conflicts of interest. Rather, it is our view that the modifications in the code reflect recognition of the fact that conflicts of interest emerge in a multitude of degrees and circumstances and that a blanket, unqualified expression prohibiting engineers to avoid all activities that raise the shadow of a conflict of interest is not a workable approach. . . . We believe the new Code provisions sought to establish the ethical obligation to engage in dialogue with a client or employer on the difficult questions relating to conflicts of interest. We think that it was for this reason that the Code provisions were altered.[14]

Although I agree with the BER's decision in 85–6 and tentatively disagree with the earlier BER's decision in 69–13, the later BER's argument against an avoidance provision in the code seems stretched. Given its explicit acknowledgment that "obvious and significant conflicts of interest are easily identifiable and should always be avoided," the later BER's thoughts would seem at most to justify a toning down of the avoidance provision, not its removal. If the earlier BER had interpreted "will endeavor to avoid" as a less than absolute prohibition, they might have decided differently.

An important factor in 69–13 could have been the amount of land inherited by the engineer, although neither the early nor the later BER commented on this point. The case uses only the phrase "a tract of land." The later BER presumably did not regard the engineer in 69–13 as having an "obvious and significant" conflict of interest but did not explicitly address the question of amount of property. The tendency of the earlier BER to leave degree of risk out of consideration is also borne out in their decision on another part of the same 69–13 case that deals with a consulting electrical engineer who owns 200 stock shares (less than one-tenth of one percent of the outstanding shares) in an electrical manufacturing company that makes products often specified by persons in his field. Here again, the earlier BER took the absolutist position that the engineer should either sell the stock or refrain from specifying the manufacturing company's products; indeed, it recommended the second alternative even though recognizing that the products could have been the best for the client. In this instance, the earlier BER stated

> It would be tempting to conclude that there is no "real" conflict of interest in this situation because the degree of financial gain for En-

gineer A by the specification of the products . . . are so minimal in profit to him that his judgment would not be biased. We reject this rationalization, however, because it is impossible to define that degree of financial gain which would, in the mind of Engineer A, be so small as to not prejudice his decision.[15]

Surely, the absolutist interpretation goes too far, but the lack of an avoidance provision likewise hampers the code's applicability. There are situations in which avoidance is the proper counsel. In this regard, some corporate codes appear to be more helpful than many professional codes.

One additional characteristic of BER cases on conflict of interest worth noting is that at least half deal with engineers' relationships with public bodies, including several in which the engineer functions as an official or as an advisory board member. In a number of instances, with virtually the same wording, the professional codes have explicit recommendations for engineers who serve the public in some recognized capacity and for engineers who might do business with public bodies. The motivation of the provisions in the professional codes seems to be that of maintaining public trust in the engineer and the engineering profession. Understandably, given their setting in a competitive economy, the parts of corporate policies dealing with public service seem more concerned with the reputation of the company, the desire of the company to avoid legal troubles, and excessive noncompany use of the employee's time.

Conclusion

Both corporations and professional societies ought to be applauded for assisting engineers in understanding the ethical problems of conflict of interest not only by providing policy descriptions but often by providing useful examples. Given an all-too-common climate of distrust of public officials, business corporations, and even independent professionals, actively promoted conflict-of-interest policies appears essential.

On the other hand, writers of policies and codes should produce documents that are as helpful as possible, with clear wording, consistent reasoning, and appropriate examples. If corporate policies insist on stressing a basic commitment to company loyalty, how should they deal with the basic professional commitment of engineers—especially Professional Engineers—to public safety when it might be seen to conflict with that loyalty? Put another way, what ought to be done when the objectivity of an employed engineer is threatened to be compromised by the financial interest he or she has in the corporation? A similar problem exists for society codes and especially for those State Boards of Engineering Registration that enforce some code provisions. How do these entities deal with cases of opposition in practice between an engineer's being "a faithful agent" of a client/employer and at the same time having a professional (and sometimes a legal) obligation to report cases of substandard engineering?

Corporate policies are obviously motivated by the desire to uphold a good reputation for the company and, at the same time, to avoid costly legal problems. Society policies are motivated by a desire to uphold a good reputation for the profession, especially with the public, and to assist individual engineers in acting in professionally sanctioned ways. Given that engineering is arguably the largest profession in the United States, and possibly the most diverse, one would hope that corporations and societies seek actively to cooperate in providing unequivocal assistance to those individuals who are the real agents of technological development and change.

Notes

1. This statement incorporates through the words "have or are given" the sound distinction Michael Davis makes between "trustee" and "agent." *See* Davis, "Conflict of Interest," 3 *Encyclopedia of Applied Ethics* (1997). Virtually all engineering cases of conflict of interest involve agency.

2. See "Conflict of Interest as Risk Analyses" by Kevin C. McMunigal, Chapter 3 (in this volume).

3. This point is in contrast to the approach by Michael Davis, "Conflict of Interest," section I.C "Interest." Davis's case of a judge having a conflict of interest when a personal friend or enemy comes before his court is plausible, to my mind, only because there is an objective, historically describable relationship between the judge and the other party, not because the judge has a particular emotion while on the bench. Should a person with whom the judge has absolutely no prior contact, direct or indirect, come before the judge and the judge feels strong emotions of attraction or revulsion toward the person, I would not say a conflict of interest existed. The judge would be expected to exercise a strictly professional approach, which includes control over personal feelings.

4. Davis, "Conflict of Interest," properly terms this situation "conflicting interests" or "conflict of interests" in contrast to "conflict of interest."

5. Unfortunately, as some corporations did not give permission to name them in connection with a discussion of their policies in this work, I refer to all the corporations—including those that did give permission—by a descriptive phrase only. Even more unfortunate, one firm contacted did not even permit me to examine their policies.

6. See Charles W. Beardsley, *The Hydrolevel Case—A Retrospective*, Mechanical Engineering, June 1984, 66–79. An earlier article by Nancy Rueth appeared in *Mechanical Engineering*, June 1975, 34–36. The case's legal citations are 456 U.S. 556, 72 L. Ed. 2d 330, 102 S. Ct.1935. The appellate court's decision is found at 635 F.2d 118 (1980). Most of the first half of Paula Wells, Hardy Jones, and Michael Davis, *Conflicts of Interest in Engineering* (CSEP Module Series), (Dubuque, IA: Kendall/Hunt, 1986) is a detailed discussion of the case. Larry May, *Professional Action and the Liabilities of Professional Associations: A.S.M.E. v. Hydrolevel Corp., Bus. & Prof. Ethics J.* 1–14 (Fall 1982),

contains an excellent discussion of the arguments in the case. May defends the judgment of the Court. An on-line discussion is also available at Texas A&M University's website: http://ethics.tamu.edu/ethics/.

7. Quote from "Exhibit B" in the record of the Wednesday, March 19, 1975, *Hearing of U.S. Senate Subcommittee on Antitrust and Monopoly of the Committee on the Judiciary,* 94th Cong., 1st Sess., 153–214 (Hon. Senator Philip A. Hart, chain).

8. Both this statement from Hardin and the following from M&M's memo are quoted from "Exhibit C" of the Senate subcommittee.

9. Associated Press story appearing in the Wall St. J., Feb. 5, 1979.

10. Beardsley, note 6 *supra,* at 73.

11. Both the Conflicts of Interest Policy (P-15.8) and the ASME Ethics Policy (P-15.7) may be obtained from an ASME office or from the ASME website at http://www.asme.org/asme/policies/p15–8.html or /p15–7.html

12. The codes are available on the Internet at each society's website: www.pubs.asme.org; www.asce.org; www.ieee.org; www.nspe.org; and www.e-architect.com/institute/codeethics.asp. The Center for the Study of Ethics in the Professions at Illinois Institute of Technology maintains an on-line collection of codes of ethics at www.iit.edu/departments/csep. The National Institute for Engineering Ethics (now an independent not-for-profit corporation but previously a part of NSPE until 1996) has a useful website at www.niee.org.

13. Some NSPE cases are available on-line. *See* NSPE and NIEE websites. My thanks to Michael Pritchard who brought this change to my attention in a paper entitled "Casuistry in Engineering Ethics" presented at the Association for Practical and Professional Ethics meeting in St. Louis in 1995.

14. *Opinions of the Board of Ethical Review,* Vol. VI, 71 (1989), (Alexandria, VA: NSPE Publication No.1106-E). None of the Board members participated in the earlier case.

15. *Opinions of the Board of Ethical Review,* Vol. III, 71 (1971), (Alexandria, VA: NSPE Publication No.1106-B). Actually, Case 69–13 takes up three cases, treated together because they all concern alleged conflicts of interest regarding ownership in land or securities.

7

CONFLICT OF INTEREST
ON CORPORATE BOARDS

Eric W. Orts

This chapter reexamines legal principles governing conflicts of interest on corporate boards in the context of broader theoretical discussions of the nature of corporations and the various interests they serve. Corporations come in many varieties, ranging from small to very large firms and from nonprofit charitable entities to multinational business corporations. They are usually governed by corporate boards,[1] and members of these boards are called "directors" or sometimes "trustees."[2] Although the older use of "trustees" reflects the origins of fiduciary duties of corporate boards in the law of trusts, nothing essential turns on this distinction in practice.[3] I follow the modern practice and refer to board members of both business and nonprofit corporations as directors.[4] In addition, though differences between business and nonprofit corporations are important, I focus here on their similarities with respect to problems of conflicts of interest.[5]

Traditional conflicts-of-interest rules include requirements of disclosure, procedural approval and ratification by disinterested superiors, and judicial review for substantive fairness in situations in which financial or personal interests may compromise a director's objectivity or loyalty to the organization. For example, a director of a bank has a financial conflict if he or she sits on the board of a corporation considering a loan from the bank. Personal conflicts of interest arise when a family member of a director would benefit from a corporate decision. This chapter reviews the general legal rules that govern these kinds of situations in the United States, though roughly similar corporate conflicts-of-interest rules govern in other countries.[6] In addition, the chapter provides some guidance about how to think about corporate conflicts of interest in their social context. Most corporations, especially large ones, pursue the interests of a number of different types of individual participants. A business corporation's "patrons" or "stakeholders" include shareholders and creditors, executives and employees, suppliers and customers, and even external social interests such as the well-being of communities in which a corporation operates and the impact a company has on the natural environment.[7] Even a one-person corporation often has employees, gets loans from creditors, and focuses on the interests of its customers.[8] The scope of nonprofit corporations is often similarly broad. Although limited by the nonprofit distribution constraint, they serve the interests of political or religious members, students, children's day care, and other philanthropic purposes, as well as providing gainful employment.[9] From this perspective, the responsibility of corporate directors to balance and resolve conflicts that arise among the various interests within enterprises becomes not only more important but also more complicated and more difficult to resolve than traditional legal rules contemplate. In this chapter, I connect a social understanding of corporate conflicts of interest with an explanation of the basic legal rules that have developed in this area.

Private Interests and Corporate Roles

Conflicts-of-interest rules begin with a recognition of a distinction between the various kinds of roles a person can play in social and organizational life.[10] A person often acts in his or her own self-interest, but a position on a corporate board carries with it a role obligation to act in the best interests of the corporate enterprise.[11] In some circumstances, this duty to act on behalf of the corporation is virtually synonymous with self-interest. For example, a one-person corporation usually acts in the best interests of the single shareholder who created and governs it, whether a natural person or a large enterprise.[12] In most situations, however, a person acting as a member of a corporate board incurs a "duty of loyalty" to the corporation, which requires the individual to subordinate self-interest to the best interests of the corporation. This duty is imposed in the frequent situations in which a corporate director has a conflict of interest and therefore may engage in "self-dealing" at the expense of the interests of the corporation as a whole.[13]

Self-interest can conflict with corporate interests in two related ways: financial and personal. Most conflicts of interest arise from divergent financial interests. Three common situations are decisions and actions involving the following: (1) salary and compensation, (2) taking corporate business opportunities, and (3) mergers, acquisitions, and the sale of corporate control. Each of these general types of financial conflicts of interest are discussed briefly here.[14] A second type of conflict of interest involves a corporate decision that benefits a director's family or close friends. Legal rules govern the circumstances in which one may use corporate authority to benefit an immediate family member such as a spouse, parent, son, or daughter.

Ordinarily, a high standard of proof is required to demonstrate the procedural and substantive "fairness" of decisions that involve a personal or financial conflict of interest. In the leading case of *Bayer v. Beran*,[15] for example, the wife of a public corporation's president and director was employed to sing in an advertising campaign to promote the company's products.[16] The court upheld the transaction, but not before emphasizing that a corporate president and director must, as a fiduciary, "subordinate his individual and private interests to his duty to the corporation whenever the two conflict."[17] Although it is not necessarily "improper to appoint relatives of officers or directors to responsible positions in a company," the court found that one's "motive" is "questioned" when "selfish, personal interests might be in conflict with the duty owed" to the corporation, and such arrangements were therefore subjected to "the most rigorous scrutiny."[18] The court upheld payments to the chief executive's wife as fair to the corporation under circumstances in which (1) the compensation paid was "in conformity for that paid for comparable work," (2) the other board members preapproved the arrangement informally and formally ratified the advertising program after the fact, and (3) the corporation was doing well financially.[19] The court in *Bayer v. Beran* does not make clear, however, exactly which of these various factors it considered essential. Was it necessary that the compensation paid to the singing spouse was proven substantively fair? Was the procedural approval and subsequent ratification of the disinterested directors sufficient? Was it important that the case involved a large public corporation rather than a small family-owned one?[20] And was the fact relevant that the company was doing well financially?

An attempt has been made to provide greater legal certainty than a case-by-case approach affords by codifying corporate conflicts-of-interest rules.[21] Although codification may improve on an ambiguous case-by-case approach, poor drafting has led to other problems. In 1988, for example, the Revised Model Business Corporation Act proposed a bright-line test to define a "conflicting interest" and to prohibit lawsuits challenging conduct or transactions outside this definition.[22] But this approach was rightly criticized as too rigid and narrow.[23] For example, the model act defined financial conflicts of interest to exclude significant collateral private benefits that a director may receive in return for corporate decisions, such as membership in a coveted golf club.[24] Personal interests were limited to immediate family members, thus excluding from coverage, for example, first cousins or in-laws. Hypothetical cases of golf-obsessed executives, kissing cousins, and parents in-law can easily be imagined to challenge the wisdom of such bright-line tests. The better view is that "a general fiduciary duty of loyalty" covers various conflicts of interest.[25] The duty of loyalty is better conceived as "a residual concept that can include factual situations that no one has foreseen and categorized" which permits a "continuous evolution" of legal rules within general statutory limits.[26]

An earlier version of the Revised Model Business Corporation Act defines a conflict as a "direct or indirect interest" in a transaction as involving a "material financial interest."[27] Guidance is also provided by the American Law Institute (ALI) in its *Principles of Corporate Governance*, which defines the word "interested" as involving "a transaction or conduct" in which (1) a corporate director or officer or immediate family member "is a party" or (2) a director or officer has "a business, financial, or familial relationship," "a material pecuniary interest," or is "subject to a controlling influence" in circumstances that would "reasonably be expected to affect the director's or officer's judgment in a manner adverse to the corporation."[28] These definitions provide specific standards while also leaving room for case-by-case development of conflict-of-interest rules in particular factual situations.

The ALI's definition includes not only conflicts between one's private interest and an organizational role but also conflicts of interest that may arise when an individual enjoys more than one institutional affiliation. It is relatively common for one person to be asked to serve on a number of different corporate boards, raising the potential for conflicting fiduciaries duties owed to different corporations in circumstances in which business is done between them or when corporations compete with each other. This is known as the interlocking director problem, though other institutional affiliations may impose similar conflicts. For example, a representative of a labor union who sits on a corporate board may owe fiduciary duties to both the union and the business corporation.[29] Legal rules must be worked out to govern these kinds of organizational conflicts as well as those between private interests and corporate roles.[30]

Procedural and Substantive Fairness: Of Corporate Checks and Balances

Once a corporate conflict of interest is identified, the next problem is what to do about it. One approach would be to make any transaction or con-

duct tainted by a conflict avoidable by the corporation or its shareholders (or, in the case of a nonprofit corporation, its voting members) without regard to considerations of "reasonableness" or "fairness." Directors
have general authority to act on behalf of the corporation; thus, under
this rule either dissenting directors or shareholders could challenge a decision or transaction characterized with a conflict of interest. This inflexible rule was the original English rule followed generally by U.S.
courts in the late nineteenth century.[31] Courts gradually allowed exceptions to the rule, however, because even though a conflict of interest
may arise in a particular transaction or conduct, the best interests of
everyone concerned may still be served by allowing it. In other words,
the inflexible rule was found impractical and inefficient.[32] For example,
a banker sitting on the board of a small nonprofit corporation may be
more willing to lend money at a favorable rate because of a more intimate knowledge of the nature and risks of the enterprise, making both
sides better off if the loan is legally allowed.[33] Also, inherent conflicts of
interest occur whenever compensation is paid to a corporate director or
officer. The old rules that directors would serve without pay and that
corporate officers would not serve as directors proved too formalistic and
unworkable in both large and small corporations.[34] Even hiring a member of the family may be beneficial (or at least neutral) from a corporation's perspective, as illustrated by the singing spouse in *Bayer v. Beran*
or the present-day practice of sometimes hiring academic spouses in the
same university.[35]

Courts and legislatures have developed two alternative methods to review conflicts-of-interest transactions and conduct in order to separate
those that are abusive and harmful from those that are beneficial or at
least benign. The first method is to allow certain interests within a corporation to challenge a conflicted transaction or conduct in court and to
demand judicial review of the substantive fairness of the transaction or
conduct. In a business corporation, the interests who have the authority
to bring a legal challenge are directors themselves and shareholders who
may sometimes sue on behalf of the corporation derivatively. The second
is to develop internal procedural checks and balances within the corporation that will improve the probabilities that conflicted transactions or
conduct are substantively fair.[36] The reward for following correct procedures is a partial or complete immunity from substantive judicial review
for fairness. Both of these alternative have been followed in the United
States, but the law is complicated in this area because the relationship
between review for substantive and procedural fairness is not always
clear. The issue may be reformulated as follows: Who decides whether a
particular corporate transaction or conduct is substantively fair and
therefore worthy of an exception to the rule of voidability, a court or
another institutional body within the corporation? And how does *procedural* fairness affect determinations of *substantive* fairness?

This problem is illustrated by the conflicts-of-interest statutes that have been adopted in many states to replace the old rule of automatic voidability.[37] The Revised Model Business Corporation Act provides that "a conflict of interest transaction" is not voidable if (1) the material facts of the transaction were disclosed to the board or a committee of the board, and the board or committee "authorized, approved, or ratified" the transaction, (2) the material facts were disclosed to the shareholders who "authorized, approved, or ratified" the transaction, *or* (3) "the transaction was fair to the corporation."[38] As the italicized conjunction "or" emphasizes, the statute is ambiguous about whether the substantive fairness test is an alternative to the procedural tests or whether a court may exercise review for "fairness" in some circumstances even when procedural "authorization, approval, or ratification" has been given by disinterested board members or shareholders.[39] Despite the alternative construction used in these conflicts-of-interest statutes, courts tend to interpret them to permit review for substantive fairness even if a decision or transaction has been authorized, approved, or ratified by disinterested board members or shareholders—though the extent to which this rule is followed depends on the circumstances.[40] In the leading case of *Fliegler v. Lawrence*,[41] for example, the Delaware Supreme Court held that ratification by shareholders under a conflicts-of-interest statute "removes the 'interested director' cloud" but does not entirely remove "the transaction from judicial scrutiny" for "unfairness."[42]

Conflicts-of-interest statutes have nevertheless encouraged a general trend toward "proceduralizing" the law of corporate fiduciary duties.[43] Although courts have preserved their authority to determine that a particular transaction or conduct that involves a conflict of interest that results in "unfairness," they have also increasingly recognized the salience of following proper internal corporate procedures to insulate conflicts of interest from searching judicial review. In particular, legal mechanisms of burden shifting, standard changing, and disinterested committees of the board are employed to give force to internal procedures to justify decisions characterized by conflicts of interests. Burden shifting refers to procedures of authorization or ratification by a board or shareholders that courts hold to shift the burden of persuasion in a conflict-of-interest case from defendant directors to shareholder plaintiffs. Standard changing means that the same procedures change the standard of review from "fairness" to the more forgiving "reasonableness" standard of the duty of care and business judgment rule.[44]

The standard for duty-of-care review is one of negligence or "gross negligence," and the business judgment rule is a judicially created presumption against second-guessing informed corporate decisions made in good faith and in the absence of fraud or conflict of interest.

Traditionally, conflicted directors always had the burden of proof to demonstrate substantive fairness in order to justify a departure from a rule of voidability, but this is changing. In addition, courts increasingly recognize the authority of specially appointed independent committees of the board to circumvent intensive judicial review for substantive fairness in situations involving conflict of interests. These committees come in two forms—negotiating committees for self-dealing transactions and litigation committees to review shareholder derivative lawsuits.[45] When properly employed, the decisions of these special committees are given the benefit of the doubt by courts.[46]

An example of the first two procedural mechanisms of disinterested director approval and shareholder ratification appears in the Delaware case *In re Wheelabrator Technologies, Inc. Shareholders Litigation.*[47] Shareholders of Wheelabrator challenged a stock-for-stock merger of the company into a wholly owned subsidiary of Waste Management, Inc. (Waste).[48] Four of Wheelabrator's eleven directors were also Waste officers, and Waste held 22 percent of Wheelabrator's stock.[49] The shareholder plaintiffs argued that this conflict of interest should result in the fairness test being applied to review the terms of the merger under the duty of loyalty with the burden of proof on the directors.[50] But because Wheelabrator's disinterested directors approved the merger and because a majority of Wheelabrator's disinterested (non-Waste) shareholders ratified the merger after full and accurate disclosure of its terms, the Chancery Court held that the burden of proof shifted to the plaintiff shareholders *and* the standard of review changed to the business judgment rule, even though the transaction was at least arguably a self-dealing one.[51]

Wheelabrator's extension of the proceduralization of corporate law to allow a shareholder vote to immunize a controlling shareholder's self-dealing transaction with business judgment rule protection illustrates the potential power of internal procedures to safeguard transactions that would otherwise be subject to searching judicial review for fairness. In other cases, the Delaware Supreme Court has made sure to preserve a substantive fairness standard of review in cases in which conflicts of interest are apparent, even when procedural mechanisms are used to "unconflict" corporate decision making. In *Kahn v. Lynch Communications Systems, Inc.*[52] for example, a takeover analogous to *Wheelabrator* arose when Alcatel U.S.A. (a subsidiary of a French corporation) owned 43 percent of the stock of Lynch Communications and then proposed a merger to acquire the remaining shares by negotiating with an "independent committee" of disinterested directors set up by Lynch.[53] In reviewing the process, the court recognized that "an approval of [a self-dealing] transaction by an independent committee of directors or an informed majority of minority shareholders shifts the burden of proof on the issue of fairness from the controlling or dominating shareholder to the challenging shareholder-plaintiff," but only in some circumstances.[54] The court held that the burden of proof did not shift unless the true independence of the negotiating committee was shown, including the approximation of arm's-length bargaining and "the power to say no."[55] Full and accurate disclosure of the material details of a transaction is also a prerequisite for this procedural defense to a fiduciary duty claim.[56] Without a procedural mechanism that arguably gives decision-making authority to a disinterested body within a corporation, a test of substantive fairness with the burden of proof on directors is applied.[57]

Another procedure employed to great effect in Delaware and elsewhere is the independent litigation committee. In contrast to a negotiating committee such as the one appointed in *Kahn v. Lynch Communications* to authorize a self-dealing transaction, a litigation committee is appointed by a board in order to fend off shareholder derivative suits alleging other violations of fiduciary duties owing to conflicting interests. Independent litigation committees were invented to supplement the procedural "demand requirement" for derivative suits brought by shareholders on behalf of the corporation to challenge fiduciary violations by directors and officers. In essence, the demand requirement allows disinterested directors to dismiss a derivative shareholder action through an application of the business judgment standard of review.[58] Demand is "excused" in conflict-of-interest cases because of the obvious inability of directors who are self-interested in a transaction or decision to pass judgment on it objectively.[59] Even in these cases, however, courts have begun to recognize a procedural mechanism of appointing new disinterested directors to a special committee to review the merits of a shareholder derivative litigation and to recommend an appropriate remedy or settlement.[60] For example, in the Delaware case of *Carlton Investments v. TLC Beatrice International Holdings, Inc.*,[61] an institutional shareholder challenged various self-interested transactions by Beatrice's chief executive officer (CEO), including excessive compensation, illegal payments for various expenses, misuse of the corporate jet, and other payments relating to personal rather than corporate business which were alleged to amount to more than $38 million.[62] The Beatrice board appointed two new disinterested directors with impeccable resumes—Clifford Alexander, a former Secretary of the Army, and William Webster, a former federal judge and director of the Central Intelligence Agency—to serve on a special litigation committee.[63] Working with independent legal counsel, executive compensation experts, and accountants, the special committee recommended a settlement of the claims for approximately $15 million, which was approved by the court over the shareholder's objections.[64] In this case, the procedural use of a special litigation committee enabled the corporation to avoid a trial on the merits, though the court scrutinized the litigation committee's recommendations for "independence and good faith" and in accordance with the court's "own business judgment . . . considering both the corporation's best interests and matters of law and policy."[65]

This summary of procedures that corporate boards may use in conflict-of-interest cases shows the complexity of corporate law in this area. Unfortunately, no easy answers can be given to questions about when a corporate conflict of interest can be challenged successfully. Instead, the cases often depend on the facts and circumstances. A few general principles may nevertheless be gleaned from the major relevant corporate statutes and cases. First, corporate conflicts of interests may ordinarily be challenged only by other directors, by shareholders, or, in nonprofit corporations, by members.[66] Second, conflicts of interests that are fully and accurately disclosed either to disinterested board members or to disinterested shareholders or both, and then approved or ratified by these disinterested bodies, usually obtain benefits when challenged through burden shifting and even standard shifting, the demand requirement for derivative litigation, and judicial deference to independent board committees. Third, courts tend to reserve the right to intervene in egregious cases of self-dealing that cannot be justified through procedural and substantive tests of fairness. Other than these generalizations, particular kinds of common situations in which corporate conflicts of interest arise must be considered more specifically.[67]

Salary and Compensation

Perhaps the most fundamental conflict of interest in most corporations involves the general one between (1) the self-interests of both executive and rank-and-file employees to be paid salary and compensation and (2) the self-interests of capital contributors to corporations, namely, shareholders and creditors, to make money on their investments. In a one-person, self-employed, and self-financed corporation, this conflict can sometimes be eliminated, but as soon as outside financing is sought or workers hired, a business becomes more economically complex and must accommodate conflicting economic demands among its various participants.[68] Corporate boards enable the dynamic management of the inevitable conflicts of interests between the self-seeking demands of capital and labor in business enterprise by appointing executives to manage the firm (which includes dealing with the everyday labor negotiations of lower-level employees) and authorizing decisions to be made about the capital structure of the firm within the limits of the corporate charter and bylaws (including the issuance or repurchase of shares and the procurement or payment of debt). Of course, business life is more complex than this theoretical sketch suggests because of the blurring of corporate roles and interests in practice. For example, hybrid financial instruments combine the properties of debt and equity.[69] Employees own shares through the increasing use of employee stock ownership plans.[70] Executive officers often also act as directors, as indicated by the ubiquitous combined title "Chairman of the Board and Chief Executive Officer."[71] And directors often hold large quantities of shares. Nevertheless, a general division of interests between those of capital and labor is a useful starting point for understanding corporate conflicts of interests from a social perspective. Corporate boards are structurally useful as a mechanism to resolve the general social conflict between labor and capital through the specialization of executive management, employees acting under their authority, and investment from shareholders and creditors. In other words, the invention of corporate boards as an institution enables the practical organization of trade-offs among competing specialized interests needed in business enterprise, including the interests of shareholders, creditors, managers, and employees. In addition, corporate boards have the responsibility to require appropriate internal procedures and practices to ensure basic compliance with legal rules and ethical principles.[72]

In the corporate law of conflicts of interest, the most significant difficulty arises in the payment of executive compensation. Salary and compensation of lower-level employees are handled in negotiation with corporate management.[73] The problem with respect to executive compensation is that corporate officers, especially CEOs, often exercise extraordinary de facto power over the corporate boards which are supposed in legal theory to oversee them.[74] To the extent the real power of CEOs overcomes formal board structures that are answerable to shareholders, the problem of excessive payment of executive compensation may arise. Some empirical evidence supports the claim that levels of executive compensation have become problematic from a social perspective, at least in the United States.[75] In 1996, for example, the CEOs of the largest thirty U.S. corporations made more than 200 times more in compensation than did the average U.S. employee, almost a fivefold increase in this ratio since 1965.[76]

In general, the corporate law in the United States (in combination with a nonprogressive income tax) enables corporate executives in large public corporations to shield high salary and compensation packages from challenge through a relatively simple procedural mechanism, namely, an independent compensation committee composed of outside disinterested directors. When executives set their own salaries directly in their roles on corporate boards, then an obvious conflict of interest triggers substantive fairness review with the burden of proof on the self-dealing executive directors.[77] However, as long as an executive is paid through the device of an independent compensation committee, the decision is virtually impregnable unless there is no rational basis for considering the payments justifiable. Under these circumstances, the procedural fairness mechanisms discussed previously—including the demand requirement for derivative lawsuits challenging the business judgment of uninterested, nonconflicted directors and the judicial respect given to independent board committees—combine to eliminate successful challenges of large compensation packages for corporate executives of public corporations.[78]

For example, in *Zupnick v. Goizueta*,[79] a plaintiff shareholder challenged the retroactive grant of one million stock options to the CEO of Coca-Cola Company on the grounds that it had no contractual consideration and therefore amounted to corporate "waste."[80] The Delaware Chancery Court dismissed the complaint for failing to make a demand on the board. Demand was not excused because disinterested directors on the compensation committee made the decision.[81] In addition, the court held that no "reasonable doubt" arose concerning the question of whether one million stock options worth approximately $25 million and given as a "bonus" for extraordinary stock price performance (which amounted to an increase of $69 billion over 14 years under the CEO's leadership) was justified as "a fair exchange" for the services rendered.[82] Therefore, the "extreme test, very rarely satisfied by a shareholder plaintiff" to show waste was not met, and the case was dismissed.[83] *Zupnick v. Goizueta* provides a good example because Coke's CEO was one of the highest-paid corporate executives in the United States in the 1990s, and the options granted in this case arguably bore no reasonable relation to providing incentive to performance because they were granted retroactively as a "bonus."[84] Other cases challenging lower and forward-looking pay packages stand even less chance of success.

Another Delaware case, *Lewis v. Vogelstein*,[85] illustrates the procedural effectiveness of shareholder ratification as a defense to a challenge of a board's adoption of a stock option pricing plan for itself. Mattel's board of directors adopted stock options for directors (15,000 options each valued according to the plaintiff at $180,000 per director).[86] The shareholders ratified the transaction after full disclosure of the exact terms of the options, though the estimated present value of the options according to any financial formula was not disclosed.[87] After an extensive discussion of the effect of shareholder ratification, the Delaware Chancery Court held that shareholder ratification in these circumstances shifted the standard of proof from the substantive "fairness" test with the burden of proof on the directors to the more forgiving "waste" standard.[88] Given the novelty of director's stock options as compared with executive's stock options approved by disinterested directors in cases such as *Zupnick v. Goizueta*, the court refused to grant dismissal with respect to whether the stock options at issue amounted to waste. But it was unlikely that the Mattel directors' self-issued but shareholder-ratified options would be found unreasonable in later proceedings.[89]

Corporate Opportunities

Another situation in which corporate directors and executives may be tempted to act in their own interests rather than those of the corporations they serve involves cases of conflict with respect to business opportunities. The general rule is that if a corporate director or executive hears about an opportunity for an investment that is characterized as "an interest or expectancy" or "in the line of business" of the corporation, then the opportunity must first be offered to disinterested representatives of the corporation (usually the disinterested board members or the shareholders) and the interested director or executive may then pursue the opportunity only if the corporation declines it.[90] In other words, directors and officers "cannot utilize their strategic positions or their powers and opportunities for their personal advantage to the detriment of other corporate constituencies" and interests.[91] This "corporate opportunities doctrine" has been "a mainstay" in corporate law for more than a century.[92] It operates on the assumption that the corporate fiduciary duty of loyalty requires directors and officers to refuse "secret profits" and to resist temptations to convert corporate information or new business opportunities to their own use.[93] The penalty for stealing a corporate opportunity is harsh: a "constructive trust" which returns all gains from the opportunity to the corporation and sometimes even punitive damages.[94] The doctrine has given rise to difficult line-drawing problems with respect to what constitutes a "corporate opportunity" as compared with an opportunity that one may pursue in one's personal capacity and what manner of procedural authorization or ratification is sufficient to permit taking a corporate opportunity.

Two leading cases that illustrate different outcomes are *Broz v. Cellular Information Systems, Inc.*[95] and *Energy Resources Corp. v. Porter*[96] In *Broz,* the Delaware Supreme Court addressed a corporate opportunity claim in the context of an acquisition of a financially strapped company. Broz was the president and sole shareholder of RFB Cellular, Inc. (RFB), and he served also as an outside director of Cellular Information Systems (CIS), a public corporation.[97] Both companies competed in the cellular telephone business in Michigan. In 1994, another company solicited bids for the Michigan-2 rural cellular license, which happened to border RFB's Michigan-4 license. Broz and RFB were invited to bid, and they did so. Informally, Broz asked the CEO and his other fellow directors of CIS whether they had an interest in also bidding, but they declined because CIS had just emerged from bankruptcy reorganization and had divested itself of a number of other cellular licenses.[98] At approximately the same time, however, Pricellular, Inc. was negotiating a takeover of CIS, and after its successful completion of a tender offer for control of CIS, Pricellular caused the company to sue Broz for the usurpation of a corporate opportunity. (Pricellular had previously negotiated an option on Michigan-2, but Broz and RFB trumped it by agreeing to a higher exercise price.[99] For several reasons, the court held that Broz did not violate his fiduciary duty to CIS by diverting a corporate opportunity to his own use. First, Broz had heard about the sale of Michigan-2 in his capacity as president of RFB rather than as a director of CIS.[100] Second, he had informally consulted with the CEO of CIS and several directors who indicated no interest in the Michigan-2 license (even though the board did not formally approve Broz's purchase).[101] Third, the court found that CIS was "not financially capable" of pursuing the Michigan-2 opportunity; Pricellular's "own financial situation was not particularly stable"; and, in any event, the impending takeover of CIS did not put Pricellular in a position to claim an interest or expectancy in opportunities CIS may have had.[102]

In contrast to the facts and holding of *Broz*, *Energy Resources v. Porter* held that a violation of the corporate opportunity doctrine occurred when Porter, who was vice president and chief scientist of Energy Resources, formed a new corporation called Energy & Environment Engineering, Inc. (EEE) to develop a method of burning high sulphur coal with less air pollution than current technologies.[103] Unlike Broz, Porter did not inform any peer or superior at Energy Resources of the opportunity. In fact, Porter had led Energy Resources to believe that he was pursuing a grant with the U.S. Department of Energy to develop the coal-burning technology for Energy Resources. Instead, Porter decided to leave Energy Resources when he obtained a grant on behalf of EEE, which Porter and some other coventurers had substituted for Energy Resources in the proposal.[104] Also unlike the facts in *Broz*, there was no indication that Energy Resources lacked the financial means to pursue the opportunity. In fact, the company arguably had a present interest and expectancy in the opportunity given its sponsorship of Porter's efforts to obtain a grant in the first place.

Like other areas of corporate conflict-of-interest law, the corporate opportunity doctrine has several significant uncertainties in its application.[105] First, the substantive definition of a corporate opportunity is disputed. Some courts use an "in the line of business" test; others require a present "interest or expectancy;" and still others employ a hybrid or general "fairness" tests.[106] Second, courts disagree about various affirmative defenses, such as whether financial incapacity should excuse taking an opportunity—a factor which might distinguish *Broz* and *Energy Resources*—as well as the degree of formality required to permit disclosure and disinterested approval to operate as a defense.[107] Third, there is argument about whether the corporate opportunity doctrine should be applied more strictly against insiders (like Porter) than against outside directors (like Broz) and whether public corporations should have stricter rules against usurping opportunities than do close corporations.[108] In general, the corporate opportunity doctrine illustrates the continuing concern with substantive and procedural fairness in reviewing corporate conflicts of interest.[109] In contemporary corporate conflicts-of-interest law, these considerations of fairness vie with those of economic efficiency to determine the ground rules for distinguishing self-interest and corporate interest—and mediating the inevitable boundary disputes between them.

Self-Dealing and Control

One last general and complex area of corporate conflicts-of-interest law relates to transactions in corporate control that involve inside directors and officers. These kinds of transactions include "squeezeouts" and "freezouts" of minority shareholder,[110] various mergers and acquisitions that result in a shift of control to inside directors and officers (such as a management-led leveraged buyout),[111] the sale of a controlling interest in a corporation by a controlling shareholder, and tender offers or proxy fights for control of a corporation which current directors and officers oppose. Although it is not possible to treat all these different kinds of situations here, it is useful to get a flavor of the conflicts of interest that are involved.

As an example, consider the Delaware case of *Thorpe v. CERBCO, Inc.*,[112] which provides a bridge between classical corporate opportunities and sales of control. In *Thorpe*, the Erikson brothers were controlling shareholders, directors, and executives of CERBCO, a holding company, the only profitable subsidiary of which owned a regional license for a new pipe-repair technology owned by Instiform of North America, Inc. (INA).[113] INA approached the Eriksons as directors of CERBCO about acquiring this subsidiary. The Eriksons refused INA's offer to purchase the subsidiary from CERBCO but offered instead to sell their controlling interest as shareholders of CERBCO.[114] Although the Eriksons as shareholders could have legitimately prevented the sale of the subsidiary because of the statutory requirement of shareholder approval for any sale of substantially all the assets of a corporation,[115] the court held that the Erikson brothers violated their fiduciary duty to CERBCO by failing to inform its outside directors of the opportunity to sell its subsidiary to INA.[116] This case therefore illustrates how the same parties must adhere to different corporate roles depending on the circumstances. Here, the Erikson brothers were not liable for transactional damages for selling their controlling interest as shareholders of CERBCO to INA.[117] But they were held liable to CERBCO (and its other shareholders) for $75,000 in fees received from INA and for legal and other expenses related to the acquisition because they failed to fulfill their duty of loyalty to act in good faith on behalf of CERBCO as directors.[118]

Another important Delaware case illustrates the interplay between substantive and procedural fairness in the context of mergers and acquisitions. *Weinberger v. UOP, Inc.*[119] involved a minority shareholder challenge to a cashout merger between two publicly traded corporations.[120] Signal, Inc. owned 50.5 percent of UOP after a previous transaction, and at issue was a subsequent cashout merger to purchase the remaining 49.5 percent of UOP shares for a price of $21 per share.[121] UOP's CEO was also a Signal vice president, and five other UOP directors were also Signal directors or employees.[122] Two Signal executives (the chief financial officer and a vice president for planning) prepared a study indicating that an acquisition of the minority UOP shares would be a "good investment" up to a price of $24 per share.[123] However, this price was not disclosed to UOP's directors or shareholders.[124] UOP's CEO and the Signal-dominated board agreed to accept the $21 per share price, received a "fairness opinion" from an investment bank that this price was substantively fair, and won a favorable shareholders' vote.[125] Even though UOP's stock was trading at only $14.50 per share prior to this transaction,[126] the Delaware Supreme Court held that the transaction violated the "entire fairness" standard that combines "fair dealing and fair price."[127] The "fair dealing" requirement refers to procedural questions, such as "when the transaction was timed, how it was initiated, structured, negotiated, disclosed to the directors, and how the approval of the directors and the stockholders was obtained."[128] The merger failed to demonstrate procedural fairness because (1) the financial study indicating that $24 per share for UOP would be a "good investment" was not disclosed to UOP directors or shareholders (which vitiated the burden-shifting effect of an otherwise valid approval by a "majority of a minority" of shareholders), (2) the fairness opinion was unnecessarily "hurried," and (3) the alternative of an independent negotiating committee was not used to resolve the obvious conflict of interest among interlocking directors and officers.[129] The court held that the substantive "fair price" standard allowed a showing of actual unfairness through expert opinions based on "discounted cash flow analysis" or other "techniques or methods which are generally considered acceptable to the financial community."[130] The case was remanded to determine damages.[131]

Some Lessons from Corporate Conflicts of Interest

The foregoing description is necessarily brief in comparison with the breadth and complexity of the topic, but it is sufficient to suggest a few general lessons for other disciplines concerned with conflicts of interest in this book. First, corporate law recognizes the importance of procedural and substantive standards of fairness in judging whether transactions or conduct involving a conflict of interest may be justified. For some kinds of conflicts of interest—for example in the law of conflicts of interest for judges—a complete ban and routine condemnation may be appropriate.[132] Some types of conflicted transactions in corporations may also warrant a flat prohibition.[133] In business cases, however, there is a general reluctance for courts to second-guess decisions made in good faith by corporate officers, directors, and shareholders.[134] Especially when procedural safeguards are followed through which the major interests implicated in corporate decisions are given voice (or at least notice), conflicts of interest are permitted if the procedures and results seem generally to be fair. This kind of attention to both procedural and substantive fairness might be usefully applied in other social contexts and to other professions.

Second, an appreciation of conflicts of interest in corporations emphasizes the importance of intermediary social institutions (including corporations and nonprofit associations) between the state (and its courts) and individual citizens. Institutional mechanisms may often be a useful supplement to the apparatus of the state in resolving conflicts of interest and providing at least a rough form of justice in governing them. In corporations, the board of directors itself is a useful institutional adaptation that provides a forum to resolve the conflicting specialized interests within corporate form, including capital and labor, management and employees, and shareholders and creditors—as well as a focus for overseeing corporate compliance with legal and ethical duties. Subservient to the board, committees of nonmanagement directors can also play a useful role to provide procedural assurances of fairness, even though the substantive fairness of these decisions may be suspect and require some form of supervising judicial review. Procedures alone run the risk of being "an easy tool, deferential, glad to be of use." [135] But institutional adaptations of corporate law may be useful to consider in other social situations of conflict.

Third, the corporate law of conflicts of interest reflects the increasing complexity of its social institutional context.[136] Corporations—and especially large ones—are becoming increasingly complex in terms of their organizational and financial structure. It is important for judges and commentators to understand and cut through this complexity in order to reveal the core conflicts of interest that occur and are resolved within corporations. Awareness of these conflicts from a social perspective should guide the development of standards in corporate law—as well as other areas in which social complexity threatens to obscure trade-offs of conflicting interests. For example, conflicts of interest of managers who serve also as directors, officers who are also controlling shareholders, or corporate managers or directors who owe conflicting loyalties to different organizations should encourage courts to submit these kinds of conflicts to close scrutiny for both procedural and substantive fairness. It is the nature of both business and nonprofit corporations to organize within them a number of different interests. Depending on the circumstances, those responsible for running corporate enterprises owe legal as well as ethical duties to consider these various social interests when making their decisions.

Notes

1. Exceptions include some small and closely held corporations that some states allow to dispense with a formal board structure by shareholder agreement. Corporate boards are otherwise required. See, e.g., Rev. Model Business Corp. Act §§ 7.32(a)(1) & 8.01(a). Partnerships and limited liability companies also do not usually have formal boards, and they are left outside the scope of this chapter even though conflicts of interest often arise within them.

2. Not-for-profit organizations sometimes have boards of trustees rather than directors. See, e.g., Cal. Gov. Code § 37603 (hospital board of trustees). But see, e.g., Cal. Corp. Code § 9500 (nonprofit board of directors); N.Y. Not-for-Profit Corp. Law § 701 (board of directors).

3. *See* Deborah A. DeMott, *Beyond Metaphor: An Analysis of Fiduciary Obligation,* 1988 Duke L. J. 879, 880–1 ("The term 'fiduciary' itself was adopted to apply to situations falling short of 'trusts,' but in which one person was nonetheless obliged to act like a trustee. . . . A corporation's directors occupy a trustee-like position: unlike trustees, directors do not themselves have legal ownership interests in transferable property beneficially owned by others, but, like trustees, directors are entrusted with powers to use in the interests of others."); Harold Marsh, Jr., *Are Directors Trustees? Conflicts of Interest and Corporate Morality,* 22 Bus. Law. 35, 40–1 (1966) (describing historical relationship between corporate conflicts-of-interest rules and trust law). Commercial trusts have become very important in contemporary law, but I do not include a consideration of the conflicts-of-interest rules applied in them. For an overview of commercial trusts, see Henry Hansmann & Ugo Mattei, *The Functions of Trust Law: A Comparative Legal and Economic Analysis,* 7: N.Y.U.L. Rev. 434 (1998); John H. Langbein, *The Secret Life of the Trust: The Trust as an Instrument in Commerce,* 107 Yale L. J. 165 (1997).

4. See, e.g., 8 Del. Code § 141 (1998); Rev. Model Nonprofit Corp. Act § 8.01 (1987).

5. In general, nonprofit corporations may demand higher standards of review for conflicts of interest given the lack of disclosure requirements under the securities law and the relative weakness of membership lawsuits as compared with shareholder derivative litigation. See Deborah A. DeMott, *Self-Dealing Transactions in Non-Profit Corporations,* 59 Brooklyn L. Rev. 131, 139–45 (1993) (arguing for voidability of all self-dealing transactions in non-profit corporations unless directors carry a burden of proof to show fairness); Harvey J. Goldschmid, *The Fiduciary Duties of Nonprofit Directors and Officers: Paradoxes, Problems, and Proposed Reforms,* 23 J. Corp. L. 631, 650–3 (1998) (arguing for fairness or at least intermediate standard of review for conflicts of interests transactions, disclosure requirements for nonprofit to profit corporate conversions, and increased government oversight of nonprofit organ-

izations); Henry B. Hansmann, *Reforming Nonprofit Corporation Law*, 129 U. Pa. L. Rev. 497, 569 (1981) (arguing for "a flat prohibition against all self-dealing transactions" in nonprofit organizations).

6. See, e.g., Luca Enriques, *The Law on Corporate Directors' Self-Dealing: A Comparative Analysis* (October 1998) (unpublished manuscript on file with author) (comparing Italy, France, Germany, the United Kingdom and the United States) Even within the United States there are differences among the states because the basic principles of corporate law are usually a matter of state rather than federal jurisdiction. See, e.g., CTS Corp. v. Dynamics Corp. of America, 481 U.S. 69, 89 (1987) ("No principle of corporation law and practice is more firmly established than a State's authority to regulate domestic corporations.").

7. See, e.g., Henry Hansmann, *The Ownership of Enterprise* 12 (1996) (describing "patrons" as "all persons who transact with a firm either as purchasers of the firm's products or as sellers to the firm of supplies, labor, or other factors of production"); Thomas Donaldson & Lee E. Preston, *The Stakeholder Theory of the Corporation: Concepts, Evidence, and Implications*, 20 Acad. Mgmt. Rev. 65 (1995) (giving descriptive and normative account of "stakeholders"). A number of state statutes specifically provide that corporate directors and nonprofit trustees should consider an array of constituent or stakeholder interests in making corporate decisions. See, e.g., 15 Pa. Cons. Stat. §§ 1715–16 (business corporations), §§ 5715–16 (nonprofit corporations) (1995). See also Lawrence E. Mitchell, *A Theoretical and Practical Framework for Enforcing Corporate Constituency Statutes*, 70 Tex. L. Rev. 579 (1992) (discussing these statues and issues they raise); Eric W. Orts, *Beyond Shareholders: Interpreting Corporate Constituency Statutes*, 61 Geo. Wash. L. Rev. 14 (1992) Even states which have not adopted these statutes, such as Delaware, recognize that considering interests beyond shareholders is permitted in some circumstances. See, e.g., Unocal Corp. v. Mesa Petroleum Co., 493 A.2d 946, 955 (Del. 1985) (directors may consider "the impact on 'constituencies' other than shareholders (i.e., creditors, customers, employees, and perhaps even the community generally)" in certain decisions).

8. For a theoretical account of the nature of the firm from this perspective, see Eric W. Orts, *Shirking and Sharking: A Legal Theory of the Firm*, 16 Yale L. & Pol'y Rev. 265, 300–09 (1998).

9. Nonprofit corporations represent a significant percentage of the private economy, by some estimates as much as 15 percent of gross domestic product in the United States, including two-thirds of all hospital care, half of children's day care, and a quarter of college education. The nondistribution constraint does not prevent large salaries often to be paid to executives, doctors, and sometimes even professors. See Hansmann, *supra* nots 7 at 227–8; *Developments in the Law—Nonprofit Corporations*, 105 Harv. L. Rev. 1578, 1581 (1992).

10. A social role, according to one definition, "involves a patterned set of expectations regarding modes of behavior as well as the mental states, such as intentions, desires, and beliefs, that are thought to properly underlie or accompany the expected behavior." Meir Dan-Cohen, *Between Selves and Collectivities: Toward a Jurisprudence of Identity*, 61 U. Chi. L. Rev. 1213, 1218 (1994). For a conception of the self as a collection of various social roles, see Erving Goffman, *The Presentation of Self in Everyday Life* (1956). On the general relationship between social roles and law, see David Luban, *Lawyers and*

Justice: An Ethical Study 104–47 (1988); Cass R. Sunstein, *Social Norms and Social Roles*, 96 Colum. L. Rev. 903, 921–2 (1996).

11. A discussion of the problem of moral roles in corporate law is given in Lawrence E. Mitchell, *Cooperation and Constraint in the Modern Corporation: An Inquiry into the Causes of Corporate Morality*, 73 Tex. L. Rev. 477, 513–27 (1995). Cf. also Marleen A. O'Connor, *How Should We Talk about Fiduciary Duty? Directors Conflict-of-Interest Transactions and the ALI's Principles of Corporate Governance*, 61 Geo. Wash. L. Rev. 954, 965–6 (1993) (arguing for the "socializing role" played by "fiduciary rhetoric"); Edward B. Rock, *Saints and Sinners: How Does Delaware Corporate Law Work?*, 44 UCLA L. Rev. 1009, 1016–17 (1997) (arguing for a normative understanding of "the narrative quality" of standards developed in Delaware corporate law decisions "leading to a set of stories" that provide guidance).

12. Single-shareholder corporations are ordinarily created in order to gain the advantage of limited liability for corporate activities. Large enterprises create wholly owned subsidiaries for various reasons, including ease of management, legal requirements (such as a requirement of domestic incorporation of a foreign subsidiary), or shell structures for mergers and acquisitions.

13. See Robert Charles Clark, *Corporate Law* 141–7 (1986) (giving an overview of "the conflict-of-interest paradigms" and the basic types of self-dealing). One empirical survey found instances of self-dealing in both public and close corporations to be frequent and often material. See Jayne W. Barnard, *Curbing Management Conflicts of Interest—The Search for an Effective Deterrent*, 40 Rutgers L. Rev. 303, 372–82 (1988) (finding conflicts-of-interest transactions including insider loans, property leases, consulting arrangements, and other deals between corporations and their directors or officers to "constitute a substantial business phenomenon in corporations of all sizes").

14. These three types of financial conflicts serve well as illustrations, but they do not constitute an exhaustive list. See infra note 26 (listing categories recognized by the American Law Institute).

15. 49 N.Y.S.2d 2 (N.Y. Sup. Ct. 1944).

16. *Id.* at 10.

17. *Id.* at 5.

18. *Id.* at 9.

19. *Id.* at 10–12.

20. There is an important legal distinction between public corporations, which are usually characterized by widely traded share ownership, and close corporations, in which shares are held by comparatively few people and not traded on public stock markets. Conflict-of-interests rules apply to both kinds of corporations, but there are important differences.

21. Forty-five states have adopted some variation of a conflict-of-interest statute. For a description of the different kinds of these statutes, see *Principles of Corporate Governance: Analysis and Recommendations* 1 A.L.I. § 501, at 235–41, reporter's n.1 (1994).

22. Rev. Model Business Corp. Act §§ 8.60, 8.61(a). See also 1 James D. Cox, Thomas Lee Hazen & F. Hodge O'Neal, *Corporations?* § 10.15 (1995).

23. See, e.g., Douglas M. Branson, *Assault on Another Citadel: Attempts to Curtail the Fiduciary Standard of Loyalty Applicable to Corporate Directors*, 57 Fordham L. Rev. 375 (1988).

24. Rev. Model Business Corp. Act § 8.61, official cmt.

25. Clark, *supra* note 13, at 141.

26. *Id.* In this spirit, the American Law Institute (ALI) addresses a number of different aspects of what it calls the general duty of fair dealing in situations that implicate real or potential conflicts of interest. 1 A.L.I., *supra* note 21 §§ 5.02 (transaction with the corporation by directors and executives), 5.03 (director and executive compensation), 5.04 (use of corporate property and information), 5.05 (corporate opportunities), 5.06 (competing with the corporation), 5.07 (transactions between interlocking directors and executives), 5.10 & 5.16 (controlling shareholder transactions), 5.15 (transfer of control when interested directors or executives are involved), 6.01 & 6.02 (responses to proposed transactions in control and tender offers).

27. Rev. Model Business Corp. Act § 8.31(a) (1984).

28. 1 A.L.I. *supra*, note 21, § 1.23.

29. See Larry W. Hunter, *Can Strategic Participation Be Institutionalized? Union Representation on American Corporate Boards*, 51 Indus. Lab. Rel. Rev. 557, 563–72 (1998) (empirical description of conflicts of interest experienced by union-nominated board members). See also Katherine Van Wezel Stone, *Labor and the Corporate Structure: Changing Conceptions and Emerging Possibilities*, 55 U. Chi. L. Rev. 73, 147–61 (describing labor conflicts of interest in theories of the firm); Klaus J. Hopt, *New Ways in Corporate Governance: European Experiments with Labor Representation on Corporate Boards*, 82 Mich. L. Rev. 1338, 1359–62 (discussing "conflicts of loyalty" of worker representatives on codetermined boards in Europe and finding them "difficult but resolvable").

30. One recommended approach to the interlocking director problem is to allow such transactions even in the absence of disclosure and ratification or approval unless an interlocking director or officer participates personally in negotiations or must vote in order to approve the transaction. See 1 A.L.I. *supra* note 21 § 5.07. The ALI does not mention other kinds of organizational conflicts, such as between labor unions and corporate boards.

31. For an historical account leading to this general conclusion, see Marsh, *supra* note 3, at 36–9. But see Norwood P. Beveridge, Jr., *The Corporate Director's Fiduciary Duty of Loyalty: Understanding the Self-Interested Director Transaction*, 41 DePaul L. Rev. 655, 659–62 (1992) (challenging the breadth of Marsh's conclusion of a general rule of voidability). In any event, the law began to change toward more liberal treatment of self-dealing corporate decisions in the early twentieth century. See Kenneth B. Davis, Jr., *Approval by Disinterested Directors*, 20 J. Corp. L. 215, 219–20 (1995); Melvin A. Eisenberg, *Self-Interested Transactions in Corporate Law*, 13 J. Corp. L. 997, 997 (1988).

32. 1 Cox et al., *supra* note 22, § 0.12.

33. James J. Fishman & Stephen Schwarz, *Cases and Materials on Nonprofit Organizations* 221(1995) (cited in Goldschmid, *supra* note 5, at 647–8).

34. See Clark, *supra* note 13, at 191 ("In former times, directors of corporations served without pay. . . . Many corporate statutes now allow them to fix their own compensation, as well as that of officers."); 1 Cox et al., *supra* note 27, § 11.1 ("presumption at common law that directors serve without pay" was overturned by statutes); Marsh, *supra* note 3, at 548 (discussing impracticability of avoiding conflicts of interests among corporate directors by insisting "that every corporation have an entirely outside board").

35. See *supra* text accompanying notes . See also Saul Levmore, *Efficiency and Conspiracy: Conflicts of Interest, Anti-Nepotism Rules, and Separation Strategies*, 66 Fordham L. Rev. 2099, 2111–12 (1998) (arguing how nepotism can

sometimes be "socially and privately efficient," for example in hiring spouses within a university).

36. Different courts use different terms to describe substantive fairness, including "intrinsic" or "inherent" fairness. *See* Beveridge, *supra* note 31, at 681.

37. See *supra* note 21 and accompanying text.

38. Rev. Model Business Corp. Act § 8.31. See also Revised Model Business Corp. Act § 8.61(b) (giving the less popular 1988 version with the same ambiguity between substantive and procedural tests). Delaware law is substantially similar. 8 Del. Code § 144 (authorization by disinterested directors or shareholder vote in "good faith" *or* "fair" if authorized, approved, or ratified by directors or shareholders).

39. For an account of these two competing view of conflicts-of-interest statutes, see 1 Cox et al., *supra* note 22, § 10.15, at 10.48 to 10.53. See also Eisenberg, *supra* note 31, at 1007 (discussing ambiguity of the statutes).

40. The interpretive argument here relies on the importance of the common statutory preface that a "conflict of interest transaction is not voidable by the corporation solely because of the director's interest in the transaction" if any of the three alternatives of disclosure and approval by disinterested directors, disclosure and approval by shareholders, or "fairness" obtain. Rev. Model Business Corp. Act § 8.31. The trouble is that neither the model statute nor various state versions specify what standard applies to review self-dealing transactions that are "not voidable" for any of these reasons. See 1 Cox et al., *supra* note 22, § 10.15, at 10.51 to 10.53.

41. 361 A.2d 218 (Del. 1976).

42. *Id.* at 222. The court then found the directors and officers concerned met their burden of proving their self-dealing transaction to be fair. Id. at 224. *Accord* Remillard Brick Co. v. Remillard-Dandini Co., 241 P.2d 66 (Cal. Ct. App. 1952) (holding that technical compliance with California's conflicts-of-interest statute does not eliminate ability of court to review a self-dealing transaction for fairness); Scott v. Multi-Amp Corp., 386 F. Supp. 44 (D.N.J. 1974) (similar result applying New Jersey law). However, the approval by a majority of disinterested shareholders may nevertheless shift the burden of proof and even change the standard of review. See infra text accompanying notes 44–46, 51, 57.

43. For a conceptual discussion of this phenomenon, see Gunther Teubner, "Corporate Fiduciaries and Their Beneficiaries," in Corporate Governance and Directors' Liabilities 166–73 (Klaus J. Hopt & Gunther Teubner, eds., 1985).

44. 1 Cox et al., *supra* note 22, §§ 10.1 to 10.3.

45. For a description of these two types of committees, see Gregorary V. Varallo, et al., *From* Kahn *to* Carlton: *Recent Developments in Special Committee Practice,* 53 Bus. Law. 397 (1998).

46. See William T. Allen, *Independent Directors in MBO Transactions: Are They Fact or Fantasy?,* 45 Bus. Law. 2055, 2060 (1990) ("When a special committee's process is perceived as reflecting a good faith, informed attempt to approximate aggressive, arm's-length bargaining, it will be accorded substantial importance by the court. When, on the other hand, it appears as artifice, ruse or charade, or when the board unduly limits the committee or when the committee fails to correctly perceive its mission—then one can expect that its decision will be accorded no respect.").

47. 663 A.2d 1194 (Del. Ch. 1995).

48. *Id.* at 1195–6.

49. *Id.* at 1196–7 & n.1.

50. *Id.* at 1198. The plaintiffs challenged the adequacy of disclosure underlying the shareholder ratification, but this argument was rejected by the court. Id. at 1198–1200. They then conceded that shareholder ratification would shift the burden of proof but not change the standard of review. *Id.* at 1200.

51. *Id.* at 1205. The court premised its holding on the fact that Waste's 22 percent interest in Wheelabrator did not amount to de facto control. The court therefore concluded that "this merger did not involve an interested and controlling shareholder." *Id.* This is at least debatable, given that a 20 percent shareholder may exercise de facto control in many situations. See Detlev Vagts, *Basic Corporation Law* 444 (3d ed. 1989) ("It is important to bear in mind that a shareholder many have control while holding less than 51% of the stock; it is familiar lore that a single, active interested shareholder . . . may dominate a corporation's affairs with 40%, 30%, or even 20% or less if the remainder of the stock is held by the scattered and semioblivious shareholders so typical of the large corporation."); Essex Universal Corp. v. Yates, 305 F.2d 572, 575 (3d Cir. 1962) ("it is commonly known that equivalent power [to exercise voting control] accrues to the owner of 28.3% of the stock").

52. 638 A.2d 1110 (Del. 1994).

53. *Id.* at 1112–13.

54. *Id.* at 1117 (citing Rosenblatt v. Getty Oil Co., 493 A.2d 929, 937–8 (Del. 1985).

55. *Id.* at 1119–21. In subsequent proceedings, the defendant directors succeeded in meeting their burden of proof that the deal was substantively fair. Kahn v. Lynch Communication Systems, Inc., 669 A.2d 79, 84–90 (Del. 1995). See also Kahn v. Tremont Corp., 694 A.2d 422, 424, 426–30 (Del. 1997) (burden shifting through negotiating committee reversed due to lack of true independence of committee members and legal and banking advisers).

56. Weinberger v. UOP, Inc., 457 A.2d 701, 703, 708–12 (Del. 1983) (holding that burden of proof did not shift with disinterested shareholder ratification when directors failed to disclose information relevant to the fairness of the merger price); see also infra text accompanying notes 119–31 (discussing *Weinberger*). This requirement is sometimes also referred to as the duty of "complete candor." See, e.g., Lynch v. Vickers Energy Corp., 383 A.2d 278, 281 (Del. 1977); *see also* Donald E. Pease, *Delaware's Disclosure Rule: The "Complete Candor" Standard, Its Application, and Why Sue in Delaware*, 14 Del. J. Corp. L. 445 (1989).

57. See, e.g., Marciano v. Nakash, 535 A.2d 400 (Del. 1987) (in a joint venture gone bad between the family owners of the makers of Guess and Jordache jeans, right to repayment on self-dealing loans of $2.5 million upheld only after directors met burden to prove substantive fairness).

58. For a more complete description of law of demand on directors including various exceptions to the rule in various jurisdictions, *see* 2 James D. Cox, Thomas Lee Hazen & F. Hodge O'Neal, *Corporations* § 15.7 (1995).

59. For a proposal for "universal demand" that would eliminate the often confusing distinction between "demand required" and "demand excused" cases, see *Principles of Corporate Governance: Analysis and Recommendations*, 2

A.L.I. § 7.03 (1994). Federal courts had begun to develop a universal demand rule, but this approach was struck down by the U.S. Supreme Court in *Kamen v. Kemper Financial Services, Inc.* 2 HS 500 U.S. 90 (1991). For a policy argument against universal demand due to added expenses that it would impose in conflicts-of-interest cases, see Clark, *supra* note 13, at 644–45.

60. This procedural innovation appears first to have arisen as a defense to shareholder lawsuits alleging corporate waste in the payment of illegal foreign bribes. See Clark, *supra*, note 13, at 645.

61. No. Civ. A. 13950, 1997 WL 305829 (Del. Ch., May 30, 1997) 23 Del. J. Corp. L. 712 (1998).

62. *Id.* at *1, 3–7.

63. *Id.* at *6. Of course, a political critic might challenge whether such military credentials deserve to be given weight in matters of corporate governance.

64. *Id.* at *7–8, 20.

65. *Id.* at *2 (citing Zapata Corp. v. Maldonado, 430 A.2d 779, 788–89 (Del. 1981)). There is considerable variation among states concerning the standard of review that courts apply to the findings of independent litigation committees, ranging from review only for procedural "good faith" and "independence" of the committee in states such as New York to strict judicial review of the substantive fairness of a committee's recommendation in North Carolina. *Compare* Auerbach v. Bennett, 393 N.E. 994 (N.Y. 1979) *with* Alford v. Shaw, 358 S.E.2d 323 (N.C. 1987). The Delaware approach is somewhere in the middle, combining a two-step process that combines both procedural and substantive fairness. For discussion of the various standards of review, see 2 Cox et al., *supra* note 58, § 15.8.

66. The effectiveness of members' standing to challenge conflicts of interests in nonprofit corporations is somewhat uncertain, as recent scandals in such organizations as the United Way of America and Adelphi University illustrate. For discussion, see Goldschmid, *supra* note 5, at 633–36.

67. *See* DeMott, *Beyond Metaphor, supra*, note 5, at 879 ("Although one can identify common core principles of fiduciary obligation, these principles apply with greater or lesser force in different contexts involving different types of parties and relationships. Recognition that the law of fiduciary obligation is situation-specific should be the starting point for any further analysis."); *see also supra* note 26 (citing various ALI sections applicable to various conflicts of interest).

68. I elaborate on this analysis in Orts, *Shirking and Sharking supra* note 8, at 298–314.

69. See id. at 306 & n.224.

70. For an overview of the trend toward increasing employee ownership, see Joseph R. Blasi & Douglas L. Kruse, *The New Owners: The Mass Emergence of Employee Ownership in Public Companies and What It Means for American Business* (1991).

71. Three-quarters of CEOs in the United States also chair their corporation's boards. *See* Laura Lin, *The Effectiveness of Outside Directors as a Corporate Governance Mechanism: Theories and Evidence*, 90 Nw. U.L. Rev. 898, 914 & n.85 (1996). But the two positions are usually split in public corporations in Great Britain. *See* Bernard S. Black & John C. Coffee, Jr., *Hail Brittania?: Institutional Investor Behavior under Limited Regulation*, 92 Mich. L. Rev. 1997, 2022 (1994). For a recommendation to require U.S. companies to disclose

whether they have separate chairs or "lead directors" of the board, see Constance E. Bagley & Richard H. Koppes, *Leader of the Pack: A Proposal for Disclosure of Board Leadership Structure*, 34 San Diego L. Rev. 149 (1997).

72. Of course, the extent to which corporate boards have responsibility to ensure legal and ethical compliance within corporations is contested, but a trend seems to be identifiable in recent U.S. corporate law toward an emerging duty to promote organizational integrity. For a discussion of this possible emerging duty and its limits, see Deborah A. DeMott, *Organizational Incentives to Care About the Law*, 60 Law & Contemp. Probs. 39 (1997).

73. I leave the issue of compensation for lower levels of employees outside the scope of this chapter, though I do not mean to denigrate its social importance. Labor law, including the law of union organization and bargaining and minimum wage statutes, as well as regulation of pensions and employment discrimination, is the primary body of law relevant to these other employees. See, e.g., Paul Weiler, *Governing the Workplace: The Future of Employment and Labor Law* (1990); Symposium, *The Changing Workplace*, 74 Tex. L. Rev. 1485 (1996); Clyde Summers, *Effective Remedies for Employment Rights: Preliminary Guidelines and Proposals*, 141 U. Pa. L. Rev. 457 (1992).

74. This empirical fact that CEOs wield considerable authority over corporate boards has been called structural bias. See, e.g., Victor Brudney, *Independent Directors—Heavenly City or Potemkin Village*, 95 Harv. L. Rev. 597 (1982); James D. Cox, *Bias in the Boardroom: Psychological Foundations and Legal Implications of Corporate Cohesion*, 48 Law & Contemp. Probs. 83 (1985).

75. For arguments that current levels of executive compensation are excessive, see, e.g., Derek Bok, *The Cost of Talent: How Executives and Professionals Are Paid and How It Affects America* 95–118 (1993); Graef Crystal, *In Search of Excess* (1991); Linda J. Barris, The Overcompensation Problem: A Collective Approach to Controlling Executive Pay, 68 Ind. L.J. 59 (1992); Carl T. Bogus, *Excessive Executive Compensation and the Failure of Corporate Democracy*, 41 Buff. L. Rev. 1 (1993).

76. Joann S. Lublin, *The Great Divide: CEO Pay Keeps Soaring, Wall St. J.*, Apr. 11, 1996, at R1.

77. *See* 1 Cox et al., *supra* note 22, § 11.5 at 11.19.

78. Few, if any, major cases striking down an executive compensation package as excessive or unreasonable have occurred since the Great Depression when the U.S. Supreme Court in 1933 upheld a cause of action against a profit-sharing scheme as "waste" if "a bonus payment has no relation to the value of services for which it is given." See Clark, *supra* note 13, at 197–98 (quoting Rogers v. Hill, 289 U.S. 582, 591–92 (1933)); see also 1 Cox et al., *supra* note 22, § 11.5 at 11.21 to 11.23.

79. 698 A.2d 384 (Del. Ch. 1997).

80. *Id.* at 385.

81. *Id.* at 386–7, 389.

82. *Id.* at 389. For the estimate of the worth of the stock options, see Jay Mathews, *Their Riches Were Your Command; Demands that Executive Pay Be Tied to Performance Are What Led to Downsizers? Bonuses*, Wash. Post, Mar. 24, 1996, at H1.

83. 698 A.2d at 387 (quoting Steiner v. Meyerson, 1995 WL 441999 (Del. Ch., July 18, 1995)).

84. Together with other options, the profits from the options upheld in

Zupnick v. Goizueta helped to inflate Mr. Goizeta's net worth to over one billion dollars at his death in 1997. See Adam Bryant, *Flying High on the Options Express*, N.Y. Times, Apr. 5, 1998, § 3, at 1. In 1996 alone, Goizeta's increase in personal wealth attributable to options rose more than $61 million. *See* Judith H. Dobrzynski, *New Road to Riches Is Paved with Options*, N.Y. Times, Mar. 30, 1997, § 3, at 1.

85. 699 A.2d 327 (Del. Ch. 1997).

86. *Id.* at 329–31.

87. The plaintiffs claimed that the failure to provide an estimate of the actual value of the options according to a standard pricing model such as the widely used Black–Scholes option pricing model violated the directors' fiduciary duty of candor. Id. at 329. See also supra note 56 and accompanying text. But the court rejected this claim on the grounds that such a pricing formula consisted of "soft information" and that the Black–Sholes model could not easily be applied to the stock options at issue, even though standard accounting standards require an estimate for financial reporting purposes. 699 A.2d at 331–3.

88. *Id.* at 333–9.

89. Interestingly, the court suggested that an enhanced standard of review may apply to directors' stock options given the self-dealing aspect of the case, but it recognized uncertainty in this area. *Id.* at 337–8. The court also did not say whether the burden of proof would lie on the plaintiffs or defendants to demonstrate waste.

90. See Clark, *supra* note 13, at 223–8, 239–41, 248–51; 1 Cox et al., *supra* note 22, § 11.7 at 11.28 to 11.40. See also A.L.I., *supra*, note 21, § 5.05.

91. 1 Cox et al., *supra* note 21, § 11.7 at 11.28.

92. Eric Talley, *Turning Servile Opportunities to Gold: A Strategic Analysis of the Corporate Opportunities Doctrine*, 108 Yale L.J. 277, 279 (1998).

93. See, e.g., General Automotive Mfg. Co. v. Singer, 120 N.W.2d 659, 662–3 (Wis. 1963) (holding corporate employee liable for secret profits from corporate opportunities obtained without disclosure or approval from the corporation).

94. See Clark, *supra* note 13, at 224; Talley, *supra* note 92, at 279, 298. In most corporate conflicts-of-interest cases, these extraordinary remedies are not usually available. See Barnard, *supra*, note 13, at 411.

95. 73 A.2d 148 (Del. 1996).

96. 38 N.E.2d 391 (Mass. App. Ct. 1982). Both of these cases are excerpted for teaching purposes in William A. Klein & J. Mark Ramseyer, *Business Associations* 333–8 (1997) & Supp. 46–51 (1998). They are also discussed in Talley, *supra* note 92, at 303–10, 336–44.

97. 73 A.2d at 150.

98. *Id.* at 151–2.

99. *Id.* at 151, 152–3.

100. *Id.* at 155.

101. *Id.* at 152 & n.5, 156 & n.7, 157–8.

102. *Id.* at 155–57.

103. Energy Resources Corp. v. Porter, 438 N.E.2d 391, 392 (Mass. App. Ct. 1982).

104. *Id.* at 393. Porter also stated falsely—or at least misleadingly—that his intention in leaving was to "work in the area of computerized cars." *Id.* at 393, 395.

105. See, e.g., Talley, *supra* note 92, at 351 (noting that the corporate opportunity doctrine "has never been a paragon of analytical precision").

106. See Clark, Corporate Law, *supra* note 13, at 225–30; Talley, *supra* note 92, at 289–96.

107. Talley argues that "disparate informational structures" distinguish *Broz* and *Energy Resources*, and he buttresses this argument with a contractarian economic analysis emphasizing the importance of information in economic decisionmaking. Talley, *supra*, note 92, at 308–9, 310–50. This approach emphasizes the need to disclose an opportunity based on what Talley calls "private information" before the opportunity may be taken—which Porter failed to do in *Energy Resources*—and is more forgiving toward breaches of fiduciary duty in situations when relatively complete information may be assumed to be more widely available as in *Broz. Id.* at 322–9, 336–8, 351–2.

108. For example, Clark argues that a "functional relationship" and "interest or expectancy" test should be applied in close corporations, but disclosure and advance consent by other directors or shareholders would authorize taking an opportunity. The defense of corporate financial or legal incapacity would not be allowed. Clark, *supra* note 13, at 234–43. But in public corporations, he argues that the difficulty of policing self-dealing justifies a categorical rule against full-time executives taking any corporate opportunity, even if they get prior consent. *Id.* at 243–50. For outside public directors, Clark advocates a modified prohibition against any use of "the corporation's resources, including its information, to develop or acquire personal business opportunities." *Id.* at 252.

109. Both Clark and Talley dismiss "fairness" as an appropriate test for the "definition" of a corporate opportunity, and both argue in favor of "efficiency" as a guide to what they see as the correct doctrine. See Clark, *supra* note 13, at 227, 228–9; Talley, *supra* note 92, at 281–2, 293–5. But it seems clear that both substantive and procedural fairness are implicated in their treatments of the importance of disclosure, access to information, and their own definitions of the nature of corporate opportunities—even if they see "fairness" in the service of a broader and more important concept of "efficiency." See *supra* notes 105–08.

110. A freezeout is a transaction in which the minority interest is involuntarily eliminated, such as through a short-form or other merger. *See* Clark, *supra* note 13, at 499, 502. A squeezeout is a transaction that does not directly eliminate the minority shareholder but "has the purpose and practical effect of making his situation so unrewarding that he is virtually disinvested or so unpleasant that he will inevitably sell out on the insider's terms." *Id.* at 500.

111. See, e.g., Rock, *supra* note 11 (providing an account of the law of Management-led leveraged buyouts in Delaware).

112. 676 A.2d 436 (Del. 1996).

113. *Id.* at 437–8.

114. *Id.* at 438.

115. 8 Del. Code § 271 (requiring majority shareholder approval for the sale of "all or substantially all of [a corporation's] property and assets").

116. 676 A.2d at 439–40, 444–5.

117. *Id.* at 444. In the United States, controlling shareholders usually have a right to obtain a "control premium" when they sell their interest to another party. The rule is different in other countries where "control premium" is deemed an asset of the corporation as a whole to be shared pro rata with

noncontrolling shareholders. See John C. Coffee, Jr., *Transfers of Control and the Quest for Efficiency: Can Delaware Law Encourage Efficient Transactions While Chilling Inefficient Ones?*, 21 Del. J. Corp. L. 359, 360 & n.2 (1996) (discussing "widely prevailing rule that a controlling shareholder may receive a control premium for its shares" but noting that "the United States stands virtually alone [compared with other countries] in failing to accord minority shareholders any presumptive right to share in a control premium").

118. 676 A.2d at 445.

119. 457 A.2d 701 (Del. 1983).

120. A cashout merger is a corporate combination that requires shareholders in at least one of the corporations to accept a specified amount of cash for their shares rather than to continue as equity-owning shareholders. See Robert W. Hamilton, *Business Organizations: Essential Terms and Concepts* 430 (1996).

121. 457 A.2d at 704–5.

122. The UOP board had thirteen directors. In addition to the six Signal-affiliated directors described in the text, a representative of Signal's investment bank was also a UOP director. *Id.* at 704.

123. *Id.* at 705.

124. *Id.* at 707–8, 712.

125. *Id.* at 705–8.

126. *Id.* at 706.

127. *Id.* at 711.

128. *Id.*

129. *Id.* at 703, 711–12. The court noted that "the result here could have been entirely different" if the conflicted UOP board "had appointed an independent negotiating committee of its outside directors to deal with Signal at arm's length." *Id.* at 709 n.7. See also supra notes 43–57 and accompanying text (discussing the law of burden shifting and the use of negotiating committees).

130. *Id.* at 711–13.

131. On remand, the plaintiffs were awarded $1 per share. Weinberger v. UOP, Inc., 1985 WL 11546 (Del. Ch., Jan. 30, 1985), *aff'd* 497 A.2d 792 (Del. 1985). This amounts to more than $5.6 million according to the original case's estimate. 457 A.2d at 709 (estimating difference between $21 and $24 per share as over $17 million).

132. For further discussion, see David Luban's chapter in this book.

133. *See* Barnard, *supra* note 13, at 388–90 (arguing some cases such as theft of corporate property or changed terms in self-dealing loans without consideration are "unacceptable conflicts of interest" under any circumstances).

134. This is the premise of the widely used "business judgment rule," but it is also applicable to other kinds of cases. See *supra* notes 44 and accompanying text.

Procedures alone run the risk of being "an easy tool, deferential, glad to be of use."

135. Allen, *supra* note 46, at 2061 (quoting T. S. Eliot).

136. See Eisenberg, *supra* note 31, at 998 (recognizing "structural complexities" in corporations and corporate law). For a normative elaboration on this point, see Eric W. Orts, *The Complexity and Legitimacy of Corporate Law*, 50 Wash. & Lee L. Rev. 1565 (1993).

III

Academics

8

COUNSELORS WHO TEACH
AND TEACHERS WHO COUNSEL

Some Conflicts of Interest in Psychological and
Philosophical Counseling

Elliot D. Cohen

This chapter develops two case studies that explore morally problematic dual role relationships arising from the blending of teaching and counseling. The first case pertains to psychological counseling; the second to philosophical counseling. Although similarities between both forms of counseling will become apparent, the newly instituted practice of philosophical counseling, with its less clearly delineated role expectations, will be shown to present special problems for philosophical practice. Standards of practice regarding ethical management of dual role relationships, which expand on existing codes of ethics in psychological and philosophical counseling, will be adduced from analyses of each case. The method used to articulate these practical guidelines resemble that of legal reasoning in which case analyses provide precedents (*stare decises*) from which rules can be derived.

Dual Role Relationships:
Some Preliminary Concepts
and Definitions

Psychological counselors include psychologists, mental health counselors, social workers, marriage and family counselors, human service workers, and other mental health professionals. Often, these professionals also teach in colleges and universities. They may be full-time faculty members and part-time counselors, or they may be adjunct faculty members who work full time in mental health. They may teach in graduate counselor education programs as well as other graduate and undergraduate programs related to mental health. Being both teacher and counselor can have significant professional advantages. Keeping current as a practitioner in the field can give instructors a note of credibility that nonpractitioners may lack. Ongoing practical experience can provide the instructor with a fresh stream of practical experience from which to draw in classroom instruction and discussion.

Philosophical counselors are practitioners of philosophy who try to help their clients deal with personal problems of living through the application of philosophical theories, ideas, and methods. Philosophical counseling is new. It was first introduced in Germany by Gerd B. Achenbach, who opened his practice in 1981 (Lahav & Tillmanns, 1995). Although philosophers who make their living by doing philosophical counseling are still rare in the United State as well as abroad, the movement appears to be growing. Associations of philosophical practitioners have formed in several nations, including Germany, Holland, Canada, France, England, South Africa, Israel, and the United States. In the United States, the American Society for Philosophy, Counseling, and Psychotherapy (ASPCP) was founded in 1992 by Elliot D. Cohen and Paul W. Sharkey—two philosophers certified in the counseling modality known as rational-emotive behavior therapy—with the goal of exploring the relationships between practice of psychological counseling and philosophy. The ASPCP has since expanded its mission to include regulation of practice through Standards of Practice and Certification.

As those trained in philosophy have traditionally been college and university teachers, it is likely that many prospective practitioners of philosophical counseling will also be teachers of philosophy or that they will at least teach in an adjunct capacity. We may therefore justly expect to find a significant number of both psychological and philosophical counselors in the classroom. Unfortunately, when these professionals occupy dual roles as teachers and counselors there is potential for collision, creating conflicts of interest.

A conflict of interest arises for a counselor when he or she has a special interest that has potential for adversely affecting professional judgment on behalf of a client. Conflicts of interest sometimes arise for counselors when they take on or maintain "dual (or multiple) role relationships" with their clients. Such relationships exist when counselors occupy two or more different (professional or personal) roles with respect to the *same* clients.

Dual role relationships may be either *consecutive* or *simultaneous* (National Association of Social Workers, 1997, 1.06.c). An example of a consecutive dual role relationship is a counselor who agrees to counselor a *former* student. An example of a simultaneous dual role relationship is one in which a counselor agrees to counsel a *current* student. As will become apparent, simultaneous dual role relationships may be more morally problematic than consecutive ones when expectations and responsibilities arising from the dual roles are incompatible.

Dual role relationships may also be *elective* or *nonelective*. An elective dual role relationship occurs when the counselor freely decides to *enter into* the relationship, as when the counselor consents to counsel a (current or former) student. A *nonelective* dual role relationship arises as a result of the (prospective) *client's decision*, not that of the counselor. For example, such a dual role relationship arises when a (current or former) client decides to become a student of her counselor. The counselor in question does not decide to *enter into* the relationship although she may elect to *maintain* the dual role relationship.

Dual role relationships do not always involve conflicts of interest; nor are they necessarily morally problematic. For example, a psychological counselor educator in a graduate program who is both teacher and supervisor to a graduate student/intern need not encounter a conflict of interest. However, dual role relationships that involve conflicts of interest are invariably morally problematic. For example, dual role relationships in which a counselor counsels a client with whom he shares (or has formerly shared) a *personal* relationship (e.g., friend or sexual partner) typically involve conflicts of interest and should be avoided (American Counselling Association, 1995, A.6.a).

Dual role relationships can be morally problematic if the client *thinks* the counselor has a conflict of interest or the client otherwise feels uncomfortable about the dual role relationship even if the counselor does not encounter any conflict of interest. For example, in a counseling relationship based on bartering for services (the client provides the counselor with some service in exchange for counseling), the efficacy of counseling may suffer if the client *thinks*, contrary to fact, that the counselor may be dissatisfied with the specific service rendered.

Dual role relationships can also be morally problematic because they involve *a public appearance* of conflict of interest. For example, counselors who engage in sexual relationships with former clients (regardless of whether counseling was terminated for the sake of pursuing such a relationship) can adversely affect the public image of counselors, thereby deterring prospective clients from seeking counseling services.

Case 1

Doing Psychological Counseling with a Student: A Case of a Nonelective Dual Role Relationship

Dr. Carver is a professor of counselor education at a local university. He also has a private counseling practice. Dr. Carver's students sometimes request counseling for themselves or family members, but he has been careful not to take on his students or their family members as clients, referring them instead to other local, qualified therapists. However, he has occasionally agreed to see other university employees, (e.g., he once counseled his departmental secretary). He has also sometimes taken referrals from his students, (e.g., friends of students). He also once counseled a former student.

One such referral, Christi Compton, was a friend of a student in one of Dr. Carver's courses. Christi, a twenty-six-year-old women, sought counseling for depression. She had been institutionalized three years earlier for attempting to commit suicide by overdosing on sleeping pills. Prior to Dr. Carver's joining the faculty, Christi had been a graduate student at the university enrolled in the counseling program. When she became seriously depressed, she withdrew from classes. Three weeks later, she attempted suicide.

At the time Christi began therapy with Dr. Carver, she lived alone and was working as a salesperson in a women's clothing store. Christi, a gay woman, had nobody special whom see was seeing. She had previously lived with a partner who abruptly left her for someone else. She sought therapy with Dr. Carver for purposes of helping her to overcome feelings of grief related to the loss of her partner and to find meaning in what she described as a "mean, insensitive, homophobic universe."

As therapy progressed, Christi began to express greater optimism about the prospects for the future. She began to date again and was now seeing someone steadily. Christi reaffirmed her earlier plan to become a therapist. She reentered the counseling program at the university and signed up for her remaining coursework, including Dr. Carver's counseling ethics course, which was a degree requirement.

When Christi informed Dr. Carver (after the fact) that she had signed up for his class, Dr. Carver was taken aback. He informed her that doing so would create a conflict of interest for him. Christi proclaimed, however, that it was through Dr. Carver's support that she was ready to return to school in the first place. She pointed out that she needed the course in order to sit for her comprehensive exams, that the course would not be offered again until the following year (which would only postpone her graduation another year), that there was just one section of the course being offered, and that no other university within commuting distance offered the course.

When Dr. Carver suggested referring her to another therapist, Christi became very upset and stated that she did not want to see anyone else. She proclaimed, "just when things are getting better for me, you want to walk out on me. That's the way things always go for me." And she pleaded with him to continue the therapeutic relationship. Dr. Carver told her he would think about it and let her know at their next weekly session. In the beginning of the next session, he told her that he had decided to retain her as his client. He also informed her that he might find it useful to consult with colleagues on this case from time to time. He also asked her not to disclose to anyone in the class that she was his client. Christi expressed satisfaction with that arrangement.

The semester began and Christi attended Dr. Carver's class. Christi appeared comfortable with the arrangement, but Dr. Carver found the situation increasingly uncomfortable. In discussing "dual role relationships" in class, for example, he felt particularly uncomfortable, especially when Christi actively argued in class that there was "nothing wrong with them as long as the therapist and client were in agreement." Dr. Carver did not challenge her argument. Feeling constrained by her presence, he instead glossed quickly over the subject, omitting careful explication of the problematic nature of counseling students and supervisees (in contrast to previous semesters in which he treated this subject in great length).

In grading essay exams, Dr. Carver felt even more uncomfortable. In deciding whether, for example, to give her essay a "C" or a "B" he found it difficult to bracket the question of how hard his client, whom he knew was aiming at getting "A's" and "B's," might take the disappointment of getting a "C." Although, on the one hand, he believed that she needed to learn to cope with disappointment, he also worried about her present ability to do so. Although Dr. Carver was able to "get through" the semester, he felt that his discomfort with the situation had negatively affected his ability to teach the course as well as his objectivity in grading.

In therapy, Christi would sometimes talk to Dr. Carver about course material and discussions that had transpired in class. Upon consideration, however, he believed that the class was now a significant part of her life and that it would be frustrating and counterproductive for Christi to disallow her from speaking freely about matters related to class. Some sessions, however, began to sound more like ethics class than therapy sessions. Dr. Carver did not, however, think it necessary to consult or seek supervision. Moreover, he was reluctant to do so because his colleagues were instructors at the university; he worried about disclosing to them that he was counseling a client because the university had a policy forbidding the counseling of students.

Nevertheless, as therapy progressed, Christi began to express renewed vitality for life. She and the person whom she was dating became intimate and decided to live together. Upon completion of the course, she enrolled in classes for the following session. Dr. Carver began phasing down sessions to once every two weeks. Thus, when Christi, after having a falling out with her partner, attempted suicide again (albeit unsuccessfully), Dr. Carver was shocked and regretful for the manner in which he had handled her case.[1]

This case raises questions surrounding the morality of several types of dual role relationships: accepting coworkers as clients, accepting (current) students or their close relatives as clients, accepting referrals from students, and maintaining counseling relationships with clients *after* they become students.

Counselors have a moral responsibility to maintain independence of judgment in acting in matters related to clients' treatment and to take reasonable precautions against loss of such judgment. However, in accepting *coworkers* as his clients, Dr. Carver voluntarily placed himself in dual role relationships in which serious potential existed for loss of independence of judgment by both client and counselor. For example, the departmental secretary could feel compelled to do special favors for Dr. Carver, which she would not feel obliged to do for other department members, or she could feel intimidated about making disclosures in therapy for fear of how Dr. Carver might view her professionally. Similarly, Dr. Carver could allow his professional interest in secretarial services to color his counseling services, for example, avoiding confrontation in order not to disrupt the work relationship. Although such losses of objectivity and exploitation *need not* result, given their serious *potential*, Dr. Carver had a professional responsibility to *avoid* these dual relationships (American Counseling Association, 1995, A.6.a). Had Dr. Carver agreed to counseling an adjunct on the faculty of another discipline whom he neither knew nor worked with professionally, the case would have been otherwise. In such a case, the potential for loss of independence of judgment would not be significant because there would be affiliation without a proximate working relationship.

Professional standards generally also prohibit psychological counselors from *recruiting* clients for private practice through their place of employment (American Counseling Association, 1995, C.3.d). While it is not clear that Dr. Carver actively solicited or recruited clients through his workplace, his willingness to take on co-employees as clients violated the spirit of this proscription, which is to prevent conflicts of interest, real or apparent. Even if Dr. Carver encountered no actual conflict of interest, the *appearance* of such can also harm a profession by raising public distrust. A counselor dedicated to the prosperity of his profession should avoid apparent conflicts of interest.

Dr. Carver's refusal to take on (current) students and family members appropriately avoided serious potential for loss of independence of judgment. The policy of referring rather than counseling students as well as supervisees has standardly been underwritten by professional codes of ethics in psychological counseling. For example, according to the American Counseling Association's (1995) *Code of Ethics*, "[i]f students or supervisees request counseling, supervisors or counselor educators provide them with acceptable referrals. Supervisors or counselor educators do not serve as counselor to students or supervisees over whom they hold administrative, teaching, or evaluative roles unless this is a brief role associated with a training program" (F.3.c).

A conflict need not arise in the instruction of *former clients*. In contrast to simultaneous dual role relationships wherein therapy and instruction are concurrent and ongoing, the instructional role (goals and evaluation) is less likely to adversely affect therapeutic concerns, and conversely. Admittedly, the problem may not be entirely moot insofar as "once a client always a client" is true. The nature of the former counselor–client relation as well as the success of prior therapy may also be significant factors. In addition, former clients may, and often do, seek additional therapy. It is therefore important that counselors be alert to the possibility that their former clients could request additional therapy *while they are students*. In such cases, conflict of interest could be avoided by making a suitable referral.

Counseling *former students* may also have potential for creating *future* conflicts of interest. If the former student Dr. Carver agreed to counsel was likely to enroll in further courses with Dr. Carver, his acceptance of this individual as client would have been shortsighted, indeed. On the other hand, had the student in question already graduated and received his degree, the potential for future conflict might have been minimal. Due care for avoidance of problematic, future dual role relationships would therefore support a professional responsibility of counselors to verify the statuses of former students *before* accepting them as clients. More generally, such a standard of due care supports a professional responsibility of counselors who teach to decline accepting as a client anyone they know or have good reason to believe will become a student in the course of therapy.

In the case of *family members of students*, the relationship often goes beyond affiliation. Because counseling clients often requires involvement by other family members (especially the client's immediate family), the risk that the student will also become a client can be substantial. Dr. Carver's refusal to counsel family members of students was therefore on firm ground.

The issue whether to accept referrals *from* students is another matter. Inasmuch as accepting these referrals cannot be expected to result in dual role relationships in which the client also becomes a student of the counselor, a policy of accepting *unsolicited* referrals made by students need not present an ethical problem. It is true that as a friend of the client, the student may become indirectly involved in the counseling relationship, for instance, as a subject of counseling sessions. Counselors can thereby learn things about their students that may have bearing on the counselor's assessment of the student in her role as teacher. However, the counselor is still afforded some insulation from the student by virtue of not having a counseling relationship with the student. Further, there are many other ways in which teachers may learn things about their students outside the teaching context. Insofar as teachers and students are members of the same community, they are likely to have mutual acquaintances or to encounter other avenues through which information is disseminated within the community. The professor may, for example, have his next door neighbor as his student.

The case of Christi presents a more difficult moral problem. There are several competing interests at stake in this case. First Dr. Carver must regard Christi's physical and mental welfare as well as her interest in advancing her education. Second, Dr. Carver has an interest in providing competent and fair instructional services to all his students. Third, Dr. Carver's professionalism as an instructor is on the line. His violation of a university policy proscribing counseling of students is a breach of a professional trust he has assumed with the university. Fourth, such a violation might well have untoward effects on his career (e.g., disciplinary action by the university and perhaps the loss of his job, especially if he is a relatively new, untenured faculty member). Dr. Carver's moral problem is that of addressing such welfare, interests, and needs of the concerned parties without any unnecessary (avoidable) sacrifices. Because Dr. Carver is a psychological counselor, his primary professional responsibility is to the welfare, interests, and needs of his client (American Counseling Association, 1995, A.1.a). On the other hand, in his capacity as professor, Dr. Carver's primary professional responsibility is to provide fair and competent instruction. Unfortunately, Dr. Carver is torn in incompatible directions in trying to address each of these professional responsibilities at once.

As an instructor, he is expected not to place any of his students at any unfair advantage or disadvantage. Each student should get the grade she deserves. Thus, in its Statement on Professional Ethics, the American Association of University Professors (AAUP) asserts that "[p]rofessors make every reasonable effort to foster honest academic conduct and to ensure that their evaluations of students reflect each student's true merit" (American Association of University Professors, 1987, II). As a counselor educator, Dr. Carver has the specific responsibility to train prospective counselors. He therefore has a responsibility *to the public* not to misrepresent the qualifications of these prospective counselors.

Further, such a public trust requires that any relationships with students tending to thwart teaching effectiveness should be avoided. "As members of an academic institution, professors seek above all to be effective teachers and scholars" (AAUP, 1987, IV). Insofar as counseling Christi has compromised his ability to provide fair and effective instructional and evaluation services, Dr. Carver's role as counselor is incompatible with his role as counselor educator.

On the other side, the teacher–student relationship that Dr. Carver has established with Christi is incompatible with promotion of client welfare because therapy is most likely to be effective when counselors possess and display personal attributes that encourage clients to become more self-directive and independent (Cohen & Cohen, 1999). In particular, counselors must possess and display unconditional positive regard for their clients (Rogers, 1977). That is, they should accept clients as the persons they are, not the persons counselors want them to be. Counselors should encourage clients to have their own ideas and feelings, to freely explore them, and to decide for themselves.

Although teachers as well as counselors have a responsibility to "demonstrate respect for students as individuals and adhere to their proper roles as intellectual guides and counselors" (AAUP, 1987, II), it is not part of the role of a counselor to formally, objectively, and officially evaluate and grade their clients. This belongs instead to the role of professor, and in particular to the role of a counselor educator who is expected to fairly evaluate student performance as a matter of public trust. When Dr. Carver became Christi's teacher, he also assumed a public trust to grade and assess her according to her merit.

This evaluative role is not necessarily inconsistent with a counselor's unconditional positive regard for his client. Nevertheless, it can be confusing to the client, who may well wonder whether what she says in therapy will affect her grade, or whether it is even appropriate (let alone safe) to get worked up emotionally, or to express irrational desires and inner conflicts to a counselor who, as her teacher, is expecting her to be rational. In Christi's case, such client confusion and loss of independence of judgment may have helped to impede therapeutic progress.

The blending of the teacher–student relationship with the counselor–client relationship also probably diverted valuable time from significant, personal issues to course-related matters that would otherwise have been better left for the classroom. Dr. Carver's reasoning that class materials were relevant to Christi's therapy was, if true, itself a negative consequence of a confusion of professional roles. A diligent counselor would have avoided such role blending in the first place insofar as this could reasonably be expected to impair the quality of services rendered.

As an instructor, Dr. Carver had a professional responsibility to be intellectually honest (AAUP, 1987, I). In the present context, this would include standing behind his moral convictions. Unless Professor Carver were to rationalize away and deny the dangerous consequences of counseling a student, he was remiss in not clearly and carefully emphasizing the dangers of such relationships in a class on professional ethics for prospective counselors. Inasmuch as he failed to do so, he violated a public trust. His failure to present thorough coverage of dual role relationships to his class, and to correct any misunderstandings about such relationships, was dishonest. It was also a breach of the primary responsibility that professors have to their subject "to state the truth as they see it" (AAUP, 1987, I).

Yet, with his client seated before him in his class, the execution of this professional responsibility ran some risk of undermining (or appearing to undermine) the very position he had subscribed to in agreeing to counsel that student. To his client, he might have thereby emerged as disingenuous, incongruent, and unworthy of trust. In agreeing to counsel his student, Dr. Carver therefore undertook a dual role relationship with inherent conflict of responsibilities and risks to both student and client.

Dr. Carver did not *initiate* the dual role relationship. He did not intentionally take on a student as his client. Rather, a client elected to become his student. The emerging relationship was a *nonelective* dual role relationship, that is, one not created by his own actions but rather by those of someone else (his client, in this case). Dr. Carver's decision to counsel Christi was thus more precisely a decision to *maintain* the dual role relationship rather than to create one. This, however, did not release Dr. Carver of the moral responsibility to address the problem raised by such a relationship.

Christi had previously been a student at the same university and counseling program in which Dr. Carver taught. Before accepting her as his client, Dr. Carver could have explored with Christi the possibility of her returning to the program. Although Christi might not have then had any intention of returning, Dr. Carver's informing Christi at the inception of therapy of his policy not to counsel his students might have set the stage for a more careful approach to the issue by both parties later on. It also would have given Christi the opportunity (before establishing a bond with Dr. Carver) to seriously consider pursuing therapy with a different counselor, allowing herself the future option of returning to school. Further, because Dr. Carver at least had reason to suspect that Christi *might* some day return to school, he had a moral responsibility to provide her with this information as part of her informed consent to therapy.

Once initiated, Dr. Carver still faced the challenge of deciding whether and how to *discontinue* the dual role relationship. In confronting this challenge, Dr. Carver needed to empathize with his client's subjective perspective. Christi perceived the world as "mean, insensitive, and homophobic." As a gay woman, she had apparently encountered antagonism and prejudice from others who lacked moral sensitivity. She had also experienced the loss of a significant other who left her for someone else. With a history of sensitivity to what she perceived as rejection of *her*, coupled with a history of attempted suicide, it is understandable that Dr. Carver did not want to place any unnecessary strain on her emotions. He cared for her and wanted to shelter her from harm, even at the expense of violating other important professional responsibilities. Unfortunately, in his zeal to protect her, he also supported her lack of self-assurance and independence, which probably contributed to her second suicide attempt.

Dr. Carver accepted Christi's reasons for maintaining a dual relationship without carefully exploring the implications of doing so. Although he informed her that such an arrangement would create a conflict of interest for him, he failed to inform her of the potential risks of such a dual role relationship (American Counseling Association, 1995, A.3.6) and therefore failed to be candid. These risks, as mentioned, included the potential for loss of independence of judgment for *both* client and counselor.

Dr. Carver also failed to inform Christi that counseling a student was against university policy, and that doing so could cost him his job. Christi wanted to take the course with Dr. Carver out of concern for professional advancement. Dr. Carver missed an opportunity to allow Christi to draw out the consistent applications of her own logic.

Dr. Carver also failed to consult on a complex ethical problem about which he apparently had questions. He indicated to Christi that he might seek consultation with colleagues, but he was instead motivated to conceal his predicament from professional colleagues for fear that he would be exposed for his violation. However, according to the ACA's (1995) *Code of Ethics*, counselors should "take reasonable steps to consult with other counselors or related professionals when they have questions regarding their ethical obligations or professional practice" (C.2.e).

In accepting Christi's reasons for taking the course with him without careful exploration, Dr. Carver missed an opportunity to work together with Christi toward a reasonable alternative. For example, he did not raise the possibility of asking another qualified professor to do a directed independent study.

In the end, however, if no such alternatives were feasible, the joint exploration of the problem at hand would have made the prospect of a referral appear more reasonable and not merely just another rejection. Such a mutual bond of respect, candor, honesty, congruence, and unconditional regard would have forged an opportunity to promote greater self-assurance and independence in the client. It would have empowered Christi to make a free and informed decision whether to wait another year to take the class and continue in therapy with Dr. Carver or to take the class with Dr. Carver and accept his referral. Such client empowerment based on mutual respect and understanding would have better promoted client welfare. Instead, Dr. Carver jeopardized client progress toward greater self-assurance, self-directiveness, and independence when he chose to remain in a dual role relationship that mutually impaired independence of judgment and strained counselor–client trust.

Case 2

Doing Philosophical Counseling with a Student: A Case of an Elective Dual Role Relationship

Timothy Stanza, a professor of philosophy at a large state university, also practiced philosophical counseling on the side. A member in good standing of the American Society for Philosophy, Counseling, and Psychotherapy, he held a doctorate in philosophy from an accredited institution. Philosophical practice was not regulated by law in his state; nor was he especially attracted to the idea of professional licensure or certification. Like many of his peers, he was skeptical about the value of licensing or certifying philosophical counselors because of the potentially damaging effect he thought this might have on the freedom to explore philosophical ideas.

Professor Stanza also believed that philosophical counseling should not be provided for a fee but should instead be offered gratis, just as Socrates did in ancient Athens. For Professor Stanza, philosophical counseling provided an outlet for philosophers, like other professionals, to apply their special skills in doing pro bono work. Thus when, on occasion, his students came to him for counseling, Professor Stanza saw no conflict in consenting. In fact, each semester, Professor Stanza made known to his classes that he did philosophical counseling and, without hesitation, distributed business cards to interested students. Professor Stanza sometimes met in his university office, sometimes in coffee houses, and sometimes on park benches. He conducted both individual and group sessions.

Mary Cartright, a seventeen-year-old freshman, who was enrolled in his introduction to philosophy class, often participated in class discussions and, while undecided about her major, found philosophy "fascinating." Mary was especially interested in existential philosophy and thought that it might be useful in helping her to confront her own existential angst. Thus, she asked Professor Stanza if he would agree to counsel her individually, and he readily agreed.

Mary's presenting problem was the desire to find meaning in her life, which she characterized as an "existential vacuum." She explained that she wanted to explore her own belief system from both theistic and atheistic perspectives. She was especially interested in "Nietzsche's idea that God is dead" and in Martin Buber's idea that one could not find God by looking outside the world. She explained that, for her, it seemed that God was dead, or at least just not listening to her prayers, and that, perhaps, she was looking for God in the wrong "places."

The two met weekly for one hour in Professor Stanza's office. Mary was given a reading list that included a number of selections by Nietzsche and Buber as well as other selections Stanza thought relevant to her interests. These readings supplemented the ones that were assigned in the class unit on philosophy of religion.

As the sessions progressed Mary became increasingly open about her personal life, sharing with Professor Stanza many of her deep secrets. On the other hand, it was also apparent to Professor Stanza that Mary's participation in her introduction to philosophy class had diminished, and she often sat in class sometimes nodding assent to the statements of her teacher but said little or nothing herself. After about five weeks of sessions, Mary disclosed to Professor Stanza that she had been sexually molested by her stepfather from the age of seven to fifteen when her stepfather divorced her mother. She explained that she had tried to tell her mother about the abuse, but her mother accused her of lying in order to "cause trouble" and blamed Mary for the divorce. Mary also explained that she was now seeing a twenty-five-year-old man—whom she referred to as her boyfriend—with whom she was currently having an ongoing sexual relationship.

Upon consulting with his peers, it became apparent to Professor Stanza that he had a legal responsibility to report Mary's case to the state sexual abuse hotline. Because Professor Stanza considered that he was "only doing philosophy" with his clients, he did not think that it was necessary to discuss the limits of client confidentiality with his client upon inception of counseling. So it came as a shock to Mary when Professor Stanza informed Mary that he had a responsibility to report what she had disclosed to him in confidence.

At this point, Mary terminated the counseling relationship and she stopped coming to class. Whereas she had previously been receiving "A's" in the class, it was just about midsemester, and she had not completed enough work to receive a passing grade. Professor Stanza tried calling Mary on a number of occasions, leaving messages to call him, but she did not return his phone calls. With regret, he failed her for the semester.

Philosophical practitioners are supposed to help their clients to "clarify, articulate, explore, and comprehend philosophical aspects of their belief systems," including "epistemological, metaphysical, axiological, and logical issues." Among the problems for which a client may seek philosophical counseling are midlife crises, career changes, stress, emotions, assertiveness, physical illness, death and dying, aging, meaning of life, and morality (ASPCP, 1997, Preamble). Philosophical counselors thus resemble psychological counselors insofar as they help clients to confront personal problems of living. Although it may be true that in some contexts philosophical counselors act as teachers or mentors rather than as therapists, this distinction may be moot when clients seek philosophical counseling not merely for the intrinsic pleasure of doing philosophy but for relief from problems of depression, low self-esteem, inability to handle stress, or other affective problems. Philosophical counselors must therefore be prepared to deal with the exigencies of psychological crises which may undergird clients' desire to explore philosophical aspects of their belief systems.

The desire to render philosophical counseling an independent profession, distinct from psychology, has led one group to define the activities of philosophical counseling as "nonmedical, noniatrogenic and not allied intrinsically with psychiatry or psychology" and as being "educational, axiological and noetic" (American Philosophical Practitioners Association, 1998). Whether the activities of philosophical counseling can appropriately be regarded as "intrinsically" distinct from psychiatry and psychology is an unsettled issue because "there is no consensus on the issue of how philosophical counseling differs from, or resembles, psychotherapies" (Lahav & Tillmanns, 1995). However, the *practical* danger of so polarizing these activities is that of not acting responsibly in the face of psychological exigencies that are likely to arise in the course of philosophical practice. As Jon Mills (in press) suggests, those who wish to deny that philosophical counseling is a psychological hence therapeutic activity are simply living in denial.

If the role of philosophical counselor and that of philosophy teacher were fundamentally the same, there would in fact be no problematic dual role relationship in philosophically counseling a student. However, given the intimacy of the philosophical counselor–client relationship, philosophical counselors have responsibilities that derive from their fiduciary relationship with their clients. Philosophical counselors should "seek to maintain the freely given and informed consent of the client" (ASPCP, 1997, p. 12), "refrain from manipulating or coercing the client, as well as any form of fraud or deceit" (ASPCP, 1997, p. 7); "avoid creating dependency relations in clients" (ASPCP, 1997, 5), and "safeguard a client's right to privacy by treating as confidential all information obtained from the client except where disclosure is required by law or is justified in order to prevent imminent, substantial harm to client or to others" (ASPCP, 1997, p. 14).

These responsibilities apply to the teaching role also. As teachers, professors are expected to "respect the confidential nature of the relationship between professor and student" as well as "avoid any exploitation, harassment, or discriminatory treatment of students" (AAUP, 1987, II). Teachers can manipulate students, say by threatening them with lowering their grades, and students can come to view teachers as authority figures on whom they rely for emotional support. Nevertheless, the intimacy of the counseling relationship defines and qualifies these responsibilities. By encouraging and becoming privy to intimate details of the client's personal life as a fundamental part of what they do, philosophical counselors have special responsibilities to take due care not to abuse this trust. Philosophical counselors, as recipients of confidential information about the private lives of persons, may find themselves in possession of information that raises both legal as well as moral problems.

The confidentiality between teacher and student does not normally extend to the intimate details of the student's life. When professors do become privy to personal details of the student's life, the personal information is not solicited by the professor as a part of the instructional or learning process although it may be pertinent to the student's performance in the class. Although students may also elect to disclose personal information during class and therefore share it with classmates, such information is usually disclosed without any explicit agreement among classmates that the information is to be kept confidential. This public dimension of a classroom distinguishes it from a counseling group wherein "the moral responsibility to respect confidentiality extends beyond the therapist to each group participant. Each group member shares intimate, personal information with the others, and each is dependent on the others for maintaining privacy" (Cohen & Cohen, 1999, p. 87).

Timothy Stanza's assumption that he was "only doing philosophy" and that there was parity with what he did in class was therefore erroneous. Stanza's desire to conduct philosophy outside the classroom within the institutional setting might have been legitimately satisfied by his sponsorship of a philosophy club where students could gather to do philosophy in a casual forum. However, club meetings and classes are not counseling sessions. Counseling sessions tend by their nature to be personal. As Gerd Achenbach (1995) suggests, philosophical counseling rests upon the accommodation of "subjective reason." The philosophical counselor or practitioner provides a companion for "the completely subjective personal feeling that is being excluded from all interactions with, or acknowledgments by others" (Achenbach, 1995, p. 71).

When Mary first described her life as an "existential vacuum," this was a sign that something might be seriously wrong in her life, or at least that personal and emotional problems would emerge in the course of philosophical counseling. This is not to say that Stanza, as a philosopher, had no business in entering Mary's world, but his lack of insight into the nature and significance of intimacy in the counseling relationship prevented him from realizing the risks in doing philosophical counseling with a student.

Nor would it have been sufficient for Stanza to have first assessed whether Mary's problem for which she sought philosophical counseling was compatible with teaching and counseling her simultaneously. This is so because it is often difficult to predict what will emerge in the course of counseling. For example, in Mary's case, the fact of her childhood abuse by her stepfather was not evident from the description of her presenting problem alone. Not everyone who has encountered loss of meaning in his or her life was sexually abused, and it would have been presumptuous to suppose such at the outset.

As Mary's professor, Stanza was expected to evaluate her academic performance in a manner that was fair and impartial according to objective criteria. However, as Mary's philosophical counselor, he was not expected to "grade her." Teachers are generally required to give grades, but this is no essential part of what philosophical counselors do. As both teacher and counselor of Mary, Stanza placed himself in the position of sharing in the intimate details of her life, including her abusive past, while remaining steadfastly detached in assigning her the grades she deserved.

The potential for conflict of interest in such cases should be evident. The problem is not merely whether Stanza can himself remain objective. As in the case of psychological counseling, Stanza must be concerned with whether his client can remain objective. The fact that Mary's level of participation in class diminished during the course of counseling was an indication that, in this case, Mary encountered a problem in functioning simultaneously as both student and client of Stanza. Perhaps the intimacy of the counseling relationship coupled with her vulnerability due to an abusive background and lack of a support system fostered her dependency on Stanza. Mary's deference to Stanza instead of healthy philosophical debate and disagreement may have been a result of such dependency. Stanza was remiss in executing both counseling and teaching responsibilities by failing to realize how the dynamics and interplay of the two roles could create a conflict for his client/student.

The ASPCP's *Standards of Ethical Practice* explicitly provide that philosophical practitioners should not use their affiliations with colleges and universities as a means of recruiting clients for their private practices (p. 19). Stanza's efforts at promoting his practice through circulating business cards among interested students was in clear violation of this provision. Further, because the proscription against recruiting students for private practice is not contingent upon remuneration, the fact that Stanza did not charge for his services had no bearing on the violation. The point of such a provision, as mentioned earlier in connection with psychological counseling, is to prevent the occasion for conflict of interest. While monetary incentive could lead to loss of teachers' independence of judgment in grading practices, this is not the only factor that can cause a conflict of interest. As is evident in the case at hand, Mary's independence of judgment as a student was adversely affected notwithstanding Stanza's refusal to charge her for his services.

It is true that the line between teaching and counseling may be blurred when a student comes to an instructor with a personal problem that might bear upon the student's performance in class. Thus, there may appear to be a supportive relationship between the roles of teaching and counseling of students. Granted it is sometimes difficult to know precisely where instruction leaves off and counseling begins, but it does not mean that there are no discernable boundaries and that the roles of teacher and counselor are indistinguishable. In the case at hand, such boundaries were clearly breached with Stanza's deliberate and contrived attempts at openly inviting, encouraging, and sustaining students' disclosure of their personal problems.

When an instructor (philosophy or other) finds a student in his or her office seeking counseling for personal problems, it is not conducive to promoting student welfare to turn the student away to fend for him- or herself. On the other hand, electing a dual role relationship with conflicting role expectations is not conducive to student welfare. In such instances, instructors have a responsibility to assist students in obtaining the help they need. Colleges and universities typically have counselors on staff or else have referral networks in place for these purposes. By placing students in contact with the appropriate professionals, instructors provide a valuable, supportive service to students. While not turning their backs on student needs, they do not risk sabotaging student welfare by embarking on incompatible dual roles.

Stanza's receptiveness and outright aggressive pursuit of doing philosophical counseling with his students constituted unethical behavior for which he was duly responsible. As a member of the ASPCP, it was expected that he should have been aware of the pertinent standard of practice militating against recruiting students for his practice. Stanza's lack of regard for informed consent and confidentiality were also transgressions he could easily have gleaned from the code of ethics. Further, such standards could also have been gleaned from the wider body of literature in professional ethics. For example, there are established principles governing medical and mental heath practice from which Stanza could have extrapolated. There are also well articulated codes of ethics (for instance, the American Medical Association, the American Counseling Association, and the American Psychological Association) that could have provided useful insight had Stanza taken the time to read and reflect on such literature as it might apply to his own practice. As a philosopher, and indeed one interested in applied philosophy, familiarity with such literature would not have been an unreasonable expectation.

Nevertheless, the lack of clear, articulate standards of practice for philosophical counseling might also have played a role in Stanza's case. Thus, Standard 18 of the ASPCP *Standards of Practice* states that "philosophical practitioners should avoid sexual intimacy with clients or any other form of dual role relation which might compromise the integrity of the professional relationship." However, given the fact that many philosophers are also employed by colleges and universities as teachers, it might have been useful to have explicitly codified the proscription against counseling students.

The problem of lack of specificity is largely a result of the newness of philosophical counseling as a profession. Professional codes of ethics do not typically emerge as fully mature doctrines at their inception. Rather, they evolve over time as the profession evolves and experience grows. Given a multitude of conflicting opinions at the outset about what should be included in a code of ethics for a new profession, it is easy enough to err on the side of leaving something out only to later regret it. (This has been my own experience as drafter of the ASPCP Standards.)

The foregoing considerations point to the need for expanding standards of practice to guide philosophical practitioners. Stanza's own skepticism about certification standards thus reflected a counterproductive mind-set, one that, in the end, led him to embark on a problematic dual role relationship without clear insight into the welfare, interests, and needs of his client.

Ethical Standards for Addressing Dual Role Relationships

The following rules of dual role relationships may be gathered from the two case studies and discussions provided in this chapter.[2] Although they are not intended to be exhaustive of all such possible rules, they are intended to supplement and expand on those contained in psychological and philosophical codes of ethics. The term "counselor" as used in these rules is intended to apply to *both* psychological and philosophical counseling.

General Rules Regarding Dual Role Relationships

GR 1 In considering whether a dual role relationship is morally problematic and should be avoided or terminated, counselors consider the potential for loss of the *client's* independence of judgment as well as that of their own.

GR 2 Counselors consider the adverse effects that pursuing certain types of dual role relationships (for instance, sexual relations with former clients or counseling current students) might have on the public image of their profession and avoid apparent conflicts of interest as well as actual ones.

GR 3 Counselors avoid any dual role relationship in which a serious potential exists for the use of confidential information in a manner contrary to client welfare.

GR 4 Counselors who have institutional affiliations (for instance, teach at colleges or universities or work in agencies) avoid provision of counseling to other employees with whom they have or are likely to have working relations.

GR 5 Counselors establish and maintain contact with other qualified professionals available to render competent, independent *ethics* consultation or supervision in case conflicts of interest make the counselor's own judgment questionable.

GR's 1 through 4 are based on the premise that counselors, both psychological and philosophical, should take reasonable measures to avoid all dual role relationships for which there exists serious potential for loss of independence of judgment—the client's or student's as well as the counselor's or teacher's. The aforementioned rules provide some key considerations for avoiding such relationships.

When counselors cannot feasibly avoid a conflict of interest, they should fully inform the affected clients about the conflict and, with the clients' consent, seek consultation and/or supervision from other qualified professionals (ACA, 1995, A.6.a). GR 5 has been advanced in support of the latter premise. In satisfying GR 5, psychological counselors who work in agencies should establish and maintain contact with other competent professionals who practice *outside* their agencies and are therefore more likely to provide independent, nonbiased consultation or supervision. Ones who practice in isolated rural areas have an especially compelling interest in establishing and maintaining such contacts. Philosophical counselors who teach at colleges and universities are not as likely as agency counselors to encounter a problem of bias in consulting ethicists teaching in the same (philosophy) departments, at least insofar as these counselors abstain from counseling students.

GR 3 not only proscribes self-serving and intentionally manipulative uses of confidentially disclosed client information but also the nonintentional psychological influences that such information may have on a practitioner. Thus, the philosophical or psychological counselor who simultaneously teaches and counsels the same student may find it difficult to bracket confidentially disclosed counseling information for purposes of assigning an objective grade.

As is true with respect to other rules, the present ones are intended to help in guiding counselors' decisions regarding dual role relationships but are not intended as a substitute for careful ethical reflection. For instance, although avoidance of *apparent* conflicts of interest is important for maintaining professional image, GR 2 must be applied with regard for the welfare, interests, and needs of particular clients. For example, a psychological counselor might justly tolerate public appearance of a conflict of interest in order to prevent serious harm to an identifiable client whereas such involvement purely for personal gain would be unacceptable.

GR 2 has special application to philosophical counseling arising from its novel status. Philosophical counseling is most likely to prosper as a profession and to make a significant contribution to society if it achieves a favorable public image. Philosophical counselors who engage in extra-professional relationships such as socializing with clients, pursuing sexual relations with them, or counseling those whom they instruct, risk casting dispersion on the profession itself in the public eye. As many potential consumers of philosophical counseling may not presently be aware of the existence of this upstart profession, it would be unfortunate if their first exposure to it were negative. Those who are presently in the trenches thus have a special responsibility to set a reputable example for others to follow.

GR 1 underscores that morally problematic dual role relationships can arise not only when a psychological or philosophical counselor encounters a conflict of interest but also when the *client's* independence of judgment is impaired. Because either case can result in ineffective or self-defeating counseling as well as teaching, a counselor may have a compelling reason for avoiding or terminating a dual role relationship even when it is only the client's judgment that is adversely affected.

The use of the term "qualified professional" in GR 5 refers to another competent counselor as well as to a competent professional in a related area such as a professional ethicist. The term "working relations" in GR 4 means *direct employee relations arising out of the cooperative performance of specific job-related tasks.* Such tasks include (but are not limited to) secretarial, administrative, custodial, maintenance, committee, and departmental functions. Working relations must involve *direct contact,* which means exchange of information by face-to-face contact or other channels such as e-mail, phone, or interoffice memo. In general, the more frequent and intimate the job-related contact between counselor and client, the greater the potential for loss of independence of judgment by both parties. Thus, an occasional interoffice memo may not be as risky as ongoing face-to-face contact. The term "working relation" does not apply simply because two individuals have the same employer. In a large institution such as a state university, it is possible that two employees have no working relation, but this is less likely to be true in smaller academic institutions and counseling agencies.

Rules Regarding Counseling Students

TS 1 Counselors do not engage in counseling with current students or those with whom current students have intimate relationships. Consistent with client welfare, counselors may engage in therapy with former students.

TS 2 Although counselors may not solicit students for referrals, they may accept unsolicited referrals from students.

TS 3 If, during the course of counseling, counselors' clients also become their students, counselors take reasonable steps to terminate the ensuing dual role relationships, including terminating counseling and providing appropriate referrals. Counselors inform their clients of all significant risks related to maintaining such dual role relationships and, consistent with client welfare, decline to remain in both roles. Counselors support and encourage their clients' own informed, autonomous choices in resolving the conflict.

TS 4 Counselors who ascertain that prospective clients are likely to become their students decline to accept such individuals as clients. As part of their clients' informed consent to therapy, counselors who teach inform potential students (clients whose profiles suggest that they might become students) of a professional responsibility not to engage in counseling with their students.

In TS 1, the term "intimate relationships" includes family members such as parents, stepparents, grandparents, and siblings. The term also includes significant others such as boyfriends or girlfriends, fiancees, and sexual partners. Although an individual may not have a close relationship with all family members, the probability that the family bond will implicate the student is substantial enough to justify a strict rule against counseling family members of students. Although TS 2 permits counselors to accept as clients the unsolicited referrals from students, it is noteworthy that, in concert with TS 1, such permissible, unsolicited referrals do not include individuals with whom students have intimate relationships.

TS 3 provides that counselors should take "reasonable measures" to terminate *nonelective dual role relationships* with students. In the context of counseling, this means measures that are consistent with client welfare, and that accordingly promote client trust and autonomy. The rule provides that clients be afforded maximal autonomy in deciding *how* the dual role relationship will be resolved, for example, whether the student–teacher relationship will be preserved and the counselor–client relationship terminated, or the converse.

TS 4 recognizes the utility of taking *preventative measures* to increase the likelihood that a nonelective dual role relationship with students is avoided before it is established by the student. It also makes clear, from the start, the counselor's professional responsibility not to counsel students. In this way, the counselor's move to discontinue such a relationship (should one later be established) comes as no surprise to the client.

Summary

Dual role relationships exist when a professional assumes at least one additional role with respect to a given client(s). Such relationships are morally problematic when they involve *conflicts of interest*. Conflicts of interest exist when the assumption of dual roles places a strain on the professional's ability to maintain independence of judgment. Dual role relationships can also be morally problematic when the *client's* independence of judgment is affected by her assumption of dual roles. Even if the counselor encounters no conflict of interest, the client's own inability to cope with the assumption of the dual roles can be (and usually is) a compelling reason for avoiding or terminating the dual role relationship.

Two cases have been presented and analyzed. The first case concerned a *nonelective* dual role relationship with a student in psychological counseling. Such a relationship arises when a current client assumes the role of the therapist's student. The case in point also raised issues regarding dual role relationships with former students, the family of students, and coworkers within an academic institution.

The second case concerned an *elective* dual role relationship with a student in philosophical counseling. Such a relationship arises when the therapist chooses to take on one of his or her students as a client.

Although the case analyses presented in this chapter are not intended to provide an account of all varieties of dual role relationships teachers/counselors may encounter, *rules* addressing dual (and multiple) role relationships have been extracted from these cases and given formulation concerning psychological and philosophical counseling with students. These rules collectively help to define ethical conduct for counselors who teach and for teachers who counsel. These rules cannot be mechanically applied, however. At the root of their application is moral sensitivity to the welfare, interests, and needs of clients. Without that, a counselor could not even appreciate the potential for client or student harm inherent in a problematic dual role relationship, let alone avoid it.

Notes

1. This case study has been adapted from Cohen & Cohen (1999).
2. Versions of these rules also appear in Cohen & Cohen (1999).

References

Achenbach, G. B. (1995). Philosophy, philosophical practice, and psychotherapy. In R. Lahav & M. D. Tillmanns (Eds.), *Essays on philosophical counseling*. New York: University Press of America, 61–74.

American Association of University Professors. (1987). *Statement on professional ethics*. Washington, DC.

American Counseling Association. (1995). *Code of ethics.* Alexandria, VA.

American Philosophical Practitioners Association. (1998). *Constitution* [Mission Statement]. New York.

American Society for Philosophy, Counseling, and Psychotherapy. (1997). *Standards of ethical practice.* Fort Pierce, FL: ASPCP. Available on-line: http://www.aspcp.org/Documents/Ethics/ethics.html

Cohen, E. D., & Cohen, G. S. (1999). *The virtuous counselor: Ethical practice of counseling and psychotherapy.* Pacific Grove, CA: Brooks/Cole.

Lahav, R., & Tillmanns M. D. (Eds.). (1995). *Essays on philosophical counseling.* Lanham, MD: University Press of America.

Mills, J. (1999). Ethical considerations and training recommendations for philosophical counseling. *International Journal of Applied Philosophy, 13*(2).

National Association of Social Workers. (1997). *Code of ethics.* Washington, DC.

Rogers, C. R. (1977). *Carl Rogers on personal power.* New York: Dalcourt Press.

9

RESISTING REASONABLENESS

Jane Gallop

In *Feminist Accused of Sexual Harassment*, in the chapter "Consensual Amorous Relations," I argued that whatever the actual policy on consensual relations, the *very inclusion* of such relations within harassment policies is a theoretical mistake with far-reaching practical consequences. As I wrote in the book:

> *Their very inclusion within harassment policies* indicates that consensual relations are themselves considered a type of sexual harassment. Sexual harassment has always been defined as unwanted sexual attention. But with this expansion into the realm of consensual relations, the concept can now encompass sexual attention that is reciprocated and very much welcome. This reconfigures the notion of harassment, suggesting that what is undesirable finally is not unwelcome attention but sexuality per se. Rather than some sexuality being harassing because of its *unwanted* nature, the inference is that sexuality is in and of itself harassment.[1]

I would still insist on the danger of this inclusion, a danger we all ought to be able to agree upon, *however we feel about teacher–student sex.* I hope that even those who are completely opposed to any sex between teachers and students will accept the idea that consensual sex must not be treated as harassment. If we want people to take sexual harassment seriously, it is imperative to distinguish it from any form of consenting relations, even or especially those some people might find objectionable.

Campuses continue to treat consensual relations within their harassment policies, which suggests that I must continue to make my argument. But since I've already made that argument in the book, I would like here to explore another aspect of consensual relations policies, one that seems more controversial (given the response to my book, I should perhaps say even more controversial) and which I am still trying to work out.

Every single reporter who interviewed me about the book responded to my careful explanation of the danger of treating consensual relations as harassment by glibly agreeing and then quickly moving on to ask "but what about" treating consensual relations as a "conflict of interest." And in every single interview, I felt I did not answer that question well. I am hoping finally to give this question the thoughtful response it deserves.

Let us start with a couple I know. Two women madly in love with each other for about a year now—one in her early forties, the other in her mid-thirties, both out lesbians through their adult lives. This feels to them like real love, the kind that lasts, and both have been around enough to make that sort of judgment. When one woman speaks of the other, her eyes glisten and her face radiates. In conversation she is often voicing anger at various injustices, but when the subject of their relationship comes up, the muscles in her neck and face relax, her breathing slows—witnessing this feels like a glimpse of love. Now, given my topic, I'm sure you have already guessed what I am about to tell you. Not only are these women lovers, they are also teacher and student. Both are in the anthropology department of a state university in the Pacific Northwest. The younger one is a doctoral student writing her dissertation; the older a tenured professor supervising that dissertation. After they were already working together, they found themselves in love. They chose both to act on their feelings for each other and to maintain their productive working relation. They thus are proceeding in complete and utter violation of their university's policy on consensual relations. Their love must remain a secret. If they were discovered, it could destroy both of their careers. Yet they are planning to spend their lives together.

This couple has the good luck to work in a department that is unusually lesbian friendly. Both have long lived comfortably in a lesbian subculture. Yet they find themselves now in a dark and scary closet.

As I have emphasized, perhaps to the point of some sappiness, these two women find themselves not just in heat but in love. In the sort of love that makes them constitute themselves as a couple. Now, although some of us have reservations about coupledom, it is worth noting that, in the context of today's academic policies, it is the romantic couple that runs the greatest risk.

Consensual relations policies actually pose little threat to all the teachers and students who continue to have the occasional fling, the moment of passion, the friendly "shtup". Not only is it much easier to hide a casual or short-term sexual connection, it might even be sexier to hide it.

But something in the nature of the romantic couple longs for public recognition. Marriage, of course, immediately comes to mind. Although we may indeed be suspicious of that peculiar institution, we probably want at least the possibility of having our love recognized. We might not want marriage, but we don't want the closet either.

I find this antiromantic twist in contemporary academic policy quite interesting, but it is not really what I need my couple to exemplify. They're here because I need their romance to disrupt the consensus of reasonableness which currently dominates the conversation on teacher–student sex.

Whereas teacher–student sex has certainly been portrayed in the lurid tones of incest and pedophilia, suggesting it to be an abomination against nature for any teacher and any student to lay together or even play together, nowadays the official discussion is more likely to be in the moderate and legalistic tones of "conflict of interest." Although it seems relatively easy to demonstrate the dangers of erotophobic moralizing, it is not so easy to voice objection to policies that appear designed not to prohibit sexuality but simply to avoid "conflict of interest." While it may be heroic to appear prosex and antimoralism, it's not so cool to seem irresponsible and unreasonable.

In 1990, the university where I teach had a policy stating that "consenting amorous or sexual relationships between instructor and student are unacceptable." That was it, simply "unacceptable," a blanket prohibition on sex between two categories of people, an absolute generality which could even mean that because teaching assistants find themselves in the indelicate situation of being at once both instructors and students, the policy would forbid them from masturbating.

Sometime around 1993 our university became aware of the immoderate nature of this policy and adopted a new, thoroughly reasonable policy. The new policy recognizes that students and teachers will enter into amorous relations and tells us what to do when that happens. The faculty member should notify her dean in writing of the relationship and arrange to avoid conflict of interest by immediately giving up any supervisory or evaluative relation to the student. If the student is in the teacher's class, arrangements should be made for someone else to grade the student; if the professor is on a graduate student's committee, she should immediately be replaced by another faculty member.

The new policy represents a clear advance over the old one. From just about any point of view, it is more practical, more realistic, more liberal, easier to live with, easier to enforce—not to mention less vulnerable to jokes and ridicule than the primitive version. It sounds more like a policy, less like a taboo.

As we moved from the early to the mid-1990s, the nationwide trend was toward this sort of reasoning. More and more campuses adopted such moderate policies, and everyone seemed to agree that the issue was not really sex but rather conflict of interest.

I felt disarmed by the new policies. They did not say sex was bad, only that if you had to have sex, you needed to stop being teacher and student. It was all so reasonable, who could resist?

Well, that lesbian couple I was just telling you about, for one. They work at a university with a similar policy. When they realized they were in love, all they had to do was stop working together: the student find another dissertation director, the professor resign from the student's committee. Had they done that, their love would have been legit, their careers safe. But instead they chose to violate the policy and risk their careers.

In the realm of the old moralistic taboo, the question would have been, how could they sleep together? But in our new, apparently less moralistic terms, the scandalous question is, how *could* they refuse to do the reasonable thing?

It is precisely this refusal to comply that put them here. Their disobedience suggests that they might help us see beyond the new policies' seeming universal reasonableness.

Let's look at this situation from the student's point of view. The student is in her mid-thirties; she entered the doctoral program after having worked for more than a decade as a well-paid, respected professional. Her research interests had grown out of her professional experience. When she began her doctoral studies, she was dismayed to find herself "treated like a student," by which she means treated like someone who has no knowledge, whose professional experience does not count, a receptacle for the professors' knowledge, in short, she felt treated like a child.

In contrast with the general attitude in her department, there was one professor who treated her like an adult and respected her professional experience, the knowledge she brought with her, and her ideas. This respect did not preclude criticism. On the contrary, this professor was more critical of her writing, setting higher standards and demanding more than did the other faculty.

The criticism was intrinsic to the respect; it meant she didn't feel she was being babied, patronized, and spoken down to. She chose to work with the one professor who regarded her as an adult. This teacher didn't impose her own ideas on the student but rather fostered the development of the student's thinking. The student felt this was the sort of relation in which she could work best, in which she would do her best work.

Our student here is, admittedly, a particular sort of student, a strong-willed, highly motivated older student who comes into graduate school with a clear sense of purpose. She needed a particular sort of mentoring relation, one that would not insult her sense of her own considerable experience. She found that in only one teacher in her department; she knew she would not be able to replace it.

For this student, the reasonable policy demanded an unreasonable sacrifice. To be in compliance, she was supposed to find a new professor with whom to work. To change dissertation directors was, however, no small thing: It meant putting her work at risk.

This unusually self-possessed doctoral student found one professor who respected her as an adult, who recognized her as a person. And that teacher who recognized her—who saw her worth, her merit, and her power—desired her and came to love her. The one professor who saw her as a person rather than a student came to want more of a relation to that person than one defined by the roles of teacher and student. I want to suggest that the very recognition and respect which made this such a productive professional relation are inseparable from the possibility of a fling in love. The policy asks the student to make what it assumes is a reasonable choice: Would you rather love this woman or work with her? The policy demands that she sort out her feelings and decide whether those feelings are sexual or intellectual, professional or romantic. Do I love her for how she teaches me, or do I love her so much that I want to replace her with another teacher? The policy does not recognize that we might not want to have a reasonable, moderate relation either to our love or to our work.

This couple takes us outside the logic of the policy. Whereas the policy represents the norm, they inhabit the extreme of both the amorous and the pedagogical relation: In each other they feel they've found their one true love; they have an intense one-on-one working relation which likewise denies the possibility of substitution. This sense of "the only one" bespeaks passion and represents a logic alien to the world of reasonable calculation where the policy makes its sense. In the world of their relation, the reasonableness of choice and substitution can only represent loss, tragedy, betrayal, and incomprehension. I take this couple as exemplary not because they are the norm but because they represent an extreme we disregard at great risk. Where the policy would regulate us based on a norm, I would resist this regulation in the name of a relation far better than the norm. I see in this extreme a sort of ideal, an old-fashioned romantic ideal, that work and life, mind and body, thought and passion can come together across the divide which too often separates them. Such separations are regrettably all too normal in academic life: Do we want an ethics based on that sad norm? Do we want policies to enforce that norm? To punish those queer enough to pursue the ideal?

I'd like to look at consensual relations policy from the standpoint of this extreme relation. I initially signaled the couple's exorbitance by introducing them as "madly in love." While I want to hold on to the romantic force of their excessiveness, I would now like to situate it within their academic relation. I want to suggest that from the point of view of the pedagogical norm, the dissertator–supervisor relation is already in itself an exorbitant relation.

First of all, because a dissertator is, by definition, at the very edge of student identity, literally at the end of her studies, the dissertator is no longer simply a student, already within the rite of passage to professor. Dissertator is a liminal identity: A dissertator is a student who cannot be comfortable with being a student. Although our exemplary dissertator returned to graduate school with more independence than the norm, impatience with being treated "like a student" is no doubt endemic to dissertator status.

The student who is no longer quite a student works within an unusual pedagogical relation. Whereas the most common pedagogical relation lasts for a few months, with teacher and student meeting only in the company of dozens of other students, this is a long-term, one-on-one relation. Dissertator and supervisor commonly work together for several years and normally meet tête-à-tête. If we take as the norm the relation between a student and the instructor whose course she takes for one term, the relation between dissertator and supervisor is exorbitant.

In the realm of pedagogy, the dissertator–supervisor couple represents an extreme like the romantic couple in the realm of amorous relations. My point in drawing this analogy is not to suggest that dissertator–supervisor pairs are latent romantic couples. The romantic couple is here rather to put us in the mood to prize excessiveness. The moderate policies with their reasonable concern about conflict of interest are in fact based on a conception of teaching as an uncaring, impersonal relation, a relation where simple calculations of interest are possible, teaching reduced to its lowest common denominator.

Earlier I noted that current academic relations policies are in fact more hospitable to casual sex than to serious romance. I see this now not as an anomaly but as entirely consistent with the norm of casual, short-term relations upon which the policies are based. In the view of these policies, it is normal human behavior to contract relations, whether amorous *or* pedagogical, which involve minimal entanglement, relations where it is easy to maintain separation between the parties, which don't involve excessive investment or confusion of interest, relations easy to dissolve should things become complicated.

Upon reading an early draft of this chapter, one of my dissertators, who is rather militantly antimonogamous, was bothered by its celebration of the romantic couple, its privileging the couple over casual sex in our contemporary antipromiscuous era. Her query is well taken, and one to which I would like to respond.

My argument is with the casual, no-entanglement norms of academic policy. In this context, in the context of this argument, in the context of academic policy, I feel romantic love can provide a discourse with the power to counter the businesslike, legalistic reasonableness which would regulate our pedagogical relations. While in the amorous realm long-term, one-on-one is certainly normative, in the pedagogical realm it is practically queer.

My celebration of romance here is not about sex; it's about teaching. My exemplary couple resisted the consensus of reasonableness not by having sex but by refusing to give up their pedagogical relation. I too want to resist contemporary policy by prizing pedagogical relations. Whereas the policies take as their model the standard casual short-term pedagogical encounter, I prefer the dissertator–supervisor relation because it deviates from the norm in an ideal way, a way that allows us to think about pedagogy not as it all too often is but as it sometimes can be, fortunately.

I hope my dissertator will understand what I'm saying here not through her sexual politics but through her pedagogical experience, that she will understand what I'm saying through the complicated, intense, and productive relation we share. She and I are not in love, we're not having sex (at least not with each other), but we have been working together for five years, since she entered our doctoral program. She took her first class from me in the fall of 1993 and two more graduate seminars in the next year. Four years ago I chaired her academic review; two and a half years ago, her preliminary examinations. Since then we've been working together on her dissertation. In those years, we've met countless times one on one for advising, to talk about her writing, and more recently to prepare her for the job market.

It is of course my role to evaluate her. When she took my classes, I graded her papers and oral presentations and gave her semester grades. On her examinations, I had to say whether or not I thought she should pass. At her dissertation defense I had to pronounce whether or not I thought she had earned a Ph.D. In my evaluations, I embody some version of professional standards, judging whether or not she has met those standards.

Teaching her is not, however, merely evaluation. By advising her on how to revise her writing, how to prepare for her examinations, I help her meet my standards, get her ready to pass my evaluations. The supervisor is not only judge but also coach.

When academic relations policies worry about "conflict of interest," they are thinking about the professor's evaluation of the student. If the professor cares too much about the student, loves or desires the student, or feels hurt and rejected by the student, then it will affect the evaluation—taint it with subjectivity.

But can a professor objectively evaluate the work of someone whom she has been coaching for years? I would argue that the supervisor is, by the very nature of her role, inevitably too close, too invested, and definitely cares too much. I want my dissertator to succeed because she is "my student," because her success reflects on me, her achievements afford me prestige. My considerable investment of time and energy in her progress as well as my narcissistic investment in my own excellence as a teacher make me an interested party in the dissertator's success.

The policy assumes that if we can separate pedagogy from amorous relations, we can avoid conflict of interest. But thinking about the relation between dissertator and supervisor suggests that no policy can shield us from the potential for conflict of interest, that in fact conflict of interest goes with the territory.

Supervising a dissertator not only involves evaluation and advising; it also includes actual advocacy, an aspect most prominent during the student's job seeking. When my dissertator went on the job market this fall, I advised her on her application letters, her vita, and other supporting material. But my most important task was to write a letter of recommendation for her dossier, to say what I could to persuade hiring committees of her excellence. This letter, a standard part of the dissertation supervisor's job description, is an act of advocacy whose conflicted relation to evaluation bears remarking.

Everyone complains that recommendations are inflated prose, impossible exercises in which the writer is forced to both exaggerate and convey authenticity. I consider this stylistic problem symptomatic of a basic contradiction in the professor's position. We are supposed to write as if we were objective evaluators, judging the student by the application of professional standards, but we are in fact writing as devoted advocates trying to get our students jobs. We cannot admit that we are writing as advocates, a fact everyone nonetheless knows. The recommendation writer's relation to her student is a devotion that dare not speak its name.

We don't need to fall in love with our dissertators to find ourselves in a compromising situation. Our academic relation in itself is enough to produce conflict of interest. The conflict is not between pedagogy and love but between two aspects of the pedagogical relation, evaluation and advocacy.

In mid-December I got a phone call from my dissertator, announcing she had gotten an interview at the MLA (the annual convention of the Modern Language Association). She called knowing her news would make me happy, and it did. I felt very much like I did when I myself got job interviews.

A few days later I got a similar call from another of my grad students. Same tone of excitement in her voice, exact same opening statement— "I have good news"—except this student was not on the job market. Not quite a dissertator yet, this student is currently working with me to prepare for her preliminary examinations. She called to announce that all her 101 students had passed. This was her first time teaching English 101, a freshman composition course in which the instructor does not determine who passes and in which a significant number of students fail.

Having one's students pass freshman comp at our university turns out to be not unlike having one's students get MLA interviews. In both cases the student succeeds in the eyes of outside evaluators, professional colleagues who don't know the student except on paper. In both cases, the actual teacher advises and roots for the student but is outside the evaluation process.

The first-time 101 TA was overjoyed her students all passed, and she wanted to share her sense of accomplishment with me, her teacher. When she phoned, her students' achievement became my student's achievement too. This almost uncanny redoubling between her pride in her students and my pride in her suggests a connection between the two extremes of teaching in our department, between English 101 and English 990 (the number under which she is registered as my dissertator).

I've been talking about pedagogy in 990 for a while; I'd like now to tell you a bit about 101. In fact, I have never taught 101, but I have learned a good deal about it from my dissertators who all have. As they have explained to me, freshman composition at our university is organized to isolate evaluation from all other aspects of the student–teacher relation. At the end of the semester, the students' writing is evaluated by other 101 instructors. The actual teacher functions only as a coach, preparing the students for evaluation by someone else, and then possibly as an advocate. For example, the TA who phoned to say all her students passed went on to correct herself: Actually, two had not passed, but she had appealed and they had passed on appeal.

A teacher who cares about her students, who knows how hard they have worked, knows the sort of obstacles they have faced; in short, a teacher who sees students as people may not be able to evaluate their work objectively. In freshman composition, this problem is solved by divorcing the functions of evaluation and coaching.

I believe that the conflict addressed by the composition-grading structure is a conflict endemic to pedagogy, the conflict between judging and caring. *And* that this is also the conflict of interest addressed by consensual relations policies, designed to keep instructors from evaluating students about whom the instructor cares too much to be objective. In fact, our composition administrators seem to have hit upon a solution to pedagogical conflict of interest that is *essentially the same* as our campus's consensual relations policy.

In both cases, the structure is designed to guard against a teacher grading a person she cares about. But the recognition that this can be a problem not only in cases of amorous relations but also in the normal course of teaching composition suggests that it is a problem not likely to be solved by anything as simple as separating out those instructors romantically involved with their students. What consensual relations policy presumes to be a conflict between love and pedagogy is actually a conflict *within* pedagogy.

Earlier I insisted that I wanted to view pedagogy from the standpoint of the dissertator–supervisor relation. And although this excursion into freshman comp may seem to have taken us from one extreme to the other of the university teaching spectrum, we have, in fact, never left the confines of the relation to my dissertators. As I specified when introducing 101 into this chapter, everything I know about it I know from them.

A look at 101 provided me with something quite useful for this chapter—a confirmation of the claim that conflict of interest is intrinsic to pedagogy—and I got that look at 101 in and through my relation to dissertators. It is this peculiar structure which this chapter would propose as a model. I propose we look at university pedagogy in general through the lens of the quite particular dissertator–supervisor relation.

Such a method is undoubtedly perverse. Perhaps even literally. Rather than reach a general understanding via the norm, I choose to theorize via a relatively rare and marginal case, but it is one that *happens to be my own personal pedagogical preference.*

I would like to rephrase a remark I once made in haste, in the heat of the moment, one that was widely misunderstood. Seven years ago, at another lesbian and gay academic colloquium, I stated that graduate students were my sexual preference. Today, after thinking it through, I would say rather that "dissertators are my pedagogical preference."

With this chapter, I am trying to theorize pedagogy in a way that resists the norm and that bases itself in my own particular preference, a way of theorizing I might want to call queer if that word didn't already have another meaning in the present context. Rather than queer theorizing then, let me call it exorbitant, or maybe romantic.

I prefer teaching dissertators precisely because they are liminal students, students who do not comfortably fit the role, who are not simply students. For example, dissertators are generally in the indelicate situation of being both students and teachers. This means teaching someone who also has some experience on the other side of the pedagogical relation. When I work with dissertators on the obstacles in their writing, they often come to understand what I'm saying when they realize its resemblance to things they tell their composition students. Of course, this doesn't mean our roles are interchangeable, but it does mean our relation is not as unidimensional as it would be with someone who is more simply a student.

Not only do I often talk about teaching with my dissertators, comparing notes from our different but related practices, I also sometimes get help from them with my own writing. Such is the situation which led to my dissertator complaining that in this chapter I privilege the romantic couple. The fact that a dissertator is someone who can help me with my writing by judging it (in this case, negatively) suggests the greater range and flexibility of this relation, one in which I am not always teaching and she not always learning.

I prefer teaching someone who is not just a student to me. I prefer a wider, more diverse, more human relation. Although that is my preference, I am not trying to claim it as the pedagogical norm. Most of my teaching is not as fulfilling, as intense, as rounded. In fact, most of my teaching unfortunately resembles the casual, short-term, impersonal, uncaring relation that is the norm.

I believe, however, that it would benefit us to take as our pedagogical model not the norm but the best. Whereas impatience with student identity is, as I said, endemic to dissertators, it is not restricted to them. There are sometimes in our classes, not only grad but undergrad, students who don't want to be "treated like students"—students who are older, or just bolder, who want to learn but find the student role demeaning and constrictive. I think our pedagogical policies ought to honor these students.

This chapter takes as its pedagogical model the couple I began with. It is, to be sure, an exorbitant model. Doubly exorbitant: as far from the norm of dissertator–supervisor relations as the standard dissertator–supervisor relation is from the campus pedagogical norm.

This amorous couple is my model because they prize their pedagogical relation unreasonably and at considerable risk. I am hoping that by showing us the exorbitant value of their pedagogical relation, they will help us view pedagogy with a less cost-effective, more romantic gaze.

Notes

This chapter was originally written for a February 1998 symposium at the Center for Lesbian and Gay Studies at the City University of New York Graduate Center. I want to thank Jill Dolan and Nancy Miller for that invitation. I would also like to thank my dissertation advisees Astrid Henry and Gary Weissman for their critical readings of this chapter.

1. Jane Gallop, *Feminist Accused of Sexual Harrassment* (Durham: Duke UP, 1997), p. 32.

A Response,
by Eric Hayot & Jeff King

We are, it would seem, uniquely positioned to respond to Jane Gallop's chapter, "Resisting Reasonableness." You see, Jane is our teacher, we her students for five or six years now. We are both currently writing our dissertations, which she supervises. But our individual relationships with Jane are each more than that of teacher and student, supervisor and advisee; we're good friends. And like many good friends, we're a bit infatuated with each other. We wouldn't work so well together if we weren't.

We both like to think that when we're at our best, when we're in love with working together, we approximate Jane's ideal pedagogical relationship, the "exorbitant" and "unreasonable" one exemplified by the lesbian couple in her essay. Although we don't have sex with Jane and aren't having what they call a "romance," our time spent together is frequently both sexy and romantic, to the delight of us all and to the benefit of our work.

At the same time, however, the kind of relationship Jane has with us, she has with other students as well, her graduate students at least. Those relationships no doubt vary by virtue of the different personalities involved, but they nonetheless appear to be similar to ours on many levels. And so our relationship, the one each of us has with Jane, the one undone by the very "we" of this response, is not unique. As a teacher, Jane has many students, many friends, many loves. We are compelled to share her (and not only with each other) and she is compelled to acknowledge our other loves, teacherly and otherwise. Even though our relationships may at times provoke the emotions we recognize as typical of being in "true" love, neither of us plan to spend our lives with Jane, nor she with us. Ultimately, then, our relationships can only approximate that of her ideal lesbian couple, who "in each other . . . feel they've found their one true love."

This isn't to say that our relationships to Jane are lacking; we both agree that most of the time they're pretty ideal. Sometimes we like not only having our relationships to Jane but also sharing our relationship to her with one another. We have taken great pleasure, for instance, in writing this response together, and there exists between us, as among some of Jane's other students, the feeling that we are part of a group affair. That is part of why we chose Jane to be our adviser.

Her other students do complicate things though. Sharing Jane with other students and with each other means that we also get to know the less pleasant side effects of such relationships: There is jealousy, possessiveness, and competition. Such moments lead us at times to wish that we each were Jane's only student, or at least her favorite, rather than simply one of many. We recognize this as a longing to be in something like the relationship between the two lesbians of Jane's essay. But that hasn't happened, and in the end that's probably the way we want it.

Such a multiple relationship nonetheless raises a question about the ideal Jane proposes in her chapter, the lesbian relationship that "denies the possibility of substitution." If the intimately conjoined romantic couple exemplifies the ideal pedagogical relation, as Jane suggests it should, can the teacher in that relation ever have more than one student at a time? All joking aside, we wonder whether the exclusivity of the romantic couple doesn't prevent us from developing a fuller, more inclusive model of the ideal pedagogical relationship, an ideal that can afford us the space to love a number of students and a number of teachers (not to mention other people) at the same time. Which brings to mind a related concern we have about Jane's chapter: "its privileging of the couple over casual sex in our contemporary antipromiscuous era," as she puts it, a criticism made by another of Jane's students. Indeed, Jane's ideal couple would seem to afford little space for "casual or short-term sexual [and academic] connection." They seem unlikely to be out looking for a one-night stand, unlikely to be looking for a little extra loving on the side. They seem pretty content in their coupledom, perhaps even longing for the possibility of "marriage," of having their love "publicly recognized." Their couple-dom, in fact, at least as Jane characterizes it, would seem to exclude third parties, the menage (sexual or academic), the friendly "shtup" with some-one else.

Jane justifies her focus on the romantic couple to the exclusion of casual sex by arguing that the ideal of the "long-term, one-on-one" ro-mance can "counter the businesslike, legalistic reasonableness that would regulate our pedagogical relations," that the romantic couple, normative in the culture at large, is non-normative, indeed, "practically queer," in the context of pedagogy as usual. Although this is certainly true, we find ourselves wanting room for a more open relationship—not just because we live in an "antipromiscuous" era but because Jane's model of the romantic couple doesn't quite ring true for us.

Several times in her chapter Jane refers to the ideal pedagogical rela-tionship as "queer," and yet she ultimately rejects this term because it has "another meaning in today's academic context." While she settles for calling the relationship "exorbitant or maybe romantic" we want to pro-pose retaining the word "queer" to mark the ideal pedagogical (and per-haps sexual) relationship. By "queer," however, we would mean some-thing different than Jane does. We mean it as the name of a different kind of relationship than that of the lesbian couple. Our queer couple (be they lesbian, gay, bi, or straight) would have what they used to call an "open marriage," a long-term commitment to one another that not only admits but enjoys other lovers and other learners.

10

CONFLICT OF INTEREST
IN ANTHROPOLOGY

Merrilee Salmon

An anthropologist, Richard Wilk, who works with the Kekchi people of Southern Belize, published research on the history of their occupation of the area (Wilk, 1999). His sources indicated that during the nineteenth century, the Kekchi moved into vacated territory that had once been occupied by Chol Maya speakers. The latter group had been forcibly removed at the time of European contact. Kekchi lived on that land in a government-designated "forest reserve" for about 150 years without interference. Their occupation was threatened in the 1990s, however, when the Belize Government sold logging concessions for the forest reserve. Some logging companies proceeded to clear-cut the land. Legal battles followed between the government on one side and environmentalists and Kekchi on the other. In one court case, the government cited Wilk's publications as scientific evidence for the claim that the Kekchi had no ancestral claims on the land because they were "recent" immigrants. As an anthropologist whose primary ethical duty was to avoid harm to his host people, Wilk was put in the position of seeing this interest conflict with his professional interest in scholarly publication. His attempt to resolve this problem was philosophically perceptive and scientifically sound. Wilk (1999) challenged some current assumptions about land tenure and rights of ownership and introduced an historically better informed conception of property as a "bundle of rights that can be divided from each other." He proposed a system of *stakeholding* that "acknowledges the legitimate interests of diverse individuals and groups" and "recognizes that all rights to natural resources are partial and divisible" (p. 373). Wilk argues that the goodwill on the part of anthropologists is not sufficient to avoid harm. They also need good science. By questioning basic assumptions and being clear about theoretical principles, they are in a much better position to avoid and resolve conflicts of interest.

Anthropologists face many such conflicts of interest. In this chapter, I examine the nature and sources of these conflicts as well as some institutional and individual attempts to resolve them.

Introduction

Anthropology is the study of humans—who we are and how we came to be as we are. The discipline embraces the physical, cultural, social, linguistic, ecological, and economic aspects of human life both in the present and back to prehistoric times. Interest in human origins and the variety of physical appearances, customs, and languages is at least as old as human history. Herodotus, for example, who wrote in the fifth century B.C., was an acute observer and reporter of anthropological detail. Academic departments of anthropology, however, are relatively new. Franz Boas founded the first one in the United States at Columbia University, where he was appointed in 1896. In England, E. B. Tylor was the first professor of anthropology. He took up this position at Oxford in 1896, where he had been reader in anthropology since 1884.

Traditionally, anthropology is divided into four major subareas:

1. Physical, or biological, anthropology studies how modern humans came to assume their present physical form, and how their biological characteristics determine their relationships to the rest of their environment.
2. Social and cultural anthropology studies the diverse human social and cultural arrangements, including interactions among various social and cultural systems, interactions among the members of these systems, and interactions with the environment.
3. Linguistic anthropology studies human development and diversity through the history and structure of human languages.
4. Archaeology studies the development and diversity of humans through the remains of their material culture.

Even from this brief description of anthropology, it is easy to see that work in this field inevitably involves interactions with other humans with diverse goals and interests.

Anthropological fieldwork has in this century become the *sine qua non* of professional anthropological training. Boas in the United States and B. Malinowski in Britain, both masterful fieldworkers, developed the techniques of participant observation for gathering and recording anthropological data. They required their students, who included the future founders of departments of anthropology in many major universities, to undergo this rite of passage. Fieldwork requires a close cooperative effort engaging the anthropologist, the people studied, and often an interpreter or informant as well. Even when the people studied are no longer alive, as in archaeology, anthropologists need the cooperation of the host people on whose land they work, and who may even be descendants of the people studied. To do anthropological research or to apply their anthropological skills, anthropologists also regularly depend on the cooperation of coworkers, students, patrons, employers, curators of collections of cultural resources, and government agencies, among others.

In all human interactions—from brief conversational interchanges between strangers to the more complex familial interactions, relations among workers, relations between employees and employer, relations between students and teachers, physicians and patients—each participant has a set of expectations regarding appropriate behavior on the part of the others involved in the interaction. These expectations are widely agreed on and are acquired as we are socialized or habituated to various situations. Sometimes only minor social friction results from disappointed expectations, but in other situations important negative consequences may result. When we anticipate that serious harm would result from failure to comply with what is expected, we regard the obligation to meet the expectations as a *duty*.

To say that appropriate behavior is widely agreed on is not to say that agreement is universal or unproblematic. Differing expectations, misunderstandings, and disagreements of all sorts are common—particularly when dealing with other cultures—and the application of blame for failure to meet responsibilities is a highly negotiable matter. Nevertheless, the duty to behave in appropriate ways toward people with diverse interests adds an ethical dimension that permeates both anthropological research and applied anthropology.

Concern about the social responsibility of scientists is for the most part a post-World War II phenomenon in such disciplines as physics. However, anthropologists have been aware of the ethical dimensions of their profession from the beginning. This is not surprising as their daily work involves them in complex human interactions with the people they study. Boas (1940), for example, found the racist evolutionary theories of the anthropology of his day morally repugnant as well as scientifically indefensible. These theories ranked different ethnic groups according to their evolutionary "progress." One popular scale involved dividing human evolution into stages proceeding from savagery to barbarism to civilization, with characteristic markers for each stage. Other scales ranked contemporary peoples in terms of their degree of "civilization" or cultural achievements, putting Australian aborigines in the lowest position and northern Europeans in the highest. Boas's anthropological investigations of the people of the Baffin Islands and the American Northwest convinced him that such scales were inappropriate and demeaning. The scales did not reflect the resourcefulness and sophistication of the people he studied. Boas rejected the idea that culture is attributable only to so-called high civilizations, such as those of western Europe in his own day. He argued instead that each ethnic group has a culture that needs to be understood in terms of its own development in a particular historical and environmental context.

While Britain was still expanding its empire before World War II, concerns about ethics in anthropology were closely tied to the role anthropologists played in supporting the colonial government. The British government funded anthropological research as part of its policy of "indirect rule." The British tried to govern their farflung colonies by enlisting the support of local political structures. Anthropologists were employed by London's Home Office to help them understand tribal cultures and gain access to their political structures. The government depended on anthropologists' advice about how to preserve the stability of local arrangements, especially in Africa and India. The students of Malinowski and others who went into the field to do research thus had two professional goals: to carry out their own research programs and to provide the government with useful information. Although the expression "conflict of interest" was not used to describe these possibly conflicting goals, anthropologists were sensitive to claims that they were being used as instruments of oppression in the colonial society. They essentially denied that they faced a conflict and maintained that in the process of pursuing their own scientific studies they worked to protect native custom and tradition (Kuklick, 1991, chap. 5).

In the United States, too, conflict of interest (though not designated as such) was recognized as a problem in situations in which anthropologists were employed by the government. In 1919, Boas caused a furor when he accused four anthropologists of using their profession as a cover to spy for the U.S. government in Central America (Stocking 1968, p. 273). Boas regarded the behavior of the four anthropologists as a betrayal of science and condemned them for violating the most fundamental principles of professional ethics. Boas, who published his denunciation in *The Nation*, was then himself censured and threatened with expulsion from the American Anthropological Association for this act. Stocking's (1968, chap. 11) discussion of Boas's condemnation argues that whereas patriotism was the official reason given for censuring Boas, other motives such as professional jealousy and a scientific reaction against cultural anthropology were operative. Boas's negative views about whether anthropologists could serve as military advisers and maintain their ethical principles reemerged during the era of the war in Vietnam, this time with greater support from anthropologists. For some at that time, ethical behavior was simply defined as refusing to work for a government involved in military action (Berreman, 1968).

Professional Codes of Ethics in Anthropology

To gain some insight on contemporary anthropologists' views on ethics, and particularly on the problem of *conflict of interest*, we turn now to the ethical code that has been developed by the main professional society of anthropologists in the United States: the American Anthropological Association (AAA). The AAA was founded in 1902. It is a democratic and nonexclusive organization with approximately 5,000 members, consisting of professional anthropologists from all subareas of anthropology, as well as students and other interested persons. The AAA works to promote anthropological research and to disseminate anthropological knowledge. It tries to represent and speak for all members of this diverse body of people who have anthropological training or a special interest in the field.

The AAA Code of Ethics is a work in progress that has been reviewed and amended many times.[1] The stated purpose of the most recent version is to educate anthropologists about the ethical issues that arise in their field and to try to give them tools to develop an ethical framework for doing anthropology. The code is one element of a comprehensive program in ethical education for anthropologists. The newsletter of the AAA regularly publishes case studies of ethical dilemmas.

While recognizing that anthropologists interact with and have duties to many different groups, including sponsors, students, and fellow anthropologists, the AAA has always been concerned most particularly with the duties of anthropologists to the persons whom they study. In the previous AAA statement on ethics, the "Principles of Professional Responsibility" (adopted in 1971 and amended through November, 1986), the first principle consisted of three related statements: (1) In research, anthropologists' paramount responsibility is to those they study. (2) When there is a conflict of interest, these individuals must come first. (3) Anthropologists must do everything in their power to protect the physical, social, and psychological welfare and to honor the dignity and privacy of those studied. This principle clearly recognizes both the potential for conflict anthropologists face as participant observers and the special duty owed to host people. The first statement also implicitly suggests that anthropologists may have other professional duties that put some strain on the duty to those they study. The second statement gives straightforward advice about which duties must prevail when there is a conflict of interest but does not say what constitutes a conflict of interest.

In the early 1990s, a commission was charged to review the Principles of Professional Responsibility to examine its purposes, content, and procedures. The commission discussed its work with ethics committees of other professional societies, and with people knowledgeable about ethics in the professions, including the philosopher B. Gert. Gert's (1992) "Morality, moral theory, and applied and professional ethics" provided some of the guidelines that the anthropologists incorporated into their report.

When the commission issued its final report in 1995, the primary focus of attention remained the relationships between researchers and the people whom they studied. The commission felt, however, that the earlier principle concerning this relationship needed to be modified and clarified to take better account of new situations and the varied roles of anthropologists in contemporary society. The commission found the last sentence of the principle particularly problematic, in part because of doubts about how and why anthropologists should protect and be advocates for the people with whom they worked and who they studied. The duty to protect suggests paternalism and seems to assume that anthropologists know best what the people they study need. The commission found the assumptions implicit in the third statement inconsistent with the work of contemporary anthropologists, who no longer typically study small groups of people in settings isolated from contact with the outside world. In addition, it is unclear why all groups studied by anthropologists, which include, for example, terrorists and drug dealers, are deserving of protection.

The final report of the commission tried to clarify responsibilities of anthropologists by distinguishing two sets of responsibilities, one to people who provide information and another to people who are studied by anthropologists. In the case of informants, the report maintained that anthropologists have the duty to protect the identity of people who provide information, but it notes the difficulty of maintaining anonymity in some circumstances. It recommends that anthropologist warn informants that this is so. To the second group, the people studied, the duties include "doing no harm or wrong, full disclosure and informed consent, warnings of possible outcomes (good or bad) of the research for the people involved, and a careful weighing of the risks and benefits for the people being studied." The report rejected the idea that anthropologists have a duty to play any advocacy role in relation to the people studied.

Interestingly, the duties of anthropologists to the host people that are outlined in the final report closely resemble duties that other ethical codes specify for medical researchers who enroll patients in clinical trials. Conflicts of interest often arise in clinical trials, and despite many obvious differences between medical research and anthropological research, both types of conflict involve issues of informed consent and full disclosure.[2] Some argue that any stigma that might attach to conflict of interest can be minimized by obtaining informed consent of the persons in the clinical trial, but this issue is controversial in both anthropology and medicine (Jonas, 1969).

The "conflict of interest" statement from the anthropologists' earlier Principles of Professional Responsibility is not explicitly mentioned in the commission's final report. Section G of the report, however, discusses the broader problem of conflicting ethical demands.

The report recognizes that the varied and concurrently occupied professional roles of most anthropologists—researchers, teachers, appliers of anthropological knowledge—as well as their extraprofessional societal roles, make them subject to conflicting ethical demands. Instead of resolving all conflicting ethical demands by stating simply that duties to the people studied always take precedence over any other duties, the report recognizes the complexity of determining the consequences of various courses of action and the many factors to be considered in making moral decisions. It advises anthropologists to weigh carefully all the ethical demands before deciding a course of action and recommends forgoing or ending participation in a project if on balance the researcher decides that the project is unethical

For several years after the publication of the committee's final report, AAA members discussed and reflected on its recommendations in symposia at meetings of the AAA and in the AAA newsletter. In June 1998, the membership of the AAA approved a revised Code of Ethics.

The new code has separate sections of guidelines for research, teaching, and application. Whereas it gives most attention to the research section (III), it states explicitly in the section on applied anthropology (V) that the same ethical guidelines apply to all anthropological work. Moreover, the code interprets anthropological research broadly. "Anthropological research" in this context covers applied and proprietary research as well as basic and pure research and does not discriminate between publicly and privately funded research.

In accord with the earlier principles, and the final report of the committee charged with examining that document, the ethical guidelines for research in the revised code once again emphasize the responsibilities of anthropologists to the people they study. The new code, however, broadens the scope of the principles to address specifically issues faced by physical anthropologists and archaeologists. The code states first of all the obligation "to avoid harm or wrong, understanding that the development of knowledge can lead to change which may be positive or negative for the people or animals worked with or studied" (III. A). Other obligations stated in the same section on research include respecting the well-being of humans and nonhuman primates and working to conserve historical, archaeological, and fossil records.

In contrast to the older statement, the new code no longer requires anthropologists to protect or be advocates for the people they study. The code recognizes the autonomy of the latter and recommends consulting actively with all affected individuals or groups to develop a working relationship that benefits both sides. In contrast to the final report's recommendation that anonymity of anthropological subjects be preserved, the new code stipulates that people who provide information or act as hosts should be consulted about whether they prefer anonymity or recognition. The code recommends that they should be treated accordingly but that they be warned that anonymity may not be possible.

This section on research (III. A) also requires the informed consent of people being studied and of anyone else whose interests might be affected by the research. This means that the anthropologist must obtain the consent of the host people after informing them that they are being studied and explaining as clearly as possible the purpose of the study and how the results of the study will be used. This clause is relevant to the problem of conflict of interest because it requires anthropologists to reveal whether their interest is solely in obtaining anthropological knowledge for the sake of science or whether they also have an interest in providing information to a sponsor who wants to use the information for another purpose, such as to obtain some economic or military advantage. The relationship of trust that the anthropologist establishes with the host people is both a relationship with the group and with individual members of the group who are involved with the anthropologist. The fiduciary bond is particularly important between the anthropologist and his or her informant(s), as the code specifies.

Another part of the research section of the new code (III. B) covers responsibilities to scholarship and science, and includes the obligation to preserve opportunities for future fieldworkers, and to disseminate findings to the scientific and scholarly community. Section III. C imposes the obligation of putting the results of research into a proper context and making it appropriately available to sponsors, students, and other members of the public. Clearly, the anthropologist's duty to disseminate findings—a fundamental duty of all scientists—needs careful interpretation in some cases to avoid straining the duty to do no harm. Revealing some kinds of knowledge about the host people can harm them or make them vulnerable.

Sometimes, but not always, anthropologists can reduce the potential for harm by presenting sensitive information in its broader anthropological context. For example, publishing information about customs that seem discriminatory to a segment of the population could draw unfavorable attention from human rights groups. The offending practices might lose their appearance of discrimination—and be recognized as a division of burdens—if presented in the fuller context of the social framework of the society.

The foregoing example brings out a (recognized) difficulty with the principle of doing no harm to "the people studied." The problem is that groups studied by anthropologists are made up of individuals with different and sometimes opposing interests. Clearly, real discrimination exists in many societies studied by anthropologists—against women in some, against children in others; and against various ethnic or religious minorities in still others. If the social fabric of a society depends on subjugating its women or on slave labor, publishing this information can cause social disruption, which in some sense "harms" the society, though its oppressed members may benefit. Anthropologists differ in opinions about these matters. Some still cling to a version of ethical relativism that links the good with what is culturally approved. They maintain that practices, such as female genital mutilation, that are accepted in societies radically different from our own should be deemed acceptable "if [they] can be demonstrated to have some social or cultural good" (Crossette, 1999). Other anthropologists believe that as participants in the group they study, they have an ethical responsibility to interfere in the interest of justice (Scheper-Hughes, 1995).

I am omitting discussion of the code's outline of responsibilities for teachers (IV) because that section introduces no obligations that are relevant to the problem of conflict of interest which are not already covered in Sections III (Research) and V (Application).

Section V addresses the problem of conflict of interest more directly than the other sections. It recognizes that the work of applied anthropologists affects "individuals and groups with diverse and sometimes conflicting interests." It states that the anthropologist "must make carefully considered ethical choices and be prepared to make clear the assumptions, facts and issues on which those choices are based." The code warns applied anthropologists to be careful not to promise or imply acceptance of conditions of employment contrary to professional ethics or competing commitments.

What Constitutes a Situation of Conflict of Interest for an Anthropologist?

Mindful of the considerations covered in the AAA Code of Ethics, and the remarks of M. Davis in his Introduction to this volume, I want to try to elucidate the notion of conflict of interest for anthropology. In doing so, I am indebted to work done by Stacey Welch (1998).

In the first place, "conflict of interest" should not be defined so broadly that it includes every situation in which an anthropologist faces an ethical dilemma or must make a choice that involves conflicting desires or even conflicting duties. Anthropologists have duties and interests that are not related to their profession, and given limited time and resources, sometimes one duty strains another.

Despite the widespread use of the term "conflict of interest," it has a brief history in the English language. Davis (2001, p. 17) cites a 1949 court case in which the term appears. *Webster's Ninth Collegiate Dictionary* gives the date 1951 for "a conflict between private interests and the official responsibilities of a person in a position of trust (as a government or corporate official)." In developing an appropriate definition of the term for anthropologists, I want to focus on the notion of "official responsibilities of a person in a position of trust." By "official responsibilities," I do not mean responsibilities of a person who holds some public office but, rather, the responsibilities or duties involving confidence or trust (fiduciary duties) that go with some profession. For the purposes of understanding conflict of interest in the profession of anthropology, I propose the following characterization:

> A situation of conflict of interest obtains when a person's ability to meet a professional responsibility to perform a fiduciary duty is strained by a competing interest.

A clear case of conflict of interest is one in which a trustee (e.g., a trust officer at a bank) who has the professional duty to manage a trust fund for the benefit of a client finds that duty strained by an interest in investing the client's funds in a way that benefits him- or herself. The trustee receives the client's assets with the understanding that the assets will be managed solely for the client's benefit. The trustee thus has a *fiduciary* duty toward the client. If that fiduciary duty is strained by some other interest of the trustee (e.g., to increase his own assets), the trustee is in a situation of conflict of interest.

Note that "conflict of interest" describes a situation rather than the feeling that the person in the situation might have. That is, the trustee need not *feel* any conflict or stress from his own interests that could threaten his client's assets, but the situation is nevertheless one of conflict of interest. The recognition that the term "conflict of interest" describes a situation is common to many writers on the topic. Welch (1998), for example, concurs, and so does Davis (2001).

While Davis (2001) characterizes conflicts of interest as *situations*, however, he also believes that the bad thing about these situations is that they "render one's judgment less reliable than normal" (p. 12). Clearly in many situations, such as when judges recuse themselves from cases, the risk to reliable judgment may be present. I prefer to characterize the situation of conflict of interest, however, as one in which a professional duty is strained by a competing interest, whether or not it gives rise to deficiencies in judgment. An unscrupulous trustee, for example, might be clearly aware of what he is doing and of the possible consequences when he invests the assets of the client in a precarious business that the trustee owns. The trustee who needs whatever assets he can garner to prop up his business is in a situation of conflict of interest whether or not his judgment is rendered less reliable than normal. It seems likely also that the strain that another interest imposes on a fiduciary duty in a situation of conflict of interest may affect the *will* to meet one's professional duty rather than the *understanding* of what that duty is.

Failure to meet responsibilities is particularly significant when the person to whom the duty is owed depends on the professional expertise of the one who has the duty. We thus feel strongly that trustees with fiduciary duties toward minors or others incapable of managing their own affairs should avoid situations of conflict of interest.

Situations of conflict of interest, as we have characterized them, are neither good nor bad—they are situations, morally neutral. Those who are in such situations, however, may be tempted to forgo some fiduciary responsibility. For this reason, and to avoid even the appearance of yielding to such temptations, sometimes it is wise and even morally obligatory to avoid situations of conflict. This is why public officials often put their own assets in a "blind trust." They want to avoid any suggestion that their public responsibilities are strained by their private interest. Attorneys avoid some conflicts of interest by refusing to represent two parties whose interests in the outcome of a lawsuit may not coincide. Judges similarly avoid even the appearance of inappropriately dispensing justice by recusing themselves from cases in which they have some interest other than the desire to make the correct decision.

Physicians are another professional group with fiduciary responsibilities. The physician's professional training imposes a strict duty to give patients, who depend on and trust in the physician's skills, the best possible care. The skill of the physician gives rise to the trust of the patient, and it is that trust that constitutes the basis for the *fiduciary* duty of the physician to the patient. In this sense, the relationship between the patient and the physician resembles the (fiduciary) relationship based on confidence or trust of the client who depends on a trustee.

Physicians may also have private interests or other professional interests that strain their fiduciary duty as caregiver. Some physicians, for example, conduct research. Consider a situation in which a physician is a member of a research team that is studying the effectiveness of a new cancer drug. The physician has the fiduciary duty of providing the best care for his or her patients and as a researcher also has a professional interest in finding a cure for the disease that affects his or her patients. Suppose that the physician suggests that a patient enroll in a clinical trial of the new drug in which the patient may receive a placebo or a therapeutically ineffective drug. If it becomes apparent that the patient is not being helped by the experimental treatment, the physician as caregiver has the duty to advise the patient to drop out of the trial, but the physician as researcher has an interest in having subjects remain in the experiment until its completion. If the physician is both caregiver and researcher, he or she is clearly involved in a conflict of interest (Welch, 1998). Welch argues that physician researchers should avoid this conflict of interest by refusing to enroll their own patients in clinical trials in which they are involved.

To summarize the view I am presenting of "conflict of interest," the term refers to a situation in which a person's professional fiduciary duty is under strain from some competing interest of the person. The competing interest may involve another duty brought about by the person's having more than one role, as in the physician researcher case. However, the strain on the professional duty may come from some private interest as well. Clear examples of fiduciary duties are the physician's duty to care for patients and the trustee's duty to manage trusts for the clients' benefit. In both of these examples it is possible and usually appropriate to avoid putting oneself in a situation of conflict of interest or to remove oneself from the situation. In the case of the physician researcher, some have argued that the problematic features of a situation of conflict of interest are resolved by obtaining the patient's informed consent. Welch (1998) disagrees, at least in cases in which the patient is seriously ill. She argues that the vulnerability of the patient and trust in the physician prevent or pose a serious barrier to informed consent.

Let us now turn to the question whether the professional training and skills of anthropologists place them in fiduciary relationships that are comparable to those of physicians or trustees. Anthropologists' professional training is designed to enhance their skills of observing, interpreting, and reporting on humans' biological, cultural (including material culture), social, and linguistic behavior. This is anthropologists' expertise. To use that expertise, anthropologists must interact with the people they study or with whom they apply their anthropological training. To enter into these relationships and maintain them successfully, anthropologists must gain the confidence and trust of their host people.

Now, clearly the host people are not dependent on the skills of the anthropologist in the same way that patients are dependent on the skills of their physicians, or the way that beneficiaries are dependent on their trustees. In the first place, in most cases the host people are not the primary beneficiaries of anthropologists' studies. In the second place, unlike patients and beneficiaries of trusts, the host people do not seek out anthropologists for their expertise. The anthropologists' skill is not comparable to that of trustees or physicians in terms of special benefits for the people studied.

Nevertheless, anthropologists do have fiduciary duties to their host people. Anthropologists use their professional credentials to try to win the confidence and trust of informants and host people. If they succeed, and if the basis for trust is the anthropologist's professional role, then the crucial element of the fiduciary relationship exists. The duty of the anthropologist—not to harm the people with whom he or she studies or works is a fiduciary duty. With a fiduciary relationship in place, situations of conflict of interest are possible.

The major professional duty of the anthropologist is the duty not to harm. But this is such a nonspecific duty—don't all humans have the duty not to harm one another?—that it seems superfluous in a code of professional conduct. In the context of anthropologists' professional duties, however, the duty not to harm should be understood in a way similar to the physician's understanding of the first principle of the Hippocratic oath. That is, anthropologists have a special duty not to use their *professional expertise* to do harm. The code gives further details: "Anthropological researchers must do everything in their power to ensure that their research does not harm the safety, dignity, or privacy of the people with whom they work, conduct research, or perform other professional activities" (III A.2).

In the course of their research, for example, anthropologists gain access to knowledge that could do harm if it were revealed. Obvious examples of knowledge to be guarded include the hidden locations of culturally valuable artifacts. If these artifacts were stolen or destroyed as a result of a careless anthropologist revealing their location, the people who own and value them would be harmed. Other more subtle examples involve societies that have a social structure based on the possession of esoteric knowledge. An anthropologist may be in a position to learn things that are known to only a few members of the society. If the esoteric knowledge becomes widely dispersed throughout the society, the social structure could be undermined and members of the society harmed as a result.

Some Examples of Conflicts of Interest and Attempts to Resolve Them

Some anthropologists are researchers; some are teachers. Some work in museums, as curators or directors. Some work for local, state, or federal governments. Some work for nonprofit corporations; some for industry; some in medical settings. Each of these roles carries a set of expectations and duties. More often than not, anthropologists fill more than one role. As a result, they frequently find themselves in situations in which the duty arising from one of those roles is strained because of conflict with what is expected from them in another professional role. Even before becoming professionals, anthropologists in training find themselves in situations in which the duty of being scientific observers can be strained because of conflict with expectations from their role as participants. Conflict of interest is a big issue in anthropology. In what follows, I discuss conflicts that arise in a few of the many varied roles anthropologists assume.

Anthropologists as Museum Directors and Curators

There is a reasonable expectation that the anthropologists who manage museum collections will preserve and maintain the collections for the benefit of the museum's patrons. Thus, in a situation closely analogous to that in trust law, the anthropologists' professional expertise produces an expectation of a fiduciary relationship between the anthropologists and those availing themselves of that expertise.

Many museums now possess important cultural artifacts that their original owners—or the descendants or fellow members of the tribe of the original owners—want to recover for the tribe. The tribal members may believe that the return of these artifacts is essential to the dignity, privacy, or well-being of their group. Sometimes these claims are supported by law. The transfer of ownership of cultural artifacts acquired since World War II (or, in some cases, 1970) is now regulated by laws and agreements at the local, state, federal, and international level. In these cases, conflicts that might arise can be resolved by obeying the law (assuming that interpretation of the law is not problematic). The laws, however, do not adequately cover the earlier period when many of the collections of the great museums were being built (Sabloff, 1999). Museum personnel thus see their professional duty as anthropologists strained by their duty to maintain and preserve collections.

Unlike the trustee and the physician researcher, the anthropologist who is entrusted with museum collections cannot resolve the issue by avoiding such situations of conflict of interest. Nor is it feasible for an anthropologist who is a museum director to ignore either an interest in the welfare of the tribe or the competing interest in achieving the mission of the museum. Without minimizing the difficulty of the issue, Sabloff (1999), who is the director of a major anthropological museum, emphasizes the importance of dialogue and consultation with representatives of all the groups that have a legitimate interest in the artifacts. Sometimes, but not always, a resolution acceptable to both sides can be reached. For example, a group might ask for return of artifacts. When they learn what is involved in the protection and maintenance of their cultural treasures, however, they might prefer to work with the museum. The museum might respond to the tribe's requests either by removing certain items from display, by enhancing the way some items are presented so their significance can be more easily recognized, by allowing tribal members special access for ceremonies, or by arranging some sort of shared custody. When such accommodations succeed, the anthropologist's conflict of interest is eliminated or alleviated by bringing into harmony the conflicting interests of the two groups that have claims on his duty. Even when no solution that satisfies both sides emerges, the participants in the dialogue may each learn from the others, and the result could enhance the preservation and accessibility of artifacts and understanding of the cultures that created them.

Anthropologists as Government Employees

Governments employ anthropologists to give advice on such matters as the impact that government policy decisions will have on various cultural subgroups, how to reach prospective clients for government health or educational benefits, how to prepare foreign service and military personnel for living in other cultures and (at least in the past) for gathering military intelligence. Anthropologists who are also government employees have the duty to uphold the laws and policies of the governments they serve. The anthropologists' expertise produces an expectation on the part of their government employers that they will use that knowledge to carry out government policy, excluding of course, any actions that are clearly immoral or unethical.

J. Watkins (1999), an anthropologist/archaeologist, a Native American, and an employee of the Federal Bureau of Indian Affairs, has written insightfully about the conflicts of interest he faces in his attempts to fulfill all his professional duties. Many of these issues can be illustrated in the controversy surrounding the recent discovery of a human skeleton on federally controlled land. Problems about the disposition of this skeleton, dubbed "Kennewick Man," demonstrate the difficulty in reconciling anthropological codes of ethics with some government regulations. Unfortunately, the issue has also been characterized as a conflict between scientific and humanist values.

The skeleton, with a projectile point embedded in its hip, was judged by the two anthropologists who discovered it to be the remains of a Caucasian male. They guessed that it dated from the nineteenth or early part of the twentieth century. Radiocarbon dating of a bone sample put its age at an astonishing 9,200–9,600 years. Once the age of the skeleton became known, five tribes filed a claim for the remains, appealing to the a newly enacted federal law, the Native American Graves Protection and Repatriation Act (NAGPRA). The tribes wanted to rebury the skeleton without allowing any further scientific tests. Eight distinguished anthropologists, worried about the loss to science, sued to block repatriation. The progress of this lawsuit, scheduled to go to trial in June 2001, will be closely watched, as it poses the first major test of the vaguely worded law. Some anthropologists fear that the tribes will be clear winners, a result that they think may force archaeology to abandon the study of Native American culture. If that is the result, Watkins writes, "Imagine the personal anguish most governmental archaeologists would feel if forced to uphold a federal policy in regard to materials equally as important to science and Native American cultures as 'Kennewick Man'." The anguish Watkins describes as "personal" is professional as well, the result of a conflict of interest between his archaeological responsibilities and his responsibilities as a public official.

Watkins' own solution to some of the conflicts he faces is to work with members of the tribe to establish personal relationships as well as the formal relationships required by his job. In this way, he hopes to forge appropriate links of understanding and respect on both sides. A continuing dialogue that focuses in part on what archaeology is trying to find out and how it fits into the other interests of the tribe, he believes, will make it easier to resolve issues about sensitive materials when they arise. If government archaeologists understand the point of view of Native Americans, they can better explain why archaeology is relevant and valuable to the Native American point of view. This should dispel the view that science (i.e., archaeology) cannot coexist with Native American beliefs about cosmology. Neither science nor Native American values would be harmed if archaeology could be perceived as both relevant and valuable to the interests of Native Americans in preserving their history and tradition. Such understanding cannot be legislated, however, but can develop only by the patient building of relationships of understanding and trust.

The preceding discussion is typical of the sorts of conflicts of interest that anthropologists face in assuming their varied professional roles. In both the cases discussed here, the anthropologists who confront conflicts of interest attempt to resolve the conflict by adjusting perceptions of how best to pursue those interests. These perceptions are adjusted through open disclosure of the sources of the conflict, negotiation, and modification of behaviors. For example, in the museum case, the interest of avoiding harm to the tribal group is recognized as important, but when the tribe is seen to benefit from the museum's care for its artifacts, the two interests no longer conflict. At the same time, by recognizing that the museum's holding artifacts is perceived by the tribe as a harm, the museum can adjust its way of curating artifacts to accommodate tribal interests. This in turn enhances the museum's understanding of its collections.

Anthropologists employed in industry and medical anthropologists often face conflicts of interest. Employers have recently come to realize that the skills of anthropologists are useful in market research and product development. Social and cultural anthropologists are trained to engage in nonthreatening but probing conversation with people and also to observe and interpret all sorts of other behavioral cues to people's beliefs, needs, and desires. Private employers have expectations similar to that of government employers with respect to loyalty in upholding company policies and professional performance of their duties.

Anthropologists, however, must take care not to exploit the people with whom they work to accomplish the goals of industry. Thus, full disclosure on the part of the anthropologists and informed consent on the part of people with whom they work are essential. Medical anthropologists confront special issues in their dealings with institutional review boards that regulate research on humans in medical settings. Anthropologists who are engaged in research on medical practices try to establish a fiduciary relationship with both staff and patients. Sometimes, however, their fiduciary duties are strained, particularly when the anthropological research uncovers incompetence on the part of the staff or unethical behavior on the part of either staff or patients. These cases may be even more difficult to resolve than the others discussed so far because so much medical information must be kept confidential. Some cases, however, may find resolution in the methods used by museum anthropologists and government employees

Concluding Remarks

Conflicts of interest arise often in anthropology. In some cases an anthropologist can avoid them by refusing to participate in a project that will impose a strain on professional duty because of another interest. Because anthropologists have diverse professional duties, however, they cannot always avoid conflict situations. The scientific duty to publish one's work may be strained by the knowledge that publication could cause harm to the people studied. Trying to ensure that one's research does no harm to some members of a group may result in harm to other members of the group. Responding to requests for aid and advice from some members of the group one is studying may strain the duty of being a scientific observer. The anthropologist can only try to handle such situations in the most sensitive and harm-minimizing way.

Sometimes the anthropologist faces a conflict of interest because of duties to different groups of people whose interests conflict. Using examples from recent anthropological work, I have tried to show that some of these conflicts can be alleviated by increasing communication and understanding between different groups. If their interests can be brought into some degree of harmony, the conflict that the anthropologist confronts can be lessened or eliminated.

Recognizing that situations of conflict of interest are not always avoidable, the AAA has tried to provide its members with some basic ethical principles along with examples of how these principles apply to specific cases. The AAA latest Code of Ethics is more subtle than earlier versions and attempts to draw anthropologists into a process of self-education in ethics. It urges members to read and think about the issues and to realize that there are no easy recipes for always doing the right thing. It also recognizes that reasonable people can disagree about which course of action is more ethical in a situation in which difficult choices must be made. The Code of Ethics is just one part of a continuing education program in anthropological ethics, but it repays careful study by anthropologists in dealing with the conflicts of interest that they all face at one time or another in their work.

Notes

The author is grateful to the editors of this volume for their insightful comments on a draft of this chapter.

1. The American Anthropological Association maintains a web site (www.aaanet.org) which publishes the ethical statements referred to in this chapter. Statements of professional ethics are also published on the web sites of other professional associations of social scientists (American Historical Association, American Sociological Association, and American Political Science Association). These statements define various sorts of conflict of interest and advise their members about how to avoid or mitigate such conflicts.

2. Although anthropologists and clinical researchers are both bound by such requirements as obtaining informed consent and avoiding harm to their subjects, the activities of clinical researchers are usually seen as more invasive and manipulative of their subjects. After all, clinical researchers provide their subjects with experimental treatments (or withhold such treatments in the control group). Anthropologists, in contrast, presumably observe their subjects and avoid interfering with them. Nevertheless, because anthropologists are *participant* observers, they are also members of the group they study. As such, they are sometimes asked to take sides in disputes and to give aid, advice, or protection to (some of) their subjects. Furthermore, in the closely knit social groups traditionally studied by anthropologists, the mere presence of the anthropologist may be intrusive enough to shift social relationships within the group.

References

Berreman, G. (1968). Social responsibilities symposium. *Current Anthropology*, 9, 391–435.
Boas, F. (1940). *Race, language and culture*. New York: Free Press.
Crossette, B. (1999, March 6). Testing the limits of tolerance as cultures mix. *New York Times*, § A, p. 15.
Davis, M. (2001). Introduction. In M. Davis & A. Stark (Eds.), *Conflict of interest in the professions* (pp. 3–19). New York: Oxford University Press.
Gert, B. (1992). Morality, moral theory, and applied and professional ethics. *Professional Ethics*, 1 (1 & 2).

Jonas, H. (1969). Philosophical reflections on experimenting with human subjects. *Daedalus, 98,* (2), 219–247.

Kuklick, H. (1991). *The savage within: The social history of British anthropology, 1885–1945.* Cambridge: Cambridge University Press.

Sabloff, J. (1999). Scientific research, museum collections, and rights of ownership. *Science and Engineering Ethics, 5,* 347–354.

Scheper-Hughes, N. (1995). The primacy of the ethical. *Current Anthropology* 36 (3), 409–420.

Stocking, G. (1968). *Race, culture, and evolution.* New York: Free Press.

Watkins, J. (1999). Conflicting codes: Professional, ethical and legal obligations in archaeology. *Science and Engineering Ethics, 5,* 337–346.

Welch, S. (1998). *The conflict of interest of the physician-investigator.* Master's thesis, University of Pittsburgh, Department of History and Philosophy of Science.

Wilk, R. (1999). Whose forest? whose land? whose ruins? ethics and conservation. *Science and Engineering Ethics, 5,* 367–374.

IV

Markets

11

FINANCIAL SERVICES

John R. Boatright

Financial services could scarcely be provided without raising conflicts of interest. In acting as intermediaries for people's financial transactions and as custodians of their financial assets, financial service providers are often forced to choose among the competing interests of others—and weigh those interests against their own. Although personal interest plays some role, the conflicts of interest in financial services arise primarily from attempts to provide many different kinds of services to a number of different parties, often at the same time. Conflicts of interest are built into the structure of our financial institutions and could be avoided only with great difficulty. As one person has noted, "The biblical observation that no man can serve two masters, if strictly followed, would make many of Wall Street's present activities impossible."[1] In addition, the inhabitants of Wall Street are motivated primarily by self-interest and can be induced to serve any master only within limits. The challenge, therefore, is not to prevent conflicts of interest in financial services but to manage them in a workable financial system.

Conflicts in Financial Services: An Overview

The financial services industry, which encompasses a broad range of institutions and individual providers, fills two primary roles. These roles are serving as *intermediaries* in financial transactions and as *custodians* of assets. In both roles, individuals and institutions act as *agents*, acting on behalf of others, who are *principals*, and often financial services providers are *fiduciaries*, who have *fiduciary duties* toward those who are the beneficiaries of financial services. However, financial services providers do not act solely as agents and fiduciaries; they act in many other capacities, often at the same time and with respect to the same parties. For example, a broker may be in a purely buyer–seller relation with a customer when recommending a stock, even though the broker may manage a discretionary account for the same person as a client with respect to whom the broker is both an agent and a fiduciary. If the broker buys a stock at the instruction of a customer from the firm's own holdings—in which case the broker is also a dealer—the broker and the firm are acting both as an agent (in executing the stock purchase) and as a principal (in selling the stock to the client). Such multiple roles are obviously fraught with conflicts of interest.

The Financial Services Industry

A vast number of financial services are offered by a few types of institutions, which combine many services under one roof. The types of financial services institutions are determined largely by law and economic efficiency, with the result that they vary from one country to another, as well as from one period of time to another. In the United States, commercial and investment banking are conducted by separate institutions because of the Glass-Steagall Act (1933). The perceived conflict between these two banking functions was thought by Congress to be a factor in the 1929 stock market crash. In many other countries, single institutions commonly engage in both commercial and investment activities. U.S. law also prohibits banks from insurance underwriting, thus creating separate insurance companies. At one time, retail brokerage firms that served individual clients and investment banks, serving institutional investors and corporations, existed apart, but in recent years, these functions have been consolidated in all-purpose financial institutions, largely because of the perceived efficiency created by economies of scale. Pressure is building to repeal the Glass-Steagall Act and other laws that prevent banks and competing institutions from offering each others' services. For example, commercial banks now offer mutual funds, and they are seeking to enter the insurance business.

At the present time, the major financial services providers in the United States include the following: commercial and investment banks; trust institutions and trust departments of commercial banks; brokerage firms, which serve both as brokers and as dealers; mutual funds and other investment companies, such as real estate investment trusts; pension funds, which may be corporate, governmental, union or private, and which may be independently managed or managed by an investment bank or the trust department of a commercial bank; insurance companies; and investment planners. To this list may be added the institutions that operate and facilitate financial markets, such as the New York Stock Exchange and the National Association of Securities Dealers, as well as specialized roles in markets and exchanges, such as floor traders, market specialists, and block positioners.

The Definition of Conflict of Interest

Although much has been written about the definition of conflict of interest, the issues in the controversy over various definitions have little bearing on the understanding of conflicts in the financial services industry.[2] As a working definition, the following is sufficient: A conflict of interest occurs when a personal or institutional interest interferes with the ability of an individual or institution to act in the interest of another party, when the individual or institution has an ethical or legal obligation to act in that other party's interest.[3] Conflicts of interest are inherent in financial services because of the ubiquitous roles of agent and fiduciary, with their attendant duties to serve the interests of others.

Fiduciaries and Agents   A fiduciary is a person who is entrusted to act in the interest of another. Fiduciary duties are the duties of a fiduciary to act in that other person's interest without gaining any material benefit except with the knowledge and consent of that person.[4] The concepts of a fiduciary and fiduciary duty originated in common law for cases in which one person entrusts property to another, but these concepts have been expanded over time to other trust-like situations in which one person relies on another's superior knowledge or skill. Thus, a stockbroker is a fiduciary not only with respect to safekeeping funds and managing discretionary accounts but also insofar as he or she gives investment advice. The classic statement on the duties of a fiduciary was offered by Justice Benjamin Cardozo in *Meinhard v. Salmon:* "Many forms of conduct permissible in a workaday world for those acting at arm's length, are forbidden to those bound by fiduciary ties. A trustee is held to something stricter than the morals of the market place. Not honesty alone, but the punctilio of an honor the most sensitive, is then the standard of behavior."[5]

The fiduciary relation closely resembles the relation of agent and principal, in which one person (the agent) has been engaged to act on behalf of another (the principal). Whereas fiduciary relations arise when something of value is entrusted to another person, agency relations are due to the need to rely on others for their specialized knowledge and skills. For example, selling a house requires considerable knowledge and skill, as well as time and effort, and thus a seller may engage a real estate agent to act on the seller's behalf. A real estate agent becomes, in effect, an extension of the seller, with a duty to use his or her abilities solely for the seller's benefit.

The duties in both kinds of relations are generally open-ended. That is, the specific acts that ought to be performed are not fully specified in advance, and fiduciaries and agents have wide latitude in the choice of means to advance the interests of others. Aside from a positive duty of an agent to act in the interest of a principal, there is a negative duty to avoid advancing personal interests in the relation. This duty is expressed in the *Restatement (Second) on Agency* as follows: "[A]n agent is subject to a duty to his principal to act solely for the benefit of the principal in all matters connected with his agency."[6] The scope of the agency relation is left vague in this statement, but agents, as well as fiduciaries, have a clear duty to avoid self-dealing by using entrusted property or information for personal gain, even if the interests of the principal or beneficiary are unaffected.

Kinds of Conflicts of Interest   Three distinctions commonly made among conflicts of interest generally are especially relevant to conflicts in the financial services industry. First is the distinction between *actual* and *potential* conflicts of interest. An actual conflict of interest occurs when an individual or institution acts against the interest of a party whose interest that individual or institution is pledged to serve, whereas a potential conflict of interest is a situation in which an actual conflict of interest is likely to occur. Actual conflicts of interest generally constitute misconduct, but potential conflicts, while best avoided, may need to be tolerated as unavoidable features of certain situations.

Second, a distinction is made between *personal* and *impersonal* conflicts of interest. A conflict of interest is personal when the interest that actually or potentially interferes with the performance of an obligation to serve the interest of another is some gain to an individual or an institution. Thus, a lawyer who stands to benefit personally by acting against the interest of a client is in a personal conflict of interest. However, the interfering interest may also be another person's interest which an individual or institution is duty bound to serve. For example, a lawyer who has two clients with opposed interests also faces a conflict of interest, which may be described as impersonal.[7] This is the classic "two masters" problem.[8] Impersonal conflicts are more common in the financial services industry, where firms have large numbers of clients.

For example, if a broker, in managing a discretionary account, selects an inferior security because it generates a higher commission, the broker is acting in a personal conflict of interest by putting self-interest ahead of the client's interest. However, a broker who manages accounts for multiple clients may be forced to choose among the interests of these different parties when he or she decides how to allocate a security in short supply. Trust officers who manage multiple trust accounts face similar conflicts. This kind of conflict also occurs for brokers and trust officers in the utilization of market-moving information. Which accounts receive the benefit of this information, and in what order? Mutual fund advisers may be forced to decide how to allocate investment opportunities between various funds. The individuals who manage multiple accounts and funds have an incentive to favor those that are more important to them personally or to the firm, because these accounts belong to large customers, for example, or because they generate higher fees and commissions. A mutual fund adviser may allocate an especially profitable investment that is in short supply to a lagging fund in order to boost its performance or to a high-performing fund in order to gain greater publicity.

In many situations, the obligations that are owed to different parties (who may have competing interests) cannot all be fulfilled, in which case some priority must be followed in allocating gains and losses. Not every account or fund can receive a firm's undivided loyalty of the kind we expect from individual lawyers, for example. Moreover, the standard solution for a lawyer with an impersonal conflict of interest, namely, to sever the relation with at least one of two competing clients, is not available to a broker or trust officer, who, of necessity, manages dozens, if not hundreds, of accounts, or to a mutual fund company, which generally offers a variety of funds.

Third, a conflict of interest may be either *individual* or *organizational*. Organizations as well as individuals act as agents and assume fiduciary duties, and an organization can fail to serve the interests of a principal or the beneficiary of a trust even when no individual is at fault. For example, if a trust officer in the trust department of a commercial bank learns that a corporate customer of the commercial bank is in financial difficulty, should he or she be permitted or required to use that information in managing trust accounts? On the one hand, a failure to use the information could result in avoidable losses for the beneficiaries of those accounts, but, on the other hand, use of the information would violate the confidentiality that the bank owes to the corporate customer. One solution is to separate the trust and commercial functions by implementing policies on information use or by constructing "Chinese walls" to prevent the flow of information.

Because financial services are delivered primarily by institutions that offer a multitude of services to multiple customers or clients, most of the conflicts of interest in this area are *potential, impersonal,* and *organizational.* They result from the deliberate design of our financial institutions and pose a problem for those responsible for creating, regulating, and managing these institutions.

Why Conflicts Arise in
Financial Services

In broad terms, a conflict of interest arises for financial services providers when some interest interferes with the performance of an agency or fiduciary duty. Much the same could be said about conflicts of interest in other areas, including medicine and law. However, there is one important difference: The work of most financial services providers does not meet the standard criteria for a profession.[9] Among the criteria for a profession which are lacking in financial services are a high degree of organization and self-regulation, a code of ethics, and a commitment to public service. These criteria are possibly met by financial planners and insurance underwriters, but not by brokers, bankers, traders, and most other people in the financial services industry, who, in the strict sense of the term, are not professionals.

As a consequence, the obligations of financial services providers are not grounded in the structure of a profession. That is, the duties of a physician can be determined by asking what it means to practice medicine, and similarly for the duties of an attorney. By contrast, the obligations of financial services providers as agents and fiduciaries cannot be derived from some general account of a profession but must be sought elsewhere. Instead of the structure of a profession, the grounding for the obligations of financial services providers is found in *financial contracting*. Providers become agents and fiduciaries as a result of specific contracts to perform agreed-on services. Within the limits imposed by law, the obligations created by these contracts can be whatever two parties conclude by mutual agreement. The duties of a broker to a customer or client, for example, can vary widely and be adjusted continuously, and a broker and any given customer may have multiple relations, each with its own contractual terms.

The law defines many roles and specifies the duties that attach to them, especially in the design of financial institutions. For example, mutual funds and pension funds must be established and operated in conformity with the relevant laws. These laws require, among other things, control by trustees, and the duties of these trustees, which vary, are specified in some detail. However, much of the law that defines the relationship between contracting parties may be regarded as default, "off-the-shelf" contracts, whose terms the parties can alter or "contract around" by mutual agreement. In general, the law specifies obligations for common, standardized roles, such as a broker, and for roles in the governance structure of financial institutions, such as trustee of a mutual fund or a pension fund. However, even when the law is fairly specific, much still remains to be negotiated in contracts for financial services.

Because the specific obligations of financial services providers are created by financial contracting, two important practical consequences follow. First, we can seldom determine whether an individual or an institution is in a potential or actual conflict of interest without knowing the precise terms of the contract between the parties. Merely knowing the roles in question is not sufficient, except when their duties are precisely specified in law. As a result, we cannot make many generalizations about what constitutes conflicts of interest for financial services providers, as we can for professionals. Judgments must be made on a case-by-case basis.

Second, self-interest is a legitimate factor in the roles of financial services providers. Unlike professionals, whose work is conducted almost entirely as a professional and is consequently subject in all its aspects to the rules of professional ethics, financial services providers operate, in part, as self-interested economic agents who legitimately engage in financial activity on their own behalf, often while they are serving as an agent or a fiduciary.

For example, a commercial bank with a trust department may be a fiduciary in the management of a corporation's pension fund at the same time that it is acting as a seller in making a commercial loan to the corporation. Similarly, an investment bank might be an investor in a takeover for which it is also raising the capital and thus be both an agent (in its financing activities on behalf of the raider) and a principal (by being an investor on its own behalf). Portfolio managers for mutual and pension funds are generally permitted to trade for their own accounts, and in so doing they are not only fiduciaries for the fund's shareholders but also active traders, competing against them. The potential for abuse in such situations is obvious.

In each instance, we could separate the functions and require those who are agents and fiduciaries to forgo all self-interested activities. Some have suggested removing trust departments from commercial banks, for example, but such proposals for restructuring our financial institutions are generally rejected on grounds of efficiency. The gain is not worth the price. Moreover, it would be difficult, as a practical matter, to insist on wholly altruistic financial services providers. Professionals can be expected to be altruistic because of their commitment to public service. Inasmuch as financial services providers primarily enable other people to make money, they cannot easily be induced to employ their special money-making skills solely for the benefit of others. Persuading them to combine self-interested and altruistic activities is perhaps the best that can be achieved.

The Sources of Conflicts in Financial Services

The conflicts of interest in financial services are too numerous to list exhaustively, and they are even difficult to classify because of the range of activities. However, one way to classify the various types of financial activities is by imagining a world of pure market transactions and identifying the need for intermediaries and custodians. To the extent that the agent and fiduciary duties of financial services providers arise from contracting in a free market, this hypothetical device provides a useful typology of financial activities within which the possibilities for conflicts of interest can be classified.

If individuals conducted their financial affairs as rational economic agents in a free market, there would be no conflicts of interest because, by definition, each person in a market is legitimately pursuing his or her self-interest. No one has any obligation in a free market to serve the interests of anyone else. Hence, there are plenty of competing interests in a free market but no conflicts of interest. Of course, there are moral constraints on free-market exchanges, such as the impermissibility of force and fraud, but these constraints do not create the conditions for conflicts of interest. However, this world would be unsatisfactory for many reasons, and insofar as rational economic agents are free to form contracts that advance their interests, they would do so. It is from this kind of contracting in a free market that the conditions for conflicts of interest arise.

Financial Instruments

In a free market, participants would create an array of *financial instruments* that impose obligations on both parties. For example, few people have enough money saved to buy a home. Thus instead of exchanging money for a house in a single transaction, the buyer and seller might draft a mortgage, which is a secured long-term loan. Similarly, a farmer and a mill owner might seek to reduce the risk inherent in the grain market. A glut of grain at harvest time would depress prices and possibly ruin the farmer, whereas a shortage would raise prices to the detriment of the mill owner. Instead of waiting until harvest time and exchanging at the market price, which is risky for both parties, they might agree in advance to a futures contract for the delivery of grain at a predetermined price. Mortgages and futures contracts solve two critical problems at once, namely, how to create long-term financial relationships and how to manage the risks that result from our lack of knowledge of the future.

The creation of financial instruments also creates the need for a variety of financial intermediaries to handle the complex transactions between contracting parties. More important, intermediaries are necessary because the parties may not be able to contract face to face but may require the services of a third party. For example, when a savings bank collects deposits from customers and lends them to home buyers, the two parties never meet; their "transaction" is mediated by the bank, which combines the functions of saving and lending. Similarly, the farmer and the mill owner might act independently to protect themselves by operating through a futures market. Investment banks, serving as underwriters, handle the many different tasks that are involved when a corporation issues new securities, including the task of finding buyers for the securities. Insurance companies enable large numbers of people to protect themselves from risk by pooling premiums, which are then used to satisfy claims.

Financial intermediaries act as agents, performing transactions and other activities that require specialized skills that are employed for the benefit of others. In so doing, they have an obligation to act in the principal's best interest. Thus, a broker has an obligation to achieve the best execution of a trade, and a fund manager has an obligation to select brokers who will provide the best execution. Both can be swayed by a personal or an institutional interest to make decisions that result in less than the best execution. For example, if the trust department of a commercial bank allocates the commissions for trades in trust accounts to brokerage firms that maintain a customer relation with the bank—a practice known as reciprocation, or "recip" for short—then the quality of the brokerage service might be compromised. Even if a broker customer provides the best execution, the bank has still used its power to allocate brokerage commissions, which ought to be exercised solely for interest of the beneficiaries of the trust funds, in order to advance the bank's commercial interests. The bank might have been able to use this power in some other way that would secure a benefit to the trust beneficiaries instead of the bank itself.

Insofar as an intermediary is the custodian of funds, such as uninvested cash in a trust or brokerage account, the intermediary is also a fiduciary. Individual accounts often contain positive cash balances from the sale of securities that have not been reinvested and from funds deposited in anticipation of purchases. Although the amount in each account is often small, the aggregate amount is usually quite large. If the trust department of a commercial bank leaves uninvested cash in noninterest bank accounts, then the bank, not the individual trust beneficiary, is benefited. A brokerage firm can also deposit uninvested cash in interest-bearing accounts and claim the interest for themselves, or they can leave it in noninterest accounts in order to gain some other benefit from a bank. SEC Rule 15c-3 stipulates that uninvested cash can be used only to provide some benefit to customers, such as providing funds for purchases on margin and for short sales. However, trust departments and brokerage firms need not credit accounts for any interest or other benefits that they derive from invested cash. Brokerage firms defend these cash management practices on two grounds. First, funds left on deposit are for the convenience of the customer and not the firm—which, in any event, could derive greater income from the commissions generated by new investments. Second, the benefits they derive help keep their fees low, so that customers are credited with the income, albeit indirectly.

Trust departments are in a position to advance the interests of the parent commercial bank in many other ways. For example, in managing trust accounts, a trust department may buy the stock of important corporate clients and hold it when it would be prudent to sell. Trust departments may also cooperate with the management of corporate clients by voting proxies in favor of management and by helping management defend against hostile takeovers. Such practices are known as "customer accommodation." In their other trust activities, such as disposing of assets during probate, a bank can serve or accommodate its customers' interests (and perhaps its own) by selling property or other valuable assets to them. For example, a trust department may be required, in the probate of an estate, to sell controlling interest in a company which had been a bank customer. By selling the controlling interest to another bank customer, a continued relationship is assured.

Financial Markets

In addition to financial instruments, free-market participants would seek to build *financial markets*, in which financial instruments could be issued and traded. Securities, such as stocks and bonds, are sold first in a primary market and then traded in a secondary or after market. A bond, for example, can be held to maturity, but a holder may also wish to cash out of this investment, in which case another buyer must be found. Mortgages can be exchanged between institutions and even pooled to form mortgaged-backed securities that trade in markets. The liquidity of a financial instrument, which is the ease with which it can be traded, adds to its value and reduces the risk of holding it—hence the benefit of secondary markets. Many aspects of primary and secondary markets, including the obligations of the various participants, are a matter of law, specifically the Securities Act (1933) and the Securities Exchange Act (1934). Securities markets are regulated by the Securities and Exchange Commission (SEC). However, within the legal framework established by law, the obligations of participants in financial markets are flexible and subject to negotiation.

Primary and secondary markets create many different specialized roles. A major source of business for investment banks is the underwriting of new issues of securities, including not only corporate stocks and bonds but also initial public offerings (IPOs) of formerly private companies. Underwriting itself consists of several distinct roles with accompanying obligations. An underwriter serves as adviser, analyst, and distributor. As an adviser, the investment bank is an agent, providing advice on how to structure and price the offering. As an analyst, the bank serves its own customers and the investing public by certifying the value of the securities. As a distributor, the underwriter also buys the securities for sale to its customers or, at least, conducts the sale, and it may pledge to buy any unsold portion of the offering.

The commitment to sell the securities underwritten by an investment bank creates an incentive to sell the stocks or bonds to customers, whether they are suitable investments or not, and there is also a temptation to place any unsold securities in accounts that the firm manages. Because any unsold securities have been judged a poor value by informed market participants, placing them in individual accounts, without the clients' knowledge, would appear to be a violation of a firm's fiduciary duty. Furthermore, underwriters have an incentive to exert improper influence on the firm's research department. A firm that underwrites an IPO cannot issue a recommendation on the stock in the first twenty-five days, but after this "quiet period," the research department is expected to issue a "buy" recommendation as a "booster shot."[10] Reputable firms attempt to shield their research analysts from improper pressure, but the conflicting interests of researchers and underwriters is an unavoidable source of tension.

The underwriting role has a built-in conflict of interest by its very nature. As an adviser to a corporate client, the bank should seek to obtain the highest price for the securities, but it serves its investment customers by obtaining the lowest price. However, this is a "virtuous" conflict of interest because the outcome is usually fairly priced securities. The investment bank must act like an auctioneer, seeking to obtain the highest price for the corporate client consistent with selling the whole offering to the bank's customers. The price, therefore, must be fair to both parties. A "vicious" conflict of interest may result, though, from the fact that the underwriter is compensated, in part, by the spread between the amount paid to the issuer and the public offering price. Thus, an underwriter has an incentive to "buy low" from the corporate client and to "sell high" to their customers.

Conflicts of interest arise for organized markets and exchanges. In the United States, there are two national stock exchanges, the New York Stock Exchange and the American Stock Exchange, as well as smaller regional exchanges. The stocks of many smaller companies trade through NASDAQ, an over-the-counter market, operated by the National Association of Securities Dealers (NASD). Other exchanges exist for bonds, commodities, futures, and other financial instruments. These organizations serve multiple constituencies and must balance the various competing interests. For example, the NASD has recognized a conflict between its role as an association of securities brokers and dealers and as an operator of the NASDAQ market.[11]

Particular roles within organized markets and exchanges give rise to role-specific conflicts. For example, floor traders in commodities and futures exchanges are privy to market-moving information that they can exploit by timely trading on behalf of themselves or others. Such trading constitutes a misappropriation of confidential or proprietary information and is strictly prohibited. A floor trader operates in an *auction market*, which is characterized by large number of buyers and sellers trading small lots.

In an auction market, prices are known to all, and the trader operates purely as an agent in the execution of trades. By contrast, in a *dealer market*, in which large blocks of securities are traded between a few parties, trades are brokered by a dealer, known as a *block positioner*. In a dealer market, both prices and commissions are generally hidden and subject to negotiation, and the dealer may be acting as both an agent for other parties and as a principal for the firm. These conditions create potential conflicts of interest.

One market role worth noting is the *market specialist*, who has responsibility for maintaining a fair and orderly market in one or more stocks. Whenever the numbers of buyers and sellers in a stock market are mismatched, the specialist is expected to buy or sell, using his or her own inventory, in ways that approximate a market with a sufficient number of buyers and sellers. A specialist also holds a "book," which is information about calls and puts and limit orders. Because of the specialist's privileged access to the market and to sensitive information, the possibility exists for abuse. Not only can a specialist manipulate the price of stocks, but he or she is able to engage in trading as a principal with virtually no risk in so-called riskless principal transactions. For example, a specialist with an order to buy a stock when it drops to a certain price can buy the stock just above that price, with the assurance that if the price drops further the stock can be sold to the customer who placed the order. As long as the commission for the sale exceeds the loss on the transaction, the specialist takes no risk.

Advisory and Management Services

Active trading of securities in markets and the holding of diverse portfolios would lead free-market participants to seek an *investment adviser* and perhaps a *professional manager* for an investment portfolio. For example, a broker acts not only as an intermediary by executing trades but also an investment adviser, recommending suitable securities, and as a portfolio manager if the customer has given the broker discretionary authority to trade for the customer's account. If a broker is compensated only for executing trades, then he or she has an incentive to recommend frequent trading of (possibly) unsuitable securities, and especially to engage in excessive trading in discretionary accounts, a practice known as "churning." Similar practices occur in banking, when loan customers are urged to replace one loan with another, and in insurance, when agents persuade customers to replace one policy with another, in order to generate extra fees and commissions. These abuses are called "flipping" and "twisting," respectively.

Investment advisers, who must register with the SEC under the Investment Advisers Act of 1940, offer investment advice to the public. Because a conflict of interest is created when investment advisers are paid a commission on the investments selected by the client, some advisers attempt to remove this source of conflict by charging a flat fee. Investment banks derive a large portion of their income from advising corporate clients on a wide range of matters, including financial restructurings, mergers and acquisitions, and hostile takeovers. Because investment banks offer other services to the same clients and also have clients with competing interests, their advisory activities create multiple conflicts of interest. Finally, mutual funds, pension funds, and insurance companies provide professional management for large portfolios of securities. Two potential conflicts of interest for portfolio managers arise when they engage in personal trading for their own accounts and when they allocate commissions to brokers for the execution of trades in return for research and other nonmonetary benefits.

Personal Trading   Conflicts of interest from personal trading are possible for so-called access people, that is, investment company personnel such as portfolio managers, analysts, and traders who have access to proprietary research and information about pending transactions. Access people are in a position to use this information to trade ahead of a fund's purchase (called *frontrunning*) and benefit from any upward price movement. If frontrunning raises the price of a stock, then the fund pays more for a security than it would otherwise. Similarly, an access person with advance knowledge of a fund's sale of a stock could capitalize on the information by selling short. An access person might be in a position to influence transactions that serve primarily to protect or promote that person's investment in a security. In addition, a fund manager who takes advantage of an opportunity, such as a special placement, for his or her own portfolio rather than investing for the fund is also in a conflict of interest.

Soft-Dollar Transactions   Fund managers use brokers to execute the numerous trades that are made daily. In return for the commissions that fund managers pay, brokers provide not only the execution of trades but also free research and other forms of noncash compensation, known as "soft dollars." This practice developed during the period of fixed commissions, which was abolished by the SEC in May 1975. Under the fixed commission system, brokers competed by offering soft dollars to large institutional clients, and the practice continued into the era of negotiated commissions. Soft-dollar transactions create conflicts of interest insofar as they benefit the fund managers at the expense of the fund's shareholders, who pay the commissions. Critics of this practice charge that a fund manager receiving soft dollars has an incentive to trade excessively in order to generate the soft-dollar benefits, to use soft dollars to benefit him- or herself personally, and finally to select brokers on the basis of the soft-dollar benefits and not the quality of the execution.

Soft-dollar transactions appear to violate a fund manager's fiduciary duty to the fund's shareholders to secure the best execution of trades at the lowest price. However, with the abolition of fixed commissions in 1975, Congress amended the Securities Act with Section 28(e), which provides a "safe harbor" that protects fund managers from charges of breach of fiduciary duty. Section 28(e) permits fund managers to pay higher-than-market rates for brokerage services, provided that the fund manager has determined in good faith that the commissions paid are "reasonable in relation to the value of the brokerage and research services provided." The "unbundling" of the payments for execution and other services would enable fund shareholders to determine whether they were paying the lowest commission, but because fund managers would still be paying for research, such a good faith determination is unavoidable. Perhaps the main incentive for soft dollar transaction is that they inflate the fund's returns, which are reported before the payments of commissions but after research costs are paid.

Organizational Governance

Because of the complexity of providing financial services and the problem of marshaling vast resources, free-market participants would create large organizations, which require forms of governance. Just as corporate law specifies the form of governance for business corporations, so other pieces of legislation create governance structures for financial organizations. The Investment Company Act of 1940 sets forth the framework for investment companies, including mutual funds, and most private pension plans are regulated by the Employee Retirement Income Security Act of 1974 (ERISA). Each of these acts requires the fund to be under the control of trustees with a fiduciary duty to the shareholders (of a mutual fund) or the beneficiaries (of a pension fund).

The governance structure of any organization creates potential conflicts of interest, not only because of the personal interests of the responsible persons but because of the multiple roles that these persons fill. An investment banker, for example, who is a director of a corporation or a trustee of an endowment fund is offered a plethora of opportunities to advance the interests of one group to the detriment of another group's interests. Individuals who wear two or more hats may be able to compartmentalize their roles and their attendant obligations. A more difficult challenge faces institutions that attempt to fill multiple roles, in which legitimate interests are continually competing.

For example, mutual funds trustees are obligated to represent the interests of the shareholder investors of a fund. However, some are people with a close association with management who also do business with the fund in various ways. Critics have accused these trustees of paying insufficient attention to fund fees and other investor concerns and have called for a greater number of independent trustees on fund boards. Real estate investment trusts (REITs) raise special governance problems, not only because of a lack of independence among the trustees, who are often associated with the sponsoring institution, but also because of the prevalence of outside management of REITs. Unlike mutual funds, REITs can assume debt and leverage its assets, and when management fees are based on total assets of the trust, the managers have an incentive to assume more debt than may be beneficial to the investors. Because of the externalized management structure of REITs, shareholders are usually unable to evaluate the fees, which are not stated separately from REIT returns. As a result, the governance structure of REITs does not provide the degree of accountability that is present in other financial institutions.

Strategies for Managing Conflicts of Interest

Despite the prevalence of potential conflicts of interest in financial services, the occurrence of actual conflicts has been minimized by relatively effective preventive strategies.[12] These strategies are embodied in much of the regulation of the financial services industry and in accepted industry practices. They can be conveniently classified under the headings of competition, disclosure, rules and policies, and structural changes.

Competition

Fierce competition among financial services providers for customers and clients provides a powerful incentive to avoid actual conflicts of interest and even the appearance of conflicts. Because results are critical in this competition, any source of inefficiency must be eliminated. For example, "recip" in commercial banks with a trust department has been virtually eliminated because of the need for returns on trust accounts to compare favorably with those of other trust departments and mutual funds. The allocation of brokerage commissions must be based on "best execution" rather than other institutional interests. In competing for customers by keeping fees low, trust department and brokerage firms must also employ responsible cash management practices. It has been argued that competition prevents the abuse of soft dollars, because fund managers who misallocate them will pay a price in the marketplace.[13] Competition is still limited in some areas of the financial services industry, and perhaps conflicts could be further reduced by eliminating these barriers, by, for example, increasing the kinds of firms that could serve as trustees of pension funds.

However, competition also contributes to conflicts of interest. It is because of competitive pressures that firms branch out into related services and combine with other service providers. A bank that makes real estate mortgage loans might be tempted to sponsor a REIT, for example, despite the increased risk of conflicts. The entry of retail brokerage firms into underwriting puts them in direct competition with investment banks, thereby increasing competition, but the move also creates conflicts with their retail customer business. The mergers of retail brokerage firms with investment banks, which have been prompted by competitive pressures, give rise to even more conflicts. Furthermore, competition depends for its force on other factors, most notably disclosure. For example, unless fund earnings are properly disclosed, competition cannot exert pressure on firms to reduce conflicts of interest.

Disclosure

Disclosure as a strategy for managing conflicts of interest is generally understood as the disclosure of adverse interests, as when a politician discloses his or her investment holdings. This kind of disclosure is important in financial services. For example, a broker who is acting as a principal in a transaction is required by SEC Rule 10b-10 to disclose this fact to a customer. Section 17 of the Investment Company Act requires detailed disclosure of transaction involving "affiliated persons" who stand to gain personally from a mutual fund's activities. Under the Securities Act, the prospectus for a security must include a description of any material conflicts of interest held by the issuing parties.

However, disclosure in finance includes much more than disclosure of adverse interests. It has been noted that disclosure of performance data of all kinds, including levels of risk, facilitates competition, which in turn reduces conflicts of interest. In addition, conflicts of interest can be avoided by making known a firm's policies and procedures for dealing with conflicts. For example, if a trust department discloses its policies concerning the priority given to accounts or the treatment of uninvested cash, there need be no violation of fiduciary duty because the terms of the contract that create this duty have presumably been accepted by the trust beneficiaries. In this case, an informed beneficiary has no justified complaint if his or her account receives less attention than that of a corporate pension fund. Similarly, an investment bank can reduce conflicts of interest by announcing in advance its policies should two clients be involved in a hostile takeover.

Rules and Policies

Specific rules and policies serve to reduce conflicts of interest, whether they are disclosed or not, by prohibiting conduct that constitutes or facilitates conflicts. These rules and policies may address conflicts of interest directly by requiring people to avoid conflicts of interest or by prohibiting the kinds of conduct that would constitute conflicts of interest. Other rules and policies may operate indirectly by creating conditions which reduce the possibility of conflicts of interest. For example, policies on the flow of information in any financial services firm—such as who has access to what information and who must be apprised of certain information—are vital for many reasons, including the prevention of conflicts of interest. Some commercial banks require that only the securities of sound, creditworthy corporations be selected for trust accounts. Not only is such a policy a good practice for a trust department, but it also prevents the possibility of conflict if, for example, the bank is also a creditor of a corporation in danger of bankruptcy. In such a case, the sale of the stock by the trust department might endanger the bank's commercial loans, which creates a conflict of interest.

Rules and policies have many sources, including federal and state legislatures and regulatory agencies, industry associations and exchanges, and financial services firms themselves. These rules and policies need to mesh with each other and be mutually supporting. However, the prevention of conflicts of interest is probably best achieved by financial services institutions themselves; that is, an employee's own firm provides a strong first line of oversight. Every firm is different, and each one can provide better oversight if it has the flexibility to tailor measures to its own circumstances. Also, whether any given action constitutes a conflict of interest is not always easy to determine, and judgment is required for carefully evaluating each case. Thus, broad rules and policies for the whole industry are likely to be less effective than finely crafted ones from each financial service institution.

The regulation of personal trading by mutual fund managers provides an example of how rules and policies can work to reduce a conflict-of-interest problem. Personal trading has been the subject of two recent reports, one by the SEC and the other by the Investment Company Institute (ICI).[14] The SEC addressed the problem by formulating Rule 17j, which contains a general prohibition of fraudulent, manipulative, or deceptive conduct in connection with personal trading. The rule also requires that investment companies (and their investment advisers and principal underwriters) adopt codes of ethics and procedures that are reasonably designed to prevent trading prohibited by the rule. Every "access person" is required by the rule to file with the firm quarterly reports on all personal securities transactions.

In formulating Rule 17j, the SEC did not attempt to specify conduct that constituted fraudulent, manipulative, or deceptive conduct in connection with personal trading, or to mandate specific provisions of company codes. An industry organization, the ICI, offered some general principles for company codes, but like the SEC, it refrained from being specific. Among the general principles offered by the ICI are the duty at all times to place the interests of shareholders first and to avoid any actual or potential conflict of interest or any abuse of an individual's position of trust and responsibility. The task of developing rules and policies regarding personal trading has fallen mainly to the investment companies themselves. Among the more common measures are rules that prohibit personal trading in a stock purchased by the fund during a "blackout" period before and after the fund purchase, participating personally in any initial public offerings, all short-term selling (generally a security must be held for more than ninety days), and selling short any stock that is held in any of the company's funds. Each of these carefully crafted rules is designed to prohibit specific conduct that could constitute a conflict of interest, either actual or potential, or (in the case of the ban on short-selling) create even the impression of a conflict of interest.

Structural Changes

Because so many conflicts of interest in financial services result from combining different functions in one firm, these conflicts could be reduced by structural changes that separate these functions. The existence of separate institutions for commercial and investment banks, mutual funds, and insurance companies is due to laws that mandate this separation, in part, to avoid conflicts. Many conflicts could be eliminated by separating the functions of trust management and commercial banking, of underwriting and investment advising, of retail brokerage and principal trading, and so on. Addressing the problem of conflict of interest by such radical structural changes is probably unwarranted, however, because of the many advantages of such combinations. For example, underwriting a corporation's securities requires an investment bank with substantial sales capability as well as personnel with analytical skills. The trend in the financial services industry is toward more rather than less integration.

Even within multifunction institutions, many structural changes are possible and perhaps advisable. One such change is strengthening the independence and integrity of functional units. In particular, steps can be taken to strengthen the autonomy of trust departments in commercial banks and research departments in investment banks by increasing the sense of professionalism among trust officers and research analysts. Managing the flow of information is an important factor in creating autonomy. This is done, in part, by building "Chinese walls" that create impermeable barriers between functional units. Chinese walls can also be built by policies that prohibit personnel from acting on restricted information, even if it is known. There are some drawbacks to Chinese walls, however. They take away some of the gains from integrating different functions in one firm, and firms may also lose the confidence of customers, who fear, for example, that investment advice does not represent all the information possessed by a firm. However, a customer may also benefit, by being assured that a broker's investment advice is not biased by the need to place unsold stocks in an underwriting. One significant benefit of Chinese walls to firms is increased protection against charges of insider trading.

Finally, financial services providers avoid conflicts of interest by seeking parties with independent judgment in situations in which their own judgment is compromised. Examples of such independent parties include independent trustees on the boards of mutual funds, independent appraisers in determining the value of assets in cases of self-dealing, independent actuaries in the operation of corporate pension funds, and independent proxy advisory services in deciding how to vote shares held by trusts and funds.

Conclusion

The study of conflicts of interest in financial services encompasses the duties of agents and fiduciaries in financial affairs. What are the duties of financial services providers? What undermines these duties? And what can be done to support them? These questions are as old as the biblical warning about serving two masters and as new as the latest Wall Street scandal. No comprehensive answers are possible, but a few generalizations can be made. First, the duties of financial services providers result from contracting in a free market and conflicts arise from the attempt to fulfill all the contracts made. To achieve efficiency in the delivery of financial services, we have knowingly designed institutions that make conflicts of interest unavoidable. In this process, the problems with conflicts have generally been recognized and reasonably effective measures have been developed. Although individual awareness of conflicts of interest and managerial attention to them are important, the prevention of conflicts must also involve government, the industry, and especially financial services firms. At the present time, two main problems remain. These are deciding how to make the trade-off between efficiency and the reduction of conflicts and finding solutions that give the desired results.

Notes

1. Warren A. Law, "Wall Street and the Public Interest," in *Wall Street and Regulation* 169 (Samuel L. Hayes, III, ed., Boston: Harvard Business School Press, 1987).

2. Michael Davis, *Conflict of Interest*, 1 Bus. & Prof. Ethics J. 17–27 (1982); Neil R. Luebke, *Conflict of Interest as a Moral Category*, 6 Bus. & Prof. Ethics J. 66–81 (1987); John R. Boatright, "Conflict of Interest: An Agency Analysis," in *Ethics and Agency Theory: An Introduction* 187–203 (Norman E. Bowie & R. Edward Freeman, eds., New York: Oxford University Press, 1992). For criticism of these works, *see* Thomas L. Carson, *Conflict of Interest*, 13 J. Bus. Ethics 387–404 (1994); Michael Davis, *Conflict of Interest Revisited*, 12 Bus. & Prof. Ethics J. 21–41 (1993), with replies by John R. Boatright and Neil Luebke.

3. This definition is adapted from John R. Boatright, *Ethics and the Conduct of Business* (3rd ed.) 145–49 (Upper Saddle River, NJ: Prentice Hall, 2000).

4. John R. Boatright, "Fiduciary Duty," in *The Blackwell Encyclopedic Dictionary of Business Ethics* 278–80 (Patricia H. Werhane & R. Edward Freeman, eds., Malden, MA: Blackwell, 1997).

5. Meinhard v. Salmon, 249 N.Y. 458, 464; 164 N.E. 545, 546 (1928).

6. *Restatement (Second) of Agency*, § 387.

7. Rule 1.7(a) of the American Bar Association's *Model Rules of Professional Conduct* labels a situation in which a lawyer represents clients with opposing interests a conflict of interest.

8. *Matthew* 6:24. "No man can serve two masters: for either he will hate the one and love the other, or else he will hold to the one, and despise the other."

9. John R. Boatright, *Ethics in Finance* 42–44 (Malden, MA: Blackwell, 1999).

10. W. Powers, *Why Hot, New Stocks Get Booster Shots*, Wall St. J., Feb. 10, 1993, at C1.

11. Speech by Mary L. Shapiro, president, NASD Regulation, Inc., Vanderbilt University, Nashville, Tennessee, April 3, 1996.

12. This is a conclusion of a set of reports on conflicts of interest in the securities markets commissioned by the Twentieth Century Fund and published together in *Abuse on Wall Street: Conflicts of Interest in the Securities Markets* (Westport, CT: Quorum, 1980).

13. D. Bruce Johnsen, *Property Rights to Investment Research: The Agency Costs of Soft Dollar Brokerage Yale J. on Regulation*, 75–113 (1994).

14. *Report of the Advisory Group on Personal Investing*, Investment Company Institute, May 9, 1994; and *Personal Investment Activities of Investment Company Personnel*, Report of the Division of Investment Management, United States Securities and Exchange Commission, September 1994.

12

THE ECONOMICS
OF THE CRITIC

Tyler Cowen

When the time approaches for the Golden Globe awards, Hollywood studios bestow gifts, parties, and out-of-town junkets on the relevant critics. Theater, ballet, and musical companies pay critics to write their program notes, hoping to receive favorable reviews in return. It is not uncommon for critics to accept bribes to praise a product or to give it publicity.

Whether we like it or not, critics are not always selfless servants of the public good. Instead, critics actively pursue agendas of fame, profit, and influence. The relationship between critic and audience is rife with potential for conflict of interest, as is the relationship between critics and their employers.

Although critics do not have unconstrained latitude to pursue their own ends, they often face a choice between their private interest and the public interest. Most critics, for instance, pursue multiple goals. They value monetary income, fame, power, influence, and doing the world good, to varying degrees.

In this context, I define a critic as any individual or institution that offers opinions to an audience. Typically these opinions concern products or performers in the marketplace. Examples of critics include movie reviewers, literary critics, disc jockeys, and the writers of *Consumer Reports*, but the designation is a broader one. We all act as critics on a smaller scale when we praise products to our friends and families.

Praise for Sale

The most direct and obvious conflicts of interest arise when critics are paid to express particular opinions. I use "praise for sale" to indicate such cases. The best known form of praise for sale is payola. Payola occurs when record companies pay radio station disc jockeys to promote specified performers and play their songs on the air. Although payola was outlawed in 1959, payments to station program directors for airtime, or exchanges of favors, remain common. In the days of vaudeville, payola was common and indeed was legal. Performers were paid to perform the material of particular songwriters.[1]

Funders sometimes hire the critic outright through vertical integration. Book clubs, rather than paying outside critics to slant their reviews, hire an advisory board to select and recommend books to their readers. The club then publicizes these recommendations in the form of monthly book club selections. The selection may be accompanied by an explanatory newsletter or descriptive blurb, providing favorable publicity for the book.

The advisory board members, employed by the book club, have the same incentives as critics who take payola—they are encouraged to endorse works to boost the profits of the book club. Movie advertisements are a significant source of newspaper revenue, which leads editors to choose critics who will write relatively favorable movie reviews. If the newspaper critic panned all movies in the local theaters, fewer people would go and the advertisements could not be sold for as much. The newspaper critics do not praise every movie, nor do they necessarily act insincerely, but the system tends to produce reviews that are slanted in a positive direction. Product placements also may bias the critical process. The recent film *The Runaway Bride*, starring Julia Roberts and Richard Gere, portrayed Gere as a writer for *USA Today*. The paper is shown applying high standards of journalism and Gere, of course, is the sympathetic male lead. It may be sheer coincidence, but the movie received an especially favorable review from *USA Today*.[2]

Payola plays a prominent role in many other sectors. Investment advisers are paid to promote the purchase of stocks, Campbell's pays a slotting fee for its location in the grocery store, and doctors pay referral fees to hospitals, to name a few other examples. Even on the low-cost Internet, praise for sale and advertising is emerging in many forms. What is scarce on the Internet is not information or material but, rather, context and evaluation. Consumers cannot find the relevant texts at low cost, given the mass of materials competing for their attention. Internet search engines accept fees to give the paying company prominence, when consumers are searching for a particular kind of product or information.

Stars reward enthusiastic critics with exclusive interviews or by making them the authorized biographer. David Marsh was a rock and roll critic who promoted Bruce Springsteen in the early days of Springsteen's career. Subsequently, Marsh became Springsteen's friend and authorized biographer, which boosted his own fame and income. When Springsteen made his music more commercial to reap large financial rewards, Marsh did not object to this trend, as did many harder-core fans, but rather he promoted it. Marsh sought to convince the world that the new, more popular persona did not contradict Springsteen's previous ideals. Marsh's motives will remain unknown, but we again see the potential for critical conflict of interest.

Some performers pay for praise by giving critics a financial stake in their reputations. The songwriting credits to Chuck Berry's *Maybellene*, were shared with disc jockey Alan Freed. Chess Records, Berry's record company, had gone to Freed with a catalog of material. Chess offered Freed partial songwriting credits on the song of his choice, knowing he would subsequently play and promote it. Freed listened to many recordings to find the most marketable one and attached his name to *Maybellene*.[3]

Painters give away works to well-placed critics and buyers. Clement Greenberg, a leading American art critic of his time, was accused of accepting paintings from artists in return for promoting their reputations. When this practice occurs, the critic has an initial reason to praise the artist, to receive an artwork in return. Later, the critic has cause to continue praising the artist, to see the artist's reputation and prices rise.[4]

Which Performers and Products Benefit from Praise for Sale?

In economic language, praise for sale favors products whose profits are highly elastic with respect to market demand. These are not necessarily the products that consumers desire most. All other things equal, a larger market makes publicity more profitable, and in that sense praise for sale responds to consumer demands. Suppliers try to avoid promoting losers, to preserve their profits and their reputations. Nonetheless, praise for sale does not match the interests of the audience exactly. Praise for sale will be strongest when it yields the most profit, not when the promotion would produce the most audience satisfaction.

In more technical economic language, the degree of promotion for a product is determined by the profits available from increasing demand for that product, rather than by the change in social value produced (consumer surplus plus producer surplus) from increasing demand. Profits and social value, however, are not generally the same. Profits measure how much of a product's value can be captured by producers, not the total value to society.

To give one example, praise for sale favors new musical stars over older musical stars. If an advertiser promotes one particular recording of *Beethoven's Fifth*, consumers may buy a different recording of the same symphony, given the relatively small differences among good performances to most people's ears. In contrast, if an advertiser promotes Prince, a responsive fan is more likely to buy Prince than the recordings of Michael Jackson. The personality-specific popular musics produce more sharply differentiated products than does the classical arena, where skilled orchestras are near-perfect substitutes. The supplier that competes with many close substitutes has less reason to stimulate fan interest, given that fan expenditures might spill over onto the substitutes.

Performers who can give critics a stake in their fame have an advantage over performers who cannot. Many kinds of artists, such as stage actors and performers, do not produce liquid resalable outputs. A critic can hear and observe a soliloquy or watch a mime, but a critic cannot own shares in the product itself. This differs from the case of the painter, who has an easier time "buying" praise by selling artworks to the right people.

Critics also pursue fame, either because they enjoy fame for its own sake or because fame often leads to money. This quest for fame, however, skews the interest of the critic.

A critic who pans all artists will find that no artist will promote his or her reputation as critic. Film critics who rave about movies see their names reproduced in advertising blurbs more frequently than do critics who are more negative. Some critics produce a steady stream of praise for nearly all movies, whether they be good or bad, simply to have their names appear in movie ads and thus to become better known.

Other critics promote their reputations by acting the role of smart aleck. Howard Stern is one of the most influential critics in the United States. His actions, including his opinions, are geared to produce an image of being rebellious and outrageous rather than necessarily reflecting the merits of products or necessarily reflecting what Stern really thinks.

In the literary realm, critics can more easily make their reputations by interpreting an ambiguous product than by summarizing a clear one. Richard Posner (1990, p. 61) argues that Shakespeare, Nietzsche, Wittgenstein, and Kafka owe part of their reputation to the enigmatic and perhaps contradictory nature of their writings. Critics can establish their own reputations by studying the writer and by promoting one interpretation over another. These same critics will support the presence of the writer in the literary or philosophical canon to promote the importance of their own criticism.

Economists have studied the ambiguities in John Maynard Keynes's *General Theory* in great detail. The monetary writings of Milton Friedman, far clearer and most likely superior for a practical understanding of monetary policy, do not receive equal attention from historians of thought. It is more difficult to establish one's reputation as an interpreter of Milton Friedman because it is usually obvious what Friedman is trying to say.

Gatekeeper Critics

Some critics pay less attention to immediate commercial incentives, instead serving as the societal guardians of long-term renown. These well-established, conservative institutions guard entrance into canons and pantheons of achievement. Examples of these critics include Nobel Prize committees, academic literary critics, museums, and Halls of Fame. I refer to gatekeeper critics.

Gatekeeper critics endorse performers to cement and extend their own critical reputations. To the extent the chosen performers do well, the certifying critic will enjoy stature, influence, and income. Gatekeeper critics therefore look to quality and historical importance when evaluating performers, at least relative to critics who are influenced by praise for sale. Gatekeeper critics are more likely to develop reputations for reliability and high standards rather than courting the mass market for immediate profit.

Even gatekeeper critics, however, do not serve as absolute guardians of merit. Like the critics who accept payola, they find their behavior shaped by economic constraints and opportunities, albeit to a lesser degree in many cases. Gatekeeper critics are not typically cynical maximizers of profit, but they must replenish their finances if they are to survive in the marketplace of ideas.

Gatekeeper critics, to the extent they are controlled by elites, produce evaluations that overrepresent the preferences of those elites. The "multiculturalists," for instance, charge that dead white males have achieved excess prominence in historical canons. Even if "white male elites" do not deliberately downplay the role of women and minorities in history, they may simply fail to perceive the contributions of those other groups. Many older critics understand the operatic music of Verdi better than the rock-operatic music of Queen, and therefore they promote the fame of Verdi to a greater degree; many younger critics act in the opposite manner. Today, conservatives charge that a new elite—academic left-wing multiculturalists—excessively promotes some reputations over others.

Critics have discretionary powers, and they often use these powers to shape cultural and intellectual agendas. We approve of the Louvre because it displays Poussin and Watteau, but also we approve of Poussin and Watteau because their paintings hang in the Louvre. Gatekeeper critics know that their promotions will be self-validating to some extent.

The discretionary power of gatekeeper critics often comes from the market power of many gatekeeper institutions. The list of top prizes and awards does not change rapidly, not compared to changes in the for-profit sector of the economy. The Michelin guide, the Nobel Prizes, the Academy Awards, and the baseball Hall of Fame have been opinion leaders for many decades and hold relatively secure positions for the future. The second most prestigious baseball Hall of Fame, whatever or wherever it may be, has low stature relative to the most prestigious. This market stability gives gatekeepers influence over market tastes and perceptions.

The discretionary powers of gatekeeper critics can lead them to discrimination and favoritism. When endorsements are free (i.e., when there is no payola), gatekeeper critics face excess demand for their endorsements. Then they can discriminate at low or zero cost. Critics in this position often will recommend friends of the family, performers who share the same political outlook, or performers who meet their personal preferences.

Even when gatekeeper critics are fully honest and sincere, their perspective will not generally match the tastes of their audience. Audiences have a greater taste for products that are accessible, immediately entertaining, and require little in the way of background knowledge. Gatekeeper critics, especially if they are professionals, take a greater interest in products that repay careful and intensive study. The audience is more likely to prefer the movie that looks good on TV or video; critics are more likely to prefer the art house film that yields more insight with successive viewings. The films of the Russian director Tarkovsky are far more popular with critics than with audiences. The audience cannot count on the critic to recommend what the audience would like to hear about, because the critic may instead try to "educate" his or her audience, whether or not the audience wants such an education.

Nor do gatekeeper critics completely avoid the biases of praise for sale which have been discussed previously. All gatekeeper critics are tempted at the margin by market opportunities, or are forced to accommodate market constraints. University presses take increasing care to publish and promote works that will sell, rather than lengthy tomes about obscure historical events. Universities are now requiring that their presses cover their costs. Art museums now sell Monet T-shirts, greeting cards, and coffee mugs, in part to raise revenue for their other operations and expenses.

Conservative Evaluations
and the Matthew Effect

Many gatekeeper critics have conservative biases. Because many fans (and performers) cannot easily distinguish between an innovation and a lowering of standards, reputation-conscious gatekeeper critics limit their innovations, in part to secure their reputations. Gatekeeper institutions therefore may become difficult to change. Their organizational structures become rigid, they implement checks and balances on decision-making procedures, and they give conservative critics a high degree of influence.

Gatekeeper critics, to demonstrate their credibility and high standards, may try to signal that they are not swept up in current fads. They often promote the time-honored achievements of the past and praise established stars from previous eras. They may glorify the past unduly, to establish conservative credentials and to insulate themselves against outside criticism.

Gatekeeeper critics often give special praise to the dead and the retired, in part because those individuals have no further opportunity to embarrass their promoters. James Dean and Jim Morrison attained greater fame with their premature deaths than if they had lived. Dean probably would have made a string of weak movies and Morrison's musical career probably would have stumbled. Both would have lost their image as "cool" and "sexy." But with these individuals safely dead, critics can promote them without fear of being embarrassed in return. Promoting the dead identifies the critic with a reliable standard more effectively than does promoting the unpredictable living.

Academic citation practices, such as the "Matthew effect," reflect the conservative tendencies of gatekeeper critics in areas such as academia. The Matthew effect arises when citations lead to other citations. Once a scientist starts being commonly cited for a contribution, that scientist continues to receive the full credit, even if other scientists were discoverers of equal historical importance.[5]

The mechanism driving the Matthew effect is clear. When one scientist cites the work of another, he or she does not wish to take chances. A scientist cannot achieve renown by having been the first to cite a notable work, but citing an unreliable work may hurt the scientist's credibility. Risky citation practices therefore have a downside but little upside, and scientists behave conservatively in this arena, even if they are risk-loving elsewhere, such as in their choice of research topics.

The Mattew effect is simply one example of the more general phenomenon of skewed praise incentives. In the view of Arthur Schopenhauer, individuals praise others to support their own glory, not to honor the person being praised. For instance, many people praise John Milton, not as an act of real homage but rather to demonstrate their literary taste, hoping to latch onto a share of Milton's renown. For this reason, once the value of a work or individual has been widely recognized, critics will scramble to honor it, but otherwise they may condemn it.[6]

Critical praise also tends to hold steady or rise over time. Once a professor helps his or her student get a teaching position, that same adviser will probably write a favorable letter for tenure. Regardless of the reality, the adviser wishes to pretend that his or her initial recommendation was a strong one. Once fans have praised a new rock star to their friends, they are more likely to keep quiet if subsequent albums are mediocre. Again, the praiser or promoter has acquired a reputational stake in the performer's success. Subsequent success will make the promoter look good, whereas failure will make the promoter look unreliable. The famous typically have induced many critics to hold reputational stakes in their status, thus supporting a conservative inertia of praise in their favor.

Critics tend to take more risk when they enjoy little surplus relative to their alternative opportunities. Young writers for technomusic fanzines have little to lose if they are fired, given their low or zero wage. For this reason, they are willing to offer risky evaluations. Alternatively, older critics with valuable sinecures and perks tend to act more conservatively, not only out of natural inclination but also in part to ensure that they do not lose their jobs.

The large corporate structures that are prevalent in the entertainment industry frequently discourage critical innovations. The larger the corporation, the greater the likelihood that the manager has built an empire of perks and personal relationships. Such managers usually play it safe and produce relatively conservative evaluations of talent. The manager bears large losses from making a mistake (i.e., he or she can be fired) but does not reap all the benefits from pulling off a gamble. That is one reason that so much of the innovation in modern popular music has come from the smaller independent record companies rather than from the established majors (Cowen, 1998). In smaller firms, the interests of the evaluating critic are more closely aligned with the interests of the shareholders. If we imagine a one person firm in which the same person is owner and talent evaluater, that person will capture the upside returns from successful gambles. He or she will face greater incentives to take chances. Motown was highly innovative when it was owned and run by Berry Gordy, but eventually it was sold to outside investors, lost its special flair, and entered the musical mainstream.

Why I Remain an Optimist about Criticism and Critics

The presence of a conflict of interest does not itself indicate a problem. A branch of economics, "principal–agent theory," demonstrates that conflicts of interest are virtually ubiquitous when individuals act jointly in pursuit of their goals. Conflicts of interest are not desirable per se, but we are willing to accept some conflicts of interest to lower the costs of doing business and to enlist the cooperative efforts of many people. A conflict of interest, when chosen by contract or of voluntary patronage, is likely to be beneficial, all things considered.

Praise for sale sounds dubious to most observers, but it often benefits consumers, as evidenced by the fact that consumers voluntarily patronize critics "on the take." Payola promotion, however unappealing to some outside observers, allows the audience to hear a critic without paying the full price.

Payola may be the best source of information audiences have, relative to its cost of acquisition. Praise for sale brings numerous and enthusiastic promotions to audiences, often for free. Sometimes fans are paid to see, listen to, or read messages of praise. Fans have entire industries at their doorstep trying to figure out which promotions will interest them most. These commercial forces often promote products with greater skill and interest than would "objective" critics with no financial interest at stake.

Audiences can limit the biases of praise for sale when they so wish. Rather than listening to mainstream radio stations for music, or consulting paid promotions, audiences can generate their own information. They can borrow recordings from friends, check recordings out from the library, consult academic experts, or patronize music shops that allow listeners to hear compact discs before purchasing them (a common practice in Europe and some U.S. stores). Audiences can limit the impact of payola by informing themselves.

Audiences often prefer praise for sale, even when more informed sources are available for free. The Tower Records chain gives away a periodical of music reviews, *Pulse*, which is highly literate, hires excellent critics, and examines nonmainstream products. In contrast, Tower window ads contain little information and target a less discriminating class of customer. Fans choose either the visual ads or *Pulse* for guidance, depending on their purposes and their degree of musical seriousness. Tower gives audiences the chance to choose the level of commercial influence which suits them best. Sometimes audiences do not know that the critics are paid to offer their praise, and in those cases praise for sale represents a mild form of fraud. Praise for sale, however, usually succeeds for other reasons. Even when audiences know that publicity is "bought," they may value the information they receive and respond by buying the product. I am more likely to buy the compact discs placed on the Tower listening stations, even though I know that the space has been sold. I have a chance to hear the music and if I like it I will buy it. Critics of commercial culture do not hesitate to check out the "New Books" table at Barnes and Noble, even though most of them know that publishers pay to have their books put on it.

Promotional campaigns often provide an important signal to consumers, who assume that an advertised CD is "hot" and therefore of potential interest. Furthermore, promoters wish to protect and extend their reputations. They would rather accept payola for popular products than for unpopular products. A critic who regularly praises inferior products will lose audience attention. Suppliers therefore find it cheaper to purchase praise for potential hits than for surefire duds; it is easier to buy a critic when the product is a plausible one. Fans, when they see payola, may rationally expect a successful and popular product.

In many cases stars purchase publicity to make themselves the "focal" performer and the center of attention. This strategy is most likely to succeed when fans do not care who the star is, but instead they simply want to follow the star that other fans follow. Payola and commercial praise, by placing a performer in the public eye, can propel that performer to stardom. When the identity of the next star is partially arbitrary in any case, fans are happy to receive an outside nomination for free rather than paying to control the choice directly.

Payola also limits the power of the critic to discriminate. When performers pay critics for endorsements, the critic is less likely to pick and choose personal favorites. Payola makes critics pay a price for discriminating; critics would forego payola income if they were to recommend their untalented nephews. Payola therefore gives individuals a chance to buy their way into markets that they otherwise might find difficult to crack. In the history of popular music, record payola has been used most intensely by outsiders and minorities, such as African Americans, who otherwise faced market discrimination (Cowen, 1998).

If audiences find that the biases of commercial promoters are too large, they can hire promoters through *subscription* to recommend products according to more specific criteria. When fans pay the entire bill through subscription, they can control their sources of information and evaluation. Under subscription finance, critics try to satisfy audiences—their immediate funders—rather than serving outside commercial interests such as distributors, advertisers, and promoters.

Watching advertisements in the motion picture theater could lower ticket prices by subsidizing the expense of the film, but fans prefer to pay for an uninterrupted movie. Many Internet users pay subscription fees to avoid the promotions that Web services flash on the screen. Again, fans choose their preferred mix of control, convenience, and price.

Payola does not give audiences the products they want most in absolute terms, but it does give them the products and promotions they are willing to pay for. The production and dissemination of critical information is costly and requires the cooperation of many outside parties, such as advertisers and promoters. Thus many people cooperate in the production of information and evaluation only because the process pays heed to profit. The critic's conflict of interest is part of the price we pay for the mobilization of information at low cost.

Fans can patronize gatekeeper critics when they wish to limit the impact of commercial promotions. Many reputation-producing institutions, such as Prizes and Halls of Fame, organize as nonprofits to signal that their endorsements are insulated from immediate commercial pressures. Some for-profit parent companies forbid their critics to take bribes to improve their reputation and marketplace standing. The Michelin Restaurant Guides are produced by a for-profit parent company, but Michelin requires its guides to rate restaurants objectively. Fewer fans would buy the Michelin guide if it were known that the critics took bribes from chefs; thus Michelin employs strict and conservative evaluators.[7]

Given that fans can reject and control advertising when they so wish, subscription finance and gatekeeper critics serve as benchmarks for understanding the role of commercial promotion in mass culture. Subscription finance and gatekeeper critics have many desirable properties, but they are too expensive to take over the entire market for criticism. Instead, we should view the market in the following terms: Fans accept critical conflict of interest because it is the best deal they can get. Marshall McLuhan pointed out that a medium shapes its messages, but he neglected to emphasize the role of audiences in choosing which medium will be used and which kind of shaping will occur. Competition, whether among media or critics, does not eliminate conflicts of interest, but it does allow audiences to select which conflicts they will encounter and therefore to minimize the costs of those conflicts.

In any particular instance, we should be wary of conflicts of interest between critics and audiences. Few particular actions of critics will provide exactly what the audience wants. But if we examine those actions in terms of their broader institutional setting, we can find logic in the observed divergence of interests between audience and critic, performer and critic, and employer and critic. The rules of the game in the marketplace for criticism are more efficient and more beneficial than they may at first appear.

Notes

Some of the themes and arguments in this essay are drawn from my books *In Praise of Commercial Culture*, and *What Price Fame?*. I wish to thank all the individuals who have assisted me with those books.

1. On the history of payola, *see* Coase (1979). One study estimated that 1985 payola payments were in the range of $70–$80 million (*see* Bogart, 1995, pp. 228–9).

2. Twitchell (1996, pp. 117–120) documents the influence of advertisers over program content; *see also* Parenti (1993). On newspapers, *see* English (1979, p. 101) and on the Golden Globe awards, *see* Waxman (1997).

3. *See* DeWitt (1985, pp. 25, 82).

4. On Greenberg, *see* English (1979, p. 98).

5. On the Matthew effect, *see* Merton (1973). On the citations literature, *see* Cronin (1984) and Lang and Lang (1990, p. 342).

6. *See* Schopenhauer (1851/1960, pp. 82–83).

7. Klein (1997) discusses how third-party certifiers face incentives to issue reliable recommendations.

References

Bogart, L. (1995). *Commercial culture: The media system and the public interest.* New York: Oxford University Press.

Booth, J. E. (1991). *The critic, power, and the performing arts.* New York: Columbia University Press.

Coase, R. (1979, October). "Payola in radio and television broadcasting." *Journal of Law and Economics, 22,* 269–328.

Cowen, T. (1998). *In praise of commercial culture.* Cambridge: Harvard University Press.

Cronin, B. (1984). *The citation process: The role and significance of citations in scientific communication.* London: Taylor Graham.

DeWitt, H. A., & Berry, C. (1985). *Rock 'n' roll music.* Ann Arbor, Michigan: Pierian Press.

English, J. W. (1979). *Criticizing the critics.* New York: Hastings House.

Keynes, John Maynard. (1936). *The general theory of employment, interest, and money.* London: Macmillan.

Klein, D. B. (Ed.). (1997). *Reputation: Studies in the voluntary elicitation of good conduct.* Ann Arbor: University of Michigan Press.

Lang, G. E., & Lang, K. (1990). *Etched in memory: The building and survival of artistic reputation.* Chapel Hill: University of North Carolina Press.

Merton, R. K. (1973). *The sociology of science: Theoretical and empirical investigations.* Chicago: University of Chicago Press.

Parenti, M. (1993). *Inventing: The politics of news media reality.* New York: St. Martin's Press.

Posner, Richard A. (1990). *Cardozo: A study in reputation.* Chicago: University of Chicago Press.

Schopenhauer, A. (1960). *The art of literature.* Ann Arbor: University of Michigan Press. (Original work published 1851)

Shrum, W. M. Jr. (1996). *Fringe and fortune: The role of critics in high and popular art.* Princeton: Princeton University Press.

Twitchell, J. B. (1996). *ADCULTusa: The triumph of advertising in American culture.* New York: Columbia University Press.

Waxman, S. (1997, Dec. 18). "Golden Globes' new spin: Hollywood press group admits problems." *The Washington Post,* pp. C1, C14.

13

CONFLICT OF INTEREST IN THE HOLLYWOOD FILM INDUSTRY

Coming to America—Tales from the Casting Couch, Gross and Net, in a Risky Business

Thomas E. Borcherding & Darren Filson

It's very difficult to identify conflict of interest.
Life is full of them.

—Warren Beatty

Making a film is an uncertain enterprise, not just because of the fickleness of moviegoers, but because of the immense complexity of the process. From its initial conception in the "pitch" to its ultimate exhibition at the movie complex or placement at the local video store, the coordination process in the making of a film is a team effort with enormous potential for economic dissonance. The Hollywood problem inheres in motivating the myriad economic agents in this process—actors, agents and managers; directors, producers and other production talent, and writers; marketers and the all-important financial backers—to serve the collective interest of the enterprise, not just their narrower ones. For artistic as well as pecuniary reasons Hollywood film industry participants often have incompatible incentives.

One of the keys to understanding the Hollywood problem is that everyone's information is imprecise. Because postcontractual separation of what follows from chance and from chiseling in the making of a film is difficult, opportunism in this environment is commonplace, if not rampant. Disputes over rights to "points" and to future syndication, profit-sharing controversies, allegations of the "casting couch" and other forms of favoritism or sexual harassment, failures to acknowledge the contribution of others in movie credits, and outright theft of concepts occasionally make the news in Middle America, but they are quotidian fare in *Daily Variety*, *Entertainment Weekly*, *The Hollywood Reporter*, *Premiere*, and the "Company Town" column in the *Los Angeles Times*. Understanding these fractious linkages helps explain how from the 1920s through the 1940s the Hollywood Studio System (HSS) developed as an ingeniously economic way of harmonizing these disputes, albeit imperfectly.[1]

In this chapter we use the movie business as a case study to show how the potential for conflicts of interest in an industry is influenced in important ways by fundamental properties of both the industry's production process and demand. We show how three key characteristics of the movie business—collaboration on a large scale, large upfront expenses, and tremendous uncertainty—have led to peculiar organizational and contractual practices. These practices appear to be noncompetitive and even coercive when they are viewed through an all-inclusive lens such as the Sherman Antitrust Act, which is designed to deal with monopolization issues in all industries and, therefore, leads courts to ignore or underestimate the importance of underlying fundamentals in any particular case.[2] We argue, however, that the unique and fascinating practices are reasonable responses to industry conditions. The organizational and contractual practices that we describe are mechanisms that align the incentives of industry participants to prevent conflicts of interest, facilitate the acquisition of information, and insure against risk. Our analysis suggests that in order to properly understand, mitigate, and adjudicate disputes among professionals, it is essential to have an understanding of the industry conditions that led to the disputes in the first place.

We approach the analysis of conflicts of interest from an economist's perspective.[3] Production and distribution involve more than a mechanical exercise in win–win cooperation. When parties to an exchange interact in the real world in a principal–agent relationship—stockholders with managers, managers with workers, customers with sellers, and so on—they seldom, if ever, have exactly the same goals. Conflicts of interest occur when a single agent has to use his judgment to either (1) balance the goals of two or more of his principals or (2) balance an interest of his own against the goals of one or more principals. Because parties to an exchange typically anticipate conflicts of interest, one of the goals in designing contracts and organizations is the minimization of such conflicts. Contracts provide agents with incentives to take appropriate actions. By doing so, contracts remove the need for a principal to trust the agent so much, because as long as the agent is self-interested, he can be expected to perform more as the principal desires. Organizations centralize decision making and use authority relationships instead of relying on independent judgement.

Nevertheless, contracts are always incomplete and organizations are imperfect; economic agents always have some opportunity to chisel on the explicit and implicit conditions agreed on. The way organizations develop and adapt to internalize these opportunistic proclivities is the subject of much of modern economic theory and is the economist's way of understanding how conflicts of interest are faced up to and mitigated (though never "solved") in the contractual process.

In what follows, we begin by describing the key characteristics of the movie business that shape the rest of our discussion and then describe how industry participants have anticipated and mitigated conflicts of interest. We organize our discussion around the rise and fall of the HSS.

Though the HSS emerged in response to industry conditions in the 1920s, several antitrust cases and consent decrees in the late 1940s and early 1950s led to the end of the vertical integration practices and the related contractual arrangements used by the major Hollywood studios in the glory days of the studio era. We describe how modern contractual arrangements between distributors and exhibitors attempt to accomplish the goals that the HSS was designed to achieve. We then discuss the net-profits controversy, which has received considerable attention in the press and in the courts in several cases, including *Art Buchwald v. Paramount Pictures Corporation* (1990) and other disputes between various Hollywood participants. Finally, we describe the controversies surrounding the "casting couch."

In our analysis we benefit from previous work by several economists and from various histories and commentaries on the industry cited in the bibliography. Four sources deserve special mention. Much of our analysis of the rise and fall of the HSS summarizes arguments made by De Vany and Eckert (1991), much of our analysis of modern exhibition contracts summarizes arguments made by Filson et al. (2000, 2001), and much of our analysis of the net-profits controversy summarizes arguments made by Weinstein (1998). Though not designed to explicitly deal with conflicts of interest, these papers analyze the relationship between the key characteristics of the business and the peculiar organizational and contractual practices we describe.

The Movie Business

A film brings together a combustible partnership
of ideas, skills, and temperaments. A tightly
controlled bottom line is for the most part an
impossibility.

—David Puttnam

Three key characteristics of the movie business have not changed since the emergence of the full-length motion picture in the early 1900s (Robertson, 1991). First, financing, manufacturing, and marketing movies requires the collaboration of several economic agents, including creators, producers, financiers, writers, directors, actors, distributors, and exhibitors. Thus, movie making is a team effort on a grand scale. To arrive at a rough estimate of the scale involved in a modern production, consider the following statistics: The Motion Picture Association of America (MPAA) reports that in 1998, a total of 490 new movies were released in the United States and 564,800 people were employed by the industry, with 240,200 employed in production and services, 133,500 employed in theatrical exhibition, and the remainder involved in videotape rental and other activities.[4] Although not all the people employed by the industry are involved in making new movies, many are involved in several projects at once. The employment figures suggest that a typical project employs a large number of people. Clearly each movie project requires a considerable amount of coordinated action.

The second key characteristic of the movie business is that movie making requires substantial upfront costs that must be incurred before the final product reaches the market. Again, the MPAA provides useful statistics. The MPAA breaks costs down into several components. The first component is the "negative costs," the costs of manufacturing the master print. The negative costs include any upfront payments to writers, directors, actors, and other employees; costs for sets; and other costs incurred during the production process. If the movie is a studio production (currently there are six major studios: Disney, Fox, Paramount, Sony, Universal, and Warner Brothers), the studio also charges an overhead fee for use of its facilities. The studio also charges interest on the negative cost and the overhead. Other important costs include print costs (the costs of making copies of the movie to distribute to theaters) and advertising costs. In 1998, the MPAA estimates that the average movie made by one of its members had negative costs, overhead, and capitalized interest of $52.7 million; print costs of $3.2 million; and advertising costs of $22.1 million—for a total cost of $78 million.

The third key characteristic of the movie business is that every movie is different; thus at the financing stage there is tremendous uncertainty about demand for the final product. Therefore, movie making is a risky business. When describing the movie, business economists frequently quote screenwriter William Goldman (1989), who said, "Nobody knows anything" (p. 39). Economists De Vany and Walls (1996, 1999) show that Goldman's statement is supported by the data. Using a sample of 2,015 movies released in the period 1984–1996, De Vany and Walls compute the cumulative box office revenues from the U.S. theatrical market for each movie. Using the cumulative revenues for each movie, De Vany and Walls show that the distribution of cumulative revenues is best approximated by a Pareto distribution with an *infinite variance*.[5] This implies that if we think of each new movie as a random draw from the distribution suggested by past outcomes, *there is no way to forecast cumulative revenues.* Because every forecast has a forecast error with an infinite variance, forecasts have no predictive power.[6]

Because financing decisions need to be made on the basis of little more than an idea (the "pitch"), it is quite reasonable to think of studio executives making financing decisions in an environment in which they are unable to forecast. In addition to De Vany and Walls's formal analysis, there are several examples in history of executives making decisions that after the fact appear to be huge mistakes. Vogel (1998) reports that *Star Wars*, the first movie in the most successful series ever (which includes *Empire Strikes Back, Return of the Jedi*, and *Phantom Menace: Episode 1*) was pitched to several studios before Twentieth-Century Fox agreed to finance and distribute it. *Titanic*, the highest grossing movie of all time, and other successful movies including *Back to the Future* and *Raiders of the Lost Ark*, were treated similarly. The list of poor box-office performers that generated tremendous initial optimism is equally impressive: *Heaven's Gate, Howard the Duck, Ishtar, Pennies from Heaven*, and *Star!* are prominent examples.

De Vany and Walls's results yield another stylized fact: the Pareto distribution has the property that the likelihood of observing any given level of revenue falls as the level of revenue rises. This fact, combined with the result that cumulative revenues have an infinite variance, implies that low revenue is the most likely outcome but when a hit occurs, the upside has no limit. This result, when combined with the fact that movie making involves large upfront costs, implies that many movies do not earn a positive return on investment. Although De Vany and Walls's data include only the U.S. theatrical market, revenues in later markets tend to be in rough proportion to revenues in the United States; thus it is unlikely that the results would change if the other markets were included. Vogel (1998) claims that most movies do not earn a positive return on investment even after taking into account home video, cable and television income, and income from other sources. Thus, the few big winners seemingly pay for the many losers.

Conflicts and Solutions in the Movie Business

As Hollywood classics . . . are recirculated and rediscovered
by successive generations, it is little wonder that
filmmakers would want to revive the system that produced
them.

—Thomas Schatz

The Emergence of the Hollywood Studio System

During the peak of the studio era (roughly from the 1930s through the
late 1940s), a few large Hollywood studios integrated finance, production,
distribution, and exhibition and dominated the industry. Each major studio had long-term exclusive contracts with its actors and other talent and
owned its own first-run theaters. Unfortunately for the HSS, its highly
hierarchical and economically successful structure—involving exceedingly long-term contracts for its numerous talent, and its putatively oli-
gopolistic rather than atomistically competitive market—invited state intervention. In the late 1940s and early 1950s a series of antitrust cases
and consent decrees collectively referred to as the *Paramount* decrees en-
sued, exceedingly adverse to the HSS. The 1950s also brought the rise of
television, a potent substitute for theater screens, causing even more
problems for the major studios. By the end of the 1950s, the HSS effectively was no more. Hollywood itself was alive, however, and many of
the major studios remained, but their structures were hollowed out. Vertical integration and temporal relations were shortened up and scale was
reduced. With the HSS gone, the market was formally more competitive,
though whether more effectively so is a matter of controversy among
scholars and industry insiders.[7]

In this section, we argue that the vertical integration and related contractual practices employed by the HSS were natural responses from firms
that had to deal with the three key characteristics of the movie business
described previously. We show how the industry structure that resulted
from the firms' choices led to legal disputes and explain why the courts
were persuaded that many of the industry's practices were the result of
abuses of market power rather than adaptive responses to fundamental
conditions. Following our analysis of the breakup of the HSS, we describe
how modern nonintegrated studios deal with the problems that the HSS
was designed to solve. De Vany and Eckert (1991) have analyzed the
events surrounding the *Paramount* decrees and provide a more detailed
analysis of many of the arguments we make.

Our first point is that the HSS emerged in response to the key characteristics outlined in the previous section. The major Hollywood studios were a solution to the problem of coordinating large numbers of inputs and financing large, risky projects. Combining finance, production, distribution, and exhibition in one organization and using long-term exclusive contracts helped the studios assemble the various participants in a project and align their incentives with the studios'. This mitigated conflicts of interest. In the movie-making process, famous actors have to balance their contractual goal of completing the movie and their private goal of gaining more recognition from fans and other studios. Actors may hold up production by demanding more lines to speak or other types of special treatment. Directors have to balance their contractual goal to not spend more than the budget allows and their private goal of pursuing their artistic aims. Short-term contracts cannot align incentives in a satisfactory way because it is impossible to write a complete contract that specifies each party's rights and responsibilities in every possible state of the world. By using long-term exclusive contracts, studios were able to economize on the transactions costs (the costs of negotiating, monitoring, and enforcing contracts) associated with dealing with the many project participants. The ongoing integrated organization avoided the cost of re-contracting every time a new movie was made and could punish chiselers more effectively because contracts lasted beyond a single project.[8]

The large studios were able to produce several movies within one organization during a relatively short amount of time. This allowed the studios to overcome the financing problem described previously, because movies in the theater provided cash to finance new projects. Other aspects of the organization of the HSS also contributed to resolving the financing problem. The studios needed access to screens in order to generate cash flow, and they used both contracts and integration to ensure access. Owning theaters provided the studios with insurance, because they could be sure of having access to the screens they owned. It also allowed them to more easily monitor box-office performance and learn about how successful their movies were.

Operating on a large scale was essential too, not only for cash flow purposes but also to diversify risks in the movie-making environment. Because success is unpredictable in advance, for a production–distribution company to survive it needs many movies in order for the hits to make up for the flops. Otherwise, as time goes by the firm eventually experiences a string of flops and must exit the industry. Several of the studios experienced ups and downs in the HSS era, and in modern times there are several examples of smaller studios and independent producers and distributors experiencing financial failure. Modern independents must experience success in their first few tries or go out of business (Levy, 1999).

In sum, the need for firms in the movie business to economize on transactions costs and diversify risks led to the emergence of the HSS, in which a few large vertically integrated firms controlled most of movie production and distribution.

The Organization of Theatrical Exhibition during the Studio Era

The theater system during the studio era was organized to allow for different "runs." Major motion pictures would open in first-run theaters, many of which were located in the downtown areas of major metropolitan centers. After showing in the first-run theaters, the movies would move to the second-run theaters, and later to third-run theaters. Then, as now, movie attendance was typically highest in the first few weeks following the opening of the movie, so the first-run theaters were the plushest and most successful theaters.

Even during the peak of the studio era, most theaters were not studio owned. Nevertheless, the studios did own several first-run theaters in major metropolitan centers, which allowed them to accomplish three main goals: First, as discussed further later, it made it easier for studios to manage the allocation of their movies to theaters. Second, the studios needed to generate cash flow as quickly as possible in order to finance their current production. Third, the studios needed to monitor box-office performance. Integration assisted the studios in planning the second and later runs of their movies by allowing the studios to obtain precise estimates of demand.[9] However, studio ownership of first-run theaters created an environment in which the studios controlled many of the most successful theaters in the industry, which led in part to the *Paramount* decrees in the late 1940s and early 1950s.[10]

The fact that studios and independent exhibitors could not predict the demand for each movie made it difficult to manage runs and release dates to maximize revenues while avoiding disputes. To see why, consider a simple scenario in which an exhibitor has a theater with a single screen. Suppose the exhibitor agrees to show distributor 1's movie A and then distributor 2 arrives with movie B. When should the exhibitor begin showing B and stop showing A? In a world free of transactions costs and with complete trust, the exhibitor could be a fiduciary of the distributors: The exhibitor could determine the switching point by maximizing the sum of the revenues from the two movies and then divide the revenues in a "fair" way between himself and the two distributors.

However, because in reality the distributors do not trust each other or independent exhibitors, each distributor uses a contract to restrict the exhibitor's behavior. A typical exhibition contract might specify a final showing date while allowing for possible renegotiation or continued showing if the revenues are sufficiently high. Although these contracts avoid the need for distributors to trust the exhibitor, they may not lead to the maximum revenues. No matter which final showing date the exhibitor agrees to, there is a high chance that after demand for A has been observed, the exhibitor will regret his choice. Renegotiation will be difficult, too, because in most cases any change that benefits distributor 1 hurts distributor 2 and vice versa.

To attempt to maximize revenues while avoiding disputes, some contracting practices emerged that were on their face unusual but reasonable under the circumstances. When studios contracted with independent exhibitors, they typically used a *block booking* contract. The basic feature of such a contract is that the studio and exhibitor would sign a contract in which the exhibitor agreed to show all the studio's movies during a season. Both sides benefited from block booking—the studios were sure of placing their products in the theaters, and theaters were sure of having something to sell. Further, block booking facilitated renegotiation. In the foregoing example, if distributor 1 and the exhibitor signed a block booking contract, then if it became desirable to extend the run of one of distributor 1's movies, distributor 1 could agree to delay the opening of one of his other movies in the block. Because block booking was typically combined with a revenue-sharing agreement, both sides had the incentive to agree to the renegotiation as long as it increased total revenues.

Though it had some advantages, block booking appeared to be coercive and the practices that accompanied it made it look even more so. For example, block booking was accompanied by *blind selling*: Typically, independent exhibitors had to accept films in the block without having the opportunity to screen the movies in advance. Each exhibitor would receive a list of the studio's movies with a basic outline of the plot, director, and actors for each feature. Blind selling was necessary under the circumstances. For block booking to occur in the absence of blind selling, a studio would have to have its entire season of movies ready to be released at the beginning of the season. As mentioned earlier, movies have large upfront costs that cannot be recouped until the movie is released, so the opportunity cost of keeping a movie in inventory is quite high. Part of the interest costs of keeping a movie in inventory would have to be passed on to exhibitors and consumers; thus it was in the interest of everyone to minimize such costs.

De Vany and Eckert (1991) argue that some of the problems that might be associated with blind selling were avoided by the HSS. For example, one potential problem with blind selling—essentially the selling of a product that does not yet exist—is that the seller may never deliver the promised good. Exhibitors might fear that the studio would promise a particular movie with particular stars and other talent and then fail to deliver. The Hollywood studios were able to avoid this problem because they were integrated into production. The studio system allowed the studios to credibly commit to making the movies on the list because all the directors and actors were in the studio's stable of stars.

Further, Hanssen (2000) argues that block booking and blind selling in practice did not restrict exhibitor choice as much as they might have. A simple-minded interpretation is that the large, powerful studios used the contracts to force the small independent exhibitors to take all the bad movies along with the good ones, and to have no opportunity to screen the movies in advance. In reality, the contracts were not so coercive. Exhibitors were typically allowed to refuse to show some percentage of the movies (perhaps 10 percent) once the movies were available for screening. Both parties agreed in advance on the number of movies the exhibitor could refuse to show. Hanssen shows that exhibitors typically refused fewer movies than permitted under the contract, which suggests that exhibitors were not unduly constrained by these long-term contracts.

In sum, block booking and blind selling allowed distributors and exhibitors to deal with the tremendous uncertainty in the movie business. Because no one can forecast a movie's likelihood of success before it has been produced, all parties operate under a veil of uncertainty at the point of contracting when blind selling is used. Thus, overall risk is reduced to the extent that distributors can be sure of placing all their movies in theatres, whether or not they are hits, and exhibitors are assured of obtaining movies for their screens. Nevertheless, disputes can occur. Once demand is realized, the distributor would like to force the exhibitor to keep the flops, but give up the hits so that they could be put up for competitive bidding! On the other side, in some situations the exhibitors might prefer to refuse more movies than they are allowed to by the contract. Given the obvious potential for disagreements after the movies have been released, it is easy to see why early on studios pursued vertical integration as a way to avoid endless contract negotiations and renegotiations and why long-term relationships were important.

The Collapse of the HSS

The fact that movie making came to be dominated by a few large firms that integrated finance, production, distribution, and exhibition and used contracts that were integrative in nature made the movie business a target for the antitrust authorities. The courts, unfamiliar with the details of how the industry operated and why its particular organizational forms emerged, applied a one-size-fits-all solution, the Sherman Antitrust Act, and decided that integration, block booking, and blind selling involved an abuse of market power on the part of the studios. In a series of court decisions that began in the late 1940s and continued into the 1950s, the studios were forced to sell off their theaters and to stop using block booking and blind selling and other features of contracts that were integrative in nature.

In part as a result of the *Paramount* decrees, the HSS collapsed in the late 1940s and early 1950s. It is difficult to estimate the full impact of the decrees because the collapse of the HSS was in part due to the diffusion effects of television. In the 1950s, television became increasingly popular. With the advent of television, demand for "B" movies, which tended to have the same characters in similar stories again and again, dropped considerably, because people could get that type of entertainment on television for free. As a result, studios found it necessary to produce large blockbusters in order to attract an audience (De Vany and Eckert, 1991). Thus, studios began making fewer but much bigger films. Once the studios stopped making B movies, it was no longer optimal to keep a large stable of talent on long-term exclusive contracts, because the talent could not be continuously employed.[11]

Interestingly, even though industry conditions have changed somewhat, some modern organizations still model themselves after the old studios when developing relationships with talent. For example, in the 1990s TriStar pictures maintained long-term relationships with several production companies. Generally, TriStar obtained exclusive rights to pictures the production companies generated for a given period, and the production companies benefited because they did not have to deal with a distributor each time they produced a picture (Medavoy, 1992). Also, modern multidivision talent agencies such as William Morris Agency, International Creative Management, and Creative Artists Agency have taken the place of the old studios in many ways. The large agencies have long-term contracts with their talent and often do package production deals that combine several actors with a director. Further, in modern times, often a single individual is both the producer and star or director and star of a movie. The individual in the combined role may internalize many of the externalities typically created in the dealings between the artistic and business sides in the movie-making process.

The HSS eliminated much of the potential for conflicts of interest because the business was dominated by large studios throughout the vertical chain, from "pitch to popcorn."[12] In the next section, we describe contractual arrangements in the post-HSS era that were designed to mitigate conflicts of interest in the absence of authoritarian relationships.

Post-Paramount Distributor–Exhibitor Contractual Arrangements

By the late 1950s studios still financed production and controlled distribution but no longer owned theaters and no longer had long-term contracts with talent. However, the underlying key characteristics of the industry remained: The studios needed outlets for their movies, the exhibitors needed movies to put on their screens, and movie making still involved tremendous uncertainty and large upfront costs. Integration of distribution and exhibition was no longer an option and in any case, with the advent of television, may not have been optimal. It is interesting to consider the two solutions the firms adopted in lieu of integration.

First, short-term contracts replaced integration and long-term contracts as the means of aligning incentives of the various parties involved. Because studios did not own theaters and could not use long-term contracts, they had to rely on short-term contracts to attempt to align the incentives of theater owners with the studio. Second, long-term relationships developed that allowed the studios and the exhibitors to avoid much of the shortsighted noncooperative chiseling that might otherwise have emerged. Today, most exhibitors are independent theater chains, so the large studios negotiate many of their exhibition contracts with these large firms. For the most part, even though contracts with exhibitors are on a movie-by-movie basis, distributors still maintain long-term relationships that help them resolve disputes.

Exhibition contracts vary from exhibitor to exhibitor and from movie to movie, but they generally have some features in common. Each week, the distributor gets the maximum of three possible payments. In the first, the distributor gets 90 percent of the movie's gross over some agreed-on "house nut," where the house nut is a fixed amount paid to the exhibitor. In the second, the distributor gets a "floor payment," some percentage of the gross that declines as the weeks go by. The share might start at 70 percent in the first week, be 60 percent by the third week, and eventually fall as low as 40 percent. In the third possible payment, the distributor simply receives a flat payment. For hits early on in their runs, the 90 percent over the house nut is the relevant payment. For most other movies the floor is relevant, and for complete failures the flat payment applies. Of course, if the distributor and the exhibitor have a long-term relationship, renegotiation is possible in the event of a complete failure.

Although the courts were in favor of distributors relying on competitive bidding as a way to allocate movies to theaters, they realized that they lacked the resources to monitor the bidding process on a movie-by-movie basis and thus did not impose such a procedure on the industry. In modern times, the use of bidding varies by distributor and by region, but in general most exhibition contracts are negotiated with exhibitors (Friedberg, 1992). Even when competitive bidding is used it is not binding, and it often serves as a point of departure for negotiations between the distributor and the exhibitor. When evaluating bids, distributors consider a variety of factors other than the contract terms, such as the demographics surrounding the theater, the location itself, and the decor.

De Vany and Eckert (1991) and Filson et al. (2000) argue that the short-term exhibition contract attempts to accomplish in a decentralized fashion many of the same goals that integration and block booking attempted to accomplish in the studio era. One of the main goals is the mitigation of exhibitor conflicts of interest.[13] To see how a short-term contract aligns the incentives of the exhibitor with the interests of the distributors, consider the problem faced by a modern exhibitor, who typically runs a multiplex (a theater with several screens). The exhibitor first must choose among the movies that different distributors have to offer and then must allocate movies to its various screens in a way that maximizes its revenue. Filson et al. (2000) have analyzed this setting and we summarize their arguments here.

The exhibitor's revenue from each movie depends on its contract terms with each distributor for each movie *and* on the entire slate of movies it selects. To see why the slate of movies matters, consider a multiplex with two screens and simply note that some movies are fairly close substitutes (e.g., Horror A and Horror B) while others are not (Horror A and Drama C). Showing two horror movies at the same time attracts only those consumers who like horror movies (typically the under-25 crowd) and splits those consumers between the two movies, whereas showing Horror A with Drama C allows the exhibitor to continue to attract many horror fans as well as to attract consumers who like dramas (the over-25 group). Thus, the demand for Horror A depends on which other movie it is paired with.

Now consider a group of distributors who have to design contracts to offer the exhibitor. In a world with zero transactions costs and no regulations, each distributor would like to negotiate a contract with the exhibitor that specifies the exhibitor's *entire slate of movies*. That way, each distributor would be sure that the exhibitor would take into account the cross effects on the demand for its movies. Because such a contract is prohibited by the *Paramount* decrees and is likely prohibitively expensive to negotiate, monitor, and enforce in any case, distributors use instead an incentive contract of the type described above. This contract provides the exhibitor with the incentive to maximize the revenue from each of its movies. Because hits are rare and have high revenues, the exhibitor can be expected to show a hit even if its share of the revenue is low. Thus in this case, the 90/10 split applies. Revenue is lower for movies later in their runs, so the exhibitor's share of the revenue must rise, and the 70/30 or 60/40 splits apply. Without the increased share the exhibitor would drop the old movie and show a new one instead.

Other contractual arrangements between distributors and exhibitors are also interesting (see Filson et al. 2001). For example, the distributor receives no share of concession revenues. To those not in the industry, this may not seem important, but concession profits may account for half of an exhibitor's profit! Given this, exhibitors may have a conflict of interest because they have to balance their own desires against the goals of their principal, the distributor. Exhibitors want to get as many people to come to the theater as possible and sell as much food and drinks as possible, but they typically get only a small percentage of the ticket revenue. As a result, exhibitors will be tempted to keep ticket prices quite low in order to encourage attendance. On the other hand, the distributor wants to maximize ticket revenue and does not care about concession sales, so the distributor prefers a higher ticket price.

To understand why concession sales are left out of the contract, it is important to think about the overall goal of the exhibition contract and then think about the optimal way to implement that goal (or at least come as close as possible to achieving it). Ideally, the distributor and exhibitor would like to maximize the sum of ticket sales plus concession sales and then divide the two in an appropriate way. This is the overall goal. While attempting to implement this goal, the two parties must economize on transactions costs.

One simple solution that distributors could use to align the exhibitor's pricing incentives with their own is to simply include ticket prices in the contract. Distributors could force exhibitors to charge a certain price for admission, and thereby provide incentives for exhibitors to keep prices up. Unfortunately, such a contract is known as a vertical restraint and is frowned on by the courts as an anticompetitive practice. Many economists believe that such practices should not be discouraged, in part because they allow contracting parties to economize on transactions costs (for a discussion, see Carleton and Perloff, 1994).

The concession sales create different incentives for distributors and exhibitors, so why not align their incentives by putting concession sales in the sharing contract? One explanation is that distributors would find it difficult to monitor concession sales and attribute the sales to the various movies showing in the multiplex. Without monitoring, the best the contract could do is assign the concession revenues to the various movies based on the number of tickets sold. This suggests that contracting on the number of tickets sold (rather than ticket revenues) could keep ticket prices up. The number of tickets sold is sometimes used in exhibition contracts but does not appear to be common (De Vany and Eckert, 1991).

The most compelling explanation for how ticket prices are kept up has to do with the structure of long-term relationships. As mentioned previously, distributors typically negotiate with exhibitors, and even when competitive bidding is used they are by no means required to accept the highest bid. If an exhibitor has delayed payment or been otherwise uncooperative in the past, the distributor can be expected to prefer the exhibitor's competitors. This "threat" encourages exhibitors to keep admission prices in a reasonable range from the point of view of the distributors.

Further, as long as the exhibitor's ticket price can be observed at the time of contracting, the parties can set their contract terms while taking the ticket price into account, and contract terms will vary across theaters with different ticket prices. Other things equal, lower ticket prices should be associated with a higher flat payment from the exhibitor to the distributor and a higher distributor share of ticket revenues, so that the expected payment to the distributor ends up being the same as when ticket prices are high. Because the exhibitor can predict that the contract terms he is offered will depend on the price he charges (though not explicitly), the exhibitor may be provided with the incentive to set the ticket price in a way that maximizes the sum of total revenues. By giving all the concession sales to the exhibitor, the contract ensures that the exhibitor has an incentive to maximize concession sales while economizing on the distributor's monitoring costs.

Compensating the Participants: The Net-Profits Controversy

In this section we describe disputes surrounding the division of distributor rentals (the distributor's share of movie revenues) between the major studios and the talent they employ. Contracts in which prominent writers, actors, directors, or producers receive a share of the revenue or a share of the profit in addition to an upfront payment have a long history in Hollywood, but since the collapse of the HSS they have become increasingly common.[14] As sharing contracts have been more widely used, their complexity has increased as well, and many have argued that the contract terms are unfair. Much of the controversy has to do with the definition of "profit" used in the contracts.

The most common type of sharing contract in Hollywood is a net-profits contract in which net profits is a *contractually defined term*, not profit as calculated according to Generally Accepted Accounting Principles (GAAP). Several disputes have arisen over the ex-post interpretation of the contracts, because on several extremely high-grossing movies the net profits were never positive. Litigation between individuals and studios has been frequent (Biederman et al., 1996) but often unsuccessful from the individuals' perspective. The first serious challenge to the net-profits contract was *Art Buchwald v. Paramount Pictures Corporation* (1990), a dispute over the net profits from the movie *Coming to America*, an extremely high-grossing movie. In the case, among other charges, plaintiff Alain Bernheim (a producer) charged that his net-profits contract was unconscionable, and that Paramount owed him a fiduciary duty. In the end, the court invalidated a number of provisions of Paramount's standard net-profits contract and awarded $900,000 (small compared to the request) to the plaintiffs, and the case was eventually settled (Biederman et al., 1996).[15] However, the court concluded that Paramount was not a fiduciary except with respect to its duty to render an accounting.

In this section, we apply the same type of reasoning used earlier to explain that the net-profits contracts employed by the Hollywood studios are responses to the three key characteristics of the movie business. We provide some insight into why the court in *Buchwald v. Paramount* was persuaded that many of the contract terms were the result of abuses of market power rather than adaptive responses to fundamental underlying conditions. In our description of the contracts and the reasons for their use, we rely heavily on a detailed analysis by Weinstein (1998). We describe the potential for the studio to experience a conflict of interest in its accounting role and some factors that mitigate this potential conflict.

A considerable amount of the controversy and confusion is related to the definition of net profits. Because net profit is defined contractually, the definition can vary from contract to contract. Typically, however, net-profits contracts use a fairly standard formula for computing net profits. Garey (1992) and Weinstein (1998) provide useful descriptions. Start with a dollar of box-office revenue (the gross). As noted previously, the distributor (the studio) and the exhibitor typically use a sharing contract, so the distributor does not obtain the full dollar. Suppose that the movie is a hit, so the 90/10 split applies once the house nut has been subtracted. Suppose the house nut is 10 percent of the gross; thus, out of each dollar the distributor gets 90 percent of 90 cents, which is 81 cents. From the distributor's share, approximately 30 percent is deducted as a distribution fee, leaving 56 cents. The distribution fee pays for the distributor's distribution expenses and includes some profit for the distributor. Next, advertising and promotion expenses, including interest costs on advertising and prints, are deducted. These costs are typically 25 percent of the distributor's rentals (the 81 cents), which leaves 36 cents. Then an overhead charge of 10 percent of advertising and promotion is deducted, leaving approximately 32 cents. From the 32 cents, "negative costs" (the costs of developing and producing the movie) plus interest on negative costs are deducted. An overhead charge on negative costs is also deducted. From what is left, any additional loans, plus interest, are deducted. If there are any gross participants, their share also gets deducted as a cost, and interest and overhead charges on the gross participation are also deducted.[16] Anything left of the initial dollar is *net profits*. From net profits, the distributor (the studio) gets a share ranging from 50 percent to 80 percent, and the producer (if independent) gets the rest. The talent (writers, actors, and directors) is paid from the producer's share.

It is easy to see from the foregoing description that the standard net-profits contract appears to be one-sided and unfair. Even large-grossing pictures, such as *Coming to America* and *Batman*, often never generate positive net profits. As the movie continues its run, the gross goes up and up, but so do the distribution, print, and promotion costs, and interest is accumulating all the time. Interest and overhead must be paid off before the principal starts to be reduced. Cynics claim that only in rare cases in which low budget pictures that have hardly been advertised surprise everyone and gross $100 million or more are net-profits participants ever paid, and even then it only occurs because the studio's creative accountants cannot hide the money. Yet, it is clear that even when net profits are negative, the studio often still earns a profit according to GAAP. The studio's profit comes from the distribution fee, the advertising fee, the interest and overhead charges, and its share of net profits. Each "cost" component has some margin of profit calculated into it. The studio has a potential conflict of interest because it must be trusted to perform the accounting properly. It has an incentive to use creative accounting to increase its own profits. The threat of lawsuits, the likelihood of repeated dealings with the same talent, and the risk of adverse publicity imperfectly mitigate this conflict of interest.

Although several of the contract terms appear to be weighted in the studio's favor, Weinstein (1998) argues that net-profits contracts have a long history in Hollywood, and that because of this modern net-profits participants know what they are getting into when they sign a net-profits contract and negotiate accordingly. Sharing contracts were used as early as 1923. These early sharing contracts tended to be used more by the small studios than the large successful ones. This alone provides some insight into the reasons for their use—smaller studios were more subject to failure and had a greater incentive to reduce upfront costs and share risk.

As an early example of a net-profits contract, consider the contract used in 1950 when Universal was experiencing financial difficulties but wanted to hire Jimmy Stewart for the movie *Winchester '73*. Universal could not afford Stewart's normal salary of $250,000 per movie so it offered him a contract with no upfront payment but 50 percent of the "net profits." Net profits were defined in the contract as the gross in excess of twice the negative cost. The break-even point of twice the negative cost was chosen because it was calculated to be the point at which the studio would recover its distribution and advertising expenses as well as its production costs.

Although Stewart's contract lacked many of the features of the modern net-profits contract, the reason for its use is instructive: knowing that movie making involves substantial upfront costs that may not be recouped (because of uncertain demand), the studio reduces the possible downside by lowering the upfront payments to its talent. Doing so does not come without cost—any risk-averse economic agent who is forced to bear risk must be compensated with a higher expected payment—but the cost is worth bearing, because the studio only has to pay if the movie is a success, in which case there is enough money for everyone. Thus, the key characteristics of the industry—its high upfront costs and its tremendous uncertainty—explain why net-profits contracts were and continue to be used.

The other key characteristic of the movie business, the need for collaboration on a large scale, also plays a part in the use of modern net-profits contracts. Movie production involves several opportunities for major stars to hold up production in a variety of ways. Stars can be difficult to work with, insist on special treatment in a variety of forms, and drive production costs up considerably. Chisholm (1997) argues that one of the things a net-profits contract accomplishes is that it aligns the incentives of the net-profit participants with the incentives of the studio. However, this effect is likely not as important as risk sharing. Reputation effects also contribute to incentive alignment; news travels fast, and an actor with a reputation as someone with whom it is difficult to work can expect to be shunned accordingly.[17] Further, because only a small fraction of net-profits contracts ever have positive net profits (perhaps 10 to 20 percent) it is unlikely that prominent actors can make marginal adjustments in their performance that have any substantial effect on the likelihood of earning positive net profits—most of the time their choices will be infra-marginal. The contracts only pay off in the event of an unanticipated success.

The use of net-profits contracts increased once the HSS began to collapse (Weinstein, 1998). With the introduction of television and the abandoning of B-movie production, the studios began to make fewer movies with larger budgets. This increased upfront costs per movie and also made the business more risky. Further, once the HSS collapsed, few prominent actors had long-term contracts with studios; movie-by-movie contracts became the norm. Studios became less stable places. Weinstein reports that the average tenure in office for executives in charge of production was around twenty years during the 1940s and declined to four years by the 1970s and 1980s. Turnover was even higher at weaker studios.[18] Weinstein argues that wealthy stars in the post-HSS era were often in a better position to absorb risk than the production executives they worked for, hence the increased use of sharing contracts.

In sum, the broad features of the modern net-profits contract have a long history in Hollywood, so it is reasonable to assume that all Hollywood agents and lawyers are familiar with what they imply. Several independent distributors exist, so there are substitutes for the studios. The reason that writers, producers, directors, and actors continue to work with the studios is that the studios provide development, production, and distribution services in one firm and put the credibility of their names behind projects. These services allow the studios to compete with entrepreneurs' other production and distribution alternatives, and if participants willingly sign the studios' net-profit contracts, it suggests that the overall benefits of working with studios offset the potential for dissonance.[19]

However, even though the broad features of the net-profits contracts have sound reasoning behind them, in *Buchwald v. Paramount* several of the features of the net profits contract were found to be *unconscionable*. Some of these features include charging a fixed, predetermined overhead on production costs and advertising expenses instead of computing the overhead charge by taking into account all of the movies produced in a given period and charging overhead and interest on payments to gross participants.

Weinstein, nevertheless, offers plausible explanations for the practices that appear to be unreasonable; many of these practices facilitate auditing and thus mitigate potential conflicts of interest for the studio in its accounting role. For example, as noted previously, one of the "costs" deducted when computing net profit is the cost of compensating the gross participants. Further, an overhead charge is attributed to this expense, even though compensating gross participants involves little more than writing a check. Weinstein's explanation is as follows: The studios need to be able to spread their overhead costs among a variety of movies and must do so in a way that allows net-profits participants to audit their contracts without having access to the studio's cost data on every movie it makes. As a result, the studios charge a fixed-percentage overhead charge. By itself, this may lead to an inefficient allocation of overhead, because efficiency requires that more expensive movies receive a larger overhead charge. Because movies with gross participants are likely to be expensive, charging overhead on the gross participation increases the overhead attributed to expensive movies and brings the studio closer to an efficient allocation of overhead while still allowing the net-profits participants to audit their contracts.

Still, some problems with auditing may remain because the costs included in the calculation of net profits are typically the studio's costs; studios have been accused of using creative accounting methods to transfer costs and benefits between projects in order to cheat net-profit participants. One response of independent producers to the studio's ability to manipulate costs is to avoid studios as much as possible until the final product is ready to distribute. However, even once distribution starts, studios still have the ability to control a variety of costs. As noted previously, studios have long-term, ongoing relationships with exhibitors. Studios have been accused of negotiating deals with exhibitors in order to shift reported revenue away from movies with high net-profits participation and toward movies with low net-profits participation (Cones, 1997).

Further, even though modern agents are familiar with the standard contract terms, problems can arise if agents do not represent the talent effectively. Agents' private incentives are often incompatible with the interests of their clients. One potential conflict between agents and talent is developing as we write (Bates & Eller, 2000). Agents to date, by agreement with the Screen Actor's Guild (SAG), by California state law, and by old federal consent decrees, are not permitted to have financial interests in either television or movie productions or distributions. Agents would like to do this, however, and one can imagine that agencies might even become part of the large entertainment conglomerates. Clearly, if an agent is part of the studio, the actor may end up with no effective representation. Opponents to agents participating in production and distribution in the SAG are many, however, and very powerful (e.g., Warren Beatty). It is doubtful that Disney or Viacom soon will be teaming up with top agencies, as SAG seems much opposed, as is the Department of Justice.

Managers, whose functions are close to that of agents, are not, in fact, so restricted, but they generally represent only well-established talent, who are capable of hiring high-priced Hollywood lawyers to keep their managers honest.[20] However, stories of bad managers are common, and even the most famous stars fall victim now and again. Clearly, reputation effects, morality, and the law of fraud are not perfect prophylactics against studied malfeasance. A prominent recent example involved the comedian Garry Shandling and his former manager Brad Grey. Shandling accused Grey of exploiting his two positions as Shandling's manager and the executive producer of Shandling's popular *Larry Sanders Show* to obtain excess fees and also to create several new shows using talent that had been involved with Shandling's show. The case was eventually settled out of court.

The Casting Couch:
If You Want to Get Ahead,
You Have to Give a Little

The famous "casting couch" and the alleged sexual exploitation of young men and women entering the movie industry are well-known to the lay public. Biographies of those in the business are awash with these stories. Although little more than strings of anecdotes are available, all agree that it is a problem for newcomers who have not established themselves in the industry but not for veterans. In this section, we argue that the big-project, big-budget, hit-driven nature of the business creates an environment that can lead to exchanges of sexual favors of newcomers.[21]

The exchange of sexual favors may lead to conflicts of interest if decision makers end up choosing talent on the basis of sexual exchanges instead of merit. The reason is that the decision maker's principal, the studio, wants the best talent available. However, the potential for conflicts of interest is not as severe as it first appears. The nature of the business makes it difficult to judge "merit" in many cases. Previously we linked uncertainty in the movie business to executives' difficulties in judging the quality of movie projects, but a second source of uncertainty comes from difficulties in judging the quality of unknown talent. Does a particular actor have the potential to be a "star," one of the few performers who can attract large crowds on opening night? On extremely rare occasions there may be new actors whose obvious talent allows them to stand out from the rest, but within broad categories most newcomers trying to make it in Hollywood are essentially indistinguishable from each other, and Goldman's Law described earlier applies to star making as well as to movie making: It is extremely difficult to predict who will become a star and who will not.

This environment, in which executives are uncertain about the potential of newcomers and in which hits earn tremendously high revenues, naturally creates a "superstar" effect that has been described by Rosen (1981) and MacDonald (1988): The pool of newcomers attempting to enter the business will always be large, and the newcomers will willingly accept wages well below what they can earn in their best current alternative. Newcomers accept low wages because success in the movie business, though rare, is rewarded highly, and the returns may be out of proportion to talent. The superstar effect means that small differences in talent can lead to huge differences in pay.[22]

We argue that, in fact, if their need for subsistence did not prevent it, most new actors and actresses would accept no wage at all and even pay for the opportunity to appear in a film.[23] Lacking money, many choose to "sell" their sexual services in an attempt to influence producers, who otherwise have few ways to distinguish one newcomer from another. According to this view, hanky-panky though common is not really coercive but represents *quid pro quo* exchanges.[24] Though the casting couch exchange is counter to state and federal law, it may be a crime without a victim.[25] As one lawyer who talked with us off the record said, "It's part of the wages on both sides of the exchange."[26]

Further, sexual exploitation is taken less seriously in this extremely sophisticated, if not wholly cynical, industry than one might expect. The industry is built in part on sex, so sexy talk off the set is common and a selling point in the gossip network which generates a great deal of valuable publicity. Exchanges of all sorts of favors are routine among those in this business, and *quid pro quo* sex may be one of the commodities. In any case complaints to the Equal Employment Opportunity Commission are rare, and suits under California law are as well.[27]

Still, it is worth noting that UCLA, USC, and various other groups run extension courses and workshops on sexual harassment. This suggests that not all sexual advances involve voluntary exchange. Further, it is not at all clear that newcomers who attempt to use sex to get ahead in the business are all successful. It seems likely that a type of "prisoner's dilemma" exists here—individuals who attempt to use sexual favors to distinguish themselves from other newcomers likely find that many other newcomers are attempting to use such favors for the same purpose. The end result may be that trading sexual favors becomes necessary for entry into the business but it is difficult to distinguish oneself through such trading because so many are engaged in the same practice.

Although precise figures are not available, it seems likely to us that sexual exploitation has been reduced since the collapse of the HSS. Under the HSS, studios had great power. Contracts were long-term and lucrative, and sexual demands were, it would appear from the "buzz" of the time and biographical materials today, part of the entry costs. It is said that one famous director had a sign on the ceiling above his couch in his Culver City studio office that read, "Don't forget, darling, tomorrow you're going to be a star" (Franke and Kasinor, 1975). With the breakup of the HSS and the death of the long-term contract, bargaining power of powerful people to make the careers of young actors has been considerably diminished.

Conclusion

For all their grandiosity, for all their ability to infuriate, movie people are rarely stupid.

—John Gregory Dunne

In the movie business, three key characteristics—collaboration on a large scale, large upfront expenses, and tremendous uncertainty—have influenced firms' choices of organizational forms and contracts. These choices have structured the disputes that have emerged between the studios on the one side and the antitrust authorities, exhibitors, and talent on the other side. Our analysis suggests that understanding the key characteristics that shape competitive behavior is important for adjudicating disputes, and we believe that this conclusion extends beyond the movie business: An in-depth industry study should be one of the first steps in any legal action involving industry participants in an industry with which the court is unfamiliar.

Notes

The authors are Professor and Assistant Professor of Economics, respectively, School of Politics and Economics, Claremont Graduate University, 160 E. Tenth St., Claremont, CA 91711. Email: Thomas.Borcherding@cgu.edu, Darren.Filson@cgu.edu. We would like to acknowledge useful conversations with Keith Acheson, Fernando Fabre, Stephen Ferris, Scot Lewis, Alfredo Nava, Michael Riley, and Paola Rodriguez. Matthew Borcherding, the senior author's son and a graduate of Hastings College of Law, University of California, shared his expertise drawn from an entertainment law course taught by Professor James Kennedy in the spring of 1999. Darlene Chisholm, Art De Vany, Sherwin Rosen, Gary Segura, Karyn Williams, and the editors provided useful comments on this chapter, and Nancy Lumpkin helped us with the literature search. Of course, all errors and misinterpretations are our responsibility.

1. Imperfect may still be efficient, however, when given the costs of further improvement, the returns are unfavorable.

2. As we write, the *Microsoft* case is underscoring the tensions between off-the-rack interpretations of law by the U.S. Department of Justice and Microsoft's team of lawyers and economists who wish to emphasize the idiosyncratic nature of the software industry.

3. Conflicts of interest are implicitly dealt with in the neoinstitutional version of economic theory (North, 1990) and game-theoretic models of agency problems (Mas-Colell et al., 1995).

4. All the MPAA figures reported here and below can be obtained from the MPAA website, http://www.mpaa.org.

5. The Pareto distribution has a peak at a low level of revenue and is skewed to the right. When the variance is infinite, the right tail is very fat.

6. It is important to distinguish between forecasts made at the financing stage and forecasts made once the master print is complete. Once the master print is complete, studios can use test audiences to assist in forecasting, and even third parties such as *Premiere* magazine can *sometimes*, but not always, compute accurate forecasts based on industry "buzz" about the movie (Bart, 1999; Shamsie, 1999). The problem is that *at the financing stage*, when the money must be committed to the project, there is no way to forecast.

As the idea is developed into a script and moves into production, the studio's forecast becomes increasingly accurate. When improved forecasts are available, the studio might reevaluate the project and shut it down. However, it appears that such shut-down decisions either occur before production has begun (in the development stage, when not much money has been committed) or not at all. Perhaps it is too difficult and expensive to transact with all the resources if the studio retains the right to cancel or renegotiate all contracts once production has begun.

In any case, the preproduction forecasts, though based on a script instead of just a pitch, are also notoriously inaccurate. For example, Goldman (1989) reports that Columbia passed on *E.T.* after developing it for $1 million because a survey suggested that the audience would be small. Universal picked it up and *E.T.* went on to become one of the most successful movies of all time.

7. Although the decline of the majors gave way to the growth in numbers and relative stature of new studios and independent producers and distributors, agency costs and scale/scope economy losses necessarily rose. De Vany and Eckert (1991) argue that the *Paramount* decrees raised costs, reduced output, and ultimately hurt consumers. Whether the recent mergers of studios and television networks in entertainment conglomerates are a substitute for the defunct HSS is not at all clear because these links are more horizontal than vertical.

8. Authority and long-term contracts provided the studios with more control over budgets as well. It is interesting to note that modern independent producers often rely on "completion guarantors" to control budgets. Completion guarantors provide a form of insurance to financiers. They are paid a fee up front, and in return they agree to provide the funds to complete the picture if it goes over budget. Of course, this is an imperfect solution, because the completion guarantor may accomplish this budget-control goal by taking over the production of the film, and this can result in a poor final product (Rudman, 1992).

9. When dealing with independent exhibitors, studios sometimes employed individuals to count the number of patrons at a theater to monitor

the box-office performance and prevent exhibitor chiseling. Also, exhibition contracts sometimes based the distributor's payment on the *national* revenues instead of the individual theater's revenues. This effectively severed the connection between the exhibitor's own revenues and the amount he needed to pay the distributor and effectively removed the exhibitor's incentive to misreport his revenues. De Vany and Eckert (1991) discuss these issues further.

10. The *Paramount* decrees were, according to De Vany and Eckert (1991), brought on by the complaints of several independently owned theaters in major metropolitan areas which felt denied the right to show first-run studioproduced films: "During the 1950s, one-third of the correspondence received by the Antitrust Division of the Department of Justice was from exhibitors complaining about distributor decisions concerning runs, clearances, and criteria for selecting winning bids" (p. 98).

11. Actors also preferred to abandon long-term contracts once the studios cut back production and stopped making B movies because they could no longer make a career out of playing a single character. Thus, the incentives for making relationship-specific investments diminished on both sides (Chisholm, 1993).

12. We thank our colleague Gary Segura for suggesting this catchy phrase.

13. It is interesting to note that in 1984, the U.S. Department of Justice gave studios permission to forward integrate into exhibition again (Mansfield, 1997). Some distributors did so, including Sony, which bought the Loew's theatre chain. Block booking is still frowned on, and the use of blind bidding varies by state. However, the lack of integration suggests that short-term contracts and long-term relationships allow the studios to accomplish many of the same goals that integration and long-term contracts accomplished in the studio era.

14. Talent at the technical end of the business—the lighting people, electricians, set constructionists, wardrobe assistants, etc.—is called *talent below the line* by those in the business (Resnick & Trost, 1996). This no doubt has to do with the placement of credits shown in the movie. They tend to be represented by their respective unions which watch out for their interests. It is the above-the-line folks—the creative people: the actors, directors, writers, etc.—who make the high salaries and receive sharing contracts.

15. Despite this case, studios have not abandoned net-profits contracts, and in a more recent case, *Batfilm Productions v. Warner Brothers Incorporated* (1994), which disputed the net profits from *Batman*, the court sided with the studio. It seems likely that disputes over the definition of net profits will continue to occur.

Stars involved in television series have had similar complaints. Vogel (1998) describes how television star James Garner became involved in a dispute with Universal Studios over the popular television series *The Rockford Files* (1974–80). Garner initially agreed to a deferred compensation contract and the studio later claimed that there were no profits to share. The case was reportedly settled out of court for $10 million.

16. In a gross participation contract, the payment is a function of the movie's gross (the revenues) instead of net profits. Only the most famous actors and directors receive such contracts, and "first-dollar" gross contracts, which begin to pay as soon as the first dollar of revenue is earned, are the

most favorable participation contracts in Hollywood. However, most gross contracts involve contingent payments, and this effectively blurs the distinction between a gross-participation contract and a net-profits contract. The net-profits formula provided here shows that net profit is essentially a function of gross receipts; the only additional terms that affect the computation are production and distribution costs. Because most gross-participation contracts involve contingent payments that are not made until these costs are covered, a typical net-profits contract can be transformed into a typical gross-participation contract and vice versa (see Weinstein, 1998, for further discussion).

17. As a qualification to this, note that it seems likely that not all of a participant's reputation may depend on the bottom line. For example, a director may value respect from peers more than the bottom line and may be willing to go over budget if it improves the artistic quality of the final product, whereas a studio may prefer to appeal to the masses and keep costs down, a point Putnam (1998) dwells on.

18. It is not obvious that dismissals should be frequent in an environment in which no one is able to forecast at the financing stage. Filson (2000) shows why rapid executive turnover can be an optimal response when firms operate in stochastic environments with hits and flops. The explanation is that it is difficult to distinguish the effects of a poor project from the effects of managerial incompetence; thus, if an executive has a string of flops even though optimizing decision makers in the firm think there is a high probability that the projects were poor, they also believe that there is a high probability that the executive is incompetent.

19. Although the data for formally evaluating the fairness of net-profits contracts are not available, Ravid (1999) presents indirect evidence that supports the claim that famous stars are paid their marginal value—their compensation reflects their contribution to making the film. This is further evidence that suggests that the contracts stars sign do not systematically cheat them.

20. Managers provide a broad range of career-management services, many of which may also be provided by agents. The main distinction between agents and managers is the following: Agents are *primarily* involved in seeking employment and the financial aspects of contract negotiations, whereas managers are *primarily* involved in the other aspects of managing the client's career (career development, financial management, public appearances, etc.). However, because both are involved in the business of advancing their client's career, there is no precise distinction between the two functions, and courts sometimes have to use judgment to determine which is which. This is not to say that the distinction is unimportant; the consequences of being a manager who acts as an agent are quite serious. Biederman et al. (1996) describe several court cases.

21. Dutka (1991), Francke and Kasindorf (1975), and McCreadie (1990) describe the Hollywood casting couch.

22. The music business and professional sports also appear to exhibit superstar effects (Frank & Cook, 1996).

23. In fact, payments of this type occur. The fraud division of the Los Angeles Police Department devotes considerable resources to chasing down persons promising, for upfront dollars, to find employment for new talent.

However, mitigations in the form of cheap information are available. New-comers can learn of what is "legit" from a plethora of extension courses, workshops, books, and information on the Internet. Still, many learn the hard way.

24. Of course, producers are not the only ones who have something to trade in return for sexual favors—writers may provide more lines (and thus more exposure) in return for sex, a director may agree to feature an actor in more scenes, and so on. For an account of such practices, we refer the reader to the recent movie *Bowfinger*, a movie about making a movie. In *Bowfinger*, the character played by Heather Graham advances her career by having sex with essentially everyone else involved in making the movie.

25. Of course, even if neither of the parties to the exchange is a victim, sexual exchanges may have victims outside the exchange. For example, a newcomer who does not get an audition may be considered a "victim" if an audition is allocated to another in return for sex. Whether these externalities are internalized by the implicit contracts involving sexual exchanges is not clear.

26. Note that this statement suggests another reason why the decision maker's principals might tolerate decisions based on sexual exchanges: If the decision maker receives sex on the job, the sex becomes part of his or her compensation, and the principals can pay the decision maker lower wages than they would have to otherwise.

27. Interestingly, other than the odd case law decision—which is rare because most complaints are settled out of court—little has been written about Hollywood sexual harassment in the law or policy journals, nor is there a book or dissertation on the subject as far as we could determine.

References

Biederman, D. E., Pierson, E. P. Silfen, M. E., Glasser, J. A., Berry, R. C., & Sobel, L. S. (1996). *Law and Business of the Entertainment Industries*. 3rd ed., New York: Praeger.

Carlton, D. W., & Perloff, J. M. (1994). *Modern industrial organization*. 2nd ed., HarperCollins.

Chisholm, D. C. (1993, Spring). Asset specificity and long-term contracts: The case of the motion-pictures industry. *Eastern Economic Journal*, 19 (2), 143–55.

———. (1997). Profit-sharing versus fixed-payment contracts: Evidence from the motion pictures industry. *Journal of Law, Economics & Organization*, 13 (1): 169–201.

Cones, J. W. (1997). *The feature film distribution deal: A critical analysis of the single most important industry agreement*. Carbondale: Southern Illinois University Press.

De Vany, A., & Eckert, R. D. (1991). Motion picture antitrust: The *Paramount* cases revisited. *Research in Law and Economics*, 14 51–112.

De Vany, A. S., & Walls, D. W. (1996). Bose–Einstein dynamics and adaptive contracting in the motion picture Industry. *Economic Journal*, 106, 1493–1514.

———. (1999, Nov.). Uncertainty in the movie industry: Does star power reduce the terror of the box office? *Journal of Cultural Economics*, 23, 285–318.

Filson, D. (2000, Oct.). The dynamics of resource allocation in research organizations. *Journal of Economic Behavior and Organization, 13* (2), 263–277.

Filson, D., Fabre, F., Nava, A., & Rodriguez, P. (2000). Avoiding head-to-head competition on the big screen: The economics of movie distribution, working paper, Claremont Graduate University.

————. (2001). At the movies: Risk sharing and the economics of exhibition contracts, working paper, Claremont Graduate University.

Frank, R. H., & Cook, P. J. (1996). *The winner-take-all society.* New York: Penguin Books.

Friedberg, A. A. (1992). The theatrical exhibitor. In J. E. Squire (Ed.), *The movie business book.* 2nd ed., New York: Fireside.

Garey, N. H. (1992). Elements of feature financing. In J. E., Squire (Ed.), *The movie business book.* 2nd ed., New York: Fireside.

Hanssen, F. A. (2000, Oct.) The block-booking of films: A re-examination. *Journal of Law and Economics XLIII,* 395–426.

Kenney, R., Klein, B. (1983, Oct.). The economics of block booking. *Journal of Law and Economics,* 497–540.

MacDonald, G. M. (1988, March). The economics of rising stars. *American Economic Review, 78* (1) 155–66.

Mansfield, E. (1997). *Applied microeconomics.* 2nd ed., New York: W. W. Norton.

Mas-Colell, A., Whinston, M. D., & Green, J. R. (1995). *Microeconomic theory.* New York: Oxford University Press.

Medavoy, M. (1992). A chairman's perspective. In J. E. Squire (Ed.), *The movie business book.* 2nd ed., New York: Fireside.

North, D. C. (1990). *Institutions, institutional change and economic performance.* New York: Cambridge University Press.

Prag, J., Cassavant, J. (1994). An empirical study of determinants of revenues and marketing expenditures in the motion picture industry. *Journal of Cultural Economics, 18,* 217–35.

Ravid, S. A. (1999, Oct.). Information, blockbusters, and stars: A study of the film industry. *Journal of Business, 72,* 463–92.

Rosen, S. (1981, Dec.). The economics of superstars. *American Economic Review, 71,* 845–58.

Rudman, N. G. (1992). The finishing touch: The completion guarantee. In J. E. Squire (Ed.), *The movie business book.* 2nd ed., New York: Fireside.

Shamsie, J. (1999, Oct. 22). *Adam Smith goes to Hollywood: Demystifying the economics of the entertainment industry.* Paper presented at conference, California State University, Northridge.

Squire, J. E. (Ed.), *The movie business book.* 2nd ed., New York: Fireside.

Vogel, H. L. (1998). *Entertainment industry economics: A guide for financial analysis.* 4th ed., New York: Cambridge University Press.

Weinstein, M. (1998, Jan.). Profit sharing contracts in Hollywood: Evolution and analysis. *Journal of Legal Studies, 27,* 67–112.

Industry Background and History

Bart, P. (1999). *The gross: The hits, the flops—The summer that ate hollywood.* New York: St. Martin's Press.

Biskind, P. (1998). *Easy riders, raging bulls: How the sex–drugs–rock n roll generation saved Hollywood.* New York: Simon & Schuster.

Brouwer, A., & Wright, T. L. (1990). *Working in Hollywood*. New York: Avon.

Cassidy, J. (1997, Mar. 31). Chaos in Hollywood. *The New Yorker*, pp. 36–44.

Dunne, J. G. (1998). *The studio*. New York: Vintage Books. (Original work published 1968.)

Dutka, E. (1991, Oct. 15). Scenes from the home of the casting couch. *Los Angeles Times*, calendar section, p. 1.

Francke, L. B., & Kasindorf, M. (1975, Aug. 18). The casting couch. *Newsweek* p. 54.

Gabler, N. (1988). *An empire of their own: How the Jews invented Hollywood*. New York: Crown.

Goldman, W. (1989). *Adventures in the screen trade: A personal view of Hollywood and screenwriting*. New York: Warner Books.

Levy, E. (1999). *Cinema of outsiders: The rise of American independent films*. New York: New York University Press.

McCreadie, M. (1990). *The casting couch and other front row seats*. New York: Praeger.

McDougal, D. (1998). *The last mogul: Lew Wasserman, MCA, and the hidden history of Hollywood*. New York: Crown.

Prindle, D. F. (1993). *Risky business: The political economy of Hollywood*. Boulder, CO: Westview Press.

Puttnam, D. (1998). *Movies and money*. New York: Alfred A. Knopf.

Resnick, G., & Trost, S. (1996). *All you need to know about the movie and T.V. business*. New York: Simon and Schuster.

Robertson, P. (1991). *The Guiness book of movie facts and feats*. 4th ed., Enfield, UK: Guiness Publishing.

Schatz, T. (1998). *The genius of the system: Hollywood filmmaking in the studio era*. New York: Holt.

Sklar, R. (1994). *Movie-made America: A cultural history of American movies*. New York: Vintage Books.

Weinstein, M. (1999, Summer). The economics of Hollywood. *Marshall School of Business Alumni Magazine—University of Southern California*, 45–9.

Workshop: Sexual harassment in the entertainment industry. (1997, May 10). UCLA Extension Program.

V

Health Care

14

CONFLICT OF INTEREST IN MEDICAL PRACTICE

Stephen R. Latham

But even skill is enthralled by love of gain.

—Pindar, *Pythian Odes*, iii:54

Conflicts of interest are an ineradicable part of medical practice, though not every kind of conflict of interest currently encountered in medical practice is ineradicable. Of those conflicts of interest that cannot be eradicated, many can be limited so that they do not result in harms to patients or to the public. In this chapter, I attempt to lay out a few of the most important types of conflict of interest in medical practice and to discuss the means by which they might best be eradicated or limited. I confine my discussion to certain of the most important conflicts faced by practicing physicians as such, leaving aside the many difficult conflict-of-interest questions raised when physicians act, for example, as researchers, educators, administrators, and lobbyists; and leaving aside, also, consideration of conflicts faced by non-MD medical practitioners.

Before discussing conflicts of interest in the context of medical practice, I offer some preliminary analysis of the general term "conflict of interest." The analysis should focus the subsequent inquiry and will support some later arguments about ways in which conflicts of interest in medical practice might be "tamed." I address, first, the relevant conception of "interests" and then consider which kinds of conflicts involving interests are properly termed "conflicts of interest." I then hazard a definition—and offer a quick justification for having done so.

Interests, Conflicts, and Conflicts of Interest

"Conflicts of interests," unsurprisingly, involve conflicting interests. But what are *interests?* Clearly, they are sources of motivation: that doing something is in our interest supplies us with some motivation for doing it. Contemporary social theorists—economists, social choice and positive political theorists, sociologists—frequently use "interest" as a loose term for any and every source of human motivation. From the economist's premise, *through his choices, the preferences of self-interested man are revealed,* it seems to follow that *man has an interest in anything he chooses.* In this vein we find Erde (1996), in his analysis of medical conflicts of interest, assimilating "interest" to all motivation, whether moral, prudential, or emotional. This broad usage is aptly described by Albert Hirschman (1986) as tautological, because, if every motivation is a variety of interest, then every action, no matter how motivated, is self-interested (Hirschman, 1986; see also Mansfield, 1996). The inevitable result for Erde is that an astonishingly broad array of events "count" as instances of conflict of interest.

But in other usage—including in legal analysis, which makes extensive use of the idea of state's and citizens' interests, and in the ordinary language that condemns politicians who sacrifice the "public interest" by pandering to "special interest groups"—the term "interest" is reserved for a particular brand of motivations—the instrumental or calculative.

Here, Hirschman's work in uncovering the term's history is of central importance. Hirschman (1997, 1986). Hirschman charts the rise, from the late seventeenth through the eighteenth century, of a certain doctrine of the interests, according to which the interests could be counted upon to tame the passions. The orderly pursuit of interests was thought to prevent first princes then states, individuals, and social groups, from giving in to their disorderly and destructive passions for fame, power, and wealth.

This doctrine of interest differentiates interests from reason on the one hand and from passion on the other. Reason is notoriously ineffectual; it can fail utterly to motivate. Passion is violent, destructive, and unpredictable; it motivates all too well. Interest "partakes of the better nature of both": It tames the passions by subjecting them to reason's long-term calculus and coaxes reason into action by tying it to passions (Hirschman, 1986). A prince with a passion for glory or power may act impulsively and destructively, but a prince pursuing his interests in "securing his place in the history books" or "consolidating his position" will act only after careful calculation. A passion for wealth may tempt us to theft or gambling, but the rational pursuit of gain makes nonimpulsive, industrious workers of us all. Adam Smith (1776) supplied the capstone to the doctrine when, in the most famous passage of his *The Wealth of Nations*, he argued that the pursuit of interest did not merely keep more destructive passions at bay but, under the guidance of the Invisible Hand, actually served as the engine of social prosperity.

In Smith's work, "interest" refers primarily to pecuniary interest—the passionate love of gain as that has been transformed through its subjection to the calculative rule of reason. This transformation involves stripping wealth of its destructively erotic character. We may sense something of this transformation by paying close attention to a delightfully topical story of Pindar's: The poet informs us that the great healer Asclepius, son of Apollo, father of Panacea and Hygieia, was tempted by the "love of gain" into agreeing to raise a rich man from the dead. For their presumption in attempting to appropriate to man the immortality of the gods, an enraged Zeus hurled a single thunderbolt through the chests of both physician and patient. Asclepius was literally seduced into his act of hubris not by the prospect of future wealth but by the immediate physical allure of the money itself—Pindar speaks of him as having been "enthralled" and "turned" by the "gold shining in his hand." By way of contrast, Smithian pecuniary interest is distinctly unerotic, impersonal, predictable, imposed on us by the calculus of reason; it is "a motive that pushes you toward an object, as opposed to an attraction in the object itself." (Mansfield, 1996, p. 60).

Importantly, however, it is not only the passion for wealth that can be tamed through its transformation into an interest. Smith's assimilation of "interest" to "pecuniary interest" is admittedly the dominant use of the term, but it is by no means universal. The passions for ease, for power, for glory, can all be tamed, and the pursuit of their objects be made less destructive, more predictable, and even socially productive, by their being transformed into interests.

Turning now from consideration of "interests" to consideration of "conflict," we may make the equally unsurprising assertion that conflicts of interest involve *conflicting* interests. But not every instance of "interests in conflict" gives rise to a conflict of interest. We can make successive cuts toward the core idea of conflict of interest by thinking about the criteria elicited by the following examples. In working through the examples, I offer no proof other than an appeal to the reader's sense of the ordinary connotations of the phrase "conflict of interest."

Consider, first, the interests of a buyer and a seller of some commodity.[1] It is in the buyer's interest to sell the commodity for the highest possible price, and in the seller's to buy it for the lowest. But though the interests of the buyer and seller conflict, we would not say that either one of them has a "conflict of interest." It would seem, therefore, that in addition to the presence of interests in conflict, "conflict of interest" requires that *a single person be simultaneously motivated to do two conflicting things*. In the case posited, though the buyer's and seller's motivations conflict with one another, the conflict is located, so to speak, in the space between them rather than within either of them. Consider, next, a single person who has simultaneous interests in enjoying leisure and in amassing wealth. Such a person has conflicting interests—is simultaneously motivated both to work and to relax—but we would still, I think, be reluctant to say he had a "conflict of interest." Conflict of interest entails not only that a single actor entertain conflicting motives but that the conflict be driven by that actor's consideration of the interests of *more than one person*. Consider, next, the employee who is simultaneously ordered by two superiors to do two mutually exclusive tasks. This poor fellow is motivated to do two conflicting things, each of which would further the interest of a different person—but, here again, although he has a difficult problem, he has no "conflict of interest." It would seem that for a person to have a conflict of interest, that person must simultaneously be motivated to do conflicting things, each of which is in a different person's interest—and that *one of the conflicting interests must be his own*. Consider, finally, the goodhearted woman who entertains simultaneous desires to give financial assistance to an impoverished friend and to save for her own retirement. This is a single person who is simultaneously motivated to do conflicting things, one of which is in her own interest and one of which is in the interest of another. And yet I think we would *still* not be tempted to claim that she has a "conflict of interest." This is because her friend's interest has come into conflict with her own, as it were, "gratuitously." She is under no duty to give financial assistance to her friend; her very consideration of his interests—her gratuitous elevation of them into a position where they can conflict with her own—is a kind of gift. With a few additional facts, however, we might start to feel differently: If she has promised him assistance in the past; if she promised his mother she would look after him; if he is retarded and she is his appointed guardian—in any of these cases, we are tempted in the direction of thinking that she now has a conflict of interest. The key notion is that her attention to her own interests is somehow interfering with a *duty* to advance his. People acquire duties to pursue the interests of others in all sorts of ways. Such duties are sometimes the explicit creations of law (as, for example, in the case of the appointed guardian); they are sometimes taken on voluntarily, through a promise or contract.

And they are sometimes read into relationships by custom. In particular, they are read into relationships in which one party is seen to be dependent on the judgment and goodwill of another, as a child upon a parent, a layman upon an expert, an investor upon a manager.

Provided that we bear in mind both the pecuniary and nonpecuniary senses of the word "interest," the following formulation seems to capture the kinds of conflicting interests that amount to "conflict of interest": A person has a conflict of interest when, in the presence of some duty to pursue the interests of another, she is motivated by self-interest to do something inconsistent with that duty. Thus a physician has a conflict of interest when, in the presence of some duty to promote the interests of another (usually, though not always, a patient), she is motivated by self-interest to do something inconsistent with that duty.

It follows from the foregoing, relatively narrow definition that there are numerous occasions when physicians' failures to serve their patients' best interests are not due to conflicts of interest. Thus, for example, a company physician who examines an employee prior to enrolling him in the company health plan may do injury to the examinee's interests by discovering and disclosing to the employer a preexisting condition that the examinee had wanted to keep secret. Such a physician may have conflicting obligations—the contractual one to the company and a professional one to the examinee as patient. But he is probably not in a conflict-of-interest situation. First, it is arguable whether he has any duty to advance the interests of the examinee in this case; second, his immediate motive for reporting his findings to the company is not properly characterized as "self-interested." It is of course open to us to argue that the physician has an "interest" in reporting this examinee's condition, insofar as his failure to make the report might result in the physician's being fired. But this way lies the tautological usage decried by Hirschman: We might just as easily say that a draftee "has an interest" in engaging in combat, because his refusal to do so might result in court martial. In the case at hand, it is easier and more direct to think of the physician's reporting obligation, rather than of his interest in fulfilling it.[2]

Similarly, we may think of the emergency-room physician who is compelled by law to report a patient's gunshot wound. The physician may or may not, in so reporting, be serving the patient's best interests, but his or her decision to report, because it is not driven by self-interest, is not the product of a conflict of interest as here defined. On the other hand, consider the pediatrician who declines to obey a law requiring her broadly to report to the state every sign of possible child abuse, including "borderline" or inconclusive signs. Suppose her reason for declining is that she is afraid of the business effects on her practice of gaining a reputation for being overly suspicious of parents, and for being an overzealous "reporter."[3] This is indeed a conflict-of-interest case, because the physician is allowing her self-interest to interfere with her obligation (as determined by the state) to pursue the best interests of her pediatric patients through a policy of liberal reporting of suspicious signs.

Finally, according to this definition, the physician who has sex with his patient may not have a conflict-of-interest problem. It may be that he is drawn into improperly exploiting his power over his patient not by his pursuit of self-interest but by his failure of self-control—that is, that his problem may have its roots in passion rather than in interest.

We cannot, of course, depend on the proposed—or any—definition to sort the world neatly into instances of "conflict of interest" and "other." Conflict of interest involves motivation, and peoples' motivations do not parse so cleanly. Nonetheless, the sloppiness of the real world does not eliminate the utility of relatively sharp definitions. Consider, for example, the problem faced by the physician in the by-now-infamous case *Spaulding v. Zimmerman* (Luban, 1988; Hazard et al., 1994; Applbaum, 1999). He is hired by defense counsel in an auto-accident personal-injury case to make a pretrial examination of the injured plaintiff, David Spaulding. He discovers that Spaulding has an aortic aneurysm—a potentially lethal but surgically correctable condition that may well have been caused by the accident in question, and which, if left untreated, could kill Spaulding at any moment. The physician's contract with the defense attorney specifies that he is not to reveal any of his medical findings to Spaulding, lest his revelations enhance Spaulding's claims for damages. What should the physician do? Should he inform Spaulding of his dangerous condition and advise him to seek medical attention immediately—even though Spaulding is not his "patient" in the customary sense of that term, and even though revealing this information constitutes a betrayal by the physician of his employer's trust and a violation of his contract? Or, should he keep silent, allowing Spaulding to walk about in innocence of his near-mortal condition—and perhaps even to die for lack of having discovered it?

No matter how clear we are about our terms, it is of course impossible to answer the question whether this physician faces or does not face a "conflict-of-interest problem." This is because the question itself is off-target; it expects the wrong thing of our definition's conceptual clarity. The utility of the definition is not in its ability to divide the world into instances of "conflict of interest" and "other" but in its ability to guide analysis. We notice very different aspects of the physician's problem if we analyze it as a conflict-of-interest problem than if we analyze it as a conflict-of-obligations problem, or as a problem about how the physician should deal with the emotions that the case no doubt excites. The question, "What are the physician's (pecuniary and nonpecuniary) interests in this case?" elicits a different set of answers from the question, "What duties has the physician in this case, and to whom?" or, "What is a physician in this situation feeling?" The value of our keeping our concepts straight—of not allowing the idea of interest to expand willy-nilly into a tautological term for every source of motivation, and of not mistaking every conflict for a conflict of interest—is that doing so allows us to separate the strands of this complex problem.[4]

I turn now to consideration of some of the most common conflict-of-interest problems in medical practice: the conflicts of interest present in traditional fee-for-service payment for medical care, those present in managed care financial-incentive plans, and those created by certain pharmaceutical-company marketing strategies. For each case, I consider the central mechanisms that might be used to eliminate, or to reduce the impact of, the conflicts in question.

Fee-for-Service Conflicts and "Separation of Function"

Consider the simple case of the sole-practitioner physician who is consulted by the sick or injured patient on a fee-for-service basis. The physician diagnoses the patient's illness, prescribes some course of action, and bills the patient for diagnostic and therapeutic services. Already in this simplest of cases we find conflict of interest.

Although the physician in this case is selling a service to the patient, the case is not analogous to the case of the buyer and seller mentioned earlier. The crucial difference is that the patient here depends on the physician not only for therapy but also for the diagnosis and prescription that lead to therapy. The patient wants her physician first to determine what service, if any, the physician should sell to her—and then to sell it to her. The physician is thus her agent for the purchase of medical services as well as purveyor of those services. His conflict of interest lies in this: As her purchasing agent, he has a duty to assist her in making prudent choices among medically relevant health care services, but as a purveyor of services, he has a pecuniary interest in advising her to make rather more extravagant purchases than a disinterested prudence would counsel. Of course, he need not give in to that pecuniary interest; the honorable physician, according to traditional standards of medical ethics, would resist that temptation. But conflicts of interest remain even when they do not succeed in having a bad influence on behavior.

Hall (1996, 1997) correctly urges us to think about such conflicts in terms of the economic theory of *agency costs*. Agency costs are the costs attributable to the fact that agents generally have interests that are not precisely the same as their employers'. Agents have interests in ease, in keeping perquisites, in ensuring their own indispensability, and so on. These interests constantly tempt them away from pursuing their principals' aims efficiently. Principals incur costs—"monitoring" costs—to ensure that their agents really do act on their behalf. These include not only the costs of literally "monitoring" agents—making sure they are working as hard as they claim to be—but also all the costs of principals' efforts to align their agents' interests with their own through incentive bonuses, prizes, worker-of-the-month awards, and so on. Agents also incur costs to reassure their principals that they are pursuing the principal's interests and not their own. These are termed "bonding costs" because they include, paradigmatically, the costs of posting performance bonds, but they include, also, the costs of producing reassuring reports, of establishing public reputations for diligence and honesty, and so on. Finally, some agency costs result from the failure, despite monitoring and bonding, of agents to act perfectly on behalf of their principals. Such "residual losses" occur whenever an employee blocks progress he perceives as threatening to his position, or takes an overlong lunch break, or undermines a talented coworker in order to make himself look better.

The conflict of interest inherent in the simple doctor/patient encounter mentioned previously can give rise to all three kinds of agency costs. There can be residual losses, insofar as a physician violates his or her fiduciary duty to the patient and successfully persuades the patient to purchase, for example, an unnecessary test. There can be monitoring costs, as when the cautious patient pays for a second opinion before going forward with the recommended treatment. And there can be bonding costs, as when physicians promulgate ethics rules requiring that they hold their patients' interests paramount and above their own pecuniary interests.

Theoretically, much of the conflict of interest present in the simple fee-for-service situation could be eliminated by enforcing a separation of physicians' diagnostic and prescribing functions from their treatment functions. For example, imagine a world in which a patient visits one physician for diagnosis, paying her a simple hourly rate, and is given a sheet of paper describing the relevant course of treatment. She takes this paper to another physician of her choice, who implements that treatment for a fee. In this world, the diagnosing physician, as the patient's agent for health care decision making, has no interest in prescribing any but the most appropriate therapy, and the treating physician is an ordinary seller of services.

Unfortunately, the costs of creating such a world would be enormous. Patients would have to select multiple physicians, and travel back and forth between them when ill. Diagnosing physicians would have to create, in every case, a medical record of sufficient clarity and detail to serve as authorization and explanation to any subsequent treating physician. And there would be the inevitable costs of misunderstandings and disagreements between diagnosing and treating physicians. It seems much more sensible and efficient to allow the diagnostic and treatment functions to blur together, even at the risk of some conflict of interest. Moreover, the separation-of-functions scheme would not eliminate agency conflicts entirely. After all, the diagnosing physician would still exercise considerable judgment in determining the cost of diagnosis itself—the amount of time spent taking the history, the number of tests given, and so on.

It costs too much to eliminate the conflicts of interest inhering in the single-patient/single-physician fee-for-service encounter, where what is being sold are the physician's own services. But there are a large number of slightly more complicated fee-for-service situations in which the separation-of-functions strategy makes sense. In particular, separation of functions is an efficient means of eliminating conflicts of interest whenever physicians are prescribing goods or services which are easily deliverable by another: more or less fungible, easily described. The best example is the provision of prescription drugs in the United States. Physicians are not allowed to sell these directly to patients. Instead, a diagnosing physician determines the proper prescription and gives it to the patient, and the patient takes the prescription and purchases the drug at the pharmacy of his or her choice. In many states, physicians are prohibited by law from owning interests in pharmacies and are subject to various restrictions regarding referrals to pharmacies owned by health facilities where they work. Thus, the state enforces a separation between the physician's function as "agent for drug purchasing" and any role the physician might play as "purveyor of drugs."

The separation-of-functions analysis also applies to the familiar case of "fee splitting," or payment by one physician (usually a specialist) to another (usually a general practitioner) as compensation for, or to induce, a referral. Physicians' ethics and the law have prohibited such payments for referral for decades (CEJA, 1998; Opinions 6.02 et seq.). That prohibition is soundly grounded in an effort to eliminate conflicts of interest and preserve physicians' effectiveness as agents for referral on their patients' behalf. If a family physician is paid by a specialist for referring patients to the specialist, then in effect the family physician acquires an interest in the specialty service being sold. This puts the family physician in the same situation we have been discussing: The physician is both the patient's agent for referral and a seller of referral services. This is a conflict of interest and could result in overreferral (referral for a specialty examination that is not really necessary) or in misreferral (referral to the specialist who pays the family physician the most rather than to the specialist who would be best for the patient). The prohibition on fee splitting enforces a separation between physicians' function as agents for referral and their function as sellers of referral services.

In the last decade, the separation-of-functions approach has become the favorite method of defusing potential conflicts of interest in a fee-for-service environment. Medicare and Medicaid regulations have applied this approach broadly to referrals by physicians to (for example) clinical laboratories, hospitals, other physicians, and purveyors of durable medical equipment (Furrow et al., 1995, secs. 15-7, 15-8). Interestingly, the laws have made exceptions for services provided onsite by (or under the supervision of) the referring physician him- or herself or members of his or her group practice. Of course, the fact that a service is available onsite does not eliminate the conflict of interest inherent in the physician's having both the opportunity to advise patients to purchase that service and the opportunity to charge for its sale. The existence of the exception therefore seems to acknowledge that the onsite availability of various services offers enormous convenience and time saving to patients and physicians alike. The law thus deliberately runs some risk of conflict of interest in order to capture transaction-cost savings.

There are still more gains to be had from the separation-of-functions strategy, however. In recent years, there has been a growing trend of physicians selling "nutriceuticals"—dietary supplements, vitamins, special meals and so on—to their patients in the office setting. Physicians have defended this practice by claiming that the products are good for their patients' health. But that is decidedly beside the point: After all, drugs and specialty referrals are also good for patients' health if they are medically indicated, but we still prohibit physicians from selling them to patients directly or indirectly, because of the conflict-of-interest problems such arrangements create. If a physician feels, for example, that a patient would benefit from taking vitamins, he should do just as he would if he felt that the patient would benefit from taking a prescription drug: Prescribe the therapy and allow the patient to purchase the product elsewhere. This would eliminate the potential for conflict of interest and of unnecessary purchases by patients whose physicians succumb to such conflict.

Another area in which the separation-of-functions strategy might further reduce conflicts of interest is in the burgeoning area of complementary and alternative medicine. The ethics rules and laws designed to limit fee splitting have, for historical reasons, concentrated on referrals for services offered by licensed medical personnel. But the conflict-of-interest analysis remains the same, whether one is talking about a referral to a dermatologist or to a Chinese herbalist. Physicians should avoid fee splitting with alternative practitioners on precisely the same grounds as they avoid fee splitting with traditional doctors.

When the separation-of-functions strategy is inefficient, efforts have been made to tame physicians' conflicts of interest by other means. Foremost among these are the various mechanisms put in place by managed care companies and indemnity insurers to prevent physicians from supplying unnecessary care: prospective approval requirements for costly treatments, retrospective record review to capture "overutilization," and the establishment of bonuses designed to reward physicians who keep their costs down. The first of these is designed to foil physicians who are prepared to give in to their fee-for-service conflicts by prescribing unnecessary care; the second to catch those who have already done so; the third to eliminate, through financial counterbalancing, the temptation to overcare which fee-for-service provides. All three techniques continue to be of vital importance, because a great deal of care is still provided on a fee-for-service basis. Though contemporary discussion of physician payment is more apt to focus on the incentive effects of capitation, it is still the case that most Medicare payments are fee for service. Many health maintenance organizations (HMOs) pay at least some of their participating physicians—particularly specialists—on a fee-for-service basis. Finally, even when physician group practices contract to accept capitated payments from HMOs, those group practices may choose to pay their participating physicians fee for service.

Managed Care Payment Schemes and Intensity Reduction

Contemporary interest in conflicts of interest in medical practice centers not on the older fee-for-service model of patient care but on the new payment models being experimented with by various cost-conscious health plans in the United States' competitive health insurance market. The variety and complexity of these payment methodologies is stunning, and a full catalogue, even if it were possible to offer one, is not in order here. I shall instead make only brief mention of some of the main payment types and then turn to consideration of the general means by which the conflict-of-interest threats they pose might be tempered.[5]

HMOs and other managed care health plans often contract with their enrollees for both the financing and the delivery of health care services. They receive premium payments from enrollees (or from their employers), in return for which they arrange for the delivery of health care to the enrollees through a series of contracts with individual physicians, physician-practice groups, hospitals, and other health-service providers. Our present concern is with the ways in which physicians might be paid under those contracts, and with the conflicts of interest that might arise under those payment schemes.

It is first worth recalling that, in the world of managed care, physicians are not always paid directly by the health plan. The plan may make a payment to an intermediary group of some sort—a physician-practice partnership or a hospital/physician joint venture. That intermediary may then make its own, independent determination of how best to pay its participating physicians for the care they give to plan enrollees. Indeed, a single health plan or intermediary organization may pay some of its physicians on one basis and others on another. Though for simplicity I refer in what follows to "plans" paying physicians, readers should bear in mind that it is often fellow physicians or other health-service provider groups who put physicians' financial incentives in place.

Another preliminary and quite complexifying fact is that individual physicians may have contracts to treat patients from multiple plans. One can easily imagine a physician who, in a single day, sees some Medicare fee-for-service patients, some Medicare and Medicaid managed care patients, one emergency patient from an out-of-state plan with which the physician has no contract, and several patients from each of a half dozen different plans with which he or she contracts—on slightly different financial terms. Such variety may well negate the incentive effects that might otherwise be created by any one of the plans. On the other hand, some physicians exclusively see patients from a single health plan. The analysis that follows focuses on the conflict-of-interest problems that would flow from a physician's being paid exclusively according to one scheme or another.

The basic means of physician payment are three: salary, fee for service, and capitation. Each of these basic means of payment gives rise to certain well-known strategies by which the physician's pecuniary self-interest is best served. Each may be modified by various financial incentive schemes designed better to align the physician's pecuniary self-interest with various external goals of the health-plan—cost control, quality assurance, and so on.

Fee-for-service payment, as we have seen, rewards physicians for supplying more services. Plans that pay on a fee-for-service basis therefore often attempt to control costs and to limit unnecessary care by imposing practice-management techniques on physicians (required second opinions, advance approvals, etc.). They also use their market power—their credible threat of dropping a high-cost physician from a plan, for example—to encourage physicians to keep their costs down and to negotiate low fees.

Relatively few plans pay salaries to physicians. Physicians on salary have no pecuniary interest in offering more or fewer services than the patient requires—though, because their wage is not tied to service delivery, they do have a nonpecuniary interest in working as little as possible, and therefore in avoiding difficult patients or cases. That interest, however, is easily outweighed by the nonpecuniary interest in reputation and by the pecuniary interest in not being fired.

Finally, physicians may be paid by capitation. In capitation, the plan pays the physician or practice group a fixed amount per enrolled patient per month. In return, the physician or group agrees to provide all necessary care to the enrollees. Capitated base pay gives physicians an incentive to keep costs down, because their payment is fixed up front without regard to the amount of time or resources they spend on any particular patient's care. The less expensive care they offer in a given period, the more of the original capitated payments they get to take home at period's end.

I turn now to consideration of the three most common incentive schemes used by plans to modify the incentives provided by fee for service, capitation, or salary. They are bonuses, referral budgets, and withholds. *Bonuses* are the most straightforward. A plan may seek to encourage cost control by offering, in addition to its base pay, a bonus geared to a formula that rewards physicians for good case-management technique. In *referral-budget* schemes, the plan supplies a group of physicians with a fund from which the physicians are expected to pay for all the "referral services" they authorize for the year. "Referral services" may include visits to specialists, inpatient stays in the hospital, or offsite laboratory tests. At the end of the year, the group is allowed to keep some or all of whatever cash remains in the referral-budget fund. (In some plans, the group is also liable to make up for any shortfalls.) The group is thus at financial risk for arranging the supply of referral services within the limits of the referral budget and gets a "bonus" for keeping referral costs low. This they achieve by limiting the number of referrals they authorize, and by negotiating for rate reductions (or even subreferral budgets) with specialists, hospitals, and labs. Under *withhold* schemes, a percentage of each physician's base pay (whether a capitated rate, a salary, or a negotiated fee) is withheld and placed into a "risk pool." Some plans use the funds in the risk pool as a referral budget. In others, the risk pool is used to fund fee-for-service payments to participating physicians for services beyond budgeted expectations. In either case, the risk pool acts as a buffer, insuring that the total amount set aside for patient care under the plan is not exceeded. At the end of the year, the participating physicians share whatever is left in the pool, either pro rata or according to a bonus formula

There is no end to the amount of tinkering that may be done to financial incentive schemes. Capitation rates may be varied according to patient risk. Stop-loss plans may place a cap on the amount of money that any physician can lose in a year, or that any physician can lose as a result of treating any particular high-cost patient. And plans can modify cost-based incentives by tying bonuses to such noncost factors as patient complaint experience, number of patient encounters, number of overtime hours, or administrative work.

All the foregoing incentive schemes have this in common: Insofar as they aim at cost control, they aim at it precisely by *creating conflicts of interest*. In each case, the scheme is designed to give the physician a pecuniary self-interest in limiting the amount of care given. The structure of the conflict is an inversion of the problem with fee for service: The physician is the patient's agent for the purchase of health care but has a financial interest in making sure that the patient does not purchase much. This pecuniary interest can naturally be expected to collide with the legitimate interests of some patients in receiving expensive care or referral services.

Some version of the separation-of-functions solution would work here, too, but only at the cost of eliminating the physician's incentive to control costs. If we assume, *arguendo*, the social value of encouraging cost control with financial incentives, we must look elsewhere for a means by which conflicts of interest may be, if not eliminated, then tamed.

There are such means at hand; they are what might be termed "intensity-reduction techniques." From the patient's point of view, what is most worrisome about managed care financial incentive schemes is the possibility that the pecuniary interest they give physicians in not providing costly medical care may result in their failure—to the detriment of the patient's health—to provide necessary care. The patient's worry, in other words, is focused on the degree to which a given incentive scheme might affect individual clinical decisions—the decisions, for example, to make a specialty referral, to order another test, or to recommend an inpatient hospital stay. We may refer to a scheme's potential for such impact as its *intensity*. Intense incentive plans are those which have the greatest potential to have an adverse impact on particular clinical decisions.

"Intensity-reduction techniques" can reduce the risk that the conflicts of interest created by cost-control incentive programs will actually result in harm to patients (Latham, 1996, 1998). By reducing the intensity of the physician's pecuniary interest in any given clinical decision, they reduce the risk that the physician will allow his or her clinical judgment to be overridden by self-interest. There are a number of well-recognized intensity-reduction techniques. It is important, for example, that incentive schemes be tied to financial goals relating to large numbers of clinical encounters. The cost experience of a larger patient pool is more predictable than that of a small group; small groups are more susceptible than larger groups to having unexpectedly high costs, and to the resultant intense pressure on clinical decisions made near the end of the fiscal period. To gain this large-group advantage, incentives should be based on the experience of multiple physicians' patients and calculated over a reasonably long period. Next, incentive intensity can be reduced by making sure that financial rewards are given piecemeal, on a sliding-scale basis, rather than in large blocks upon the attainment of fixed target numbers. A physician who earns a large bonus upon the attainment of a certain level of cost savings, but who gets nothing short of that attainment, will be under extreme financial pressure whenever he or she is near the borderline of attaining the goal. A better plan would give the physician financial rewards proportional to whatever level of savings he or she in fact attains. Under the latter plan, every cost saving would be rewarded, but no one clinical decision (or patient) would ever be a "bonus breaker."

Finally, plans can reduce their intensity by gearing financial rewards not only to cost savings but also to quality goals. And plans can build in stop-loss elements to ensure that no physician is ever tempted to make risky clinical decisions in order to avoid financial ruin, and no seriously ill patient is ever regarded as a "high-cost case."

There is another important tool for reducing the possible harmful impacts of physicians' conflicts-of-interest—a tool that does nothing to eliminate or reduce the conflict but which nonetheless offers important protections to the patient. This is disclosure. As an ethical matter, patients are entitled to all information bearing on the treatment decisions they make with their physicians—and this includes economic information (Morreim, 1995; CEJA, 1998, Opinions 8.13 et seq). As a practical matter, a patient who is informed of the financial incentives bearing on his or her physician's decisions is in a better position to protect him- or herself by obtaining second opinions or by asking probing questions. Finally, the act of disclosure itself can keep physicians aware of the subtle play of their own interests upon the decisions they make at the gray margins of medical care.

We have completed our quick tour of the conflict-of-interest problems created by managed care incentive plans, and of the intensity-reduction techniques which can limit their adverse impact. Before leaving the topic, however, it is worth noting that in the area of health care cost control, there are worse things than conflict of interest. Indeed, many of those "worse things" are the very things that managed care plans use when they cannot use conflict-inducing financial incentives to keep costs down. I am referring here to the various case-management, "prospective approval" and "appeal of denial" strategies used by managed care to second-guess the medical judgment of their physicians in the name of cost control. Nothing infuriates physicians more than the requirement that they get a plan's stamp of approval before going forward with costly treatments that they feel are appropriate for their patients. It is especially irksome when the required approval is to be granted by a company functionary who is armed with no medical expertise, or with a "practice protocol" whose scope and limits he or she does not understand. These techniques may well help control costs, but they aggravate physicians and patients alike, result in a certain number of poor medical decisions, waste money and time on costly internal appeals, and have lately given rise to a spate of lawsuits for denial of necessary care. One advantage of the financial-incentive, creating-conflict-of-interest approach to cost control is that it does leave the final medical judgment in the hands of physicians. Physicians who are placed into conflict-of-interest situations need not give in to them in every case. Physicians themselves get to decide when they will advance their pecuniary interests under an incentive plan, and when they will take a financial "hit" for the sake of making sure that a patient is well cared for. This gives the patient a kind of safety valve that the corporate approval techniques do not. It is perhaps for this reason—as well as to improve political relationships with their physicians—that several health plans in the United States have recently announced that they are abolishing their prospective-approval requirements and leaving all decisions in the sole discretion of physicians. These physicians have financial incentives to keep costs down and fear being deselected from the plan, but they nonetheless remain free to exercise their professional judgment in each individual case.

Pharmaceutical Marketing and Voluntary Limits

It would be difficult to overstate the impact of the pharmaceutical industry on medical practice. Pharmaceutical firms are the main funding source for continuing medical education sessions, the principal advertisers in most medical journals, and the primary sponsors of most medical-information websites. They are important sponsors of medical research. For better or for worse, pharmaceutical print and personal marketing statements are accepted by most physicians as important sources of information about the latest medical developments and techniques (Rodwin, 1993; Shimm, Spece, & DiGregorio, 1996). The recent spurt in direct-to-consumer marketing of drugs ("Ask your doctor about") has injected firms' messages into the dialogue between physician and patient.

Most of these activities do not raise important conflict-of-interest questions for practicing physicians. There are important questions about the influence of advertising on physician behavior, and about the effect of pharmaceutical sponsorship on U.S. medical education, publication, and practice, but these questions have no particular nexus to problems of physician self-interest. Where conflicts of interest *do* arise is in connection with pharmaceutical marketing techniques that involve gift giving and other payments to physicians. I shall briefly describe some of the more troubling marketing techniques and then some of the voluntary limits accepted by physicians and by the pharmaceutical industry to limit their effects.

The most common and least troubling gifts given to physicians by pharmaceutical companies are trinkets—the keychains and pens the firms hand out at their information tables at medical conferences. Free drug samples are also commonly given to physicians; these, too, raise little concern about conflict of interest, provided that physicians do not request such free samples for personal or family use, that their personal use of such drugs does not interfere with patients' access to them, and that their receipt of free samples in no way interferes with patients' access to other drugs (CEJA, 1998, Opinion 8.061(2)).

Physicians sometimes receive other, more substantial gifts from pharmaceutical companies. Firms often include a dinner or cocktail hour as part of an educational program designed to inform physicians about the uses of their new drugs. More troublingly, firms have occasionally chosen simply to entertain physicians, sometimes lavishly, presumably in hopes of creating brand recognition and goodwill. Some such entertainments have been "disguised" or packaged as conferences or educational seminars.

The foregoing practices are intended to create goodwill for firms—to create, in physicians' minds, a favorable impression of particular firms or brands. They are troubling insofar as they attempt to substitute feelings of goodwill for actual information about drugs as the physician's criterion for drug selection. Still, gift giving to generate goodwill does not give physicians actual pecuniary interests in prescribing any one drug over another. For example, a physician may, without losing anything, harbor warm feelings toward a firm that entertained her and still prescribe a competitor firm's product when she feels it medically appropriate. Most troubling, however, are marketing practices that offer physicians financial rewards, either concurrently or retrospectively, for their actual prescribing practices. Some firms have offered vacations and expensive gifts as rewards to their "high prescribers." This creates a direct and powerful conflict of interest for physicians, giving them a pecuniary interest in prescribing one product over another. This interest conflicts with their duty to their patients to base such judgments solely on medical criteria. Other firms have invited physicians to "enroll" their patients in a "study," under which the patient is switched from a competitor's drug to the firm's. The physician is paid a fee for each patient whose prescription he or she changes. This fee is characterized as payment for the physician's work in recording the "study" results, (e.g., scientifically valueless comments about "how the patient is doing" with the new drug). I have seen a number of such "studies" promulgated unblushingly by firm marketing departments; in each case, the information solicited from the physician could not reasonably be expected to add anything to the information about the drug which was already gathered pursuant to Food and Drug Administration regulations. The principal function of the sham "study" was simply to give physicians a direct financial interest in switching their patients from one brand to another.

What can be done to limit the impact of such tactics on physicians' prescribing practices? It is difficult to frame laws explicit enough to capture abusive practices without also capturing reasonable marketing techniques. For example, it is quite difficult to frame a law that can accurately capture the difference between a legitimate study and an illegitimate one, or between a firm that serves physicians refreshments during a break at an educational seminar introducing a new line of drugs and a firm that tacks sham educational content onto a lavish entertainment.

The American Medical Association's (AMA) Council on Ethical and Judicial Affairs has attempted to limit conflicts of interest created by pharmaceutical marketing practices by promulgating a set of ethical standards for physicians on accepting gifts from industry (CEJA, 1998, Opinion 8.061; and see CEJA, 1991, 1992). The guidelines require that any gifts accepted by physicians should entail benefit to patients and should not be of substantial value. Textbooks and modest meals accompanying educational seminars fit the standards; ski trips do not. The guidelines (and the interpretations of them that CEJA has issued from time to time) also attempt to differentiate legitimate from illegitimate "conferences" and "seminars"; the guidelines allow such events to be industry-sponsored but prohibit individual physicians from receiving travel subsidies or registration-fee reductions directly from the sponsoring firms. The guidelines allow physicians to be paid honoraria if they serve as consultants or as faculty at conferences but distinguish genuine faculty and consulting arrangements from "token" ones. They permit firms to sponsor scholarships for attendance by medical trainees of "carefully selected educational conferences" (e.g., "the major educational, scientific or policymaking meetings of national, regional or specialty medical associations"). Finally, gifts "with strings attached" are prohibited entirely; this includes all gifts tied in any way to physicians' actual prescribing practices (CEJA, 1998, Opinion 8.061).

The AMA guidelines are essentially voluntary; there is no meaningful enforcement mechanism for their violation, and no means even of detecting violations dependably. How effective can they be? Certainly they are not universally effective: numerous physicians violate them annually. On the other hand, numerous physicians call the AMA to make inquiries about them, and planners of Continuing Medical Education events strive to obey them.[6] And firms—particularly the largest, best-established firms—show considerable sensitivity to the existence of the rules and make a point of adhering to them. Less scrupulous firms pay a kind of homage to the guidelines by making some show of adhering to them.

Interestingly, there is an argument to be made that the pharmaceutical industry itself has some interest in adopting the AMA's (or some similar) voluntary guidelines. With regard to gift giving as a marketing strategy, the firms find themselves with a collective-action problem: Each would ideally like to be the only firm that entertains or gives gifts to physicians, because it could then be assured of capturing physician goodwill. This leads multiple firms to engage in the practices. This very multiplicity makes the gift-giving strategy less effective; physicians who are entertained or paid by multiple firms are less likely to develop goodwill and loyalty toward any one of them. Given this development, firms would then like to cease the costly, and not very effective, entertainments—but only if all the other firms do so as well, so that abstinence confers no competitive disadvantage. This theory may explain the fact that PhRMA, the industry trade association, has attempted to secure its members' voluntary compliance with the guidelines from time to time.

Medical Professionalism
and Self-Interests

We have just seen that the conflicts of interest created by fee-for-service payments, by managed care cost-cutting incentives, and by pharmaceutical company gifts and incentives can be eliminated or dampened by the use of certain techniques. The separation-of-functions strategy, the intensity-reduction strategies, and the AMA's strategy of promulgating voluntary guidelines all work to minimize the threat to patients of conflicts of interest. They achieve this by preventing certain particularly strong conflicts of interest from arising. One advantage of these techniques is that they protect not only physicians' conscious decisions but also their unconscious decisions from undue influence by pecuniary self-interest.

But the battle against conflict of interest need not only be fought on the field of prevention. If the threat to patients from physicians' conflicts of interest can be reduced by preventing strong conflicts from arising, the actual damage done by conflicts can also be eliminated or reduced by the cultivation, among physicians, of an attitude which allows them to resist those conflicts that do arise. It is presumably toward the end of cultivating such an attitude that the AMA's Code of Ethics contains the admonition that "[i]f a conflict develops between the physician's financial interest and the physician's responsibilities to the patient, the conflict must be resolved to the patient's benefit" (CEJA, 1998, Opinion 8.03). Yet the skeptic might be forgiven for wondering whether, assuming the admonition was sincerely meant by its draftsmen, the laudable attitude it preaches can seriously be cultivated by a professional organization that spends so much of its time in the ardent pursuit of physicians' financial interests (Buchanan, 1996; Wolinsky & Brune, 1994).

In this connection it is worth remembering the special role that interests were once thought to play in the organization of medicine and the other professions. The social theory of the professions in this country was for decades dominated by the structural–functionalist school of Talcott Parsons and his followers (Abel, 1989; Freidson, 1994; Rueschemeyer, 1986; Vollmer & Mills, 1966). On Parsons's view, professionals in modern capitalist society serve the special function of harmonizing public with private interests. In effect, professionals serve as interstitial go-betweens, sometimes nudging their private clients better to align their private interests with the public interest and sometimes pressing public interests better to accommodate their clients' private interests (Parsons, 1954a, 1954b; Parsons & Fox, 1951). Thus, lawyers might sometimes prod their clients into regulatory compliance and at other times lobby for relaxed public regulation so that private interests might more easily be pursued. Physicians might work to cure a patient in order to return the patient to a productive position in society, but they might also use their authority to secure for their patient various excuses from her duties, or accommodations of her needs. It was of central importance to Parsons that professionals could only play this interstitial role if their own interests were of a certain cast. In particular, Parsons assumed that these interstitial services could be delivered by a self-regulatory profession only because the individual professional's dominant interests were nonpecuniary. Professionals, Parsons argued, were as self-interested as any other successful actors in the contemporary capitalist economy, but the interests they were pursuing were in status, power, and reputation rather than in wealth (Parsons, 1954a). This afforded a crucial counterbalance to the professionals' right of self-regulation: for although the right of self-regulation guaranteed that professionals could not be induced by regulators into favoring the public interest over that of their private clients, the nonpecuniary character of professionals' dominant interests helped guarantee that they could not be induced to favor private, moneyed interests over the interests of the public. Thus professionals' nonpecuniary interests were mobilized to minimize and neutralize their pecuniary interests.

Beginning in the 1960s, this Parsonian view of professionals' interests has been subject to withering attacks from all academic quarters. Sociologists, historians, and philosophers of the professions have dismissed Parsons's vision as naïve and have instead cast professionalism as a cynical collective-mobility project, designed to secure wealth for professionals by means of monopolization and supply restriction. This attack is summarized in Rueschemeyer (1986), Abel (1989), and Freidson (1994); representative attackers of medical professionalism include Freidson (1970), Starr (1982), and Buchanan (1996).

Professionalism has more recently returned to academic favor; even former critics of professionalism are willing to speak for it as a possibly attractive alternative to markets, and to bureaucratic centralization, for the delivery of complex social services (Freidson, 1992, 1994; Gordon & Simon, 1992). But these writers importantly regard the "promise of professionalism" as contingent upon a still open question about professional *interests*. The condition of our entrusting professional institutions with self-regulatory power, they argue, must surely be that the professionals will not exploit their power harmfully in order to advance their own interests.

These waves of criticism and skeptical reassessment of medical professionalism have nearly washed away a subtle Parsonian point: Professional institutions, in order to make the professional self-regulatory regime viable—and, less grandly but more pointedly, in order to help insulate patients from the dangers of physicians' financial conflicts of interest—need not attempt to enter the business of manufacturing saints. It is sufficient both for their self-justification and for their patients' protection that they cultivate among medical professionals a certain brand of nonpecuniary self-interest. There is a certain mindfulness of one's position that can turn aside financial temptation, a certain confident single-mindedness that cannot be distracted by the prospect of gain. It is these that medical professional institutions must concentrate on creating, though the mindfulness be mistaken by laymen for overbearing pride and the single-mindedness for narrowness. If physicians can cultivate the right interests—in status, in respect, in reputation for skill, in peer recognition—then their relentless, ruthless, competitive pursuit of them cannot hurt, and may even help, the rest of us.

Notes

1. The reference to the commodity is essential here. A seller of services, as opposed to goods, nearly always has some small conflict of interest insofar as his or her interest in ease conflicts with his or her employer's interest in receiving efficiently delivered services.

2. But see Shimm and Spece (1996) considering a similar case: "We do not distinguish between conflicts of interest and conflicts of obligation or loyalty" (n. 46 and accompanying text).

3. I am grateful to my colleague Greg Loken for this example.

4. Erde (1996) is thus correct to criticize Grey (1991) for calling for a definition of "conflict of interest" that will "settle whether [a certain matter] should be considered [a conflict of interest]." (Erde, 1996, p. 15). But he is wrong to move from there to the position that "[n]o useful and strict definition of CI exists. Nor is one needed" (Erde, 1996, p. 17). On the value of conceptual analysis generally, see Bix (1995) and Bix (1996, pp. 15–32).

5. This discussion is adapted from the more detailed treatment of Latham (1996) and Latham (1999).

6. In 1996–98, the Ethics Standards Division of the AMA averaged dozens of calls weekly requesting details on the gifts guidelines.

References

Abel, R. L. (1989). *American lawyers*. New York: Oxford University Press.

Applbaum, A. I. (1999). *Ethics for adversaries: The morality of roles in public and professional life*. Princeton, NJ: Princeton University Press.

Bix, B. (1995). Conceptual questions and jurisprudence. *Legal Theory, 1,* 465–479.

———. (1996). *Jurisprudence: Theory and context*. Boulder, CO: Westview Press.

Buchanan, A. E. (1996). Is there a medical profession in the house? In R. G. Spece, Jr., D. et al., S. Shimm, & A. E. Buchanan, (Eds.), *Conflicts of interest in clinical practice and research*. New York: Oxford University Press.

Council on Ethical and Judicial Affairs. (1991). Gifts to physicians from industry. *Journal of the American Medical Association, 265,* 501.

————. (1992). Gifts to physicians from industry. *Food and Drug Law Journal,* 47, 445–458.

————. (1998). *Code of Medical Ethics: Current opinions with annotations, 1998–1999 edition.* Chicago: American Medical Association.

Erde, E. L. (1996). Conflicts of interest in medicine: A philosophical and ethical morphology. In R. G. Spece, et al. Jr., D. S. Shimm, & A. E. Buchanan (Eds.), *Conflicts of interest in clinical practice and research.* New York: Oxford University Press.

Freidson, E. (1970). *Profession of medicine: A study of the sociology of applied knowledge.* Chicago: University of Chicago Press.

————. (1992). Professionalism as model and ideology. In R. L. Nelson, D. M. Trubek, & R. L. Solomon (Eds.), *Lawyers' ideals/lawyers' practices: Transformations in the American legal profession.* Ithaca, NY: Cornell University Press.

————. (1994). *Professionalism reborn: Theory, prophecy and policy.* Chicago: University of Chicago Press.

Furrow, B. R., Greaney, T. L., Johnson, S. H., Jost, T. S. & Schwartz, R. L. (1995). *Health law (Hornbook).* St. Paul, MN: West.

Gordon, R. W., & Simon, W. H. (1992). The redemption of professionalism? In R. L. Nelson, D. M. Trubek, & R. L. Solomon (Eds.), *Lawyers' ideals/lawyers' practices: Transformations in the American legal profession.* Ithaca, NY: Cornell University Press.

Gray, B. H. (1991). *The profit motive and patient care: The changing accountability of doctors and hospitals.* Cambridge, MA: Harvard University Press.

Hall, M. A. (1996). Physician rationing and agency cost theory. In R. G. Spece, Jr., D. S. Shimm, & A. E. Buchanan (Eds.), *Conflicts of interest in clinical practice and research.* New York: Oxford University Press.

————. (1997). *Making medical spending decisions: The law, ethics and economics of rationing mechanisms.* New York: Oxford University Press.

Hazard, G. C., Jr., Koniak, S. P., & Cramton, R. C. (1994). *The law and ethics of lawyering (2d ed.).* Westbury, NY: Foundation Press.

Hirschman, A. O. (1986). The concept of interest: From euphemism to tautology. In Albert O. Hirschman (Ed.), *Rival views of market society.* Cambridge, MA: Harvard University Press.

————. (1997). *The passions and the interests: Political arguments for capitalism before its triumph.* Princeton, NJ: Princeton University Press.

Latham, S. R. (1996). Regulation of managed care incentive payments to physicians. *American Journal of Law & Medicine 22* (4), 399–432.

————. (1999). The ethics of managed care financial incentives to limit care: Some thoughts for specialists. *Clinics in Plastic Surgery, 26,* 115–121.

Luban, D. (1988). *Lawyers and justice: An ethical study.* Princeton, NJ: Princeton University Press.

Morreim, E. H. (1995). *Balancing act: The new medical ethics of medicine's new economics.* Washington, DC: Georgetown University Press.

Parsons, T. (1954a). The professions and social structure. In T. Parsons (Ed.), *Essays in sociological theory, (rev. ed.).* London: Free Press of Glencoe. (Original work published 1939)

————. (1954b). A sociologist looks at the legal profession. In T. Parsons (Ed.), *Essays in sociological theory, (rev. ed.).* London: Free Press of Glencoe. (Original work published 1952)

Parsons, T., & Fox, R. (1982). Illness and the role of the physician. In L. H.

Mayhew (Ed.), *Talcott Parsons on institutions and social evolution*. Chicago: University of Chicago Press. (Original work published 1951)

Pindar. (1997). *Pythian Olympian odes,*. Cambridge, MA: Harvard University Press.

Rodwin, M. A. (1993). *Medicine, money and morals: Physicians' conflicts of interest*. New York: Oxford University Press.

Rueschemeyer, D. (1986). *Power and the division of labor*. Stanford, CA: Stanford University Press.

Shimm, D. S., Spece, R. R., Jr., & DiGregorio, M. B. (1996). Conflicts of interest in relationships between physicians and the pharmaceutical industry. In R. G. Spece, Jr., D. S. Shimm, & A. E. Buchanan (eds.), *Conflicts of interest in clinical practice and research*, New York: Oxford University Press.

Smith, A. (1998). *An inquiry into the nature and causes of the wealth of nations*. Washington, DC: Regnery. (Original work published 1777)

———. (2000). *The theory of moral sentiments*. Amherst, NY: Prometheus Books. (Original work published 1759)

Starr, P. (1982). *The social transformation of American medicine: The rise of a sovereign profession and the making of a vast industry*. New York: Basic Books.

Vollmer, H. M., & Mills, D. L. (Eds.). (1966). *Professionalization*. Englewood Cliffs, NJ: Prentice-Hall.

Wolinsky, H., & Brune, T. (1994). *The serpent on the staff: The unhealthy politics of the American Medical Association*. New York: G. P. Putnam's Sons.

15

ETHICAL CONFLICT IN CORRECTIONAL HEALTH SERVICES

Kenneth Kipnis

Ethics may have the most to learn at societal interfaces. When differing cultural values and social practices brush up against each other in ways that force accommodation, the collision of normative systems can sometimes provide the ethics theorist with fascinating data even as it affords the ethics practitioner an opportunity to participate creatively in a process of principled reconciliation. Such an interface can be found at the boundaries of medicine and corrections. For health care professionals who work in prison settings—nurses and psychologists as well as doctors—and for the corrections personnel who sometimes work alongside them, there can be a sense of working at the margin. It is the purpose of this chapter to characterize the types of normative conflict that arise for correctional health care professionals (CHCPs) and to set out some strategies for engaging them. In the process, I make some observations about how to understand the generic nature of these insufficiently studied ethical issues.

The Incarcerative Backdrop

Much of the appeal of *M.A.S.H.*, both the film and the television series, was in its surrealistic foregrounding of a close-knit team of devoted healers against the grim backdrop of a vast military organization, optimized to inflict death and serious injury upon an enemy. The drama, with its regular doses of black humor, drew heavily on the value conflicts inherent in that context. It was easy to appreciate why most of these well-meaning doctors and nurses were cynically alienated from military life and why they drank.

In some ways, the social responsibilities of CHCPs are comparable to those of the military in wartime. Like the army, prisons are not there to promote the values of health care. The essential constituting task of penal institutions is readily grasped when we recollect that those convicted of sufficiently grave offenses are, as we say, remanded to the warden's custody. In so doing, the judicial system solemnly entrusts prison administrators to carry out the penal sentences imposed by the courts. Apart from the fines and the occasional death penalty, the retributive loss of liberty is the predominant form that judicial punishment takes: There are about two million persons in U.S. jails and prisons.

Although more philosophical work needs to be done on the nature and justification of imprisonment as a form of punishment, we should not be surprised, in our society, to see retribution take the form of loss of liberty. For it is common for those reared in liberal democracies to celebrate personal freedom as the preeminent political good: Liberal democratic societies are, perhaps by definition, informed by the value rational persons are presumed to place on liberty. Thus the first of John Rawls's two principles of justice reads: "Each person is to have an equal right to the most basic liberty compatible with a similar liberty for others."[1] And Joel Feinberg has devoted much of his career defending the Millian view that unless there are good reasons to the contrary, individuals should be at liberty to do as they choose.[2] Accordingly, if liberty is embraced as a preeminent political good, then official punishment, as a societally imposed form of hard treatment, might well take the form of imprisonment: an officially imposed, systematic suspension of liberty. Not only could loss of liberty be reasonably supposed to be undesirable enough to deter rational malefactors, but, in addition, its imposition upon those convicted of serious offenses could persuade law-abiding citizens that, so retributed, crime does not pay.

Accordingly, we shall not challenge the premises that wrongdoers should be punished; that the forfeiture of liberty is, here and now, a societally appropriate punishment in many cases; and that the prison—more or less as we understand it—is an appropriate means of implementing such a punishment. So conceived, prisons are institutions in which the presumption in favor of liberty is in large measure reversed; that is, unless there are good reasons to the contrary, inmates do not have the right to do as they choose. As socially constituted institutions, prisons exist for the purpose of systematically and generally denying opportunities to those convicted of serious offenses.

Jurisprudentially, the prison's implementation of this inverted liberal principle has historically taken the form of judicial deference to experienced prison administrators. Adopting a hands-off policy, courts have generally given wardens broad latitude to implement institutional policies that further proper penal purposes. But these purposes—a motley agglomeration of goals, some perhaps central to the prison's mission and others more or less peripheral to it—are often controversial. Along with implementing a retributive forfeiture of liberty, commentators have spoken of the value of rehabilitation, of encouraging repentance, incapacitating convicted wrongdoers, deterring extramural crime, making available a population of tightly controlled research subjects, generating revenues through the use of a monitored labor force, promoting institutional efficiency, earning profits, administering suffering, managing the surplus labor force, and so on—hence the need, noted earlier, for further philosophical inquiry.

But notwithstanding this variety, one salient fact sharply narrows the warden's focus: Prisons are, by their very nature, coercive institutions. The inmates there have been arrested, their sentences have been imposed upon them and, from the moment a prisoner first hears the heavy steel doors slam shut, the elements of everyday life are palpably shut off. Accordingly those remanded to the warden's custody are presumed to be (1) intent on taking their leave should the opportunity arise, and (2) unenthusiastic at best about deferring to the prison's de jure authority. Thus the liberties inmates will surely forfeit are those that must give way to the warden's responsibilities for prison security: the twin duties to prevent escape and riot. In this regard we point to the authoritarian model of management, the thick walls, the razor wire, the locked doors, the armed guards, the regimentation, and the secondary penal systems within the penal system. Administratively, physically and philosophically, these familiar elements of prison life betoken an absence of trust.

The Mandate of the
Correctional Health Care Professional

Although it is relatively easy to discern the warden's ethical situation in the context of prison life, the role responsibilities of the CHCP are somewhat hazier. Notwithstanding the systematic suspension of liberty, it is useful to distinguish between two types of right that inmates can claim.[3]

There are, first, what we can call "residual rights" that survive the sentence to prison. The general right to legal counsel, for example, cannot be abridged by wardens, though it is commonly contoured to comport with penal regimes. And, second, there are other rights that flow from the status of being in custody: rights, for example, to food and to other living conditions that measure up to our "evolving standards of decency."

Although prison medicine has had a long but not entirely illustrious history in the United States, courts have only occasionally scrutinized the sources and scope of the duty to treat. In 1926, for example, a North Carolina court opined in *Spicer v. Williamson*:[4] "It is but just that the public be required to care for the prisoner, who cannot by reason of the deprivation of his liberty, care for himself." But it was not until 1973 that the Supreme Court saw fit to set what one might take to be a minimum requirement. Appealing to the constitutional prohibition of "cruel and unusual punishment," the Court ruled, in *Estelle v. Gamble*,[5] as follows:

> [D]eliberate indifference to serious medical needs of prisoners constitutes the "unnecessary and wanton infliction of pain" . . . proscribed by the Eighth Amendment. This is true whether the indifference is manifested by prison doctors in their reponse to the prisoner's needs or by prison guards in intentionally denying or delaying access to medical care or intentionally interfering with the treatment once prescribed. Regardless of how evidenced, deliberate indifference to a prisoner's serious illness or injury states a cause of action under Sec. 1983.

Thus, surprisingly and thanks to *Estelle*, convicted felons are the only population in the United States with a Constitutional right to health care.

It is perhaps useful to tease apart these two quite distinct arguments for the prisoner's right to indicated medical treatment. *Estelle*—the more recent Supreme Court case—bases it on the Constitutional prohibition against "cruel and unusual" punishment. Because "deliberate" indifference to the inmate's medical needs adds an extra and illicit measure of suffering to that which is incident to the licit penalty of imprisonment (i.e., loss of liberty), the warden (and all those accountable to that office) has a derivative duty to respond to evident medical needs. It is unconstitutional cruelty to withhold needed health care. Having commonly been merely an important part of good penological practice, responsiveness to the inmate's medical requirements has evolved into a Constitutionally mandated entitlement.

On the other hand, *Spicer*, the earlier North Carolina case, derives the right from custodial obligations flowing from the prisoner's societally imposed deprivation of liberty. In this context, inmates resemble children in a jurisprudential sense. Although there are differences, it is revealing to observe how the legally narrowed liberty rights of children are comparably paired with a reciprocal prohibition against parental neglect. It is, in part, because children—like inmates—are systematically denied the legal powers needed to provide for themselves, that parents and guardians—like wardens—are properly charged with a legal duty to make needed medical services available to those in their custody. In Hohfeldian terms, the constriction of the standard range of liberty rights is tolerable, in part, because of the presence of special claim rights. Upon emancipation or completion of a sentence, the legal adult and the parolee enjoy an enhanced liberty even as they lose their claims to bed, board, and various other necessities of life.

On either of these two jurisprudential analyses, what brings health care professionals into prison are, (1) the legal requirement that prison administrators attend to the serious health needs of inmates, and (2) the legal prohibition on the unlicensed practice of medicine and nursing. Legally, wardens must provide needed health care. But—equally legally— they are generally not licensed to provide it themselves. When we take the duty (as in *Spicer* and *Estelle*) to make appropriate medical and nursing services available, and add it to the prevailing practice of health care licensure, what precipitates is the warden's special obligation to retain CHCPs to deliver health-related services in the corrections setting.

Health Care in the Corrections Setting

Now, by their very nature, health care professionals are committed to putting the patient's interests first: striving above all never to harm them, treating decisionally capacitated patients only with informed consent, and scrupulously preserving patient confidences. At the root of this attentive deference, so antithetical to the prison's punitive ambience, is the understandable vulnerability that the ill generally experience when compelled to rely on health care professionals. Infirmity can force any of us to tell uncomfortable truths to our doctors, requiring that we open ourselves in ways that, in other settings, would be embarrassing, shameful, and imprudent. This trust in the integrity of health care professionals is an indispensable element of the "therapeutic alliance." It is largely because of these well-understood professional commitments (coupled with the professions' distinctive knowledges and skills) that, (1) we as a society have delegated to duly licensed health care professionals the exclusive responsibility to deliver their distinctive services to the community (unauthorized practice being a criminal offense), and, (2) that the infirm are as willing as they are to seek out and use these specialists.

But although these health care providers serve the needs of the inmate population, they are nonetheless working, directly or indirectly, for prison administration. We have noted how the elements of prison administration betoken an absence of trust in the inmate. Against this background, the CHCP's foundational duty to nurture the trust and confidence of the inmate/patient runs directly counter to the prevailing ethic in the institution.[6]

In systematically representing a profession's normative commitments, it is often useful to organize them according to the discrete social roles encountered in generic professional practice. Preschool teachers, for example, characteristically have professional dealings with children, the children's parents, colleagues (including supra- and subordinates), specialists in other fields (psychologists and social workers, for example), and, occasionally, the public. One way of conceiving a profession's ethics is to try to specify and array the obligations practitioners have toward those who occupy each of these generic roles so the obligations are consistent with each other.

In the present context, it is a useful oversimplification to regard the responsibilities of the generic correctional health care professional as vectored toward three discrete parties. As noted earlier and as with all health care professionals, there are the familiar clinical obligations toward the inmate/patient: centrally, a duty of beneficence toward the patient within the parameters of the patient's consent. A second set of obligations involves duties as an employee of the warden/employer and, derivatively, toward other correctional officers also accountable to the warden. And, finally, there is a third set of "public health" obligations for the well-being of the inmate population taken as a whole. Although there are important differences, one can compare this third perspective with the veterinarian's accountability for the health of the herd. Quite unlike the clinician's focus on a discrete patient, husbandry can require the sacrifice of individuals to secure the well-being of the group. The public health perspective can manifest itself in a variety of strategies devised to prevent or slow the spread of illness through a population, strategies that can sometimes pit collective interests against the interests of individuals. In the most dramatic cases (e.g., an outbreak of multiple drug resistant tuberculosis), infected persons, if uncooperative, can be properly quarantined against their will.

Many of the ethical dilemmas of correctional health are understandable as conflicts arising out of these potentially competing sets of obligations. Case One: "The Gun," illustrates a characteristic clash between the first two.

Case One: "The Gun"
You are director of health services for a large correctional facility. The warden has received reliable information from an informant that a certain inmate is sequestering a gun in his rectum. The warden insists that he has probable cause to perform a search and directs you to have it carried out. The inmate will not consent to examination. Except for

members of your staff, no correctional personnel are qualified to do X rays or perform body cavity searches.

The next two cases illustrate the tension between the clinical and public health perspectives.

Case Two: "The Outbreak"
Following an outbreak of five cases of hepatitis B in one of your units, your investigation points to a prisoner tattooist as the possible source. Though it violated prison regulations, all the infected inmates had recently been tattooed. The tattooist is unwilling to cooperate, refusing to be tested for hepatitis B. Do you test him against his will? If he is a carrier, what do you do then?

Case Three: "The Diabetic"
Inmate Richard Wong is a diabetic who has been placed on a special diet by order of the medical staff. He has been hospitalized three times with life-threatening diabetic ketoacidosis following ingestion of candy bars obtained from the inmate canteen. You can initiate disciplinary procedures that will result in his loss of canteen privileges.

Case Four illustrates a conflict between public health responsibilities and duties to the warden/employer.

Case Four: "Condom Availability"
The encouragement and facilitation of condom usage is a standard and effective public health intervention for managing a sexually active population with HIV seroprevalence. Though condoms do not prevent disease in every instance, their usage significantly reduces the spread of the AIDS virus. Despite evidence that the transmission of HIV (and other sexually transmitted diseases) occurs in prison, common administrative policies barring inmates from having sexual relations have generally been invoked to justify derivative prohibitions on the distribution of condoms to inmates. These restrictions on inexpensive public health efforts contribute to the spread of a deadly and expensive-to-treat disease as they draw heavily on the financial and staff resources of fixed-budget correctional health services. Should health care professionals distribute condoms anyway?

It is useful to distinguish between conflicts of obligation and conflicts of interest.

One has a conflict of obligation when, for example, one owes it to A that one do R but also owes it to B that one not do R. A surgeon, for example, who happens to be a Jehovah's Witness might be the only doctor on duty when an injured non-Witness enters the emergency room in need of an immediate blood transfusion. As a doctor, the surgeon has a clear duty to transfuse, but as a Witness, the surgeon has an equally clear obligation not to transfuse. Jehovah's Witnesses believe that blood transfusions are contrary to God's word. Once the conflict arises, there may be no painless answer. The unfortunate clinician may have to choose between betraying his profession and betraying his religion.

Conflicts of obligation can be actual or potential. When the Witness/ surgeon is alone and on duty, there is a potential conflict. Something can happen (the appearance of a patient requiring blood) that can bring about an unmanageable dilemma. Once the exsanguinating patient presents in the clinic, the conflict is actual.

The optimal way to deal with conflicts of obligation is prophylactically. The Witness/surgeon's mistake was to be alone and on duty. Knowing of a potential conflict of interest, one must scrupulously avoid placing oneself in such a situation. Professionals need to be, (1) alert to the possibility of a conflict of obligations and, (2) empowered to configure their responsibilities in advance so that conflicts cannot arise.

In contrast, a conflict of interest occurs when, (1) the agent's role essentially involves some type of loyalty, and (2) some fact reasonably calls that loyalty into question. There is nothing wrong with refereeing a soccer game and nothing wrong with being a parent. But there is something wrong with refereeing a game in which one's own child is a player. Although each role is legitimate, one cannot discharge both at once. For we expect parents to be partial to their own children, and that simple fact calls into question the impeccable impartiality we want to see in a referee. Given a close call, the parent/referee can be suspected of bias if the judgment favors his child and can be suspected of bending over backward to avoid the appearance of favoritism if the judgment does not. Even if the referee's call is always "correct," even if the referee is wholly unmoved by parental sentiment and knows this, there is still a conflict of interest. Impartiality is called into question by the bare fact that the referee's child is the subject of the call. Persons who are supposed to have particular set of interests cannot, as a practical matter, decisively settle certain issues.

Conflicts of interest are of great concern for professionals whose abilities to serve clients are broadly dependent on their trustworthiness. We want to rely on what we are told by, for example, lawyers and journalists, and, accordingly, conscientious professionals undertake to protect the credibility of their judgment—their basic stock in trade—by avoiding even the suggestion of disloyalty. In medicine, fidelity to the patient involves an acknowledgment of the inmate's humanity. Doctors are not supposed to betray, coerce, or harm their patients. A responsible physician honors the patient's entitlement to be treated with dignity and respect: a rarity in the correctional context and yet the only way to engender a therapeutic alliance, the only way to be a doctor.

Taking these cases as illustrative, what then do CHCPs owe to the inmate/patient, what do they owe to the prison population conceived as a whole, and what do they owe to their prison-administrator employers? Although I do not claim to be able to pronounce the final word on this issue, let me propose the following principles as, perhaps, a place to start:

1. Health care professionals must have the necessary resources and latitude that they need in order to perform their job.

CHCPs have the responsibility to provide health services to inmate/patients. Because wardens are not licensed health care professionals, they cannot discharge that responsibility themselves and thus they must delegate it to doctors and nurses. In addition, crucially important in this context, they must provide these professionals with what they need to do their job. The point here is not that prison administrators are required to provide health care professionals with everything they need. From the perspective of professional ethics, it is rather that it is improper for professionals to accept responsibility for the health care of inmates unless they are provided with a level of resources adequate to discharge that responsibility. There is a difference between honestly doing one's job and maintaining an illusion of concerned attention.

In the final analysis, the judgment about what professionals need to do their work is a professional judgment. Nonprofessionals are typically not competent, for example, to decide what should be in a clinic's formulary. Likewise, because health care professionals need the trust of their patients if they are to discharge their responsibilities to them, prison administrators may not require health care professionals to act in ways that betray that trust. What doctors do to inmate/patients must be done within the framework of the doctor–patient relationship. This line of reasoning supports the second principle.

2. Health care professionals should scrupulously avoid enlisting in or being conscripted into activities that are not required as part of health care. They must especially avoid complicity in activities that would take advantage of their professional skills to promote prison security.

A doctor or nurse is not acting as a health care professional if he or she carries out a body cavity search, conducted against the will of the inmate, for reasons that have nothing to do with the health care of that inmate. The concern here is to keep the two spheres of responsibility—security and health care—separate. Only in this way can doctors and nurses continue to be seen as independent health care professionals rather than as agents of prison administration. Prison administrators will sometimes want to enlist health care providers into the incarcerative mission of the institution; to recruit them, so to speak, into secondary roles as security personnel. But wardens need to remember that success in this endeavor is likely to undermine the credibility of CHCPs and, as a consequence, damage the prison's ability to discharge its responsibility for inmate health care.

Just as wardens must respect the working space that health care professionals require, so too must health care professionals bear in mind the incarcerative mission of the prison. Reciprocally, doctors and nurses must remember that their work is to be carried out within procedures that ensure prison security. This leads to our third principle.

3. Although health care professionals should strive to be independent of the incarcerative function of the prison, they must defer to rules and procedures intended to further institutional security.

Assuming that such rules and practices do not make it impossible to discharge their health care responsibilities, health care professionals need to appreciate the overriding responsibility that wardens have for prison security. Both health care professionals and prison administrators need to work together to reach a modus vivendi, coordinating the health care and incarcerative responsibilities of prisons. Health care must not be compromised because of the prison administration's concern for security. And—equally—security must not be compromised out of the health care staff's concern for the well-being of inmates.

Applied to "Case One: The Gun," these principles would suggest that prison administrators find alternate ways of dealing with the suspected firearm. Perhaps prison security could be adequately provided for if the inmate were placed in restraints and under guard in a dry room for several days. Were the inmate eventually to request medical attention, health care professionals would then be at liberty to provide it, with the procedure being protected by physician–patient confidentiality. (I assume that the procedure will be carried out in such a way as to ensure protection of the health care staff: Restraints might be used if general anesthesia is not required.) However, once the sequestered firearm comes into the possession of the health care professional, he or she would clearly be ethically prohibited, under principle 3, from returning it to the inmate. The health care professional could convey the gun to the warden. But, because of principle 2, and apart from conveying the firearm to the inmate, the physician should not be asked to testify against the inmate.

At bottom, this approach depends on the abilities of wardens and health care professionals to draw a line between, on the one hand, health care activities that respect reasonable rules that ensure prison security and, on the other hand, activities that constitute complicity by health care staff in the incarcerative mission of the prison. Although the former behavior can properly be required of health care professionals, doctors and nurses should uniformly refuse, as a matter of professional ethics, to participate in the latter. Faced with these conscientious refusals, prison administrators should accede to them out of a concern for the effectiveness and professional integrity of their health care staff.

From a public health perspective, condom availability is a standard intervention in dealing with a sexually active population with some HIV seroprevalence. It seems likely that there will be significant morbidity and mortality, not only in prisons but outside prisons as well, as a consequence of our current prison policies. What both populations need is education in the use of prophylactic measures. It could be argued that health care professionals commit professional neglect if they withhold the means for inmate self-protection when condoms are not available from other sources and when high-risk sexual activity occurs and is expected, often, to be less than fully consensual. It could be argued that in failing to assist in the inexpensive prevention of HIV infection when the ensuing disease can result in costly drains to scarce medical resources, CHCPs are allocating scarce resources unwisely and therefore failing to honor their obligations to respect the claims of other non-HIV positive inmates with health problems of their own. It could be argued that it is manifestly improper to assume responsibility for the health care of a population when one's employer explicitly prohibits interventions that are known to be effective in preventing the spread of deadly diseases within that population.

In the early decades of this century, university professors (i.e., the American Association of University Professors) carried on a debate and political struggle over the proper dimensions of professional autonomy in higher education. There was broad agreement that it was manifestly improper for a university administration to hire a capable scholar to pursue responsible judgment in some academic arena and then to specify the conclusions that scholar could and could not defend. It was plain that if one is going to have scholarship, one has to allow scholars to pursue arguments wherever they lead; even if the arguments lead to opinions that run counter to received doctrine. The academic freedom that is so essential to responsible scholarship is a secured limitation on the employer's right to determine the conditions of employment. Trustees and presidents cannot fire academicians merely because they disapprove of the substance of their published work.

If the foregoing analysis is correct, CHCPs are at a point today that compares to the one professors occupied prior to 1919. There is some emerging awareness that if health care professionals accept responsibility for providing care to a population. they must be free from administrative restrictions that seriously impair their abilities to do that job. Alas, there are also many whose professional commitments are evaporating as they align themselves with the incarcerative imperatives that prevail in prison. It is always a political–ethical struggle to retain integrity within institutions that see it as a threat. CHCPs, perhaps more than any other group, need an ethical compass, a code, and the institutional machinery to give it purpose.

It would be a serious error to think of the problems explored in this chapter as merely discomfiting the criminal element and of small concern to the rest of us. On the contrary, we would do well to consider the meteoric ascendancy of managed care. As medicine moves away from its independent fee-for-service transactions toward large-scale, for-profit enterprises in which physicians increasingly think of themselves as employees, the very health of health care will depend on the profession's competence in managing similar pressures. Only all of us will be affected. The lessons of prison medicine (and military medicine as described in *M.A.S.H.*) are worthy of philosophical attention.

Notes

1. John Rawls, *A Theory of Justice* 60 (Cambridge, MA: Harvard University Press, 1971).

2. *See, e.g.*, Joel Feinberg, *Social Philosophy* (Englewood Cliffs, NJ: Prentice Hall, 1973).

3. Hugo Bedau, *Prisoners' Rights*, Crim. Just. Ethics, 38, vol. 1 (1982).

4. 191 N.C. 487, 490 (1926).

5. 429 U.S. 97 (1976).

6. Nancy Dubler and B. Jaye Anno, "Ethical Considerations and the Interface with Custody," in *Prison Health Care: Guidelines for the Management of an Adequate Delivery System* 55 (B. Jaye Anno, ed., Washington, DC: US Department of Justice, National Institute of Corrections, 1991).

16

CONFLICT OF INTEREST
AND PHYSICAL THERAPY

Mike W. Martin & Donald L. Gabard

Most philosophical attention to health care ethics has focused on physicians and nurses, neglecting the moral issues faced by physical therapists and other members of allied health care fields. The neglect is compounded by misperceptions that physical therapists are technicians rather than professionals, that they do not have fiduciary relationships with patients, and that they lack all discretion in allocation matters. In fact, physical therapists possess discretionary power in treatment selection, advising, and duration and intensity of therapy—all areas in which trust and trustworthiness are paramount. In addition, their work tends to make possible longer time spent with patients. And their contributions to health care are distinctive in terms of the techniques used in restoring persons to a more functional, pain-free, independent life, as well as in preventing injury and pain. For all these reasons, the neglect of physical therapy ethics fosters a lack of vigilance that sometimes masks abuses, such as those arising from conflicts of interest.

The definition of conflicts of interest is itself contested, quite apart from physical therapy ethics. We begin by proposing a definition and providing a rationale for it, using examples from several professions. Then we make a few general comments about evaluating conflicts of interest. The remainder of this chapter discusses issues of current interest in physical therapy under six headings: (1) advising and providing, (2) physician referral, (3) equipment and supplies, (4) gifts, (5) inappropriate sexual behavior, and (6) teaching and research. The categories are not exhaustive, but they suffice to illustrate an array of recurring problem areas.

Defining Conflicts of Interest

Conflicts of interest have always arisen in all forms of work, but the expression "conflict of interest" has somewhat recent vintage, as Neil R. Luebke (1987) points out. Only since the 1930s did the phrase acquire currency in law and then spread to other professions. Its original usage targeted relationships of trust in which a fiduciary acquired interests in property (money, jobs, etc.) or persons (family, friends, etc.) inimical to meeting duties to clients, employers, or the general public. Thus, judges should not try cases involving their own children, and attorneys should not accept two clients whose financial interests directly clash. Luebke (1987) contends that we should retain this original meaning. In his view, conflicts of interest involve (1) fiduciary relationships and (2) "objective interests" (rather than mere subjective biases), such as "some material right, benefit, asset, or share possessed by the fiduciary or by others with whom he/she is legally or closely associated (family members, business partners, employer, benefactor, client, or the like)" (p. 69).

Other philosophers broaden the definition by expanding the range of interests that threaten responsibilities; simultaneously they narrow the definition in other ways. Thomas Carson (1994), for example, expands interests to include altruistic desires, such as a company official's desire to help a nonprofit charity by donating corporate funds and also malicious desires such as to harm someone by not awarding their company a contract. At the same time, he also restricts conflicts of interest to employees, thereby excluding self-employed professionals. Again, Michael Davis (1982, 1998) expands the relevant interests to include virtually any desire or duty, attitude or aim, bias or benefit having a tendency to adversely affect judgment within a role. Yet he restricts conflicts of interest to situations involving the exercise of judgment or discretion, apparently ruling out occasions when one's responsibility is entirely obvious and requires no exercise of judgment.

We share Luebke's worry about losing the usefulness of the concept by stretching it too far. Nevertheless, his attempt to limit interests to material matters, "objective" relationships, and fiduciary relationships is needlessly restrictive, as is Carson's restriction to employee status and Davis's limitation to matters of judgment—even though these factors have great moral significance in the cases we discuss. In particular, we agree with Davis that most conflicts of interest involve matters of judgment, where judgment is "the capacity to make correctly decisions not as likely to be made correctly by a simple clerk with a book of rules and access to all the facts" (Davis, 1982, p. 27). Yet, conflicts of interest also arise in routine matters when sophisticated judgment is not required, and when by-the-book decisions straightforwardly indicate one's obligation in the situation. It can be entirely obvious what should be done, even to the agent who through weakness of will or outright greed fails to do what is right.

Regarding motives, we note that typically professionals have mixed motives in all areas of their work: compensation motives (income, recognition), craft motives (commitment to excellence), and moral concern (caring, integrity). (Martin, 2000). These multiple motives interact in complicated ways, usually reinforcing each other but occasionally pointing in opposing directions. In most conflicts of interest, compensation motives threaten responsibilities within professions and organizations, although occasionally altruism conflicts with professional responsibilities, as Carson points out. Complete explanations of any ensuing wrongdoing need to be contextual and to make reference to motives linked to both social influences and personal character. (Martin, 1999).

In our view, the crux of conflicts of interest resides in significant threats to role responsibilities, where role responsibilities are well-delineated duties attached to formal assignments within organizations or social practices, such as professions. Accordingly, we adopt the following definition: "Conflicts of interest are situations in which individuals have interests that significantly threaten their role responsibilities, or would do so for a typical person having their role." Although the definition is simple, thereby adding to its usefulness, we offer the following comments by way of further clarification and rationale.

Areas of vagueness in a definition can actually be helpful by identifying areas in which practical controversies are likely to arise. Consider the word "interest." Ordinarily, we might not speak of a conflict of interest when professionals' duties are only somewhat threatened by interests centered in personal life, such as family difficulties, desires for illegal drugs and excessive use of alcohol, or sundry bigotries. Our definition allows for this by speaking of "significant" threats (dangers, hindrances) to duty. We reasonably expect and demand professionals to maintain *professional distance*, that is, to avoid allowing personal biases and interests to distort their work (Martin, 1997). Some conflicts of interest arise when distance is placed at risk, as when individuals know (or should know) that their prejudices or addictions are beginning to significantly threaten their work, perhaps by tempting them to issue biased rulings (judges, referees) or to steal drugs from a hospital (health professionals).

Why does the definition refer to both individuals and typical persons? Consider a judge of such exceptional integrity that we know she would be fair in adjudicating a dispute involving a family member. The judge is still in a conflict of interest in cases involving family members because, according to ordinary usage, a typical judge in that situation would be at risk of failing to properly fulfill his or her role responsibilities. Conversely, some professionals are inclined to lose distance in particular areas (perhaps a specific religious matter) in which a typical professional would not, and hence the definition also refers to the individual involved.

The term "formal role" also deserves comment. We intend rule-structured activities with assigned responsibilities within social organizations—understood broadly to include professions, corporations, and voluntary organizations—that assign responsibilities and authority. Do families involve formal roles? We do not think of them that way, at least given their great variability within contemporary Western societies, but others might. For example, others might speak of a conflict of interest when Christian Scientists or Jehovah's Witnesses withhold essential medical care (on religious grounds) from their young children. In a similar vein, Davis (1993) suggests that parents face a conflict of interest when their desire to take a weekend trip threatens their judgment about their child's medical care. We consider these applications of conflicts of interest a bit expansive, but our definition helps us pinpoint the source of disagreement.

Again, is citizenship a formal role? We do not think so, because the role delineations and duties involved are too diffuse and disputed, but others might disagree. Consider Antigone, who has conflicting obligations (and conflicting interests): a citizenship duty to obey King Creon, who forbids the burial of her brother, and a religious duty which requires burying her brother. In our view, Antigone faces a conflict of duty (a moral dilemma) but not a conflict of interest. There would be a conflict of interest, however, if Antigone had been the King's Deputy of Burials. If others disagree, our definition at least helps explain why the disagreement arises.

Evaluating Systemic and Episodic Conflicts

Joseph Margolis (1979) suggested that Antigone is not caught in a conflict of interest for a different reason. In his view, conflicts of interest are restricted to situations in which it is morally wrong to follow the conflicting interests together. We disagree: Some conflicts of interest are inevitable or otherwise tolerable, and hence permit pursuing both interests (cf. Davis, 1982). This leads us to offer a few general comments on the moral evaluation of conflicts of interest.

Why do conflicts of interest have such great moral significance? Part of the answer is clear from the definition: They threaten responsibilities. Another part of the answer is that even the appearance of conflicts of interest can endanger the trust which is so important in professional relationships. However, to say that conflicts of interest are morally problematic, especially in raising issues of trust, does not settle how to resolve them. For there might be additional moral considerations, whether additional responsibilities or rights, that override the threat to role responsibilities and permit pursuing the (conflicting) interest. To illustrate that point, let us distinguish between episodic and systemic conflicts.

In this chapter we are interested in recurring conflicts of interest, ones that arise with frequency rather than by occasional happenstance. Recurrence takes two forms. *Episodic* conflicts of interest arise in particular situations as a result of voluntary choices (beyond simply choosing to serve in a formal role), yet they can be recurring in the sense of widespread. Giving and accepting personal gifts is a familiar example we will discuss. By contrast, *systemic* conflicts of interest arise from the very structure of formal roles. For example, there is an ongoing temptation in all professions to provide unnecessary services to clients in order to increase profits.

The last example, which we discuss in the next section, illustrates how systemic conflicts of interest can be inescapable, short of overthrowing or radically modifying social practices and economic systems (which often generates new systemic conflicts). As a second example, it is cost-effective for the Federal Aviation Agency (FAA) to select some employees of airline manufacturers to serve as government inspectors. (Martin & Schinzinger, 1996). Here the conflict of interest is internal to the individual's professional roles: professional duty versus professional duty, rather than duty versus personal gain. The dual roles of government inspector and corporate employees constitute a conflict of interest, but when individuals are carefully selected, the practice saves taxpayers the costs of a wholly independent set of inspectors for complex technology (or risking public safety by doing without inspectors).

In general, systemic conflicts of interest are *tolerable* when the relevant systems (institutions, economic structures, etc.) are morally permissible and when effective procedures of overseeing abuses are in place (laws, self-regulations within professions, consumer-group publications). We will largely take for granted the economic systems of Western democracies that combine capitalism (free enterprise), government regulation, and professional self-regulation currently established in the United States. Nevertheless, we are less sanguine about current substructures in health care, in particular many aspects of current managed health care. Capitalism takes many forms, and the rapid changes currently under way confirm that the United States has yet to achieve anything like an ideal form with regard to health care.

Calling a conflict of interest tolerable or inevitable does not banish moral concern. Such conflicts continue to be of concern because responsibilities continue to be at risk. Inevitable and inescapable conflicts of interest call for moral vigilance and conscientiousness by committed professionals and equally vigilant disciplinary structures. Notoriously, these things are in short supply in long-established professions, and difficulties are compounded in still developing professions such as physical therapy.

Regarding episodic conflicts, alternative moral responses include the following options: (1) escape from them, typically by relinquishing the conflicting interest that threatens the role responsibility; (2) avoid them in the first place; (3) disclose them to appropriate parties (e.g., employers and clients); or (4) take other steps, as appropriate, if only exercising special caution to ensure that role responsibilities are properly met (Davis, 1998). As we proceed, we will discuss which option is appropriate in a particular situation. We add a prefatory caveat about disclosure, which is too readily taken to be sufficient.

Health care exists because someone is vulnerable and in need of care. Furthermore, harm caused by mistakes frequently cannot be undone, unlike financial or legal matters. As a result, disclosure of conflict of interests is generally not enough. To undermine the trust on which care is built is to diminish the care, regardless of whether professionals profit. Unlike a profession such as law or banking, where it is desirable for all parties to be vigilant and where full disclosure helps ensure that vigilance, in health care the primary concern and focus are to achieve better health or function. To minimize the threat to trust, there is a strong presumption that therapists and other health care professionals should do everything possible to avoid conflicts of interests as they relate to patient care.

In short, to call something a conflict of interest is to raise a (moral) red flag, but it does not indicate how the flag is to be waved. As an analogy, consider the word "deception." All deception raises moral questions, but the questions are sometimes easily answered and other times sharply contested. Deception is permissible in a game of poker; it is obligatory when it is the only way to defeat a tyrant in order to save many innocent lives; its moral status is subject to debate when it is used to conceal personal sexual matters (as recent debates about President Clinton revealed). Exactly when and why conflicts of interest are morally objectionable needs to be explored contextually, a task to which we now turn.

Advising and Providing:
Intervention, Outcome,
and Payment

In physical therapy, as in other professions, the most basic systemic conflicts of interest center on the primary good served. Described in general terms, this good is shared within all health fields: to promote health while respecting patient rights. Described more specifically, the good served by physical therapy is to restore persons to a more functional, pain-free, and independent life, and also to prevent injuries and pain. Three interwoven questions arise immediately:

1. When is health care intervention warranted and at what level?
2. Who defines acceptable outcomes—patient, provider, or reimbursement organization?
3. What is the cost, and who pays?

Most of us, healthy and functional within the expectations of others, our age, and our level of activity, could profit from physical therapy services in prevention (proper body mechanics) or even improvement in such things as balance and gait. Who defines the threshold for services? If left to patients, all will draw a different line in the sand. Even when there is obvious disability, some patients are quickly resigned to a life of needless dysfunction; others want not mere average abilities but athletically competitive skills. Needs for physical therapy can be highly specialized, even within the specialties recognized by the national organization and achieved through extensive specialized training and monitored clinical experience. For example, within sports medicine, some physical therapists have specialized in treating only professional dancers due to the unique injuries and risk in that profession.

As with physicians, therapists' primary conflict of interest is inherent in the entrepreneurial method of reimbursement and acquisition of medical services. All health care providers have one foot in an ethic of equality (serving all patients to the best of one's ability) and another foot in an ethic of equity (service according to ability to pay or a plan's prenegotiated equity format). In addition, each of the methods of reimbursement carry with it potential conflicts of interest between whatever service is provided or denied and the financial well-being of the provider.

Again, as in most professions, physical therapy generates systemic conflicts of interest centered on the therapist's dual roles of adviser and provider (Green, 1990; Kipnis, 1986; May, 1996. McDowell, 1991; Rodwin 1993). Thus, most professionals advise clients about options, help decide the best course of action, and then provide the services. The implications of adviser–provider conflicts differ according to the payment systems within which health professionals function, and those systems are in the midst of turmoil on a historic scale. Many options are being experimented with, but two main categories are fee for service and managed care.

In traditional fee-for-service systems, the provider role is a systematic incentive to advise for unnecessary services, thereby raising costs dramatically. As a general tendency, fee for service brings higher costs for patients, unnecessary tests, and unnecessary procedures. Under fee for service, the therapists' self-interest is to set goals and timetables that will harvest the maximum payment, yet patients' desire to restrict cost as much as possible.

By contrast, in managed health care systems, the costs of providing services constitute a systematic incentive not to advise patients of all needed services (to minimize usage of services, given that capitation pays according to numbers of members rather than usage). In a managed care environment, the conflict of interest is between a duration of treatment which is in the best interest of the client and what is permissible under the managed care plan. The move to managed care has generated many adviser role conflicts for physical therapists: Should therapists inform and counsel clients about the true potential and risk in the minimal care they are being asked to provide? How about informing clients of options that might produce beneficial results but at extra cost for the provider? Or, should therapists proceed to limit client expectations to meet standardized pathways and time frames?

The current system encourages providing a minimum level of care rather than an optimal level. Economic realities cannot be ignored, but concern for the patient must remain paramount. When patients would probably profit from additional treatment, they should be so informed. Defending the adequacy of a managed care pathway, which is not accurate regarding the individual, is dishonest even if the employer is embarrassed. Therapists should not sign contracts that forbid them to express professional opinions ("gag orders") any more than physicians should.

The primary responsibility of physical therapists is to clients: to provide quality services and products at reasonable costs within the constraints of respect for autonomy. In addition to issues of cost, quality, and control, there are related considerations about honesty and maintaining the public trust, which often require avoiding even the appearance of objectionable conflicts of interest. In addition, there are responsibilities to employers, to other professionals with whom one works, and to the general public. Exactly when these responsibilities are sufficiently threatened requires examination of the dangers arising in particular types of situations, informed by an understanding of human propensities and historical settings.

Finally, the American Physical Therapy Association (APTA) Code of Ethics sounds the right note, although it leaves specifics to the judgment of individual practitioners. The accompanying "Guide for Professional Conduct" explicitly forbids certain types of conflicts of interest (without using the expression) (APTA, 2001). For example, section 7.1.B states that "A physical therapist shall never place her/his own financial interest above the welfare of individuals under his/her care," and 7.1.F states that "A physical therapist shall not directly or indirectly request, receive, or participate in the dividing, transfering, assigning, or rebating of an unearned fee."

Physician Referral

Physician referral constitutes one of the most discussed issues surrounding conflicts of interest in physical therapy, partly owing to historical reasons. At one time physical therapists worked more directly under physicians' supervision. As physical therapy became increasingly professionalized (a process still continuing), with greatly augmented skills required in both diagnosis and treatment, there was a strong move toward therapists working privately. As a result, referral arrangements began that allowed physicians and physical therapists to profit when physicians were paid simply for making referrals.

By the early 1980s there was increasing awareness that the practice had serious potential for abuse, and in its grossest forms it constituted kickbacks that significantly increased costs to patients, potentially affected judgments about quality of services, and threatened a loss of public trust. A consensus arose that referral is not itself a service from which physicians should be allowed to profit but essentially a type of kickback arrangement that invites numerous abuses. In 1983, the APTA forbade physical therapists from entering into arrangements that allowed physicians (or other referring practitioners) to profit simply from making a referral.

Philip Paul Tygiel (1989) cited many illustrations of instances in which patient rights were abused when physicians were allowed to profit from referrals. The cases included physicians and therapists alike providing unnecessary services, low-quality care resulting from physicians not focusing on adequate specialization of the therapists they used, and denying patients the therapist they prefer, either individuals or those in convenient locations near their home. In one case study, an orthopedic surgeon employed a physical therapist who, although well trained in treating spinal conditions, did not have an expertise in hand therapy—even though hand surgery was a primary component of the surgeon's practice. Hand therapy and the custom splinting frequently required by patients is a highly specialized area of practice for both physical and occupational therapists. The surgeon still referred his patients to the therapist in his employment, even though patients frequently had to be referred again to one of four qualified hand therapists in the community for resplinting because the therapist employed by the surgeon lacked the special skills needed. The resplinting by a qualified therapist was an additional cost to the patient.

The APTA Code of Ethics has since been clarified and strengthened to forbid physical therapists from entering into many problematic referral relationships. Regardless of how carefully a code is constructed, however, it is not possible for a single document to anticipate all possible variations on a common theme. For example, we know of a case in which the husband is a physician and the wife is a physical therapist. Although legally their practices are separate, and therefore withstand the APTA definition of conflict of interest, the private and personal perspective clearly defines a conflict in which their joint income is enhanced by referrals from the physician husband to his therapist wife. The physician responds that he wants his patients to receive the best physical therapy care available, and he believes that is provided by his wife. In this case, there is clearly a possibility for abuse. Disclosure to patients by the physician or therapist should be supplemented with a listing of other therapists in the area with similar training prior to the first appointment.

A general reading of the intent of section 7.3 in the "Guide for Professional Conduct" appears to support the spirit of this recommendation. The section states that "A physical therapist shall disclose to the patient if the referring practitioner derives compensation from the provision of physical therapy." (APTA, 1997).

Referral issues have become somewhat more convoluted with managed care where the senior physicians in the health maintenance organization (HMO) hold ownership of the HMO. Profit is still the concern, but this time underuse rather than overuse poses the more serious offense. The dilemma is compounded by the dependent role the physical therapist experiences in practice. Although in some states, such as California, the physical therapist can treat a patient without a physician's referral, the vast majority of insurance carriers will not reimburse without the referral. As a result, therapists are financially wedded to physicians, even though they have professionalized themselves to the point to which many make independent evaluations and treatments of disabilities. This financial tether is somewhat unique, and although it may disperse liability and accountability, it has the potential to bind the professional judgment of the therapists to a menu of physician-acceptable options.

Referrals to therapist-owned facilities might not be ethically resolved by a simple disclosure of interests. Patients trust therapists as they do physicians to act and recommend in the best interest of the patients. The trusting relationship is itself diminished if the patient has to monitor the provider. To maintain the more comfortable trusting relationship, patients ignore confessed disclosures as a required process that may be pertinent to others but certainly not to their relationship.

Equipment and Supplies

Frequently physical therapists make equipment for patients, such as splints and seating inserts. Usually only the therapists who work with the patient know their specific needs and have the specialized knowledge to order equipment. In private practice it is usual for the therapist to charge patients for materials and sometimes the time used to construct the equipment. Frequently these therapists supply equipment cheaper than that available through specialized vendors, but not always.

Therapists who fabricate equipment for patients often cite patient benefit as the primary motivation. Because equipment, especially splints, has to be custom made in many cases to the specification of the therapists, they argue that it is both time efficient and ultimately contributes to a better product when therapists do the fabrications. Doing so, they do not have to bring another person into the clinic and take the time to communicate in detail the patient needs. They also point out that while fabricating a piece of equipment, they are free to respond to unanticipated variables and to change the specifications of the equipment and implement those changes immediately.

Many therapists charge only for the cost of the materials and their customary practice rate, or some fraction thereof, to generate the equipment. There are, however, companies strictly dedicated to the creation of these appliances and they are quick to point out that this practice robs them of needed income for the task for which they are specifically trained. Perhaps, however, there is the greater problem of the appearance of a conflict of interest. Therapists can easily fill any downtime with equipment fabrication, thereby securing a secure and steady income in private practice. Thus, there is the temptation to create a market for equipment with a population that could not possibly get the exact appliance without going to another therapist who also manufactures appliances. The appliances are so uniquely a blend of the patient's need and the therapist's goal of correction that without the therapist's input, an outside vendor would be unable to adequately meet the patient needs.

Therapists should not have major financial interests in the company that supplies them with products they use in practice. However, there is an interesting dilemma inherent in this advice. People are advised to invest only in areas in which they know the products and the markets. If therapists are also good business persons intent on securing extra financial security through investments, their fiscal manager might advise investing in companies whose products they know to be better than the competition's. Thus even though therapists may own stock in those companies from which they make purchases, they are driven by the commitment to provide the best supplies. Only if the company supplies inferior products, offers direct kickbacks, or becomes excessive (as defined by reasonable guidelines within organizations and the profession) is the stock ownership inherently objectionable.

Gifts

The importance of context and of appearances enters into thinking about gifts. Principle 4.4 of the APTA's "Guide for Professional Conduct" states:

"A physical therapist shall not accept or offer gifts or other considerations that affect or give an appearance of affecting his/her professional judgment." This is a good, clear statement, but even so it leaves some areas of vagueness. The intent is not to forbid all gifts. That prohibition may become necessary in some professional settings, such as the defense industry. But in physical therapy, as in many other professions, hard and fast rules on gifts can cause unexpected negative consequences.

Many gifts by vendors are "reminder items" that have negligible monetary value. But as a tool to enhance a relationship, their value cannot accurately be measured in dollars. Instead, it must be considered relative to the subtle influence on the relationship and related decisions. The American Medical Association (AMA) allows small gifts, and anyone who has attended a health profession conference in this nation has experienced how widespread this practice has become. At APTA conferences, as well as at other health-related conferences, the trend has been away from promotional gifts which can be used with patients and instead toward gifts specifically for the therapists, often without any relationship to the products the vendors sell.

Other gifts raise different concerns, in both their acceptance and their rejection. In most physical therapy settings, the therapist is engaged with the client for significant lengths of time, and the quality of that time is enhanced by collaborative goal setting and assessment that frequently builds a social as well as professional relationship. Clients often see the therapist as their primary advocate and sometimes their primary hope for restoration of function. As a result, gifts from clients to therapists are common, especially in pediatric settings and often insignificant in their cost—drawings, homemade cards, and so on. Whereas with vendors small gifts may be objectionable because they build a relationship that will influence products purchased and used, in this case they appear to actually strengthen a component of care and caregiving that is advantageous for the client.

It is also true that in some cultures gifts are given to health care providers out of custom and appreciation, without any intended influence to acquire more or better services. In those cases, to refuse such a gift is considered an insult. It symbolically states that the giver and the gift are unappreciated and thereby disrupts the client-therapist relationship. Because the type of work that the therapist perform requires maximum effort and cooperation from the patient, any action that diminishes the trust with the patient potentially diminishes the effectiveness of the intervention.

At the same time, no therapist is immune to attempts by clients to influence them to provide more services in appreciation of a gift. Patients sometimes try to influence therapists to continue treatment after the point at which, in the therapist's judgment, the patient has the capability of benefiting from treatment. As long as the therapist continues to treat the patient, many believe that hope for significant recovery or restoration of function exists. No one wants patients to abandon realistic hope, nor should patients and loved ones cling to false hope when doing so undermines efficient use of services or equipment. In these ways, gift giving and receiving are caught in the nuanced interplay of hope and honesty in ways that call for good judgment rather than fixed rules.

Cost of the gift is one guide to its intent, but surely it is a fallible guide. Gifts must be assessed against the background of the economic situation of patients rather than the value relative to the therapist. What may appear to be a large gift to one therapist may be an inexpensive expression of appreciation by a client, whereas for another client it would be a considerable sacrifice. In all these cases one must assess the intent based on the history of the relationship and what is known of the client.

Despite these and other moral nuances of gift giving and receiving, in practice the difficulties are not insurmountable. Claudette Finley (1994) offers several criteria that handle most cases. Gifts should be expressions of gratitude, not manipulation or coercion; they should have minimal monetary value; they should not significantly shape relationships with vendors; they are best when they benefit people in need; the cost of gifts must not be passed on to clients; most important, one should be willing to have the gift disclosed to interested parties.

Inappropriate Sexual Behavior

Mentioning inappropriate sexual behavior immediately brings to mind misconduct initiated by professionals, but in fact patients are also initiators. If not dealt with properly, inappropriate sexual behavior by patients creates conflicts of interest for the therapist and threatens performance of their responsibilities as health care providers.

Physical therapists are especially at risk for these behaviors because of the close physical contact and prolonged private communication with patients. In addition, because of their physical disability and complex psychological states triggered by medications, feelings of isolation, and damaged self-esteem, patients are frequently in need of reassurance that they are desirable and lovable. Usually the therapist intervenes at a time in patients' lives when they lack their usual degree of power at work, within families, and elsewhere.

Inappropriate sexual conduct by patients expresses itself on several levels (McComas, Hebert, Giacomin, Kapla, & Dulberg, 1993). Mildly inappropriate sexual behavior by patients, characterized as suggestive stories or solicitations for dates may, depending on the setting, best be handled by the therapists ignoring or being nonresponsive to the behavior, thus in effect escaping from the conflict. Moderate (deliberate touching, direct propositions, etc.) and severe (forceful fondling and attempts to secure sexual intercourse) inappropriate sexual behavior by patients present the therapist with difficulties as well as temptations.

According to a study conducted in Canada, 92.9% of surveyed practicing physical therapists had experienced some level of inappropriate patient sexual behavior in the work environment (McComas et al., 1993). Of those, 32.8 percent of female physical therapists and 37.5 percent of male physical therapists had experienced severe inappropriate sexual behavior by patients. More than 66 percent of students in physical therapy, by the end of their training, had experienced inappropriate sexual behavior by patients. In the United States, a national study published in 1997 found that 86 percent of physical therapists had experienced some form of inappropriate sexual behavior by clients and 63 percent reported at least one incident of sexual harassment by clients (DeMayo, 1997). The problem is recognized as sufficiently prevalent that some educational institutions are implementing instruction on this subject in their curriculum.

The role of power is one of the most frequently discussed components of sexual harassment, of which sexually inappropriate behavior is a component. Paradoxically for therapists, the relevant question is whether there is truly a power differential between therapists and patient and, if so, who has the power? The patient is dependent on the delivery of service by the therapists, but dependency alone does not mean there is a power differential in favor of the provider. In restaurants we do not assume that the server has an elevated position over the patron even though the patron is dependent on the server for the delivery of food. In our health care system, the patient is empowered as a consumer. Indeed, within the managed care environment in which companies openly compete for patients, even the doctor's position of power has been usurped, at least in the eyes of many consumers of health care. The third-party payer or its spokesperson, the health care administrator, is seen by many as the one with ultimate authority over the dispensation of care. Although therapists have significant discretionary power, the general public perception is increasingly that the business manager controls the physician and the physician controls the therapist.

Clearly no one should be forced to compromise his or her personal or professional ethics in the performance of his or her job as health care provider. In these cases, it would seem that disclosure to appropriate parties would better secure a just outcome. However, when power is perceived to be with the consumer, it is feared that administrative efforts will downplay the offense or even blame the therapist for contributing to the situation. Administrators are concerned about keeping patients happy with the services provided in order to keep the market share necessary for survival and profit. Being portrayed to the public as repressive, lacking a sense of humor, or just being plain hard-nosed does not increase subscription rates or ensure continuing contracts.

In addition, not wishing to bring their own integrity into question, many therapists ignore the behavior and fail to report it to supervisors. Avoidance of the problem may include requesting another therapist to assume the care of that patient for fear that if rejected, the patient may retaliate with false charges of inappropriate sexual behavior toward him or her. More often, however, therapists who complain about patient behavior to supervisors are awarded the status of a whistleblower concerning an institutional secret. The therapist is left alone without any realistic means of protecting him- or herself or achieving fairness.

The institutional response should focus on the long-term survival of the organization. That means recognizing that the health care worker should be afforded the same protections from patients that are already assured legally to coworkers. Substantial numbers of therapists simply will not stay in an employment setting in which their personal integrity is sacrificed for the business of health care. When therapists are harmed by patient behaviors, the quality of care is diminished, either through avoidance or through stringent risk-reduction efforts. To meet expectations of quality care delivery and to maintain a stable work force, health care organizations must make it clear to patients and staff that sexual harassment policies extend to patients as well as to staff.

Regrettably, on occasion therapists solicit sexual favors from patients. These patients may perceive that the quality of care is dependent on their compliance with inappropriate requests. Beyond issues of coercion, there is the far more troubling matter of maintaining trust. Patients typically assume that professionals are obligated to set aside personal opinions and self-serving motivations to provide optimal and objective care. When the therapist diminishes the trust built on that assumption, all who share the assumption are damaged to the extent that they are aware of the violation. There is an unanticipated and unacceptable cost to the patient for the services requested.

What about situations in which sexual attraction is mutual and appreciated? Is there harm to the patient, the therapist, or the institution that provides the care? One troublesome part of this situation when there is no easily defined victim is the issue of the genuineness of a relationship. Formal roles (therapist, patient) can eclipse important values that support lasting committed relationships often desired by the parties. But even if we have no interest in protecting the genuineness and duration of relationships, we have concerns when the purpose of the organization is subverted by personal interests. A health care service environment is by necessity tightly focused on the services and equipment linked to the delivery of care. It has nothing to gain but potential problems and liabilities by allowing behaviors unrelated to its mission.

Teaching and Research

Physical therapists who are also professors of physical therapy have new roles and hence new conflicts. Like other professors, professors of physical therapy have enormous demands from their research, consulting, and family that can threaten teaching responsibilities. Exactly how much time, effort, and skill are morally obligatory in the teacher role is contestable, thereby inviting temptations to give more attention to prestige-promoting publication at the cost of students. But there are threats to research as well, and in general the compensation motives of personal income, job security, and prestige present threats to role responsibilities in academia, as they do in serving patients.

There are also episodic conflicts of interest shared with other professors, such as having sexual affairs with students in their classes. Are they threatening their ability to grade fairly—threatening it sufficiently to call for university policy in the matter? In our view, decidedly yes, and that applies not only to the university environment but also to instructors in the clinic setting who teach students as a part of the university program. But others disagree, and many schools continue not to have policies forbidding such affairs. Values of freedom, sexual and otherwise, are invoked to prevent anything stronger than legally mandated sexual harassment policies.

Additional conflicts of interest arise in accepting, rejecting, and supervising student internships. Physical therapy students must complete a number of months in the clinic treating patients under the supervision of a licensed physical therapist in an employment setting approved by the educational institution. The intent is that the student will be taught many clinical skills, designated by the APTA accreditation standards as part of the eligibility requirements to take the state licensing exam. Especially in a managed care environment, many therapists are simply refusing to take students because of productivity standards that leave little or no time to supervise students, thereby adding to universities' difficulties in finding internship sites. In other cases, students are treated as revenue-generating personnel with little if any instruction. Because the latter is the only situation in which the educational facility has governance, schools regularly interview students and conduct onsite visits to ensure that students receive instruction and are not used solely to increase revenue at the expense and safety of patients. However, as clinical sites continue to diminish, educational institutions will be increasingly tempted to rationalize inadequate supervision as better than having to create new university-sponsored clinics to supply the experiences necessary for completing the educational program.

Currently, an area of great concern is the selection of candidates for educational programs. The number of applicants to schools of physical therapy have recently decreased, secondary to cost-saving measures in managed care. Simultaneously, the number of accredited physical therapy programs in the United States has increased, rendering some schools unable to fill their class quotas. Like most businesses, university departments are staffed and funded on the basis of anticipated enrollment and accompanying tuition revenue. Compounding the dilemma, academic programs are encouraged by the APTA, or even required, as by the California chapter of the APTA, to convert existing programs to award a doctorate in physical therapy as the entry-level degree program. This is a transition with considerable costs in terms of labor and material resources.

Taken together, these pressures intensify commitments to select only competent students who with education will be able to pass licensure examinations, at the same time keeping enrollment levels adequate to ensure the survival of the department. In addition, the educational institutions serve as the gatekeepers to the profession and have a duty to the profession to populate it with competent professionals. Some schools have responded to these financial threats by increasing their recruitment programs, but it is feared that as competition increases for a diminished pool of applicants, compromises in admission standards are inevitable.

Even the method of selecting candidates is controversial. Basic academic abilities and skills needed to complete the academic program are clearly needed, but what additional standards are needed? Should the educational institutions focus only on the recruitment and training of future clinicians when there are other areas of the profession such as research that are seriously deficient? Given the extremely diverse areas of specialization within clinical applications, combined with the employment opportunities in teaching, supervision, and case management, the task of defining valid admission criteria in addition to academic standards is daunting. Restricting the student population too narrowly, through rigid entrance requirements of voluntary clinical experience, does a disservice to the profession, but to apply no standards invites inappropriate academic recruitment to fill revenue needs.

In all university teaching, research responsibilities are important in their own right, as well as their general contribution to teaching. Physical therapy is criticized for failing to provide documentation that treatment methods pass accepted standards of scientific inquiry for efficacy, and professors share a responsibility toward the profession to help remedy that. Practitioners also have this duty but the conflicts are significant. Especially in a managed care environment, therapists' first obligation is to provide the best care to the patients who depend on them. The patient loads and time allotted typically eliminate any hope of conducting valid scientific enquiry in the true experimental model. Even quasi-experimental models require more time and planning than most therapists in clinical practice can be expected to accommodate. In the university, typically physical therapy faculty carry heavier teaching loads than most other faculty and have limited resources to finance efficacy studies either at a public or a private level. The focus of research dollars remains, and one could argue rightly, on the most expensive elements of health care, namely, pharmacy and surgical interventions.

Even when funds and opportunities are available, there has been a reluctance to engage in double-blind studies on the grounds that it is unethical to deny treatment. That would at some level be correct if it were known that the treatment had an effect. Controlling for bias is essential given the placebo effect of treatment and researcher bias in therapy. In the absence of that knowledge, one has to question the ethics of providing care that may be of no benefit to tens of thousands of patients and the consequential opportunity cost to the patient of alternate care that may provide some benefit or simply avoiding the costs incurred. Thus the most meaningful conflict is the one between current beliefs and the reality of unsupported promises. There is also the suspicion that research is neglected because it might show procedures to be inefficacious, possibly eliminating some components of practice in physical therapy.

Conclusion

The topic of conflicts of interest is a prism for exploring both the core commitments and historic variations of professions. We have highlighted examples of enduring issues centered on the public goods served by physical therapists, such as provider–adviser conflicts and also issues arising from historically contingent institutional structures and economic settings, such as managed health care. Although we commented on possible solutions, our discussion reflected our conviction that the primary moral challenge is to identify and render salient areas in which conflicts of interest are recurring and especially likely to cause harm.

In addition, the topic of conflicts of interest is a prism for exploring areas of shared and distinctive features of professions. Thus, some conflicts of interest in physical therapy are shared with all professions (gift accepting), some are shared with other health professions in particular (adviser–provider conflicts within managed health care), some are shared with other allied health care professionals (physician referral), some have special relevance to physical therapy (patient-intitiated sexual overtures), and some are akin to other professions but have unique variations in physical therapy (equipment and supplies). These prism effects are not surprising given that conflicts of interest, by definition, involve threats to role responsibilities.

References

American Physical Therapy Association. (1997). Guide for professional conduct. *Physical Therapy, 77,* 106–108.

Carson, T. L., (1994). Conflicts of interest. *Journal of Business Ethics, 13,* 387–404.

Davis, M. (1998). Conflict of interest. In *Encyclopedia of applied ethics* (vol. 1, pp. 589–595). San Diego: Academic Press.

Davis, M. (1982). Conflict of interest. *Business and Professional Ethics Journal, 1,* 17–27.

Davis, M. (1993). Conflict of interest revisited. *Business and Professional Ethics Journal, 12,* 21–41.

DeMayo, R. (1997). Patient sexual behavior and sexual harassment: A national survey of physical therapists. *Physical Therapy, 77,* 739–743.

Finley, C. (1994). Gift-giving or influence peddling: Can you tell the difference? *Physical Therapy, 74* 143–147.

Green, R. M. (1990). Physicians, entrepreneurism and the problem of conflict of interest. *Theoretical Medicine, 11,* 287–300.

Kipnis, K. (1986). *Legal ethics.* Englewood Cliffs, NJ: Prentice-Hall.

Luebke, N. R., (1987). Conflict of interest as a moral category. *Business and Professional Ethics Journal, 6,* 66–81.

Margolis, J. (1979). Conflict of interest and conflicting interests. In T. L. Beauchamp & N. E. Bowie (Eds.), *Ethical theory and business* (pp. 361–372). Englewood Cliffs, NJ: Prentice-Hall.

Martin, M. W. (1997). Professional distance: *International Journal of Applied Philosophy, 11,* 39–50.

Martin, M. W. (1999). Explaining wrongdoing in professions. *Journal of Social Philosophy, 30,* 236–250.

Martin, M. W. (2000). *Meaningful work: Rethinking professional ethics.* New York: Oxford University Press.

Martin, M. W., & Schinzinger, R. (1996). *Ethics in engineering.* New York: McGraw-Hill.

May, L. (1996). Conflict of interest. In *The socially responsive self* (pp. 123–138). Chicago: University of Chicago Press.

McComas, J., Hebert, C., Giacomin, C., Kaplan, D., & Dulberg, C. (1993). Experiences of student and practicing physical therapists with inappropriate patient sexual behavior. *Physical Therapy, 73,* 762–770.

McDowell, B. (1991). *Ethical conduct and the professional's dilemma: Choosing between service and success.* New York: Quorum.

Rodwin, M. A. (1993). *Medicine, money, and morals.* New York: Oxford University Press.

Tygiel, P. P. (1989). Referral for profit. In J. Mathews (Ed.), *Practice issues in physical therapy* (pp. 35–43). Thorofare, NY: SLACK.

VI

Epilogue

17

COMPARING CONFLICT OF INTEREST ACROSS THE PROFESSIONS

Andrew Stark

Consider the following two situations. In the first, a government bureaucrat's decision to support a high-tech subsidy program is affected by her part ownership of—or her spouse's employment with—a software venture that would benefit from the program: a set of interests she possesses outside her role as an officeholder. In the other, her decision to support the high-tech subsidy program is affected by her desire to advance through the ranks bureaucratically, shift her career path within the department, and increase her official salary: a set of interests she possesses within her role as an officeholder. Both kinds of interest compromise her professional judgment. And yet, for a long time, scholars of conflict of interest typically have concerned themselves only with the first type, when the encumbering interest arises outside of role. For if the second type—when the impairing interest arises within role—were treated as actionable conflict of interest, all professionals would be in conflict of interest all the time.

It is also the case, however, that if the first kind of situation—when the impairing interest arises out of role—exhausts what we mean by conflict of interest, as it typically seems to have, then every profession faces exactly the same kinds of conflict of interest. There is little to say, little grist for the mill, if our purpose is to compare conflicts across professions and our focus remains confined to out-of-role interests. A personal gift from an individual external to the professional–principal relationship—a pharmaceutical manufacturer in the case of the physician–patient relationship, a mutual fund salesman in the case of the broker–client relationship, an art dealer in the case of the critic–reader relationship—impairs the professional's judgment in all three pursuits in exactly identical ways. A judge's decision-making capacity is threatened in precisely the same fashion as a journalist's—or a corporate director's— by her capacity to affect an out-of-role financial holding through her in-role decision making. It is only when we turn to conflict of interests that arise within role, to conflicts not extrinsic but intrinsic to the professional's relationship with her principal, that revealing differences emerge across the professions. Here, as we shall see, the resulting conflicts fall into two main categories: Some arise because the professional occupies more than one role with respect to the same principal, such that the existence of the second role impairs her capacity to exercise the first. Others occur because the professional must exercise the same role with respect to more than one principal, such that the presence of a second principal impairs her capacity to exercise her role on behalf of the first.[1]

It is not surprising that one gets greater traction for cross-professional comparisons from in-role rather than out-of-role conflict of interest. After all, whereas judges and journalists and directors can all have the same kinds of external interests—stocks, bonds, fees, gifts—the internal structures of their roles each differ. In Tolstoyan fashion, conflicts of interest arising from out-of-role sources are all alike, but every profession experiences in-role conflicts in its own way. And, without in any way being orchestrated, the chapters in this volume confirm this fact. Almost every contributor, perhaps led by an innate sense of where the really interesting issues reside in his or her topic profession, spends as much time on in-role or "professional" as on out-of-role or "personal" conflicts of interest; sometimes more. As a result, this volume can be seen as a turning of the page in the exploration of conflict of interest in the professions, a turning from outside to inside. And, as we shall see, some striking patterns emerge from the book as a whole.

Many Roles, One Principal

There are, as I noted, two basic kinds of in-role conflict, one that arises when a professional occupies more than one role with respect to any given principal; the other, when the professional occupies the same role with respect to many principals. Consider, to begin with, the first type, which—to judge from the contributors' chapters—is itself amenable to being divided into two classes. On the one hand, there are professions in which such multiple-role conflicts emerge because the professional simultaneously occupies a judging and an advocating role—an impartial and a partial role—in the work he does for the principal. On the other hand, conflicts inhere in a tension between the professional's diagnostic and service-provision roles, his roles as both a buyer of services for and a seller of services to the principal.

Consider first the professions that fuse a judging with an advocacy role. Many officials fall into this class. Think, for example, of legislators whose role it is to advocate aggressively for various interests held by different sections of the public while, in the final analysis, judging legislation impartially in the interest of the public as a whole. Or think of agency officials who help prepare cases which they ultimately have to participate in deciding. Primary-market financial services underwriters, too, find themselves riven between judging and advocacy roles when they assess the merits of a client I.P.O. (initial public offering) which they are, at the same time, promoting. Likewise journalists, who often combine reportorial with commentative work, or who wrestle with the need to be "objective"—to judge the hard truth of a story—and yet at the same time display "balance," by rendering "all sides of the story." Literary critics, too, find the distinction between judging and advocacy, between being an arbiter and a tribune of public taste, extremely fuzzy. The same with university teachers, who, as Jane Gallop shows, must confront a conflict posed by their having to judge their graduate students—grade and assess them—while at the same time advocating for them in the professional marketplace. Show-business agents, too, can fall into an advocacy/judging form of conflict. On the one hand, the agent is obliged to represent his client—say the star of a TV show—by energetically advocating for her interests. On the other, he might also produce the show, and in that role his obligation is to judge what is best for the program and its investors, whose interests could easily diverge from the star's.[2]

Even with judges themselves, whose roles are more obviously "judgmental," if they ever find themselves in a multiple-role sort of conflict, it is because they are tugged by a competing obligation to advocate. They might, for example, find themselves torn between an obligation to assess a case "on the merits" and an obligation to advance a broader legal doctrine or "legal agenda," as David Luban puts it. Or judges might find themselves sundered by a role requirement to rule exclusively on the "legal issues" in a case and a competing imperative to show "compassion" for particular parties before them: to pursue "impartiality and universality" at the same time, as Robin West says.

True, some of these professionals—in particular, journalists, financial underwriters, show-business agents, and officials—work in organizations which, if they are suitably structured, can largely segregate those occupying judging from those occupying advocacy roles. Commentators *need* not be reporters, financial analysts need not also be salespeople, show-business agents need not double as producers, and decision-making officials—administrative judges, for example—need not at the same time fill the roles of preliminary investigators. But in the remaining three professions—judging, criticism, and university teaching—the professional operates with far greater independence from whatever organizational structure surrounds her. In these three venues, whatever fusion of judging and advocacy roles arises is thus more likely to be inveterately internal to the individual and less amenable to resolution through organizational manipulation.

It is true that Jane Gallop describes a situation, at her university, where the "freshman composition course is organized to isolate evaluation from all other aspects of the student–teacher relation"; where, specifically, "[a]t the end of the semester, the student's writing is evaluated by other [freshman composition] instructors," and the "actual teacher functions only as a coach"—and "possibly as an advocate"—"preparing [her students] for evaluation by someone else." The very exceptionalism of this arrangement, however, proves the rule that judging and advocacy combine inextricably within most university teachers. More to the point, Gallop herself uses the very incorrigibility of the professor's impartiality–partiality role conflict in the area of academic judging (evaluation) and advocacy (coaching, recommending, instructing) to say, in effect, that if we are going to allow such conflicts there, we should allow them anywhere, including situations in which the professor is both evaluator and lover. But whether or not judging and a professional advocacy roles are ultimately segregable, these are the professionals—journalists, financial underwriters, show-business agents, officials, judges, critics, and professors—who are peculiarly prey to it.

The second kind of intraprincipal role conflict arises when the professional occupies both a diagnostic and a service-providing role with respect to the same principal. Consider the accountant who provides an audit and then offers comptrolling or forensic services to deal with any shortcomings she discovers. Or the consulting engineer who recommends structural work which his firm can then supply as a contractor. Or the lawyer who reviews a client's estate and then suggests a complex series of trust arrangements. Or the corporate director whose engagement in a proxy fight involves, essentially, a conflict between her fiduciary obligation to ascertain a course of action that will best cure the company's ills and her position as someone who might be able to offer such a course of action. Or the broker who "churns," recommending "frequent trading of (possibly) unsuitable securities" on the secondary stock market in a situation where he is "compensated only for executing trades." Or, too, the official who identifies a social problem and then seeks the budget and staff to deal with it: the kind of conflict of interest public-choice scholars study. Or the physician who diagnoses a particular ailment and then prescribes a battery of tests to confirm, or who refers the patient to a specialist facility she co-owns for treatment.

In each of these cases, the professional is conflicted between a diagnostic and a service-provision role. As Stephen Latham puts it in discussing the physician in particular, in all such situations, the professional occupies the role of both buyer—the principal's agent for the purchase of services—and seller, the supplier of those services. What Latham says about the doctor is the case for each of these other professionals: "His conflict of interest is this: as [the principal's] purchasing agent, he has a duty to assist her in making prudent choices among [relevant professional] services; but as a purveyor of those services, he has a pecuniary interest in advising her to make rather more extravagant purchases than a disinterested person would counsel."

For some of these professionals—in particular, accountants, doctors, secondary-market financial brokers, and lawyers, who operate according to traditional fee-for-service principles—the fusion of diagnostic and service-providing roles will, at some level, become inveterate and incorrigible, unamenable to any kind of organizational remedy. Latham, for example, notes the impracticality of a world in which a "patient visits one physician for diagnosis, paying her a simple hourly rate, and is given a sheet of paper [which she takes] to another physician of her choice, who implements that treatment for a fee." Indeed, some physicians cite the very irremediability of the fee-for-service conflict to say, in effect, that if we are going to allow diagnostic/service-provision conflicts there, we should allow them anywhere, including situations in which "a physician refers a patient for testing to a lab that he or she owns." As Bradford H. Gray puts it:

> Because [such] conflicts of interest are so similar to the conflicts of interest that inhere in fee-for-service, criticisms of the new arrangements [such as a physician referring a patient who needs tests to a laboratory she co-owns] can be seen as criticisms of arrangements to which organized medicine is wedded. If the physician who invests in facilities to which he refers cannot be trusted to resist economic temptation and to put the patient's interest first, then why should fee-for-service physicians—who are faced with analogous decisions daily—be trusted? This logic makes the profession reluctant to condemn any economic arrangement on the basis of the temptation to which it exposes physicians.[3]

Of course, the same could be said of accounting, law, and secondary-market financial services which, like medicine, are traditionally fee-for-service professions.

By contrast, engineering, corporate directorships, and government—while they, too, risk diagnostic/service provision conflicts—are not fee-for-service professions in the same way, and hence any such conflicts are less inveterate, more amenable to organizational remediation through the segregation of those occupying diagnostic from those occupying service-provision roles. It is frequent practice, for example, for engineering clients to use separate firms, one firm as a consultant to study needs, design specifications, review proposals, and monitor performance and another as the actual contractor. Indeed, only a handful over the past thirty years of National Society of Professional Engineers Board of Ethical Review (NSPE BER) conflict-of-interest cases deal with "diagnostic-service provision" conflicts, and all find them relatively amenable to remediation through a combination of recusal, where the diagnosing firm takes itself out of the running for service-provider, and pluralism, where the diagnosing firm recommends a number of competing alternatives as service providers. As for corporate directors, there also exists the possibility of considerable daylight between diagnosis and service provision: If a director is in a position to provide services to the company, then disinterested directors, shareholders, or potential buyers of the company are available to verify the diagnosis that those services are indeed needed.[4] Government, too, has available an innumerable number of arrangements whereby it can segregate officials charged with diagnosing the need for a program or monitoring it from those developing and executing it. Finally, although primary-market financial brokers can also fall into a diagnostic/service-provision conflict, such conflict—by comparison with fee-for-service secondary brokers—is amenable to organizational resolution, to a structural segregation of those occupying diagnostic roles, determining the best stocks for a client's portfolio, from those filling service-provision roles, trying to sell a particular stock or bond that the company underwrites.[5]

In sum, when it comes to conflicts of interest that arise when the professional occupies more than one role with respect to a particular principal, the professions fall neatly into two categories: those that feature a conflict between judging and advocacy roles and those that exhibit a conflict between diagnostic and service-provision roles. And, within each category, the conflict can be more or less inveterate and incorrigible. Thus, when the conflict conflates a judging with an advocacy role, the two roles may in some situations be amenable to organizational segregation, as with journalists, primary-market financial underwriters, show-business agents, and officials. But in other circumstances—when the professional operates with some quasi-independence from the surrounding organizational structure, and hence remains beyond the reach of organizational manipulation—the judging–advocacy conflict, where it arises, may be more entrenched within the individual practitioner, as it is with judges, critics, and university teachers. Likewise, when the conflict in question fuses a diagnostic with a service-provision role, it may lend itself to resolution through organizational ecology or maneuvering—as with engineers, corporate directors, and primary-market financial underwriters—or there may come a point where such conflicts are ingrained and irremediable, as with the traditional fee-for-service professions of law, accounting, medicine, and secondary-market brokerage.

Many Principals, One Role

"Internal" conflicts of interest—those intrinsic to the professional–principal relationship—can also arise not when the professional occupies more than one role with respect to any given principal but when he or she must deal with more than one principal within the ambit of any given professional role. If, for example, the central problem with fee-for-service medicine is that it creates conflicts between the various roles (diagnostic vs. service-provision) that the physician occupies with respect to a particular patient, the central problem with its alternative—capitation—is that it fosters conflicts between the various patients whom the doctor services in any given medical role. Capitation forces doctors to choose between allocating their limited time and resources to different principals, some of whose needs pose a far greater threat to that time and those resources than do others.

But medicine is not the only profession that features conflicts between various principals on matters that come under the rubric of the professional's role. Corporate directors must deal with competing majorities and minorities among shareholders. Lawyers often face the problem of either concurrent or serial representation of adversarial clients. As Eric Hayot and Jeff King note, graduate students such as themselves fall into competition for the university teacher's attention and assistance in much the same way as patients do for their doctor's under capitation. In financial services, as Boatright says, a "broker who manages accounts for multiple clients may be forced to choose among the interests of these different parties when he or she decides how to allocate a security in short supply"; also, interprincipal conflicts arise because the broker represents both the buyer and the seller in many transactions. In fact, as far as interprincipal conflicts go, brokerage is unique. Whereas the interests of various principals might *possibly* come into conflict in medicine, law, corporate directorship, and university professorship, in brokerage, they *necessarily* fall into conflict, because they involve buyers and sellers, principals on either side of a market exchange.

But there is another set of professions which do not seem quite so afflicted by interprincipal conflicts of this sort. Perhaps that is because in their case—journalism, literary criticism, government, judging, accounting, and engineering—the public as a whole is either the principal whom the professional is obligated to serve or else is coequal to other principals. Engineers and accountants, as Neil Luebke and Len Brooks show, fall into this latter category. One analyst, Paul L. Busch, even explicitly couples the two professions by noting that in both, the professional bears an obligation to the "public interest" and not just the "client's interest." "Axiomatically," Busch writes, "engineers are expected to design for earthquake protection whether or not it is requested by the client, [while] public accountants' audits are expected to disclose what the public needs to know about their clients, whether or not the client is happy about it."[6] As for the accountant's or engineer's private clients, certainly they might fall into competition in the broader marketplace: A single engineering firm can construct stadiums for both the Chicago Bears and the San Diego Chargers; a single accounting firm can keep books for both Christie's and Sotheby's. But engineering and accounting clients are rarely adversaries— as can be doctors' patients under capitation, lawyers' clients, professors' students, and directors' shareholders—on any matter in which the engineer or accountant is responsible for serving them as a professional. [7]

When it comes to the remaining four professions for which the public is a principal—government, journalism, judging, and criticism—the public is in fact the *only* principal. Unlike with accounting or engineering, these four professions do not embrace private-party principals as well. That is not to say that, for example, journalists, in serving the public, owe no obligations to various private parties, such as their sources or subjects, or that those obligations will never trump the one owed to the public to report the news. But the obligations a journalist bears to those she interviews or covers are not ones of professional to principal; they are not, as Alan Goldman puts it, role-moral obligations—heightened fiduciary duties of singular commitment and devotion—but rather "ordinary-moral" obligations—minimalist or baseline duties to be fair and decent of the kind we bear toward anyone, including those with whom we have no special relationship.[8] Likewise, critics write for their public, not for the artists they analyze, which is not to say that they bear those artists no obligations of baseline fairness. As for officials, they, too, direct their professional or role-moral obligations to the public; toward particular agency clients or groups, they hold only ordinary moral obligations.[9]

In the same vein, judges bear a primary obligation to the public for whom they work to do justice: to faithfully interpret, clarify, improve, and rationalize the law. And yet, as Luban notes, they certainly have other kinds of obligations to the private litigants before them, obligations that might compete with their duties to the public, such as settling a case quickly without addressing the broader public values it implicates, preserving secrecy, or delving into the complexities of the case at the cost of omitting to create simple legal rules of broad application. Of course, those litigants themselves—though they do not constitute the judge's principal—not only might be, they necessarily *are*, in competition on matters that fall squarely within the judge's role responsibility. Judges share this quality with brokers, which is perhaps why David Luban even describes litigant-centered judges as "brokers."

As with the multiple-role/one-principal variety of conflict, then, so with the one-role/multiple-principal type: The professions divide themselves into two basic categories. On the one hand are those—medicine, corporate directorships, financial services, law, and university teaching— in which the private-party principals may well come into competition or conflict within the domain in which the professional is responsible. On the other hand are professions in which many individual private-party principals are replaced either wholly or partially by the public. Thus, journalists, critics, judges, and officials owe their professional responsibilities only to the public—which is not to deny that the public might sometimes fall into internal conflict on matters for which the official or judge, say, is responsible in role. And although engineers and accountants bear professional obligations to individual clients, those interests are unlikely to fall into conflict on any matter for which engineers or accountants are professionally responsible; moreover, accountants and engineers bear a coequal fiduciary obligation to the public as a whole. There is, of course, some argument to be made that physicians, especially those working in public settings or being paid through public funds, and corporate directors, laboring as they do under corporate constituency statutes, are moving toward a point at which the public will assume coequal status as a principal, along with the patient or the shareholder. Conversely, Luban suggests, judges may be moving toward a point at which litigants assume coequal status as principals along with the public. But we have not yet actually reached any of these points.[10]

Cross-Professional Patterns

There is, then, a pattern—depicted in table 17.1—to the kinds of conflicts that arise from sources internal if not external to the professional-principal relationship. It is a pattern, or more exactly a four-quadrant matrix, born of the different structures each profession displays. In the first quadrant are professions in which the professional occupies the dual roles of judge and advocate (some more integrally and others less) and the principal is the public itself: journalism, criticism, government, and the judiciary. Second come professions—accounting, engineering, government—where this time the professional occupies the dual roles of diagnostician and service provider (again, the one more integrally than the others), while the principal continues to include the public. Third, there are professions—medicine, law, corporate directorships, and financial services—in which the professional continues to occupy the dual roles of diagnostician and service provider, but in which it is only private par-

Table 17.1 Conflicts, Roles, and Principals

	ROLES Judging/Advocacy		ROLES Diagnosis/Service-Provision	
PRINCIPALS	Conflicts Less Integral	Conflicts More Integral	Conflicts More Integral	Conflicts Less Integral
Public Only or Included	Journalism Government	Criticism Judging	Accounting	Government Engineering
Private Only	Financial Services Show Business	University Teaching	Medicine Law	Corporate Boards Financial Services

ties, and no longer the public itself, who number among the principals.[11] Finally, there come the professions—university teaching, financial services again, and show business—in which the professional's dual roles are once again those of judge and advocate but the principals continue to include only private parties, not the public. This last category, I note, seems to contain a bit of an odd triumvirate: What has university teaching got to do with financial services got to do with show business? The answer is that in these professions, unique among the ones considered here, the principal is actually the product being sold by the professional. University teachers judge and advocate for their students as they propel them into the academic job market. Brokers judge and advocate for their client company as they propel its IPO into the primary stock market. Show-business agents judge and advocate for their stable of stars as they propel them into the casting market. No other profession markets its principals in the same way, which is why the three belong together.

Ex Post Decisions and Ex Ante Impairment

Overlaying this pattern is one other set of distinctions that emerges from the book's various chapters. The question which any conflict-of-interest situation raises, of course, is whether a professional's judgment has been impaired or compromised. In exactly half of the professions under discussion, we have available (at least in principle) a way of answering this question by looking at the decision the impaired principal actually makes and comparing it with an independent standard of correctness. So, for example, for both journalists and judges—at least in respect of part of what they do—there is an empirical reality, a fact of the matter, against which their reporting or judging can be measured to see whether it moved off course.[12] For both doctors, concerned as they are with health, and engineers, focused as they must be on safety, certain physical realities can be used to check a particular medical or engineering decision; peers can ascertain, in many cases, whether it was faulty or not. Finally, in both accounting—with its Generally Accepted Accounting Principles—and corporate directorships—where in a transaction involving a self-interested director, "unfairness of price . . . after the fact" can "be evidence of unfairness of process"—certain numerical realities exist against which any putatively impaired decision can be measured.[13]

None of this is to say that empirical reality for journalists and judges, or physical reality for doctors and engineers, or numerical reality for accountants and corporate directors, is always knowable, accessible, or beyond contestation. But because it exists in principle, and in some cases it provides an added means of assessing the existence of impaired judgment: by looking at the actual judgment *ex post* instead of examining only the extent of the impairment *ex ante*. And this is so whether the impairment originates in external interests such as stockholdings or fees or in internal interests such as a conflicting role or principal. The availability of such a supplementary measure distinguishes these professions in a key way. After all, just because her judgment was impaired *ex ante*, it does not follow that any professional—no matter what his or her field—was unable to rise above the impairment and produce a good judgment anyway *ex post*. In these six professions, there may be means of assessing whether this in fact happened.

Such extrinsic standards are, however, unavailable for the remaining professions. In the political world of the official, the partisan world of the lawyer, the academic world of university teaching (as distinct from university research, especially in the physical sciences), in the aesthetic (or what Tyler Cowen calls the "ambiguous") world of the critic, in the speculative world of the broker bringing a stock to market for the very first time—and in the political, partisan, aesthetic, and speculative world of the show-business agent—there are generally no independent empirical, physical or numerical standards against which to assess a professional's decision. Instead, these are realms of great and inveterate contestation. Absent such standards for assessing or second-guessing the professional's judgment *ex post*, it is not surprising that these professions (or, at least, those among them that have conflict-of-interest strictures) rely not just partially but wholly on prophylactic conflict-of-interest standards, standards which control impairments *ex ante*.

Loose Ends:
Teaching—Counseling and Anthropology

I have thus far omitted discussion of two of the chapters in the book, those on teaching–counseling and anthropology. The reason is that they are literally off the charts—or, more exactly, off Table 17.1—but in an intriguing and mutually inverse way. One breaks the mold in its treatment of roles, the other in its orientation to principals.

Teacher–counselors take the kind of intrarole conflict that inheres within other professions—between various kinds of judging–advocacy roles, say, or between diagnostic-service provision functions—and makes it an interrole conflict, a conflict better understood as one between two distinct professions, teaching and counseling. Indeed, in Elliott Cohen's example, the conflicted professional is not just any teacher, he is "a professor of counselor education"; hence, he is compromised in his teaching role when, in the presence of a student he also counsels, he instructs on the topic of professors who also counsel. Likewise, he is not just any psychological counselor; he is a counselor who is helping the student deal with her educational experiences, including experiences she has had in his class. His role as a teacher is thus one that leads him to pass judgment on what he does as a counselor; as a counselor, he must comment on his behavior as a teacher. Clearly, he is uniquely compromised in both roles. If, however, as a teacher he taught the student computer science, while as a counselor he was treating her for the psychological effects of a motorcycle accident, the same sorts of conflicts would not arise. Yes, he might be tempted to favor her in class in order to keep her business as a counselor. But that would be a conflict external not internal to the teaching role, one identical to the situation of an official who favors a businessperson who pays her a consulting fee.

If teaching–counseling externalizes a kind of conflict other professions experience intrarole, then anthropology internalizes a kind of obligation other professions leave out of role—obligations to nonprincipals—by making it an in-role obligation. As Merrilee Salmon notes, the anthropologist (as does any other professional) bears a fiduciary or role-moral duty to her principal, in this case the public for whom she writes, to positively promote its interest in gaining knowledge. And, as do all other professionals, she has the negative "duty not to harm" others—in particular, the group about whom she writes. But, unlike other professionals, for whom this duty to nonprincipals is a common moral or nonfiduciary one, for the anthropologist, the duty "not to harm the people he or she studies or works with is a fiduciary duty." Thus, anthropology varies the theme of multiple principal conflict—by internalizing, as well, competing obligations to nonprincipals—just as teaching–counseling varies the themes of multiple role conflict by externalizing conflicting obligations between roles.

But the possibilities for deepening cross-professional comparisons and contrasts—for going further and further "off the chart"—does not end with teaching–counseling or anthropology. Consider, just as one illustrative example, corporate directors and public officials. Both share certain off-chart characteristics that add texture to their respective conflict situations and distinguish them from other professions. First, within certain closely guarded limits, directors and officials are both able to draw on resources of the principal to combat any attempt to replace them with competing professionals: Think of the use of corporate resources by incumbent directors in proxy fights and the use of public resources by incumbent officials in political campaigns. Second, both are elected. Third, both are the only professions whose principals divide themselves into majorities and minorities: After all, whereas all of the director's or official's principals might find themselves interested in the same particular matter—a stock split, a budget resolution—this never happens with medical patients or engineering clients. Fourth, both are professions in which the professionals themselves might number among the principals whom they are obligated to fiduciarily serve: Officials are also citizens of the jurisdiction; directors can also be shareholders in the company.

Fifth, and finally, in directorship and officialdom the diagnostic/service-provision conflict uniquely spills out of the professional role. Consider that in other professions—accounting, engineering, medicine, or financial services—professionals, in their role as diagnosticians, might recommend services that they themselves can provide in their professional capacity. True, the official, too, might diagnose a social ill for which he then develops a service as an official, thus expanding his department. The director, likewise, might diagnose a corporate malfunction which she believes she and her incumbent colleagues are uniquely equipped—by contrast with members of a competing slate of candidates—to cure as directors. But in government and corporate directorship, alone among the professions, the professional is also regularly in a position to diagnose needs that themselves would not necessarily be served in-role—whether by herself or a fellow professional—but rather by out-of-role service providers of almost any shape, among whom she might also number. Thus, an official might use his role to diagnose a social need which nonofficial entities, among them a private company he owns, might meet, as when an agriculture department supervisor diagnoses a departmental need for warehouse space and, in his out-of-role position as a warehouse owner, supplies it.[14] Similarly, the director might use her role to diagnose a corporate need for a new office building and, happening to own one out of her directorial role—as a real estate investor—supplies it.[15] Hence, among directors and officials alone, the in-role diagnostician/service-provision conflict can spill over into a kind of out-of-role self-dealing.[16] For all these reasons, government and directorship offer but one illustration of the ways in which the structure of conflict of interest can reveal deep, and perhaps hidden, structural affinities (and, presumably, also distinctions) between professions.

Conclusion

Does a professional occupy multiple roles with respect to the same principal? Are these judging and advocacy roles? Diagnostic and service-provision roles? Are such role fusions integral to the individual professional, or are they amenable to organizational remediation? Does the professional exercise his or her role with respect to more than one competing principal? Are such interprincipal conflicts necessary or simply possible? Do her principals include the public or not? And are there external empirical, physical, or numerical standards available against which to assess the *ex post* results of any *ex ante* impaired judgment? These are the questions that separate the professions, that array them in a rich diversity—indeed, a patterned diversity—insofar as conflicts arising from within the professional–principal relationship are concerned. Conflicts arising from without that relationship, by contrast, show no such rich or patterned set of distinctions at all.

It is our hope, as editors and authors, that scholars and practitioners will build on the research reported in this volume and on the opportunities for cross-professional comparisons it affords; that they will find its analyses fruitful and informative. And plausible. In witness whereof, let me just pluck out one observation from the preceding discussion. Of all the professions, two in particular emerge from the volume as being polar opposites if we judge them by their conflict-of-interest structures. In the one—literary criticism—conflicts arise from a fusion of judging and advocacy roles, they are integral and inveterate, they involve the public as principal, and they are bereft of any established external means of assessing the outcome of a judgment *ex post*. In the other—corporate directorships—conflicts emerge from a combination of diagnostic and service-provision roles, they are frequently remediable and corrigible, they involve only private parties as principals, and external standards are often available for assessing the *ex post* quality of any decision made under some form of *ex ante* impairment. Literary critics and corporate board members, according to this analysis, could not be more dissimilar. If that does not conform to our "pretheoretical intuitions," it is hard to say what would.

Notes

1. There is, perhaps, a third kind of nonexternal conflict of interest that hovers above the other two, not so much internal as "meta." Consider Michael

Pritchard's example of "Adams," a professional of undesignated profession, who "is invited to play golf with some friends on a particularly beautiful day" at a time when he has "an appointment with a client." Pritchard believes that Adams's circumstance does not even rise to a "potential conflict of interest." But perhaps another way of understanding it is this: Adams's situation may not impair any decision he takes in role, but it does encumber his decision as to whether to enter his role in the first place—a meta-conflict of interest. See Michael Pritchard, *Conflict of Interest: Conceptual and Normative Issues*, 71 Acad. Med. 1308 (1996).

2. Eben Shapiro, *Hollywood abuzz over Shandling lawsuit*, San Diego Tribune, March 13, 1998, at E10. The core of the Garry Shandling lawsuit—perhaps the most famous to emerge in the arena of show-business agency—had to do with the internal conflicts of interest that allegedly arose because Shandling's agent, Brad Grey, "serv[ed] as both Shandling's manager and the executive producer of his show." As well, Shandling alleged several other purely "external" conflicts of interest on Grey's part, claiming that Grey had traded on Shandling's name in order to advance his own extra-professional commercial interests. See also Lynn Elber, *Shandling's suit puts managers in spotlight*, Tulsa World, July 1, 1999, at 5.

3. Bradford H. Gray, *The Profit Motive and Patient Care* 198 (Cambridge, MA: Harvard University Press, 1991).

4. See Norwood P. Beveridge, Jr., *The Corporate Director's Fiduciary Duty of Loyalty: Understanding the Self-Interested Director Transaction*, 41 De Paul L. Rev. 677 (1992).

5. I had earlier described this same financial-services role fusion as one of judging and advocacy, not of diagnostics and service provision. And so it is, from a different perspective. For what is of note here is the existence of two vantage points from which one can view the primary-market broker's role—that of the company whose stock the broker underwrites and that of the client whose portfolio the broker manages, both of whom number among the broker's principals. From the point of view of the company whose shares are being underwritten for an IPO, the broker may be conflicted as both an advocate for the stock and a judge who must execute due diligence—who must pass on it objectively in the same way a university professor must with respect to the students for whom he or she also advocates subjectively in the job market. But from the perspective of the individual client whose account the broker manages, the conflict is one between diagnostician—someone who must determine what financial services the client needs—and potential supplier of those services ("have I got an IPO for you!"), in much the same way as a physician—someone who must ascertain the medical needs of a client—might also be a potential supplier of those services ("I know of a nice MRI facility . . ."). Primary-market financial services thus fall into both classes of multiple-role conflict, judging/advocacy and diagnostic/service provision, precisely because it is the only professional activity in which the principals routinely fall on both sides of a market transaction, and who thus bear the two perspectives. I say this notwithstanding that government, too, can experience both judging/advocacy and diagnostic/service-provision conflicts, because in its case, it is usually different officials—or, at least, different official activities—that fall into one or the other kind of multiple-role conflict, not (as with primary-market financial brokerage) the same official undertaking the same official activity. Finally, although it is true that an accountant, too, can act

as a judge—in her public auditing capacity—and also advocate before the tax authorities on behalf of a client whose affairs she has audited, the accountant rarely executes both roles with respect to the same particular matter; (i.e., she rarely advocates with respect to the audit itself). Role conflicts for accountants are typically those of diagnosis and service provision.

6. Paul L. Busch, *Time for Another Look at Conflict of Interest,* http://www.nspe.org/ ethics/eh1-tim.asp.

7. I must qualify this comment. Sometimes, as NSPE ethics cases reveal, engineers do appear to fall into conflicts because they must serve different principals with competing interests on matters that fall within their professional role. But closer scrutiny shows this to happen only when they have, in essence, left the engineering and entered the legal sphere: when they find themselves acting as expert witnesses for both the plaintiff and the defendant in a particular case (see, e.g., Case 95-7). It is equally noteworthy that the only time engineers seem to fall into conflicts because of the competing (diagnostic/service provision) roles they occupy with respect to the same principal is when, in essence, they have left the engineering and entered the governmental profession. Almost all such cases involve consulting engineers brought in by government to design specifications for a project which they are then in a position to build; they involve engineers occupying, as one case (92-5) put it, a "quasi-governmental" role with whatever added obligations to the public trust such a role represents. It seems, then, that engineers fall into either type of conflict only when they assume the mantles of other professions, specifically law (more than one principal, but one role) and government (more than one role, but one principal); when they shuck those mantles, few engineering conflicts of interest seem to arise. (These National Society of Professional Engineers ethics cases can be found at http://www.niee.org/cases.)

8. Alan H. Goldman, *The Moral Foundations of Professional Ethics* (Totowa, NJ: Rowman & Littlefield, 1980); *see also* Everette E. Dennis, *The Press and the Public Interest: A Definitional Dilemma,* 23 De Paul L. Rev. 945 (1974).

9. See Andrew Stark, *Beyond Quid Pro Quo: What's Wrong with Private Gain from Public Office?* 91 Am. Pol. Sci. Rev. 115–116 (1997).

10. Prison medicine, as Kenneth Kipnis describes it, seems to differ from general medical practice in this way: The principals involved, the patients, are not individual private parties who come to the doctor willy-nilly from the general population; rather, they themselves constitute a population within a confined space. Hence, the interprincipal conflicts the prison doctor faces are heightened. Indeed, three of Kipnis's four examples place prison doctors in the kind of conflict that arises when their obligations as a physician to one of their principals—one prisoner patient—conflict with their obligations to others. If, for example, the physician tests an inmate who is potentially infected with hepatitis B against his will, she violates her obligation to him. If she does not, she violates her obligations to other inmate patients who might get infected as a result. If a diabetic inmate continues to ingest candy bars at the prison canteen, making himself ill and "draw[ing] staff and resources away from the needs of other inmate/patients," the physician could continue to assist him each time he harms himself—thus hurting other patients. Or she could initiate disciplinary procedures that would result in the inmate's loss of canteen privileges, thus partly transgressing her role obligation to the diabetic patient himself. If the prison physician is faced with the question whether she

should violate prison policy and distribute condoms in order to combat HIV, "it could be argued that in failing to assist in the inexpensive prevention of HIV infection where the ensuing disease can result in costly drains to scarce medical resources, [she is] allocating scarce resources unwisely and therefore failing to honor [her] public-health obligations to respect the claims of other non-HIV positive inmates with health problems of their own." All are conflicts not between the professional's roles but between her principals. And, Kipnis notes pointedly in concluding, as individual patients outside prison coalesce into "populations" in the way inmates do—as fee for service, in other words, is replaced by capitation—the heightened interprincipal problems of prison medicine will come to beset more and more physicians.

11. It would seem, from Donald Gabard and Mike Martin's thorough treatment, that the physical therapist is in much the same position as the physician. Physical therapists find themselves afflicted with diagnostic/service-provision role conflict with respect to any individual patient, as well as—at the level of resource allocation and devotion of attention—conflicts between the obligations they bear to many patients within any individual therapeutic role. Thus, for medicine, read, "medicine and physical therapy."

12. John Rawls distinguishes the archetypal judging situation—the "criminal trial," in which there exists an "independent criterion of a correct result" even if our means of reaching it are imperfect—from political debates over "distributive shares," in which "there is no independent criterion for the right result." For judges, in other words, there exists in principle an extrinsic standard against which to test the fruits of impaired judgment, whereas for officials, say, there often is not. See *A Theory of Justice* 85, 86 (Cambridge, MA: Harvard University Press, 1971).

13. Melvin Aron Eisenberg, *Self-Interested Transactions in Corporate Law*, 13 J. Corp. L. 1005 (1988).

14. I base this example on Smith v. United States, 305 F.2d 197 (9th Cir. 1962).

15. Supra note 13 at 999.

16. Of course, there are some gray areas here. As we have seen, physicians can under certain circumstances diagnose a need, and then refer the patient concerned to a testing lab they co-own. Here, the services provided remain medical ones—that is, they are offered as professional in-role services by medical personnel, and certainly doctors—but they are rendered outside of the doctor's own office, by another entity she owns, and hence begin provoking a debate as to whether they constitute self-dealing. By contrast, lawyers who get into "ancillary businesses"—referring clients to insurance, lobbying, mediation, financial planning, trust, real-estate development or investment banking services they provide—often find themselves in the reverse situation. Here, the services provided are not legal ones—they exist outside the profession of law—but they often are offered inside the lawyer's own firm; indeed, this is the idea of such "one-stop" shopping or "multi-disciplinary law firms." And, again, unease arises as lawyers debate whether or not such ancillary businesses fall into the class of normal, in-role professional conflicts—conflicts between a diagnostic and service-provision role of a sort inherent in fee-for-service business—or whether they cross a line into self-dealing. For some good discussion, see James Fitzpatrick, *Legal Future Shock: The Role of Large Law Firms by the End of the Century*, 64 Indiana Law Journal 467 (1989).

INDEX

Printed in the United States
98578LV00002B/373-387/A